Windows Admin Scripting

Little Black Book
Third Edition

Jesse M. Torres

PARAGLYPH™
P R E S S

President
Keith Weiskamp

Editor-at-Large
Jeff Duntemann

Vice President, Sales, Marketing, and Distribution
Steve Sayre

Vice President, International Sales and Marketing
Cynthia Caldwell

Production Manager
Kim Eoff

Cover Designer
Kris Sotelo

Windows Admin Scripting Little Black Book, Third Edition

Limits of Liability and Disclaimer of Warranty

The author and publisher of this book have used their best efforts in preparing the book and the programs contained in it. These efforts include the development, research, and testing of the theories and programs to determine their effectiveness. The author and publisher make no warranty of any kind, expressed or implied, with regard to these programs or the documentation contained in this book.

The author and publisher shall not be liable in the event of incidental or consequential damages in connection with, or arising out of, the furnishing, performance, or use of the programs, associated instructions, and/or claims of productivity gains.

Trademarks

Trademarked names appear throughout this book. Rather than list the names and entities that own the trademarks or insert a trademark symbol with each mention of the trademarked name, the publisher states that it is using the names for editorial purposes only and to the benefit of the trademark owner, with no intention of infringing upon that trademark.

Paraglyph Press, Inc.
4015 N. 78th Street, #115
Scottsdale, Arizona 85251
Phone: 602-749-8787
www.paraglyphpress.com

Paraglyph Press ISBN: 1933097108

Printed in the United States of America
10   9   8   7   6   5   4   3   2   1

Praise from Readers for *Windows Admin Scripting Little Black Book (Previous Editions)*:

"Summed in one sentence: You have got to get this book! I have bought about 3 other over-priced scripting books, and they are so fluffed with fillers. This is the first book to cover and actually explain WMI and ADSI scripting. It is packed with examples that administrators will use daily! Great for beginners (both to administrating, WiMndows 2000, and scripting). This is the first book I actually read front to back! This book isn't filled with examples like writing 'HELLO WORLD,' but with awesome ones like automating installs, updating antivirus files, and creating logon scripts. I am going to start using them at work and pass them off as my own."
—*Yari Rischkin*

"For all of us who have to gather commands and keystrokes, and do them again some time, this is the book to get. Logically organized and presented, this book will give you the starting point for just about any automated scripting task you have to take on. Get it as a reference book to look up how to do specific scripting tasks, or just browse through it, and you're bound to come across something that you had never even considered automating."
—*Amazon Reader*

"I've never seen a book like this! This guy must be an admin because everything here is what I do on a daily basis. Managing users/groups, inventory, imaging, messaging—you name it—it's in here. The other cool part is that I just bought the book for Windows Scripting Host and now I can learn KiXstart and shell scripting all in the same shot. Definately worth it!"
—*Raymond K., Amazon Reader*

"This book is a great reference. Everything is right here, and you can easily modify or combine the scripts to perform the tasks needed to get done. If you've ever bought a Little Black Book, you'll be comfortable with this book. It is a concise reference and is intended for intermediate to advanced admins/ programmers/computer geeks. It dives right into the task at hand, and shows you the results. Two thumbs up!"
—*Mike Costa*

"This book has so much information, it's almost scary. There is a script in here to do about anything and everything you could possible want to do. I specifically bought it to automate some user creation/set NTFS permission, and now I'm taking more of the book's scripts and turning them into web pages (so I can create users and manage the domain from a simple web page). This book was definately worth it!"
—*Amazon Reader*

"This book can open many doors and show you many great things. I don't think that anyone at any administrative level can read this book and not discover something new."
—*Jase T. Wolfe*

The Paraglyph Mission

This book you've purchased is a collaborative creation involving the work of many hands, from authors to editors to designers and to technical reviewers. At Paraglyph Press, we like to think that everything we create, develop, and publish is the result of one form creating another. And as this cycle continues on, we believe that your suggestions, ideas, feedback, and comments on how you've used our books is an important part of the process for us and our authors.

We've created Paraglyph Press with the sole mission of producing and publishing books that make a difference. The last thing we all need is yet another tech book on the same tired, old topic. So we ask our authors and all of the many creative hands who touch our publications to do a little extra, dig a little deeper, think a little harder, and create a better book. The founders of Paraglyph are dedicated to finding the best authors, developing the best books, and helping you find the solutions you need.

As you use this book, please take a moment to drop us a line at **feedback@paraglyphpress.com** and let us know how we are doing and how we can keep producing and publishing the kinds of books that you can't live without.

Sincerely,

Keith Weiskamp & Jeff Duntemann
Paraglyph Press Founders
4015 N. 78th Street, #115
Scottsdale, Arizona 85251
email: **feedback@paraglyphpress.com**
Web: **www.paraglyphpress.com**
Phone: 602-749-8787

About the Scripts

Throughout this book, you'll encounter a number of very useful scripts to help you perform a wide range of administrative tasks with Windows 2003, XP, and 2000. These scripts have been written with four different scripting tools including Shell Scripting, AutoIt, KiXtart, and Windows Script Host. To use these scripts, I'll show you how to get the scripting tools you will need in Chapter 1.

Because some of the scripts are just a line or two of code, you'll likely just type them in. When typing in scripts, be sure to type them in just as they appear in the text. In some cases, a line of scripting code could not fit on a single line due to the page width of this book. When this occurred, the line of scripting code was continued on the next line. Any line of code that has been formatted in this manner has been highlighted in the book. When you type in this code all you have to remember is to type in the highlighted code as a single line of code.

Since many of the scripts are longer, I have made them available on my personal Web site for you to download. This can save you a lot of time from having to type in the scripts. You can access my Web site to get updates for the scripts and support material for the book. In addition, you'll find other scripts, tricks, tips, security documents, music, and more. To visit the site, point your Web browser to:

www.jesseweb.com

In addition, you may also register your book at the site listed above to gain access to more advanced scripts that could not fit into the book.

Before visiting my Web site, make sure that you also read the appendix provided in this book. Here you'll find a set of resources and tools to help you with your scripting.

To my wife and best friend, Carina:
Your love, smile, and support mean more to me than you could
ever know. Our love is truly blessed, and for that, our children,
and for you, I am thankful. I love you, always.

To my son Ryan and daughter Bianca:
You both have helped me realize the really important things in life
and with that have brought new meaning to it. I promise to give
you all my love, guidance, support, and understanding—always.

ཐ

About the Author

Jesse M. Torres' experience in the computer industry includes the private, corporate, and government sectors. He served six years in the Air National Guard working in computer maintenance and has since worked for large corporations such as PricewaterhouseCoopers and United Technologies. His education includes a specialist's certification in electronic switching systems from the U.S. Air Force, a B.A. in Versatile Technology from the University of Connecticut, a specialist's certification in Lotus application development, and an MCSE and .NET MCAD certification from Microsoft.

Jesse has extensively scripted software and OS installations and updates, inventory procedures, desktop management, maintenance, security, and more. He has also created numerous Windows, Web, and database applications for systems automation and management. Some of his programming and automation experience includes shell scripting, AutoIt, KiXtart, Windows Script Host (WSH), Windows Management Instrumentation (WMI), Active Directory Service Interfaces (ADSI), VBScript, JavaScript, Active Server Pages (ASP), ASP.NET, Veritas WinINSTALL, Microsoft Systems Management Server (SMS), Microsoft ScriptIt, Visual Basic, Visual Basic.NET, C#, and Microsoft SQL. He has also written the book *Surviving PC Disasters, Mishaps, and Blunders* as well as an article on WSH for *Windows* and *.NET Magazine's Windows Scripting Solutions.*

Currently, Jesse is working as a senior IT developer for Bridgewater Associates, a global investment manager located in Westport, CT.

Acknowledgments

First, I would like to thank Keith Weiskamp, president of Paraglyph Press for his hard work, guidance, and continuing support.

Thanks to all the software companies and developers (Rudd van Velsen, Microsoft, Sapien Technologies, Executive Software, Hidden Software, and BellCraft Technologies) for sharing information and making quality products.

Thanks to my family, whose pride in my accomplishments clearly shines through. I love you all. Special thanks to my mom and dad for their encouragement and support.

Finally, special thanks to my wife, Carina, son Ryan, and daughter Bianca for giving up some of our time together so I could share this book with the world. At only 16 months old, my son Ryan contributed over 100 pages for the second edition of this book. Unfortunately they appear to be in some untranslatable, foreign language and were cut at the last minute from the final version. While my son has grown and lost his passion for writing, my daughter has caught the writing bug and assisted in this edition by ripping off two keys from my laptop keyboard (apparently her idea was to speed up production by removing unused keys). I love all of you and will always be here for you, as you've been for me. Thanks again.

Contents at a Glance

Contents

Contents

Chapter 3
Scripting Installations and Updates 39

Chapter 4
File Management 57

Chapter 5
Automating Windows and Applications 87

Chapter 7
Local System Management   135

Chapter 8
Remote System Management   161

Chapter 10
Managing Inventory 223

Chapter 13
Logon Scripts 295

Contents

Introduction

Welcome to *Windows Admin Scripting Little Black Book, Third Edition*. This book is specifically designed to teach you how to quickly turn routine, repetitive, time-consuming, or complex administrative tasks into simple scripts. If you're like me, you probably don't have the time to spend thumbing through books filled with general examples that you'll never use. Because of its compact size, this book is free of generic filler material (a common trait of the larger scripting books) and comes packed with information and examples that you can actually use. Whether you're a basic Windows user or a network administrator in charge of a corporate infrastructure, this book will teach you how to use scripting to become more productive and recoup some free time from your busy schedule.

This book is a concise reference detailing various scripting methods and techniques to automate all types of administrative tasks. At its core, this book explains and illustrates the four major scripting methods: shell scripting, AutoIt, KiXtart, and Windows Script Host. It will also teach you the inner workings of Active Directory Service Interfaces and Windows Management Instrumentation, and how to use the provided examples to manage an enterprise. Beyond the extensive scripting examples and information, this book also provides in-depth coverage of scripting for Windows 2000, XP, and 2003.

Is This Book for You?

If you've read this far, chances are this is the book for you. Out of all the sites where I've worked, only a small percentage of employees have even thought about using scripting. Perhaps it's because there is a common misconception that you have to be a programmer or computer genius to write scripts. This couldn't be any further from the truth. Scripts are the simplest form of programming, and anyone who uses a computer can easily create them.

The examples and information in this book are specifically focused around the daily tasks of the IT professional. For the novice administrator or scripter, this book will guide you through the world of scripting and administration, while helping you quickly build your skill set. For the experienced administrator or scripter, this book provides a wealth of information and advanced techniques to help you manage and standardize your environment.

How to Use This Book

This book is divided into 18 chapters. Each chapter begins with a brief overview followed by a set of immediate solutions to help you automate your tasks.

Chapter 1: Introduction to Scripting

Chapter 1 provides an introduction to the four major scripting methods (shell scripting, AutoIt, KiXtart, and Windows Script Host) discussed throughout the book. This chapter teaches you about the basics, limitations, and appropriate times to use each scripting method.

Chapter 2: Scripting Workstation Setups

Chapter 2 covers how to automate hard disk setups and imaging. Immediate solutions include how to script partitioning, formatting, and boot disk creation. It also includes extensive information on how to script today's most popular imaging utility Norton Ghost.

Chapter 3: Scripting Installations and Updates

Chapter 3 covers how to automate installations and updates. Immediate solutions include how to script installations and updates using built-in switches, custom routines, and the Microsoft Windows Installer. It also includes information on how to use Autoit when other scripting methods simply won't work.

Chapter 4: File Management

Chapter 4 covers how to automate file manipulation and management. Immediate solutions include how to script file renaming, replication, deletion, appending, updating, searching, and attribute modifying. It also includes information on how to use shell scripting, KiXtart, and Windows Script Host.

Chapter 5: Automating Windows and Applications

Chapter 5 covers how to automate the operating system and its applications. Immediate solutions include how to script Windows operations and settings, such as Microsoft FTP uploads, defragging, hardware devices, and Control Panel applets. It also includes information on how to script applications, such as Norton Antivirus, Microsoft Office, Internet Explorer, and Diskeeper Lite.

Chapter 6: Inside the Registry

Chapter 6 covers how to automate changes to the registry. This chapter includes in-depth information about the birth and structure of the registry while clearing up common misconceptions. Immediate solutions include how to secure, back up, restore, modify, and search the registry. It also includes information on how to modify common Windows annoyances, for example, how to disable Dr. Watson or the Welcome screens.

Chapter 7: Local System Management

Chapter 7 covers how to control and automate local system changes. Immediate solutions include how to manage shortcuts, program groups, profiles, shares, services, permissions, and more through simple scripts. It also includes information on how to script common system events, such as logging off a user or rebooting a system.

Chapter 8: Remote System Management

Chapter 8 covers how to control and automate remote systems. Immediate solutions include how to manage processes, shares, services, permissions, and more through simple scripts. This chapter includes in-depth information and examples on how to use Windows Management Instrumentation. It also includes information on how to script common system events, such as shutting down or rebooting a system.

Chapter 9: Enterprise Management

Chapter 9 covers how to automate enterprise management. Immediate solutions include how to manage user, group, and computer accounts through simple scripts. This chapter includes in-depth information and examples on how to use Active Directory Service Interfaces. It also includes information on Windows 2000/2003 Enterprise networks.

Chapter 10: Managing Inventory

Chapter 10 covers how to gather inventory information without the use of expensive management systems. Immediate solutions include how to collect software and hardware information, such as battery, operating system, Network Interface Card (NIC), processor, printer, sound card, and memory information. It also includes information on how to generate inventory reports using utilities like MSD, WINMSD, MSINFO32, and SRVINFO.

Chapter 11: Security

Chapter 11 covers how to control and automate remote systems. Immediate solutions include how to manage system and domain security settings; create, apply, and export security templates; and run a security analysis through simple scripts. This chapter includes in-depth information about authentication protocols and common security practices. It also includes information on how to use utilities to run operations under the security context of another user, such as the RunAs utility.

Chapter 12: Logging and Alerting

Chapter 12 covers how to log system events and alert users when events occur. Immediate solutions include how to manage text logs and the event log through simple scripts. The chapter also includes information on how to script alerts to a single user, group, or user list through network alerts and email.

Chapter 13: Logon Scripts

Chapter 13 covers how to create and use logon scripts to standardize your environment. Immediate solutions include how to synchronize the system time, map drives and printers, display logon script progress, and more through simple shell, KiXtart, or WSH scripts. This chapter also includes in-depth information about the logon process and file replication services.

Chapter 14: Backups and Scheduling

Chapter 14 covers how to automate backups and scheduling tasks or scripts. Immediate solutions include how to script Windows backups, IIS metabase backups, and task scheduling. It also includes information on how to script third-party backup applications, such as Backup Exec and ARCserve.

Chapter 15: SQL Processing and Automation

Chapter 15 covers how to automate the core tasks for administering a SQL server. Immediate solutions are included that show how to create scripts for processing services, databases, tables, stored procedures, linked servers, users, logins, and more. This chapter also includes information on how to script database objects to a file for quick and easy backups and restores.

Chapter 16: Exchange Server Scripting

Chapter 16 covers how to control Microsoft Exchange, mailboxes, and contacts through scripting. Through various automation objects and utilities, you can script just about any Exchange task.

Chapter 17: Fun with Multimedia

Chapter 17 covers how to play and control multimedia files using simple scripts. Immediate solutions include how to script the Microsoft Media Player and the RealPlayer G2. This chapter also includes information on how to script the Microsoft Office Assistant and Microsoft Agent characters.

Chapter 18: Windows XP/2003 Only

Chapter 18 covers scripting techniques specifically designed for the new features of Windows XP/2003. It also includes information about Product Activation, system restores, and the MMC 2.0 automation object model.

The *Little Black Book* Philosophy

Written by experienced professionals, Paraglyph *Little Black Books* are terse, easily "thumb-able" question-answerers and problem solvers. The *Little Black Book*'s unique two-part chapter format—brief technical overviews followed by practical immediate solutions—is structured to help you use your knowledge, solve problems, and quickly master complex technical issues to become an expert. By breaking down complex topics into easily manageable components, this format helps you quickly find what you're looking for.

A Final Note

I hope this book will become your essential reference in streamlining your environment and daily tasks. I welcome your comments, questions, suggestions, tips, scripts, or anything else you would like to share. Please feel free to visit my web site at www.jesseweb.com for updates.

The Essentials of Scripting

Welcome to the world of Windows Admin Scripting. This chapter introduces the basic techniques of scripting and the four major scripting methods used throughout this book: Shell Scripting, AutoIt, KiXtart, and Windows Script Host. Because this book covers a lot of ground, I have included this scripting introduction to help you get up to speed with the basic techniques that we'll be using throughout the rest of this book. By the end of this chapter, you will have learned the basics of scripting, how to approach each scripting language, how to work with their limitations, and when to use them.

The Essence of Scripting

Scripts are the simplest form of programming, and anyone who uses a computer can create them with a little practice. I cannot emphasize this enough. Scripting is a fast, simple way to instruct a computer to perform a specific set of instructions. These instructions can range from simple tasks like "delete temporary files from a computer" to more complex tasks like "install this application on every machine on the network." A script is merely a text file that contains a set of commands for performing a specific operation. The best part about scripting is that you can do a lot with a little bit of programming knowledge. The scripting tools and languages are easy to learn and the skills you develop with one scripting tool can easily be adapted to another tool. The scripting tools I've selected for this book are all especially designed to be easy to use, yet provide many powerful features so that you can perform a wide range of tasks.

Scripts vs. Programs

Computers only understand binary operations (on or off, 1 or 0). When a script runs, the scripting engine reads each line of code and translates it into machine language on the fly. This is why scripts are also called *interpreted programs*. High level languages such as Visual Basic .NET and C#

must be translated into machine language by a compiler before execution. Because scripts compile at runtime, they tend to run slower than compiled programs. The good news, however, is that the types of tasks you'll typically perform with scripts aren't so speed critical and thus the simplicity of using a scripting tool far outweighs the complexity of using a programming language.

Limitations of Scripting

While high level languages contain an extensive library or set of functions, certain scripting languages may only contain subsets of their counterparts or comparables. Scripting languages do not usually supply graphical interface elements, such as forms, dropdown lists, checkboxes, and so on. Finally, scripting languages do not typically provide advanced programming features such as object orientation, early binding, and threading.

When to Use Scripts

Scripting languages are designed to be lightweight and easier to work with than their compiled counterparts. In some cases, scripts can even perform tasks more quickly than can be performed with compiled programs simply because scripts do not contain a lot of extra baggage. Scripting is best used when you need quick solutions without a full blown interface or intensive processing. If you find a script is using a lot of system resources, taking a long time to complete, or is simply unmanageable due to its size or complexity, you should consider using a compiled program.

Scripting Basics

While this book covers several different scripting languages, they all are designed around the same basic concepts. The differences you'll encounter will mainly be in how specific features are implemented. Once you understand the basics and the subtle differences in the languages, you'll be able to switch between one to the other without much trouble.

Variables

Variables are places to store and retrieve data by a name. For example, you might want to store the user name of an account using a script you just created. To do this, you can create a variable called "LastUsername" and set it to hold the value "John Doe."

Declaring Variables

Before using a variable, you must allocate a place in memory by performing a declaration. Declaring a variable is simply a way of saying "make room for my variable." Table 1.1 shows how to declare variables with the different scripting languages.

Table 1.1   Variable declarations used in the different scripting languages.

Language	Declaration
Shell	N/A
AutoIt	DIM $VariableName
KiXtart	DIM $VariableName
WSH	DIM VariableName

NOTE: *Shell scripting does not use variable declarations. Shell scripting also stores variables in the registry as opposed to storing variables in memory.*

Assigning Variables

After declaring a variable, you may set its contents to your desired data, also known as "assigning a variable." Assigning a variable is simply a way of saying "replace whatever my variable currently contains with this new data." In shell scripting, variables can only contain strings (e.g., "Hello World"), but in AutoIt, KiXtart, and WSH, the contents of a variable can be a string, a number, or an object (not available in AutoIt). The way you assign a variable may change depending on the type of data you wish the variable to contain. Tables 1.2 through 1.4 show how to assign values to variables.

Table 1.2   String variable assignments.

Language	Assignment
Shell	SET X=Hello World
AutoIt	$X="Hello World"
KiXtart	$X="Hello World"
WSH	X="Hello World"

Table 1.3   Numeric variable assignments.

Language	Assignment
Shell	SET /A X=1
AutoIt	$X=1
KiXtart	$X=1
WSH	X=1

Table 1.4   Object variable assignments.

Language	Assignment
Shell	N/A
AutoIt	N/A
KiXtart	SET $X=CreateObject("*object*")
WSH	SET X=CreateObject("*object*")

Comments

After you code for a while, you'll go back to your scripts (or some-one else's scripts), look at them, and have no clue what a certain section does, why it was coded in a certain way, who wrote it, how old it is, and so on. That's where commenting comes in. Comments allow you to write notes in your code. They are there solely for docu-mentation. When commenting, be clear and concise. Bad comment-ing can be worse than no comments at all. In order for your comments to not be interpreted or executed as commands, you need to prefeix your comments with a special tag. Table 1.5 shows how to add a comment.

Table 1.5   Format for comments.

Language	Tag	Example
Shell	REM	REM This is a comment
Shell	(::) Double Colon	::This is also comment
AutoIt	(;) Semicolon	; This is a comment
KiXtart	(;) Semicolon	; This is a comment
WSH	(') Single Quote	' This is a comment

NOTE: While writing shell scripts, you can use either REM or :: to start a comment. Personally, I prefer to use the double colon (::) commenting style because it is a little cleaner looking and requires one less key to press :).

Subroutines

Imagine if you had to perform a series of twenty tasks on more than 1,000 files. What a pain it would be to rewrite those tasks so many times! *Subroutines* allow you to take a section of repeated code and make it accessible by simply calling the subroutine by name. Subrou-tines can accept single or multiple parameters, allowing you to pass arguments to the subroutine for manipulation. There are two types of subroutines: sub procedures and functions.

Sub Procedures

A sub procedure performs a series of actions without returning any data. A typical use of a sub procedure is to perform file manipulation tasks. Some examples might be working with text files or to display user prompts. For example, you may have a sub procedure called "ShowError" which displays an error message in a dialog box. You wouldn't need any data returned, you would just need an error message displayed. If you did need data returned, you would have to use a function.

Functions

A function is a procedure used to perform a series of actions and return data. A typical use of a function is to perform calculations, create objects, or return error codes. For example, you may have a function called "GetUsername" which returns the currently logged on username. Since you need the username returned to you, you must use a function as opposed to a sub procedure.

What in the World Is an API?

So what do you do when "what you want to do" is not available in your scripting language? the answer: you turn to an API. An API is a collection of functions that the operating system or application can call on to perform many different tasks. By using a common set of code, applications can perform operations identical to those that the operating system performs. These APIs are normally stored in DLL files. Although programmers can access DLLs through compiled applications, scripters need to find another method of access. While shell scripting and AutoIt do not provide methods to interact directly with external APIs (AutoIt kind of does, but it's too complicated to mention in this book), KiXtart and Windows Script Host allow API interaction through COM objects.

Working with COM Objects

An *object* is simply a collection of functions that perform similar tasks. COM (Component Object Model) objects expose API methods and properties, providing a safe way for scripters to access APIs in their scripts. These objects are normally stored in OCX (OLE custom control) or DLL files. To gain access to a COM object, you use the **CreateObject** function to load an object into memory, connect to the object, and set this connection to a variable. To gain access to a COM object already in memory (e.g., interact with an open Excel session), you use the **GetObject** function to connect to the object. Once these instances are created, you can use these variables throughout your script to access all the methods within the object.

Shell Scripting

Shell scripting involves running a series of commands from within a command shell (e.g., command prompt). Although these commands can be run from the command line individually (e.g., COPY *.*), they are more often stored within a script or batch file. A *batch file* is a text document with a .bat or .cmd extension. Shell scripting has been around since the inception of MS-DOS and is the easiest scripting method to learn.

Using the Command Shell

A command shell is a text-based, command interpreter application. Similar to MS-DOS, you type a command and the command shell displays a response. Windows provides two command shells: CMD.exe and COMMAND.com. The Windows command shell, CMD.exe, is a 32-bit application that contains many built-in commands (e.g., DIR, ECHO, DEL, and COPY) known as command extensions. The MS-DOS command shell, Command.com, is a 16-bit application supplied for backwards compatibility of 16-bit DOS applications. It passes all commands to CMD.exe for processing, and it does not support long file names. Whenever possible, you should use CMD.exe because it provides better performance and stability than COMMAND.com. Figure 1.1 shows the window that is displayed when CMD.exe executes. In this case, the DOS command, DIR, is being executed.

```
C:\WINDOWS\System32\cmd.exe

Microsoft Windows XP [Version 5.1.2600]
(C) Copyright 1985-2001 Microsoft Corp.

C:\Documents and Settings\Administrator>DIR
 Volume in drive C has no label.
 Volume Serial Number is B4A2-2CEE

 Directory of C:\Documents and Settings\Administrator

08/10/2003  11:04 AM    <DIR>          .
08/10/2003  11:04 AM    <DIR>          ..
07/20/2003  03:44 PM    <DIR>          Desktop
08/10/2003  11:05 AM    <DIR>          Favorites
08/10/2003  11:04 AM    <DIR>          My Documents
07/20/2003  03:44 PM    <DIR>          Start Menu
               0 File(s)              0 bytes
               6 Dir(s)  13,813,817,344 bytes free

C:\Documents and Settings\Administrator>
```

Figure 1.1   The CMD.exe command prompt window.

TIP: *A quick way to access a command shell is by clicking Start/Run from the Windows Start menu, type "CMD," and click the "OK" button.*

Variables

In Windows shell scripting, variables are known as "environment variables." There are two types of environment variables: system and user. System environment variables are available to all users. They are usually set by the operating system, and can only be modified by a system administrator. User environment variables are available to the current user and any user can add, edit, or remove them; these are the variables you typically create in your scripts.

You "set" the value of an environment variable using the SET command. For example, to store the value of "Hello World" in a user environment variable called "MyVar," you would enter the following command:

```
SET MyVar=Hello World
```

To get the value of a variable, you simply surround the variable name with %. For example, to echo the value of the user environment variable called "MyVar," you would enter:

```
ECHO %MyVar%
```

NOTE: *Whether setting or getting, environment variable names are not case sensitive (i.e., MyVar = MYVAR = myvar).*

You can also combine setting and getting values. For example, to store the value of the user environment variable called "MyVar" into another variable called "YourVar," you would enter:

```
SET YourVar=%MyVar%
```

TIP: *You can display all variable names and their values by simple typing "SET" or SET followed by part or all of the desired variable name (e.g.,. SET, SET Y, SET Your, SET YourV, SET YourVar).*

Functions

While shell scripting doesn't support true functions, we can mimic the basic concept with labels to reference a group of statements. A label is simply a word prefixed with a colon. It marks an area of code that you can jump to with either a CALL or a GOTO statement. While a GOTO statement instructs the script to jump to a specific label only, the CALL statement will jump to a label, pass it any arguments if needed (enclosed in double quotes if an argument contains spaces, multiple arguments separated by a single space), and can return to continue the script with the line following the CALL statement. Our shell script function structure is as follows:

```
CALL :FunctionName arguments
ECHO Value returned from our function is %FunctionName%
GOTO:EOF

:FunctionName
SETLOCAL

  CODE

SET RetVal=Something

ENDLOCAL&SET FunctionName=%RetVal%&GOTO:EOF
```

Here, ***FunctionName*** is the name given to the label; ***arguments*** are the parameters passed to the function; and ***Code*** are the script action(s) to perform. To return a value outside of the function, we name a variable from within the function with the same name as the function and set a value to it. While you don't have to use or construct your calls and labels like in the example just shown, I'll use this format throughout the book.

Shell Scripting Example

To help you better understand how shell scripting works, I've created a script to show you how to display the name of your computer. Later, I'll show you how to perform this same task using the other scripting tools that I will be introducing, AutoIt, KiXtart, and Windows Script Host. This will really help you understand the differences (and similarities) involved in using the different scripting tools.

Displaying the Computer Name

To display the name of your local computer using shell scripting, proceed as follows:

1. First, you'll need to create a simple script file (.bat file) and place a few commands in the file. Use a text editor and create a file named "*batchfile*.bat." Here, *batchfile* is the full path and file name of a batch file that should contain the following commands:

```
@ECHO OFF
ECHO %COMPUTERNAME%
```

Make sure that you save the file in the same directory that you will be running the command shell from (Step 2).

By default, the command shell displays (echoes) the called command before displaying the results. To suppress the called command and only display the results, the @ECHO OFF command is used. The last line uses the ECHO command to display the contents of the COMPUTERNAME environment variable, which is automatically set by the operating system at boot time.

2. Once you have created and saved the .bat file as instructed in Step 1, you can run your batch file by starting the command shell (CMD.exe) and entering the following instruction at the command prompt:

```
batchfile
```

Remember that the quickest way to run the .CMD command shell is to click Start|Run from the Windows Start menu type "CMD," and click the "OK" button.

Limitations of Shell Scripting

Although shell scripting is easy, it is a limited language. This is something I hate to admit because my scripting roots date back to the good old days of MS-DOS. Shell scripting is not a collective language, but rather a language consisting of various individual executables and commands. It has limited logical statements, no debugging capabilities, limited error-handling capabilities, and no graphical interface.

When to Use Shell Scripting

Although shell scripting continues to improve over the years, it is best used for simple scripting tasks that do not require complex calculations or extensive file manipulation. To perform more powerful tasks, you should turn to another scripting tool, such as AutoIt, KiXtart, or Windows Script Host.

AutoIt

AutoIt (**www.autoitscript.com**) is a free automation tool originally designed to automate the sending of key and mouse commands to Window objects. AutoIt can detect window titles and text and then send commands to specific windows based on that information. Although you can use other scripting send-keys methods, such as Windows Script Host (WSH) or KiXtart, AutoIt provides the easiest way to detect windows and send keys. In addition to key, mouse, and window manipulation, AutoIt has grown to become a true, lightweight scripting language. It provides the basics of any scripting language but also provides advanced features like the ability to create graphical user interfaces (forms, buttons, and so on), file manipulation, and much more.

NOTE: The scripts in this book were written and tested with AutoIt version 3.0. These scripts will not work in earlier versions of AutoIt.

Variables

Variables are used extensively in AutoIt to store values or return codes. AutoIt variable names consist of a $ sign followed by text, and should not be the same as any of the built-in AutoIt component names. Declaring a variable and assigning a value is identical to doing so in a language like KiXtart as shown here:

```
DIM $MYVARIABLE
$MYVARIABLE = "SOME VALUE"
```

Functions

An AutoIt function is structured as follows:

```
$RetVal = FunctionName(arguments)
MsgBox(0, "Return Value", $RetVal)

Func FunctionName (arguments)
   Code
   RETURN value
EndFunc
```

Here, *FunctionName* is the name given to the function; *arguments* are the parameters passed to the function (separated by commas); *Code* is the script action(s) to perform, and *value* is the value to return.

NOTE: AutoIt does not differentiate between functions and subprocedures. If you do not want to return a value (i.e., sub procedure), simply do not use "RETURN value."

Macros

AutoIt macros provide various system and user information by accessing APIs. AutoIt has over 80 built-in macros to easily return various system and network information. All macros are prefixed with an @ symbol. See the AutoIt help file for a complete list of macros.

AutoIt Example

Let's revisit our simple example of displaying the name of your local computer to see how AutoIt compares with shell scripting. If you do not currently have a copy of AutoIt on your computer, you'll need to download a copy from the Web using the instructions that I have provided.

Displaying the Computer Name

To display the name of the local computer using AutoIt, proceed as follows:

1. Create a new directory to store all files included in this example.

2. Download and install the latest version of AutoIt, from **www.autoitscript.com**, to the new directory.

3. Use your favorite text editor to create a new script file. The following instruction should be placed in the file:

```
MsgBox(0, "Computer Name", @ComputerName)
```

   The line above uses the MsgBox command to display a message box with a title of "Computer Name" and the contents of the current computer's name provided by the @ComputerName macro.

   To finish your script file, simply save it with an extension of ".au3."

4. Now you are ready to run your script. Select Start|Run and enter "*scriptfile.*"

Here, scriptfile should be the full path and file name where your file is stored (Step 3).

Limitations of AutoIt

Since AutoIt does not come with Windows, you either have to install it or precompile your scripts into executables before use (compile/decompile tool comes with AutoIt). AutoIt also does not have the ability to instantiate COM objects (easily) and has no built-in debugger. Finally and most important is that AutoIt is a Windows only scripting language. It cannot run in DOS and cannot output text to console windows.

When to Use AutoIt

AutoIt is a great alternative to shell scripting due to its ability to interact with windows, advanced key and mouse controls, and to create
graphical user interfaces. It also has built in network, file, and registry functions. With the ability to compile your scripts into executables,
you can protect your code and escape the administrative burden of
having to install AutoIt first before running your scripts. With more
and more features being added to every release, AutoIt's capabilities
are quickly becoming an extremely powerful scripting tool.

KiXtart

KiXtart is an easy-to-use scripting language available for download
from www.KiXtart.org. Some of the advanced features of KiXtart are
built-in debugging, the ability to modify the registry, COM automation, and the ability to shut down or reboot systems. KiXtart includes
both a Windows and a console engine, allowing it to interact in both
environments. Although originally designed and still primarily used
for logon scripting, KiXtart can be used as a standalone scripting solution to automate everyday tasks.

NOTE: *The scripts in this book were written and tested with KiXtart version 2010. These scripts
may not work properly in earlier versions of KiXtart.*

Variables

Variables are used extensively in KiXtart to store values or return
codes. Just like AutoIt, KiXtart variable names consist of a $ sign fol-
lowed by text, and should not be the same as any of the built-in KiXtart
component names. Declaring a variable and assigning a value is identical to doing so in AutoIt:

```
DIM $MYVARIABLE
$MYVARIABLE = "SOME VALUE"
```

Functions

A KiXtart function is structured as follows:

```
Function FunctionName (arguments)
  Code
  FunctionName = value
EndFunction
```

Here, *FunctionName* is the name given to the function; *arguments* are the parameters passed to the function (separated by commas); and *Code* is the script action(s) to perform. To return a value outside of the function, you should name a variable from within your function with the same name as your function and set a value to it.

Macros

KiXtart macros provide various system and user information by accessing Windows Application Programming Interfaces (APIs). KiXtart has over 50 built-in macros to easily return various system and network information. All macros are prefixed with an @ symbol. Some of the more commonly used macros are listed in Table 1.6.

Table 1.6   Commonly used KiXtart macros.

Macro	Definition
@ERROR	Return code of the last command or function.
@LDRIVE	Drive that maps to *LogonServer*\NETLOGON.
@LSERVER	Validating Server Name.
@SCRIPTDIR	Directory of the currently running script.
@SERROR	Description of the last error.
@USERID	Username of the current user.
@WKSTA	Local computer name.

KiXtart Example

Let's revisit our simple example of displaying the name of your local computer to see how KiXtart compares with AutoIt and Shell Scripting. If you do not currently have a copy of KiXtart on your computer, you'll need to download a copy from the Web using the instructions that I have provided.

Displaying the Computer Name

To display the name of the local computer using KiXtart, proceed as follows:

1. Create a new directory to store all files included in this example.

2. Download and extract the latest version of KiXtart, from www.kixtart.org, to the new directory.

3. Use your favorite text editor to create a new script file. The following instruction should be placed in the file:

```
? @WKSTA
sleep 5
```

This instruction might look a little unusual but it simply uses the "?" command to echo the contents of the @WKSTA macro (similar to the shell scripting ECHO comamnd).

To finish your script file, simply save it using a filename that you will remember.

4. Now you are ready to run your script. Select Start|Run and enter "*kix32"scriptfile.*"

Here, **kix32** is the full path of the kix32.exe and ***scriptfile*** should be the full path and file name where your file is stored (Step 3). The SLEEP command is used to pause script execution for 5 seconds, allowing us to view the results.

Limitations of KiXtart

Since KiXtart is not a built-in Windows feature, you must either copy it to every system or make it available by sharing it across a network. This isn't difficult but it is an administrative task you'll need to take care of. A KiXtart script also tends to run slower for remote access or linked site users than a Windows Script Host script. Finally, KiXtart is not currently supported by Microsoft.

When to Use KiXtart

KiXtart is a great alternative to shell scripting due to its built-in de-bugging, network, file, and registry functions. It's a perfect solution to simplify complex shell scripting tasks and remains a popular choice for logon scripting. With more and more features being added to every release, KiXtart's capabilities are slowly reaching those of Windows Script Host.

Windows Script Host

Microsoft's Windows Script Host (WSH) is a language-independent scripting host for 32-bit Windows operating systems. It provides the most powerful functionality of all the scripting methods discussed so far. Windows Scripting Host works seamlessly with all scriptable objects available to Windows, allowing you to create complex, scripted applications. By providing extensive scripting capabilities combined with support for multiple scripting languages, WSH is quickly becoming the scripting method of choice.

NOTE: By default, Windows Script Host supports two languages: VBScript and JScript. All the Windows Script Host examples in this book are written in VBScript.

CSCRIPT and WSCRIPT

Windows Script Host is controlled by two executables, CSCRIPT and WSCRIPT. CSCRIPT is the command-line host utility that is commonly used to run tasks in a command prompt. WSCRIPT is the graphical host utility commonly used to interact with the user or run silently in the background. These two executables support many command-line parameters, as shown in Table 1.7.

Table 1.7   Windows Script Host parameters.

Parameter	Description
//B	Disables command prompt user input.
//D	Enables active debugging.
//E:*engine*	Uses the specified engine at script execution.
//H:CSCRIPT	Sets CSCRIPT as the default execution host.
//H:WSCRIPT	Sets WSCRIPT as the default execution host.
//I	By default, enables command prompt user input.
//JOB	Executes a WSC job.
//LOGO	By default, displays logo at script execution.
//NOLOGO	Suppresses logo at script execution.
//U	For CSCRIPT only, specifies to use UNICODE for I/O operations.
//S	Saves options on a per user basis.
//T:*seconds*	Specifies the maximum time, in *seconds*, a script is allowed to run.
//X	Executes the current script within the debugger.
//?	Displays help context.

Variables

To declare a variable and assign a value, here is the format you use:

```
DIM MYVARIABLE
MYVARIABLE = "SOME VALUE"
```

This is almost identical to how to use variables in KiXtart, minus the KiXtart required $ sign.

Windows Script Host Object Model

The Windows Script Host object model (see Figure 1.2), is a hierarchal, organized collection of objects, mostly stored in a file called WSHOM.OCX located in the Windows\System or Winnt\System32

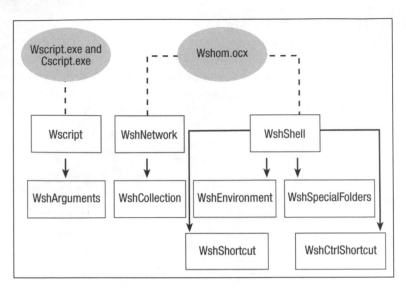

Figure 1.2   The Windows Script Host object model.

directories. Each of the core objects contains its own methods and properties to perform specific tasks.

The Wscript Object

The **Wscript** object is the core scripting object. It allows you to collect information about your script, work with arguments, and call other ActiveX objects. The **Wscript** object contains the methods to instantiate other objects and is automatically instantiated every time a script is run. The most commonly used **Wscript** method is the **Echo** method, which sends output to the screen:

```
Wscript.Echo "Some Output"
```

The WshNetwork Object

The **WshNetwork** object provides access to Windows network functions. You can use this object to work with network connections and perform various network-related tasks. The most common tasks used with this function are mapping printers and drives, and obtaining a computer's network information.

The WshShell Object

The **WshShell** object provides direct access to Windows and registry functions. You can use this object to work with shortcuts, display messages to users, manipulate the registry and environment variables, and run external commands.

The FileSystemObject Object

Is there an echo in here? Although not actually a part of the Windows Script Object model, the **FileSystemObject** object, contained in SCRRUN.DLL, can be used to access and manipulate the file system. Through this object, you can perform almost any file management task that you perform manually.

Now that you are familiar with the Windows Script Host Object model, you can start using subroutines to organize your scripts.

Subroutines

Windows Script Host provides two types of subroutines: sub procedures and functions.

Sub Procedures

A sub procedure is structured as follows:

```
Sub SubName (arguments)
  Code
End Sub
```

Here, **SubName** is the name given to the sub procedure; **arguments** are the parameters passed to the sub procedure (separated by commas); and **code** is the script action(s) to perform.

NOTE: *Any variables used within a sub procedure will not be accessible outside of the sub procedure, unless they are explicitly declared beforehand.*

Functions

Similar to KiXtart, a function is a procedure used to return data. A Windows Script Host function is structured as follows:

```
Function FunctionName (arguments)
  Code
  FunctionName = value
End Function
```

Here, **FunctionName** is the name given to the function; **arguments** are the parameters passed to the function (separated by commas); **Code** is the script action(s) to perform, and **value** is the value to return. To return a value outside of the function, you should name a variable from within your function with the same name as your function and set a value to it.

> **NOTE:** *While the KiXtart closing statement for a function is "EndFunction," Windows Script Host requires a space between the words "End" and "Function."*

Windows Script Host Example

You now probably realize why I've saved the most difficult scripting example for last. As you'll see, using Windows Script Host requires a bit more set up work but the work is worth it because of all of the flexibility and power that you gain. Let's revisit the task of displaying the name of your local computer with the help of a WSH script.

Displaying the Computer Name

To display the name of the local computer using Windows Script Host, proceed as follows:

1. Create a new directory to store all files included in this example.

2. Download and install the latest version of Windows Script Host, from **www.microsoft.com**, to the new directory.

3. Again, use your favorite text editor to create a new script file. The following instructions should be placed in the file:

```
Set WshNetwork = CreateObject("WScript.Network")
WScript.Echo  WshNetwork.ComputerName
```

The first line uses the CreateObject method to create an instance of the built-in Wscript.Network object and stores the instance in a variable called "WshNetwork." The last line accesses the Wscript.Network's ComputerName property and displays it with the Wscript.Echo method.

To finish your script file, simply save it using a filename that you will remember.

4. Select Start|Run and enter "wscript *scriptfile*.vbs."

Recall that WSCRIPT is the name of the graphical host utility. Here, *scriptfile* should be the full path and file name where your file is stored (Step 3).

Limitations of Windows Script Host

Windows Script Host's built-in graphical support is extremely limited. Although it does offer popup capability, WSH does not include the custom screen manipulation capabilities that AutoIt and even KiXtart has to offer. Finally, as the name implies, Windows Script Host can only be used under Windows or within a Windows DOS console.

When to Use Windows Script Host

Windows Script Host can be used to manipulate windows, work with files, modify the registry, and more. By itself, Windows Script Host is best suited for background tasks with little or no interface. When combined with COM automation, WMI (Windows Management Instrumentation), and ADSI (Active Directory Services Interfaces), WSH is a powerful tool that can be used for almost all of your scripting needs.

Which Scripting Method Should I Choose?

I am asked this question all the time (sometimes I ask this question myself) and the answer is always the same: whichever gets the job done. Truth is, most scripting tasks either can or must be completed using two or more scripting methods. The key is to minimize your code, complexity, maintenance, and resource usage. The more you script, the easier it will be to determine which scripting method or methods to use. After all, you wouldn't want to write a 200 line, resource intensive KiXtart script to discover you can complete the same task in a one line shell script, would you?

Chapter 2

Scripting Workstation Setups

In Brief

As a Windows administrator, you'll do your fair share of system builds, rebuilds, and images. In this chapter, you'll learn the quickest methods to automate hard disk setups and images. You'll begin learning the secrets of Microsoft FDISK and how to create partitions from the command line. You'll also learn about the scripting limitations of Microsoft FDISK and how to use Free FDISK to script creating and deleting partitions. You'll then learn about imaging and how to create and restore image files.

In order to implement all the examples in this chapter, you'll need to obtain the following files:

- Free FDISK (**www.23cc.com/free-fdisk/**)
- Norton Ghost (**www.symantec.com**)

Setting Up a New Hard Drive

For the typical PC, the core component to store user data and system files is the hard drive. A hard drive is like a wallet or purse—a place you can store your most valuable assets you need to access quickly. When you receive a new hard drive from the manufacturer, it is most likely low-level formatted with no data on it. After you physically install and configure the hard drive properly, you must partition and format it before you can put any real data on it.

Partitioning

The first step to setting up a new drive is to partition it. *Partitioning* is the act of dividing up a hard disk into logical sections, which allows one physical drive to appear as multiple drives (i.e., C:, D:, E:, and so on). When you partition a new drive, a master boot record (MBR) is created on the first physical sector on the hard drive. As a computer initially powers up, it calls the routines stored in the BIOS (Basic Input/Output System). This typically appears as a black DOS screen. The BIOS routines access the system's basic hardware devices (e.g., floppy disk, hard disk, keyboard, video). After these routines are executed, the BIOS reads and executes instructions from the MBR (i.e., Load Windows). The MBR contains the partition table, which contains four entries, allowing for various partition types.

Partition Types

When scripting the creation of a partition, you must know the type of partition and its dependencies beforehand. There are three different types of partitions: primary, extended, and logical. Each physical disk can have a maximum of four primary partitions, and only one can be marked active in order to boot. When a primary partition is marked active, it is automatically assigned the drive letter C.

Each primary partition can have only one extended partition. Within an extended partition, you can create up to 24 logical partitions (or 23 logical partitions if you have an active partition on the same drive). Each logical partition is assigned a drive letter (with A and B reserved for floppy drives).

NOTE: *Only one primary and one extended partition are allowed per physical disk.*

Partition Hierarchy

Partition types follow a hierarchy: primary, extended, and logical. They can only be created in this order, and can only be deleted in the opposite order. To begin scripting partitions, you must first familiarize yourself with Microsoft FDISK.

Microsoft FDISK

Microsoft FDISK (Fixed DISK) is a program that an experienced administrator can be all too familiar with. If only I had a nickel for each time I've used Microsoft FDISK, I'd be as rich as these IT salary surveys say I should be. Microsoft FDISK is the most commonly used partitioning utility for hard disks, but despite its popularity, most of its functionality remains highly undocumented. Microsoft FDISK is included with all versions of Windows. It allows you to create, delete, or view entries in the partition table. If you've ever used Microsoft FDISK to set up a new hard drive manually, you know how time-consuming it can be navigating through menus and waiting for drive integrity checks. Microsoft FDISK provides limited support for scripting from the command line.

NOTE: *If you want to change entries in the partition table, you must first delete and then recreate them.*

Scripting Limitations

Scripting Microsoft FDISK is like going to the casino—sometimes you win, sometimes you lose, but most of the time you lose. Microsoft FDISK does support many command-line options, but doesn't work well with command redirection input (for example, **FDISK < COMMANDS.TXT**).

Although the menu-based portion allows for deleting partitions, there's no way to delete partitions from the command line. Just as you do when you're at the casino, you have to know when it's time to collect your chips and move on to the next table. For us, that move is to Free FDISK.

Free FDISK

If Microsoft FDISK were a used car, you could slap a new engine in it and make it run just the way you like. Well, Free FDISK does just that. Free FDISK offers enhanced functionality over Microsoft's FDISK and is the official FDISK of FreeDOS (**www.freedos.org**). Free FDISK provides the same standard Microsoft FDISK interface and command-line options, while adding even more options for batch scripting. After you partition the hard drive, formatting is the last step needed before the drive is ready for data.

Formatting

Formatting is the process of preparing a disk for reading and writing. FORMAT.COM is the executable used to format both floppy and hard disks. When you format a disk, a file allocation table (FAT) and a new root directory are created, allowing you to store and retrieve files. This, in essence, places a file system on a disk for you to use.

The FAT organizes a hard disk into clusters, grouped into 512K sectors. Clusters are the smallest units for storing data and vary in size depending on the file system. Starting with the Windows 95 OSR2 release, Microsoft Windows supported the following two file system types: FAT16 and FAT32. FAT16 is a 16-bit file system that typically stores files in 32K clusters, depending on the partition size. FAT32 is a 32-bit file system that stores files more efficiently in 4K clusters. Under Windows NT, 2000, XP, and 2003, you have a third choice of using NTFS (New Technology File System). NTFS provides better protection against corruption, allows for file/folder encryption, allows for file/folder permissions (discussed in detail in Chapter 7), and more. Each file system has its advantages and disadvantages. You should choose a file system that will be compatible with the various operating systems running, provide the greatest security, be the most efficient, and can handle the partition sizes you need (see Table 2.1 for size limitations).

Table 2.1 File system partition size limitations.

Name	Max Size
FAT16	4 GB
FAT32	32 GB
NTFS	2 TB (and higher)

Imaging

Imaging is the process of taking an exact copy of a reference computer's hard drive or partition and storing it to an image file (usually compressed). That image can be stored on any storage medium (hard disk, CDR, , USB key, and so on) and restored to multiple computers, creating a standardized software and operating system environment. The basic principle of imaging is very similar to a simple disk copy.

Tools

For an administrator, deploying new PCs can become a large part of your job. With old PCs being retired and new PCs rolling in, finding a way to streamline the imaging process can help cut hours from your work day. And when you're dealing with more than a few PCs, automating the imaging process is not only helpful, but essential. An imaging tool such as Norton Ghost make it easy for an administrator to re-image multiple hard drives in a matter of minutes. While there are plenty of imaging tools available on the market, Norton Ghost is the most popular.

Symantec's Norton Ghost

Norton Ghost from Symantec (**www.symantec.com**) is the imaging package most commonly used by home users and IT (Information Technology) professionals. In addition to imaging, Norton Ghost includes cloning functionality, which allows disk-to-disk/partition-to-partition copying. Norton Ghost uses only command-line switches.

The **-CLONE** switch is the main switch used to create and restore Norton Ghost image files. The basic syntax of the **-CLONE** switch is:

```
GHOST -CLONE,MODE=m,SRC=s,DST=d
```

Here, *m* is any mode parameter, *s* is any source parameter, and *d* is any destination parameter. The **MODE** parameters are:

- **COPY**—Copies one disk to another
- **LOAD**—Restores an image to disk
- **DUMP**—Creates an image from disk
- **PCOPY**—Copies one partition to another
- **PLOAD**—Restores an image to partition
- **PDUMP**—Creates an image from partition

The rest of the parameters are dependent on the selected **MODE** parameter.

The **SRC** parameters are:

- *Drive*—Specifies a drive number (**COPY/DUMP**)
- *File*—Specifies a source image file (**LOAD**)
- *Drive:partition*—Specifies a drive and partition number (**PCOPY/PDUMP**)
- *@MTx*—Specifies a tape drive where *x* is the device number (**LOAD**)

The **DST** parameters are:

- *Drive*—Specifies a drive number (**COPY/LOAD**)
- *File*—Specifies a source image file (**DUMP/PDUMP**)
- *Drive:partition*—Specifies a drive and partition number (**PCOPY/PLOAD**)
- *@MTx*—Specifies a tape drive where *x* is the device number (**DUMP**)

NOTE: Inserting spaces between the CLONE parameters will cause script errors.

The Scripting Advantage

Since this chapter focuses on disk setups and formats, shell scripting clearly has the advantage because most of this activity occurs in DOS. AutoIt, KiXtart, and Windows Script Host cannot run in a pure DOS environment and are incapable of providing most of the functionality (if not all) of the scripts in this chapter.

A Word of Caution

This chapter contains many scripting examples on partitioning, formatting, and imaging disks. These scripts are very powerful and in the blink of an eye you can easily and accidentally destroy valuable data on a disk. As with all scripts, you should first test in an isolated testing environment to ensure the script produces the desired results before using in a production environment.

Immediate Solutions

Creating Partitions with Microsoft FDISK

Creating a partition with Microsoft FDISK from the command line is like scripting any program from the command line. The basic syntax to scripting a program from the command line is as follows:

```
program options
```

Here, **program** is the executable to be run, and **options** are the supported program parameters.

Creating a Primary Partition

To create a primary partition from the command line, enter the following:

```
FDISK /PRI: size disk
```

Here, **size** is the size of the partition in megabytes, and **disk** is the physical disk number.

TIP: *Entering a partition size greater than the drive size will set the partition to the maximum size of the drive or the maximum size allowed by the selected file system. This is useful when creating generic scripts where you will not know the drive size in advance.*

The **/PRI** option creates the primary partition and automatically sets it active. Any partition under 512MB will be set up as FAT16, and larger partitions will be set up as FAT32. To override this behavior and set up all partitions as FAT16, you can append an **O** (override) to the **/PRI** switch:

```
FDISK /PRIO: size disk
```

To have all partitions set up as FAT32, you can add the **/FPRMT** switch:

```
FDISK /FPRMT /PRI: size disk
```

Creating an Extended Partition

Scripting an extended partition creation is identical to scripting a primary partition creation, with the exception of the **/PRI** switch. To script the creation of an extended partition, enter the following:

```
FDISK /EXT: size disk
```

Here, **size** is the size of the partition in megabytes, and **disk** is the physical disk number.

The **/EXT** option creates an extended partition.

NOTE: You must already have a primary partition created before you can create an extended partition.

Creating a Logical Partition

To create a logical partition from the command line, enter the following:

```
FDISK /EXT: size disk /LOG: size
```

Here, **size** is the size of the partition in megabytes and must be less than or equal to the remaining free space, and **disk** is the physical disk number.

The **/EXT** switch is required in order to use the **/LOG** switch.

NOTE: You must already have a primary and extended partition created before you can create a logical partition.

To set up a logical partition with FAT16, you can append an **O** (override) to the **/LOG** switch:

```
FDISK /EXT: size disk /LOGO: size
```

Combining Switches

You can combine all three partition creation switches to set up a new hard drive with one line of code:

```
FDISK /PRI: size disk /EXT: size disk /LOG: size
```

NOTE: You cannot have multiple /LOG switches per one line of code. If you need to create multiple logical drives, you need to add multiple lines of code.

Rewriting the Master Boot Record

With an undocumented FDISK option, you can rewrite the master boot record without rewriting the partition table. To rewrite the MBR, proceed as follows:

```
FDISK /MBR
```

Undocumented Microsoft FDISK Options

Even though the **/?** option is supposed to display all available command-line options, Microsoft FDISK has many undocumented options. Here are some of the most common undocumented options:

- **/ACTOK**—Skips drive integrity checks (speeding up the process overall)
- **/EXT:*size disk***—Creates an extended partition
- **/FPRMT**—Skips the large drive support startup screen
- **/LOG:*size***—Creates a logical drive
- **/MBR**—Creates a new Master Boot Record
- **/PARTN**—Saves partition information to partsav.fil
- **/PRI:*size disk***—Creates a primary partition
- **/STATUS**—Displays current partition information

Working with Free FDISK

Free FDISK provides the same functionality as Microsoft FDISK while adding more useful features. Tasks like deleting, creating, and auto-sizing partitions are just as simple to perform as any other FDISK option.

Creating Auto-Sized Partitions

To create partitions to the maximum size, enter the following:

```
FDISK /AUTO
```

TIP: *You can create individual partitions by following the above command with a partition number.*

Deleting All Partitions

To delete all existing partitions (physical, extended, and logical), enter the following:

```
FDISK /CLEAR
```

TIP: You can delete individual partitions by following the above command with a partition number.

Other Free FDISK Options

Here are some of the most common options:

- **/ACTIVATE:*partition# drive#*—**Sets the specified partition active
- **/C—**Checks marked bad clusters
- **/DELETE—**Deletes individual partitions
- **/FS:*filesystem*—**Specifies the file system to format with
- **/ONCE—**Formats a floppy disk without prompting
- **/REBOOT—**Reboots the machine

Scripting Disk Formats

The main purpose of scripting is to streamline a process. Manual disk formats contain user prompts and pauses. Scripting a disk format allows you to control how much, if any, prompting is allowed.

Scripting a Hard Disk Format

To perform a completely hands-free drive format and label, enter the following:

```
FORMAT drive /AUTOTEST /V:label
```

Here, **drive** is the drive you want to format, and **label** is the label you want to give the drive.

The **/AUTOTEST** switch causes the **FORMAT** command to run while suppressing any prompts. The **/V** switch is used to assign a label to a disk. Disk labels can contain a maximum of eleven characters.

TIP: *You can follow this command with a /S to format the drive as a system drive.*

Scripting a Floppy Disk Format

Combining the **/AUTOTEST** switch with the **/V** switch does not create labels on floppy disks. Instead, you can use two separate commands:

```
FORMAT drive /AUTOTEST LABEL drive alabel
```

Here, **drive** is the drive you want to format, and **alabel** is the label you want to give the disk.

Scripting a Faster Disk Format

If the disk has already been formatted, you can run a quick disk format that simply erases the disk address tables (not the disk data). To perform a faster disk format, start the command prompt and enter the following:

```
FORMAT drive /Q /U
```

Here, **drive** is the drive you want to format; **/Q** indicates a quick format; and **/U** indicates an unconditional format.

Other Format Options

The other commonly used options are:

- **/BACKUP**—Identical to **/AUTOTEST** except prompts for disk label
- **/C**—Checks for bad clusters

Formatting a Disk to FAT32 or NTFS

By default, disks are formatted with the FAT file system. To format a disk to FAT32 or NTFS, enter the following:

```
FORMAT drive /fs:type
```

Here, **drive** is the drive you want to format (i.e "D:") and **type** is the desired file system type (FAT, FAT32, or NTFS).

NOTE: *Floppy disks can only be formatted to FAT.*

Converting a Formatted Disk to NTFS

If a disk has already been formatted as FAT or FAT32, you can convert
the disk to NTFS without losing data using the CONVERT command.
To convert an existing FAT or FAT32 disk to NTFS, start the command
prompt and enter the following:

```
CONVERT drive /fs:ntfs /v
```

Here, *drive* is the drive you want to convert to NTFS and **/v** indicates
that detailed messages should be displayed during the conversion.

WARNING! *This is a one-way conversion process. Microsoft does not provide any
method to convert an NTFS volume to FAT or FAT32. Remember, NTFS drives are not
accessible from Windows 95, 98, and ME.*

Suppressing Output when Shell Scripting

Although scripting does suppress most prompts, sometimes it does
not suppress the command output. You can suppress the output of a
shell command by sending the output to a **NUL** device (nonexistent
device). To suppress the output of a drive format, enter:

```
FORMAT drive /AUTOTEST > NUL
```

Redirecting Output when Shell Scripting

While the above example showed you how to suppress the out of a
shell script command, it really redirected the output to a nul device.
You can also redirect the output to a text file, which is useful for logging purposes. To redirect the output of a drive format to a text file,
enter the following statement:

```
FORMAT drive /AUTOTEST > FileName.txt
```

Creating Boot Disks

Any good administrator has a collection of boot disks ready and
waiting in time of need. Boot disks are used when you need to bypass

or perform a task before system bootup. Not only can you use scripting to create boot disks, but you can also use powerful scripts within them.

Creating a Hard Drive Setup Boot Disk

Follow these steps to create a boot disk that will automatically FDISK and format a hard disk:

1. Make a bootable DOS diskette. On Windows XP, this can be done by opening Windows Explorer, right clicking on the floppy drive, choosing "Format" from the context menu, selecting "Create an MS-DOS startup disk," and clicking "Start."

2. Copy FREE FDISK to the diskette.

3. Copy FORMAT.COM to the diskette.

4. Copy the script below to a file and save it as A:\AUTOEXEC.BAT:

```
@ECHO OFF
IF EXIST "A:\FORMAT.TXT" GOTO FORMAT
IF NOT EXIST "A:\FORMAT.TXT" GOTO FDISK

:FDISK
ECHO This system will reboot when complete.
ECHO.
ECHO Deleting all current partitions …
FDISK /CLEAR > NUL
ECHO Creating new partitions …
FDISK /AUTO > NUL
ECHO. > A:\FORMAT.TXT
GOTO REBOOT

:REBOOT
FDISK /REBOOT

:FORMAT
ECHO Formatting drive …
FORMAT drive /AUTOTEST /V:label /S
DEL A:\FORMAT.TXT
GOTO END

:END
CLS
ECHO FINISHED FDISK AND FORMAT
```

Here, ***drive*** is the drive you want to format, and ***label*** is the label you want to give the disk.

TIP: *To echo a blank line, use "ECHO." Notice there is no space between the word "ECHO" and the period.*

WARNING! This disk will automatically FDISK and format all partitions. You should clearly mark this disk and store it in a secure area. TRUST ME, I KNOW!

Working with the BOOT.INI

Once your drive is up and running Windows, you may need to edit the boot.ini file. The boot.ini is a hidden, read-only, system file stored in the root of the system partition (Windows Boot Drive). It contains options about which operating system to load and the timeout to load the default selection. At boot up, the boot loader will display the options contained in the boot.ini, if it contains more than one entry. You can modify the boot.ini directly (not recommended), through the System Configuration Utility (Start I Run I Msconfig), through the System control panel applet (Control Panel I System I Advanced I Startup and Recovery - Settings I System Startup), or through the Bootcfg command.

Backing up the Boot.ini

To backup the existing boot.ini, enter the following:

```
ATTRIIB -S -H DRIVELETTER:\BOOT.INI

COPY DRIVELETTER:\BOOT.INI   DRIVELETTER:\BOOT.BAK
ATTRIIB +S +H DRIVELETTER:\BOOT.INI
```

Here, the ATTRIB command is used to remove and later add the system and hidden attributes of the boot.ini.

Driveletter is the drive that contains the boot.ini file (e.g., C).

Related solution:	Found on page:
Setting File or Folder Attributes	59

Displaying the Boot.ini

The TYPE command displays the contents of a text file from the command prompt. To display the contents of the boot.ini using the TYPE command, enter the following:

```
TYPE DRIVELETTER:\BOOT.INI
```

Here, **driveletter** is the drive that contains the boot.ini file (e.g., C).

Displaying the Boot.ini Using Bootcfg

Bootcfg is a Windows XP/2003 command line tool that allows you to modify the boot.ini file of a local or remote system. To display the contents of the boot.ini on a remote system using Bootcfg, enter the following:

```
bootcfg /query
```

Here, the QUERY option displays the contents of the boot.ini.

TIP: *Many of Bootcfg options use entry ID numbers to reference each entry. Use the QUERY option to display entry ids.*

Scanning and Rebuilding the Boot.ini Using Bootcfg

Bootcfg can scan for existing Windows NT, 2000, XP, and 2003 installations and prompt to have the entries added to the boot.ini. To scan for existing installations only, enter the following:

```
bootcfg /scan /s REMOTESYSTEM /u USERDOMAIN\USERNAME /p PASSWORD
```

Here, the SCAN option displays the discovered Windows NT, 2000, XP, and 2003 installations and **remotesystem** is the name of the remote computer that contains the boot.ini file. The U and P options allow you to specify the domain name, user account name, and user account password of the user account with permissions to the remote computer.

To have Bootcfg scan and prompt to add discovered installations to the boot.ini, you can use the REBUILD option:

```
bootcfg /rebuild /s REMOTESYSTEM /u USERDOMAIN\USERNAME /p PASSWORD
```

TIP: *You can always use the U and P options to run Bootcfg against a remote system.*

Adding Safe Mode Entries Using Bootcfg

By default, Windows XP does not contain any safe mode boot.ini entries. To add safe mode entries to the default Windows XP boot.ini, enter the following:

```
bootcfg /copy /d "Safe Mode with No Network" /id 1
bootcfg /raw "/safeboot:minimal /sos /bootlog" /id 2

bootcfg /copy /d "Safe Mode with Network" /id 1
bootcfg /raw "/safeboot:network /sos /bootlog" /id 3
```

Here, the COPY option is used to copy the first entry (id 1). The /RAW option is used to replace any options with a specified string.

Deleting an Entry Using Bootcfg

To delete an entry, enter the following:

```
bootcfg /delete /id entrynumber
```

Here, *entrynumber* is the ID number of the entry to delete.

Scripting Norton Ghost

Norton Ghost is a powerful imaging tool that provides a quick and simple approach to scripting its functions: It performs all it's scripting from the command line. With just one line of code, you can create or restore an image in a snap. Although it does support the use of script files, these files are nothing more than a list of switches that can be performed at the command line.

Creating an Image

To create an image of drive 1 called image.gho on a remote drive Z, enter the following:

```
GHOST.EXE -CLONE,MODE=DUMP,SRC=1,DST=Z:\IMAGE.GHO
```

To create an image of the second partition of drive 1 called image.gho on a remote drive Z, enter the following:

```
GHOST.EXE -CLONE,MODE=PDUMP,SRC=1:2,DST=Z:\IMAGE.GHO
```

Restoring an Image

To restore an image called image.gho on a remote drive Z to drive 1, enter the following:

```
GHOST.EXE -CLONE, MODE=LOAD, SRC= Z:\IMAGE.GHO, DST=1
```

To restore an image called image.gho on a remote drive Z to the second partition on drive 1, enter the following:

```
GHOST.EXE -CLONE,MODE=PLOAD,SRC= Z:\IMAGE.GHO,DST=1:2
```

Performing a Drive Copy

To copy drive 1 to drive 2, enter the following:

```
GHOST.EXE -CLONE,MODE=COPY,SRC=1,DST=2
```

Performing a Partition Copy

To copy the first partition on drive 2 to the second partition on drive 1, enter the following:

```
GHOST.EXE -CLONE,MODE=PCOPY,SRC= 2:1,DST=1:2
```

Logging Errors

Norton Ghost records all errors in a log file called *ghost.err*. This file is normally stored in the program's root directory, but you can change the name and location of the file per use by using the **-AFILE** switch. Here is an example of how to use the **-AFILE** switch:

```
GHOST.EXE -CLONE,MODE=PCOPY,SRC= 2:1,DST=1:2 -AFILE=filename
```

Using a Script File

Norton Ghost can also read a text file that contains all or additional command-line switches. This file must be in text format, and each command-line switch must be on a different line. Here is an example of a script file:

```
-AFILE=z:\errorlog.txt
-CLONE,MODE=PCOPY,SRC= 2:1,DST=1:2
```

To run the script file, enter the following

```
GHOST.EXE @filename
```

Here, *filename* is the name of the script file.

More Switches

Different versions of Norton Ghost support different switches. To see a brief description of the available switches, type "GHOST -H" at the command prompt.

Scripting Installations and Updates

In Brief

In the previous chapter, you learned how to automate hard disk set-ups and images. Throughout this chapter, you will use various scripting methods to create unique scripting solutions to common administrative installations and updates. You will start by learning how to script installations from the command line. You will then learn how to use send keys to install windows and wizards using AutoIt.

Scripting Methods

Not all of us have the luxury of working with a centralized management system such as Systems Management Server (SMS), Lan Desk, or Tivoli. With new programs, program updates, service pack updates, and hot-fixes constantly coming out, installing all of these manually can consume most of an administrator's day. Scripting provides a way to automate these tasks with little or no user intervention.

Microsoft Command-Line Switches

Microsoft installation and update executables support many different switches to allow for shell scripting and installation customization. Switches are not case-sensitive and, more often than not, they are not standardized. To make matters worse, Microsoft tends not to document some of the most useful switches (as you saw in Chapter 2). Here are some of the most common, and possibly undocumented, switches for Microsoft installation and update executables:

- */?*—Displays unhidden switches and usage
- */C*—Extracts files to folder specified with /T switch
- */C ID*—Used to enter a 20-digit product ID
- */F*—Forces applications to close at shutdown
- */K ID*—Used to enter an 11-digit CD key
- */N*—Does not back up files for uninstall
- */N name*—Used to enter a username for registration
- */N:V*—Installs without version checking
- */O*—Overwrites OEM files without prompting
- */O organization*—Used to enter an organization name for registration

- **/Q**—Runs in quiet mode, skips all prompts
- **/Q:U**—Runs in user quiet mode, shows some dialog boxes
- **/Q:A**—Runs in admin quiet mode, shows no dialog boxes
- **/R**—Reinstalls the application
- **/R:A**—Always reboots
- **/R:I**—Reboots if necessary
- **/R:N**—Does not reboot, even if necessary
- **/R:S**—Reboots without prompting
- **/T:*path***—Specifies or extracts files to a temporary working folder
- **/U**—Runs in unattended mode or uninstalls an application, prompts for shared file removal
- **/UA**—Uninstalls an application and shared files, without prompting
- **/Z**—Does not reboot when installation is complete

Windows and Wizards

Many of the tasks of an administrator involve navigating through interactive windows and wizards. Whether installing a new program or adding a new piece of hardware, these wizards guide the user through a complicated setup process. This process involves scrolling through selections, clicking check boxes, selecting tabs, browsing, entering text, and more. Although these wizards are helpful, they frequently do not support scripting.

In the past, administrators used macro recorders to deal with these unscriptable windows and wizards. The main problem with basic macro utilities is that they are great for performing linear tasks, but they choke when dealing with complex routines that require decisions. The solution is to use a send-keys utility, such as AutoIt.

Scripting Windows with AutoIt

AutoIt (**www.autoitscript.com**) is a free automation tool that can send key and mouse commands to Windows objects. AutoIt detects window titles and text and sends commands to specific windows based on that information. Although you can use other scripting send-keys methods, such as Windows Script Host (WSH) or KiXtart, AutoIt provides the easiest way to detect windows and send keys.

Detecting Windows and Text

Sometimes multiple windows can have the same title. Luckily, AutoIt allows you to specify a combination of window title and window text to specify the exact window you want. Running the "AutoIt Windows Information" utility allows you to see the title, text, sizes, and mouse coordinates of the currently active window in real time. You can start this utility from the AutoIt start menu folder.

For example, suppose you wanted to script the Add New Hardware Wizard window (see Figure 3.1). Running the utility would show the window title and text (see Figure 3.2).

Adlibbing with AutoIt

One of the advantages that AutoIt has over using other send-key methods, such as KiXtart or WSH, is the ability to immediately intercept windows that may occur unexpectedly. AutoIt refers to the ability to handle unexpected Windows as "adlibbing." In order to use adlibbing, you must first enable it with the AdlibEnable command. When the script encounters any unforeseen error, window, and so on and adlibbing is enabled, the script can break out from its current location, execute the "handle" function you specified in the AdlibEnable command, and then return to the current location.

Figure 3.1   The Add New Hardware Wizard window.

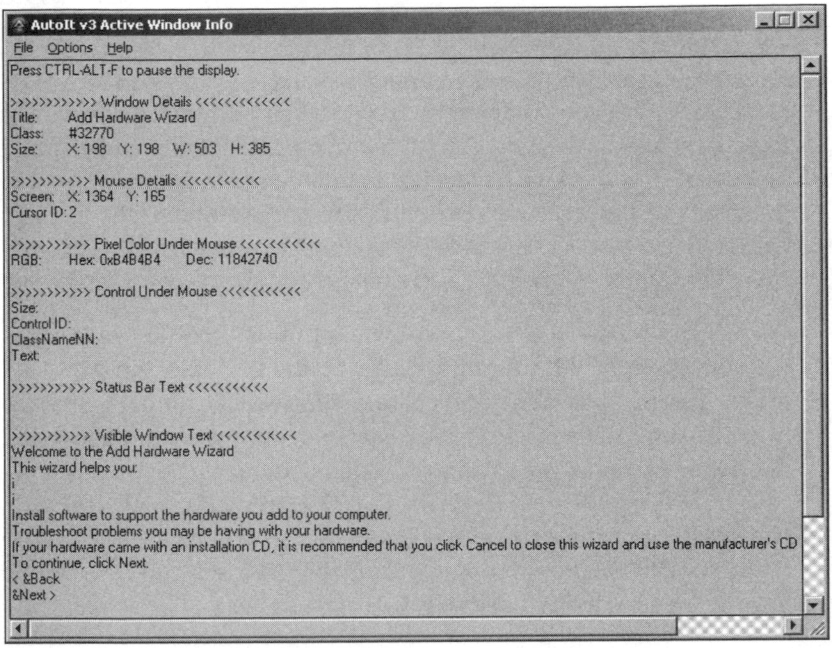

Figure 3.2   Detecting window title and text with /REVEAL AutoIt.

Convert Script Files to EXEs

Included in the AutoIt installation package is a utility called AUT2.EXE used to convert AutoIt script files into standalone executables. You can even password protect these executables from being turned back into AutoIt scripts. By converting your scripts, you can prevent users from reading your code and modifying your scripts. The conversion utility is menu-based and allows you to set your own executable icon, provided that it is 32 by 32 pixels in 16 colors.

Scripting AutoIt through COM

You can control AutoIt with KiXtart or Windows Script Host (or any language that can interact with COM) through AutoIt's COM object called AutoItX3. To gain access to AutoItX3, you must first use the **CreateObject** function and set it to a variable:

```
Set variable = CreateObject("AutoItX3.Control")
```

NOTE: *For more information and details on usage, see the AutoItX3 control documentation included in the program install.*

Microsoft Windows Installer

Before Windows 2000, installing and managing applications was a complete mess. Software companies created their own installation interfaces, each with its own set of rules, command-line options, and uninstall functions. This provided headaches for administrators who attempted to create common scripting solutions for application installations. To help reduce total cost of ownership (TCO) and provide a standardized set of installation rules, Microsoft created the Windows Installer.

The Windows Installer is a new installation and configuration service for 32-bit Windows platforms that standardizes the way programs install and uninstall. The Windows Installer is a Zero Administration Windows initiative and is required to conform to the "Designed for Microsoft Windows" logo standards. Some of the advanced features of the Windows Installer are self-repair, rollback, and install on demand. The Windows Installer comes packaged with Windows 2000 and above, and is available as a separate download for Windows $9x$ and Windows NT.

The Windows Installer runs as a two-part installation utility that consists of a client engine and a system service. The client engine (MSIEXEC.EXE) runs with user privileges and provides the interface between the system and the installation service. MSIEXEC.EXE reads the instructions from the installation package (*.MSI) and passes them to the installation service (Windows Installer).

The installation service enables the system to keep track of all program installations and system changes, providing for cleaner uninstalls. Because the installation service runs as a system service, it can be given various privileges to allow users to install their own applications.

Self-Repair

When a program file becomes corrupted or missing, a program installed with the Windows Installer can identify these files and replace them automatically. This is a handy feature for those of us with troublesome users who like to attempt their own uninstalls.

Rollback

The Windows Installer rollback feature creates a temporary backup and script of any files changed during the installation process. If a fatal error occurs during the installation, the rollback feature immediately runs the script and returns the system to its original state. All rollback files are stored in a temporary file called config.msi, and are automatically deleted when the installation successfully completes. Rollbacks can take a significant amount of disk space and can be disabled by an administrator.

TIP: You can always delete the config.msi file manually if setup fails to remove it.

Microsoft Windows Installer Switches

The MSIEXEC.EXE supports various command-line switches, allowing you to control the installer from the command shell or batch file. Here are some of the most common command-line switches for Microsoft Windows Installer:

- **/I**—Installs the program
- **/F**—Repairs an installation
- **/X**—Uninstalls the program
- **/L*V** *logfile*—Logs all information to a *logfile*
- **/QN**—No user interface
- **/QB**—Basic user interface
- **/QF**—Full user interface
- **/?** or **/H**—Displays some switches and copyright information
- **/X**—Uninstalls the program

The Scripting Advantage

Nowadays, most installations support command line switches to perform automated installs. While you could perform these type of installations using AutoIt, KiXtart, and Windows Script Host, shell scripting is clearly the most direct and easiest method to use when command line support is provided. For installations that absolutely do not offer an easy or any way to script the installation, AutoIt's mouse, keyboard, and Window control capabilities provides us with a last resort for these tough installations.

A Word of Caution

This chapter contains many scripting examples on performing application installs and uninstalls. An improper installation/uninstallation may not only leave the application inoperable, but other applications and even the operating system could be harmed as well. As with all scripts, you should first test the script in an isolated testing environment to ensure the script produces the desired results before using it in a production environment.

Immediate Solutions

Scripting a Silent .NET Framework Installation

Microsoft .NET is a collection of technologies that allow developers to build, deploy, and maintain applications using a standard set of classes. The .NET framework is the common language runtime and set of classes required to run any application built in .NET. To automate a silent installation of the .NET framework, proceed as follows:

1. Create a new directory to store all files included in this example.

2. Download the .NET framework redistributable from **www.microsoft.com** to the new directory.

3. Start the command prompt and enter the following:

```
"new directory path\dotnetfx.exe" /q:a /c:"install /l /q"
```

Here, ***new directory path*** is the complete path of the new folder created in step 1.

Scripting a Silent MDACS Installation

MDAC (Microsoft Data Access Components) is a set of drivers used to communicate with databases. While Windows 2000 and later versions come with a version of MDAC preinstalled, updating your version will provide improved performance and stability, as well as provide access to new data sources. To automate a silent installation of MDACS, proceed as follows:

1. Create a new directory to store all files included in this example.

2. Download the MDACS installer from **www.microsoft.com** to the new directory.

3. Start the command prompt and enter the following:

```
new directory path\executable
/q /C:"setup /QN1"
```

NOTE: *The highlighted code above is one continuous statement.*

Here, *new directory path* is the complete path of the new folder created in step 1, and *executable* is the name of the MDACS executable downloaded in step 2.

Scripting a Silent Windows 2000/XP Service Pack Installation

The Windows 2000/XP service packs allow you to script an install without forcing you to extract the files first. To automate a silent installation of a Windows 2000/XP service pack, proceed as follows:

1. Create a new directory to store all files included in this example.

2. Download the latest service pack, from **www.microsoft.com**, to the new directory.

3. Start the command prompt and enter the following:

```
new directory path\executable -F -N -O -Q
```

Here, *new directory path* is the complete path of the new folder created in step 1, and *executable* is the name of the service pack executable downloaded in step 2.

Scripting an Internet Explorer Download

The Internet Explorer setup utility is a 479kb file that downloads only the files needed for your operating system. If you need to install Internet Explorer on fifty systems, you'll have to sit and wait for it to download fifty times. To automate the download of Microsoft Internet Explorer 6.x, proceed as follows:

1. Create a new directory to store all files included in this example.

2. Download the Internet Explorer setup file (ie6setup.exe) from **www.microsoft.com** and store it in the new directory.

3. Start the command prompt and enter the following:

```
new directory path\-ie6setup.exe /c:"ie6wzd.exe /d /s:""#E"
```

Here, *new directory path* is the complete path of the new folder created in step 1.

Scripting a Silent Internet Explorer Install

Microsoft Internet Explorer is the most widely used Web browser for Windows and comes included with every Windows operating system. To automate the installation of Microsoft Internet Explorer 6.x, proceed as follows:

1. Create a new directory to store all files included in this example.

2. Download the Internet Explorer setup file (ie6setup.exe) from **www.microsoft.com** and store it in the new directory.

3. Start the command prompt and enter the following:

```
new directory path\ie6setup.exe /Q:A /R:N
```

Here, **new directory path** is the complete path of the new folder created in step 1.

Related solution:	Found on page:
Using Microsoft Internet Explorer as a Display Tool	98

Scripting a Silent WinZip Installation

WinZip is the most popular Windows compression utility for the ZIP format. To automate the installation of WinZip 8, 9, or 10 proceed as follows:

1. Create a new directory to store all files included in this example.

2. Download the WinZip installation executable, from **www.winzip.com**, to the new directory.

3. Download and install AutoIt, from **www.autoitscript.com**, to the new directory.

4. Double click on the *scriptfile*.

Here, **scriptfile** is a text file that contains the following:
```
Run("WinZipInstallationExecutable.exe")

WinWaitActive("WinZip® ", "http://www.winzip.com")
Send("{ENTER}")

WinWaitActive("WinZip® ", "&Setup")
Send("!s")
```

```
WinWaitActive("WinZip Setup", "Setup will install WinZip into the
following folder")
Send("{ENTER}")

WinWaitActive("WinZip Setup", "WinZip features include")
Send("!n")

WinWaitActive("License Agreement")
Send("!y")

WinWaitActive("WinZip Setup", "For helpful information on in-
stalling")
Send("!n")

WinWaitActive("WinZip Setup", "You can start with the")
Send("!c!n")

WinWaitActive("WinZip Setup", "&Express setup (recommended)")
Send("!e!n")

WinWaitActive("WinZip Setup", "Associations allow WinZip to")
Send("!n")

WinWaitActive("WinZip Setup", "Thank you for installing this
evaluation version")
Send("{ENTER}")

WinWaitActive("WinZip (")
WinClose("WinZip (")
```

NOTE: *The highlighted code above is one continuous statement.*

Scripting a Silent RealVNC Installation

RealVNC is an extremely powerful and free utility to see and control a remote computer (similar to PCAnywhere or Terminal Services). To automate a silent installation of RealVNC, proceed as follows:

1. Create a new directory to store all files included in this example.

2. Download the RealVNC installation executable, from **www.realvnc.com**, to the new directory.

3. Start the command prompt and enter the following:

```
new directory path\vnc-4_1_1-x86_win32.exe /VERYSILENT /
COMPONENTS="vncviewer, winvnc" /TASKS="quicklaunchicon,
```

```
desktopicon, installservice, launchservice"
```

Here, *new directory path* is the complete path of the new folder created in step 1.

Related solution:	Found on page:
Connecting to a Remote System through VNC	175

Scripting a Silent Windows Media Player Installation

To automate a silent installation of Windows Media Player 10, proceed as follows:

1. Create a new directory to store all files included in this example.

2. Download the Media Player 10 installation executable, from **www.microsoft.com**, to the new directory.

3. Start the command prompt and enter the following:

```
new directory path\MP10Setup.exe /q:A /c:"setup_wm.exe /Q /R:N
/P:#e"
```

Here, *new directory path* is the complete path of the new folder created in step 1.

Scripting a Silent DirectX Installation

To automate a silent installation of DirectX 9b or 9c, proceed as follows:

1. Create a new directory to store all files included in this example.

2. Download the DirectX 9b or 9c installation executable, from **www.microsoft.com**, to the new directory.

3. Start the command prompt and enter the following:

```
new directory path\DXWebSetup.exe /c:"DXwSetup.exe /
windowsupdate" /q /r:n
```

Here, *new directory path* is the complete path of the new folder created in step 1.

Working with the Windows Installer

The Windows Installer replaces the old ACME installer, adding more features and functionality. This new installer provides a standard method for application installations and an easy way for administrators to script installations.

Scripting a Silent Acrobat Reader Install

Acrobat Reader is the most widely used free PDF reader. To automate the installation of Acrobat Reader 7.0, proceed as follows:

1. Create a new directory to store all files included in this example.

2. Download the Acrobat Reader setup file (AdbeRdr70_enu_full.exe) from **www.adobe.com** and store it in the new directory.

3. Start the command prompt and enter the following:

```
new directory path\AdbeRdr70_enu_full.exe /s /v/qn
```

Here, *new directory path* is the complete path of the new folder created in step 1.

Scripting a QuickTime Install

QuickTime 7 is the latest version Apple's popular multimedia player. To automate a silent installation of QuickTime 7, proceed as follows:

1. Create a new directory to store all files included in this example.

2. Download the QuickTime setup file from **www.apple.com** and store it in the new directory.

3. Start the command prompt and enter the following:

```
new file path\QuickTimeInstaller.exe /s /v /qn
```

Here, *new directory path* is the complete path of the new folder created in step 1.

Scripting a Silent pcANYWHERE Installation

PcANYWHERE 11.5 is the latest version of remote control from Symantec (**www.symantec.com**). To automate a silent installation of pcANYWHERE 11.5, start the command prompt and enter the following:

```
MSIEXEC /I filepath\ Symantec pcAnywhere.msi /QN
```

Here, *file path* is the complete path of the pcANYWHERE 11.5 installation files.

Scripting a Silent Windows 2000 Resource Kit Installation

The Windows 2000 resource kit provides many tools and utilities that allow you to perform powerful administrative and system tasks. To automate a silent installation of a Windows 2000 resource kit, start the command prompt and enter the following:

```
MSIEXEC /I DRIVE:\W2000RKPRO.MSI /QN
```

NOTE: *Using the /QB switch may cause the installer to prompt that it is uninstalling the resource kit when in fact it is installing it.*

Here, *DRIVE* is the CD-ROM drive letter containing the Windows 2000 resource kit CD.

TIP: *You can script a silent Microsoft TechNet installation using the same install syntax and replacing the name of the msi file.*

Scripting the Windows Installer Installation

Although the Windows Installer redistributable files usually come packaged with a program that uses the Windows Installer, they can be downloaded and installed individually. To automate the installation of the Windows Installer, proceed as follows:

1. Create a new directory to store all files included in this example.

2. Download the Windows Installer redistributable from **www.microsoft.com/msdownload.platformsdk/ instmsi.htm**.

3. Select Start|Run and enter *"new directory path\wiexe /Q:A /R:A."*

Here, *new directory path* is the complete path of the new folder created in step 1, and *wiexe* is the name of the Windows Installer redistributable executable.

Scripting Microsoft Office 2000/XP

Microsoft Office 2000 was one of the first applications released by Microsoft to utilize the new Windows Installer. Although the following examples are focused toward Microsoft Office 2000 and Office XP, they can be applied to any application that utilizes the new Windows Installer.

Removing Older Versions

The Microsoft Office Removal Wizard can be used to remove older versions of Microsoft Office before installing Microsoft Office 2000/XP. To automate the removal of older versions of Microsoft Office, start the command prompt and enter the following:

```
SETUP /S /Q /R /L log file
```

Here, *log file* records all activity of the removal process.

NOTE: *The Microsoft Office Removal Wizard is included in the Microsoft Office 2000/XP Resource Kit.*

Scripting a Silent Installation

To automate the installation of Microsoft Office 2000/XP, start the command prompt and enter the following:

```
file path\SETUP /QN /L*V
install log COMPANYNAME="company"
```

Here, *file path* is the complete path of the Office installation files, *install log* is the file to store all errors and output, and *company* is the name of the company registered for Office.

TIP: *For more information about Office 2000/XP command-line switches, see the Microsoft TechNet Article Q202946 (Office 2000) and Q283686 (Office XP).*

Scripting an Uninstall

To automate the uninstallation of Microsoft Office 2000/XP, start the command prompt and enter the following:

```
file path\SETUP /QN /X msifile
```

Here, *file path* is the complete path of the Office installation files originally used to install Office, and *msifile* is the name of the msi package to uninstall.

Scripting a Repair

To automate the repair of a Microsoft Office 2000/XP installation, start the command prompt and enter the following:

```
file path\SETUP /FOCUMS msifile
```

Here, *file path* is the complete path of the Office installation files originally used to install Office, and *msifile* is the name of the msi package to repair.

Scripting a Reinstallation

To automate the reinstallation of Microsoft Office 2000/XP, start the command prompt and enter the following:

```
file path\SETUP /FECUMS msifile
```

Here, *file path* is the complete path of the Office installation files originally used to install Office, and *msifile* is the name of the msi package to reinstall.

Advertising

Instead of installing an application, you can simply set up the Start menu shortcuts that, when activated, will install the application on first use. This setup method is called *advertising*. To advertise Microsoft Office 2000/XP, start the command prompt and enter the following:

```
file path\SETUP /QN /JU msifile
```

Here, *file path* is the complete path of the Office installation files originally used to install Office, and *msifile* is the name of the msi package to advertise.

Disabling Windows Installer Rollbacks

To disable the Windows Installer Rollback feature during an installation, start the command prompt and enter the following:

```
file path\SETUP DISABLEROLLBACK=1
```

Here, *file path* is the complete path of the installation files used in the original installation.

Installing the Windows Installer Clean Up Utility

Microsoft has created a utility that allows you to delete Windows Installer registry entries from a system. This is useful when you have corrupted installations that are preventing you from successfully installing a program. Although the utility's installer states that it supports the standard Microsoft installation switches, they do not work. To automate the installation of the Windows Installer Clean Up Utility, proceed as follows:

1. Create a new directory to store all files included in this example.

2. Download the Windows Installer Clean Up Utility from Microsoft.

   For Windows 9*x*:

   ```
   download.microsoft.com/download/office2000pro/util22/1/W9X/
   EN-US/msicu.exe
   ```

NOTE: *The code above is one continuous statement.*

   For Windows 2000:

   ```
   download.microsoft.com/download/office2000pro/util20/1/NT4/
   EN-US/msicuu.exe
   ```

NOTE: *The code above is one continuous statement.*

---

3. Download and install AutoIt, from **www.autoitscript.com**, to the new directory.

4. Double click on the *scriptfile*.

Here, **scriptfile** is a text file that contains the following:

```
AdlibEnable("AdlibHandler")

RUN("executable")

WinWaitActive("Windows Installer", "It is strongly")
Send("!N")

WinWaitActive("Windows Installer", "License")
Send("!A!N")

WinWaitActive("Windows Installer", "Start")
Send("!N")

WinWaitActive("Windows Installer", "Windows Installer Clean Up has
been successfully installed")
Send("!F")

Exit

Func AdlibHandler()
  ;Used to prevent installation from unexpectedly ending
  If WinActive("Windows Installer", "Setup is not complete") Then
     WinActivate("Windows Installer", "Setup is not complete")
```

```
                Send("!R")
            EndIf
            If WinActive("Windows Installer", "Windows Installer Clean Up
                  was interrupted") Then
              WinActivate("Windows Installer", "Windows Installer Clean Up
                  was interrupted")
              Send("{ENTER}")
            EndIf

            ; Used for uninstallation
            If WinActive("Windows Installer", "This will remove") Then
              WinActivate("Windows Installer", "This will remove")
              Send("!N")
            EndIf
            If WinActive("Windows Installer", "Windows Installer Clean Up
                  has been successfully uninstalled") Then
              WinActivate("Windows Installer", "Windows Installer Clean Up
                  has been successfully uninstalled")
              Send("!F")
              EXIT
            EndIf
            ; Used if wrong version installation is attempted
            If WinActive("Installer Information") Then
              WinActivate("Installer Information")
              Send("!O")
            EndIf

            If WinActive("Fatal Error") Then
              WinActivate("Fatal Error")
              Send("{ENTER}")
              Exit
            EndIf
        EndFunc
```

Here, *executable* is the name of the Windows Installer Clean Up executable.

NOTE: *For more information about the Windows Installer Clean Up utility, see the Microsoft TechNet article Q238413 (Office 2000) and Q290301 (Office XP).*

NOTE: *The highlighted code is one continuous statement.*

Chapter 4

File Management

(continued)

4. File Management

In Brief

Files are the backbone of any information system. They hold the data you work with and make up the programs you use. As a computer user, everything you do involves interacting with files. Finding, deleting, creating, and modifying files are actions you do every day, often without even noticing it.

As administrators, we've all dealt with users who tried to back up their entire system to the server or start their own MP3 (Motion Pictures Experts Group Layer-3 Audio) server with their user directory. Although Windows 2000 provides disk quota management, it does not include a method to target and remove the offending files. In addition to eating a disk's free space, users also have a tendency to save files with strange names and extensions while storing the data anywhere they please.

And while users are slowly tearing at the file system, the system is also filling the disk with temp files, orphaned files, and system logs. With more user data and application files being placed on a system daily, keeping the file system healthy is a constant race that never ends. In this chapter, you will learn how to clean up your file system and perform file-related tasks.

A Word of Caution—Understanding NTFS Permissions

This chapter contains many scripting examples on copying and moving files. Copying and moving files and folders has various affects on NTFS encryption, compression, or permissions. For example, a task as simple as copying a file may cause you to lose NTFS permissions set on a secure file. The following list explains the affects of copying and moving NTFS files and folders:

- Copying Files/Folders within NTFS drives will cause the object to inherit NTFS permissions of the target folder.

- Moving Files/Folders between two NTFS drives will cause the object to inherit NTFS permissions of the target folder.

- Moving Files/Folders within the same NTFS drive will cause the object to retain its NTFS permissions.

- Copying Compressed Files/Folders within NTFS drives will cause the object to inherit the compression setting of the target folder.

- Moving Compressed Files/Folders between two NTFS drives will cause the object to inherit the compression setting of the target folder.

- Moving Compressed Files/Folders within the same NTFS drive will cause the object to retain its compression.

- Copying or Moving Compressed Files/Folders to a non-NTFS drive will cause the object to lose its compression.

- Copying or Moving Encrypted Files/Folders within NTFS drives will cause the object to retain its encryption.

- Copying or Moving Encrypted Files/Folders to a non-NTFS drive will cause the object to lose its encryption.

- Copying Unencrypted Files/Folders to an NTFS Encrypted Folder will cause the object to become encrypted.

- Moving Unencrypted Files/Folders to an NTFS Encrypted Folder will not cause the object to become encrypted.

The Scripting Advantage

Due to the power of the FileSystemObject object, Windows Script Host and KiXtart have the clear advantage. KiXtart has a slight advantage because it includes basic file and folder functionality without having to go through the FileSystemObject. Shell scripting is also a good choice because it provides basic and advanced file and folder functionality and you can extend it using the Windows 2000 Resource Kit and third-party utilities. Finally, while AutoIt also includes basic file and folder functionality, its inability to easily work with FileSystemObject and it's lack of extensibility in this area causes it to fall behind.

A Word of Caution

This chapter contains many scripting examples on manipulating the file system. Accidentally deleting, renaming, copying, or moving production files and folders can have disastrous effects. As with all scripts, you should first test each script in an isolated testing environment to ensure the script produces the desired results before using it in a production environment.

Immediate Solutions

Working with the File System

Files and folders are the building blocks of any system. They contain the data we treasure, the operating system we use, and the applications we work with. Shell scripting, KiXtart, and Windows Script Host provide many ways of working with the file system. Although the tasks these scripting methods perform are similar, the commands, syntax, and limitations of each method differ.

Manipulating the File System Using Shell Scripting

Shell scripting provides limited functionality for manipulating the file system. Although Resource Kit utilities extend the capabilities of shell scripting, it still cannot compare to the more powerful functions of KiXtart and Windows Script Host. So, why use shell scripting? Shell scripting comes built into every operating system, and you will run into situations where shell scripting is your only alternative.

Deleting Files Depending on Extension

The Windows 2000/XP DELETE command supports many options that the Windows 9*x* command does not. To remove files based on extension in Windows 2000/XP, start the command prompt and enter the following:

```
DEL *.ext /F /Q /S
```

Here, *ext* is the file extension of the files to delete; the **/F** switch forces the deletion of read-only files; the **/Q** switch removes prompts; and the **/S** switch performs deletions not only in the current directory, but in the subdirectories as well.

Deleting Folders and Subfolders

Windows XP includes the RMDIR (Remove Directory) command that mimics the Windows 9*x* DELTREE.EXE (Delete Tree) command. To delete a root folder and all its subfolders with RMDIR, start the command prompt and enter the following:

```
RMDIR /Q /S directory
```

Here, **directory** is the name of the directory to delete; the **/Q** switch removes prompts; and the **/S** switch performs the deletion of all files and subdirectories.

Determining File Versions

FILEVER.EXE is a Resource Kit utility to display file versions from the command line. To determine a file version, start the command prompt and enter the following:

```
FILEVER filename
```

Here, **filename** is the path and name of file to determine the file version.

NOTE: *Remember, only application files have versions.*

Updating Program Files Depending on the Version

REPLACE is a command that can be used to update older files with newer file versions. To update a file with a newer version, start the command prompt and enter the following:

```
REPLACE /R /S /U source destination
```

Here, **source** is the path and name of the source file; **destination** is the directory to start the replacement; the **/R** switch allows for read-only file replacement; the **/S** switch performs the replacement in the current directory and all subdirectories; and the **/U** switch specifies to only replace files with a newer version.

Replicating Files and Directories

You can tell users to back up their files to the server, but whether the users actually do back the files up is a different story. ROBOCOPY is a Resource Kit utility to copy, move, or replicate files from the command line. To replicate files, start the command prompt and enter the following:

```
ROBOCOPY /MIR /ETA /NP /LOG+:logfile source destination
```

Here, the **/MIR** mirrors a directory tree; the **/ETA** switch displays the estimated time of arrival of copied files; the **/NP** switch causes no copy progress to be displayed; the **/LOG+:***logfile* outputs the status to the *logfile*; and *destination* is the location to replicate the *source* to.

Displaying File or Folder Attributes

The ATTRIB command allows you to display file or folder attributes. To display the attributes of a file or folder, start the command prompt and enter the following:

```
ATTRIB filefolder
```

Here, *filefolder* is the file or folder that contains the attributes you wish to display.

Setting/Removing File or Folder Attributes

The ATTRIB command allows you to set or remove file and folder attributes. To set attributes of a file or folder, start a command prompt and enter the following:

```
ATTRIB +R +H +S filefolder
```

*TIP: Here, **filefolder** is the file or folder that contains the attributes you want to set. The **+R**, **+H**, and + **S** set **filefolder**'s Read Only , Hidden, and System attributes respectively.*

To remove attributes of a file or folder, start a command prompt and enter the following:

```
ATTRIB -R -H -S filefolder
```

Merging Files

The TYPE command combined with the redirection commands (> to overwrite, >> to append) allow you merge multiple files into a single file. To merge files, start the command prompt and enter the following:

```
TYPE FilePath1 > MergedFile
TYPE FilePath2
>>
MergedFile
```

You can also use the **COPY** command to merge multiple files:

```
COPY FilePath1 + FilePath2 MergedFile
```

Compressing Files and Folders

With Windows NT/2000/XP/2003 and a drive formatted with NTFS (New Technologies File System), you can take advantage of NTFS

4. File Management

compression to save disk space by compressing your files and folders. The COMPACT command allows you to compress/uncompress NTFS files and folders from the command line. To compress all the files and subfolders of a folder, start a command prompt and enter the following:

```
COMPACT /c /s rootfolder\*.*
```

Here, **rootfolder** is the folder that contains the files and folders you want to compress. The **/c** option sets the intended action to compress, and **/s** specifies that the intended action should be applied to all files and subfolders of the **rootfolder**.

Creating Random File Names

CMD.exe can generate a random number between 0 and 32767 and store it to an environment variable called %RANDOM%. To create a random file name, start the command prompt and enter the following:

```
Set FileName=%RANDOM%.tmp
```

Deleting a File to the Recycle Bin Using AutoIt

While AutoIt provides basic file and folder functionality, it simply cannot compete with Windows Script Host and KiXtart. Some of its disadvantages are the inability to recursively delete files or force delete files (to name a few). Due to the size limitations of this book, we'll focus on AutoIt's unique ability to delete a single or multiple files to the recycle bin. To delete a file to the recycle bin, create and then execute an AutoIt script containing the following:

```
$ReturnCode = FileRecycle("FilePath")
```

If the file deletion is successful, **$ReturnCode** will be set to 1; otherwise, it will be set to 0 (delete failed or file does not exist).

Manipulating the File System Using KiXtart

KiXtart is a scripting language introduced in Chapter 1 that is best used when you know the exact file or directory you want to manipulate. KiXtart provides poor directory parsing capabilities with its limited DIR command and lack of recursive support. To compensate, you can call external commands for indirect file management and KiXtart commands for direct file management.

Using External Commands

KiXtart provides two statements to run an external 16- or 32-bit application or command: **SHELL** and **RUN**. The **SHELL** statement will wait for the external command to complete, but the **RUN** statement will not. Both the **SHELL** and **RUN** statements have the same syntax:

```
statement "command"
```

Here, *statement* is the **RUN** or **SHELL** statement, and *command* is the command to run. To delete all the files in the temp directory using the **RUN** statement, you would enter:

```
RUN "%COMSPEC% /C DEL C:\TEMP\*.* /F /Q /S"
```

NOTE: *%COMSPEC% /C is used to run commands from the DOS environment.*

Renaming a File or Folder

KiXtart does not contain a function to rename a file or folder. Instead, you can move the current item to a new item with the desired name, providing an item with the new name does not already exist. To rename a file or folder, create and execute a KiXtart script containing the following:

```
REN('oldname', 'newname')

Function REN($OldFileName, $NewFileName)
  MOVE $OldFileName $NewfileName /h
EndFunction
```

Here, *oldname* is the name of the file or folder to rename and *newname* is the name to rename the *oldname* to. The REN function uses the MOVE command to rename the file or folder. The **/h** option specifies to include system and hidden files.

Displaying File or Folder Attributes

The KiXtart command **GetFileAttr** allows you to display file or folder attributes. To display the attributes of a file or folder, create and execute a KiXtart script containing the following:

```
DisplayAttr("path")
Sleep 5

Function DisplayAttr($FileFolder)
  $ReadOnly = 0      $Hidden = 0       $System = 0
  $Dir = 0           $Archive = 0      $Encrypt = 0
```

```
$Normal = 0        $Temp = 0        $Sparse = 0
$Reparse = 0       $Compress = 0    $Offline = 0

If GetFileAttr($FileFolder) & 1 $ReadOnly = 1 EndIf
If GetFileAttr($FileFolder) & 2 $Hidden = 1 EndIf
If GetFileAttr($FileFolder) & 4 $System = 1 EndIf
If GetFileAttr($FileFolder) & 16 $Dir = 1 EndIf
If GetFileAttr($FileFolder) & 32 $Archive = 1 EndIf
If GetFileAttr($FileFolder) & 64 $Encrypt = 1 EndIf
If GetFileAttr($FileFolder) & 128 $Normal = 1 EndIf
If GetFileAttr($FileFolder) & 256 $Temp = 1 EndIf
If GetFileAttr($FileFolder) & 512 $Sparse = 1 EndIf
If GetFileAttr($FileFolder) & 1024 $Reparse = 1 EndIf
If GetFileAttr($FileFolder) & 2046 $Compress = 1 EndIf
If GetFileAttr($FileFolder) & 4096 $Offline = 1 EndIf

? "File: " + $FileFolder
? ""
? "ReadOnly: " + $ReadOnly
? "Hidden: " + $Hidden
? "System: " + $System
? "Directory: " + $Dir
? "Archive: " + $Archive
? "Encrypted: " + $Encrypt
? "Normal: " + $Normal
? "Temporary: " + $Temp
? "Sparse: " + $Sparse
? "Reparse: " + $Reparse
? "Compressed: " + $Compress
? "Offline: " + $Offline
EndFunction
```

Here, *path* is the file or folder that contains the attributes you wish to display.

NOTE: *Windows 2000 adds several new file attributes with NTFS 5. For more information, see Chapter 17 of the Windows 2000 Professional Resource Kit.*

Setting File or Folder Attributes

The KiXtart command **SetFileAttr** allows you to set file or folder attributes. To modify the attributes of a file or folder, create and execute a KiXtart script containing the following:

```
;Sets Read Only and Hidden attributes
SetAttribs("filefolder",1,1,0,0,0,0)
Function SetAttribs($File, $ReadOnly, $Hidden, $System, $Archive,
$Temp, $Offline)
```

```
$Rcode = SetFileAttr($File,128) ;Reset file to normal

  $Attribs = 0
  If $ReadOnly = 1 $Attribs = $Attribs + 1 EndIf
  If $Hidden = 1 $Attribs = $Attribs + 2 EndIf
  If $System = 1 $Attribs = $Attribs + 4 EndIf
  If $Archive = 1 $Attribs = $Attribs + 32 EndIf
  If $Temp = 1 $Attribs = $Attribs + 256 EndIf
  If $Offline = 1 $Attribs = $Attribs + 4096 EndIf

  $SetAttribs = SetFileAttr($File,$Attribs)
EndFunction
```

NOTE: *The highligted code above must be placed on one line.*

Here, *filefolder* is the file or folder that contains the attributes you want to set. To modify *filefolder*'s attributes, change the value of the corresponding input parameters (*$ReadOnly, $Hidden, $System, $Archive, $Normal, $Offline*) to 1 to enable, or 0 to disable.

Appending Text Files

To append the contents of one text file to another, create and execute a KiXtart script containing the following:

```
$File1 = "file1"
$File2 = "file2"

$Rcode = Open(1,$File1)
$Rcode = Open(2,$File2,5)
$File1 = ReadLine(1)
While @Error=0
  If $File1
    $Rcode = WriteLine(2,$File1 + Chr(13) + Chr(10))
  EndIf
    $File1 = ReadLine(1)
Loop

$Rcode = Close(1)
$Rcode = Close(2)
```

Here, *file1* is the file whose contents you want to append to *file2*.

Searching and Replacing Lines within Files

Replacing specific lines within text files is a common administrative task. To search and replace a line within a text file, create and execute a KiXtart script containing the following:

```
$File = "somefile"
$DLine = "searchline"
$RLine = "replaceline"
$TempFile = $File + ".TMP"
$LineNum = 0

$Rcode = OPEN (1, $File, 2)
DEL $TempFile
$Rcode = OPEN (2, $TempFile, 5)
$Line = READLINE(1)
WHILE @Error = 0

$LineNum = $LineNum + 1
IF $Line = $DLine
    $Rcode = WRITELINE(2, $RLine + Chr(13) + Chr(10))
ELSE
    $Rcode = WRITELINE(2, $Line + Chr(13) + Chr(10))
ENDIF
    $Line = READLINE(1)
LOOP

$Rcode = CLOSE(1)
$Rcode = CLOSE(2)
COPY $TempFile $File
DEL $TempFile
```

Here, *somefile* is the file to parse, and *replaceline* is the text to replace the *searchline* with.

Searching and Replacing within an INI File

INI files, or initialization files, are text files that were originally created to store configuration information for 16-bit applications. KiXtart is the easiest scripting method for modifying an INI file because it has two built-in INI functions (**READPROFILESTRING** and **WRITE PROFILESTRING**). To search and replace a value in an INI file, create and execute a KiXtart script containing the following:

```
$LoadKey = ReadProfileString("inifile", section, key)
If $LoadKey = oldvalue
  WriteProfileString("inifile ", section, key, newvalue)
EndIf
```

Here, *inifile* is the complete name and path of the INI file; *section* is the name of the INI section to search (without the brackets); *key* is the name of the key to search; *oldvalue* is the value to find; and *newvalue* is the value to replace it with.

NOTE: WriteProfileString in this example replaces the old value with a new value surrounded by double quotes. If you wish to clear the value, the new value should be a space surrounded by double quotes. Simply supplying double quotes (no space) would delete the entire key and value from the INI file.

Manipulating the File System Using Windows Script Host

Many of the file management tasks administrators would like to script are too complex or cannot be done with shell scripting or KiXtart. Through the FileSystemObject object, Windows Script Host (WSH) provides direct access to the file system, allowing you to create complex and unique file management scripts.

Accessing the **FileSystemObject Object**

The **FileSystemObject** object stores all the functions that allow you to manipulate the file system through a script file. To create an instance of the **FileSystemObject**, proceed as follows:

```
Set FSO = CreateObject("Scripting.FileSystemObject")
```

Going through Subfolders

This subroutine will work through the subfolders of a main directory, calling another subroutine called **MainSub**:

```
Sub GoSubFolders(objDIR)
  If objDIR <> "\System Volume Information" Then
    MainSub objDIR
    For Each eFolder in objDIR.SubFolders
      GoSubFolders eFolder
    Next
  End If
End Sub
```

NOTE: The System Volume Information Directory is a system directory that stores system files, restores information, and encryption logs. Since this is an exclusive system directory, scripts that attempt to access it will generate an access denied error.

Connecting to a File

Before performing certain WSH actions on a file, you must first connect to it using the **GetFile** method. Here is a function to connect to a file:

```
Function GetFile(sFILE)
  On Error Resume Next
  Set GetFile = FSO.GetFile(sFILE)
  If Err.Number <> 0 Then
    Wscript.Echo "Error connecting to: " & sFILE & VBlf & _
        "[" & Err.Number & "] " & Err.Description
    Wscript.Quit Err.Number
  End If
End Function
```

TIP: On Error Resume Next *allows the script to continue to the next statement if an error occurs. This allows you to perform error checking and alerting.*

In this script, a connection to a file is attempted, and the user is prompted if any errors occur.

Connecting to a Folder

Before performing certain WSH actions on a folder, you must first connect to it using the **GetFolder** method. Here is a function to connect to a folder:

```
Function GetFolder(sFOLDER)
  On Error Resume Next
  Set GetFolder = FSO.GetFolder(sFOLDER)
  If Err.Number <> 0 Then
    Wscript.Echo "Error connecting to folder: " & sFOLDER & _
        VBlf & "[" & Err.Number & "] " & Err.Description
    Wscript.Quit Err.Number
  End If
End Function
```

Generating a Random File Name

Most applications use temporary files—files with random and or unique names. During your scripting lifetime, you will need to generate a random filename to hold temporary data. Here is a function to create a temporary file name:

```
Function GetRandomName()
  Set FSO = CreateObject("Scripting.FileSystemObject")
  GetRandomName = FSO.GetTempName
End Function
```

Generating a Directory Listing

To generate a directory list, create and execute a WSH script containing the following:

```
Set FSO = CreateObject("Scripting.FileSystemObject")
sDIR = "directory"

Set objDIR = GetFolder(sDIR)
GoSubFolders objDIR

Sub ListFiles(objDIR)
    For Each efile in objDIR.Files
        Wscript.Echo efile
    Next
End Sub

Sub GoSubFolders(objDIR)
  If objDIR <> "\System Volume Information" Then
    ListFiles objDIR
    For Each eFolder in objDIR.SubFolders
        Wscript.Echo eFolder
        GoSubFolders eFolder
    Next
  End If
End Sub
```

Here, **directory** is the root folder containing the files and folders to list. The subprocedure **ListFiles** rotates through all the files within the current directory and lists their names.

NOTE: *You need to append the **GetFolder** routine, listed earlier in this chapter, to this script in order for it to run.*

TIP: *If you want to send the directory list to a text file, you can use the DOS append command (>>) when running the script from the command line (for example, **cscript scriptfile.vbs >> textfile.txt**).*

Deleting a File

To delete a file with WSH, you can use the **DeleteFile** method. Here is a subroutine to delete a file:

```
Sub DelFile(sFILE)
  On Error Resume Next
  FSO.DeleteFile sFILE, True
  If Err.Number <> 0 Then
    Wscript.Echo "Error deleting file: " & sFILE
  End If
End Sub
```

In this script, a file deletion is attempted, and the user is prompted if any errors occur.

Deleting All Files within a Folder

To delete all files within a root folder and its subfolders, create and execute a WSH script containing the following:

```
Set FSO = CreateObject("Scripting.FileSystemObject")
sDIR = "directory"
Set objDIR = GetFolder(sDIR)
GoSubFolders objDIR

Sub MainSub(objDIR)
  For Each efile in objDIR.Files
    DelFile efile
  Next
End Sub
```

Here, **directory** is the root folder containing the files to delete.

NOTE: You need to append the **GoSubFolders**, **DelFile**, and **GetFolder** routines, listed earlier in this chapter, to this script in order for it to run.

Deleting Files Depending on Size

It happens to all of us, but every now and then a user chooses to upload hundred meg files to a public share. To delete all files within a root folder and its subfolders depending on size, create and execute a WSH script containing the following:

```
Set FSO = CreateObject("Scripting.FileSystemObject")
sDIR = "directory"
lSIZE = lowersize
uSIZE = uppersize

Set objDIR = GetFolder(sDIR)
GoSubFolders objDIR

Sub MainSub (objDIR)
  For Each efile in objDIR.Files
    If lSIZE = Null and uSIZE = Null Then
      If efile.Size = 0 Then
        DelFile efile
      End If
    ElseIf lSIZE <> Null and uSIZE = Null Then
      If efile.Size < lSIZE Then
        DelFile efile
      End If
```

```
      ElseIf lSIZE = Null and uSIZE <> "" Then
        If efile.Size > uSIZE Then
          DelFile efile
        End If
      ElseIf lSIZE = uSIZE Then
        If efile.Size = lSIZE Then
          DelFile efile
        End If
      Else
        If efile.Size > lSIZE and _
          efile.Size < uSIZE Then
          DelFile efile
        End If
      End If
    Next
End Sub
```

Here, **directory** is the folder containing the files to delete, **lowersize** is the lower size limit, and **uppersize** is the upper size limit. If both limits are null, the script will delete all empty files. If just the upper limit is null, the script will delete files smaller than the lower limit. If just the lower limit is null, the script will delete files larger than the upper limit. If both limits are not null but equal, the script will delete files equal to the limit. If both limits are not null and not equal, the script will delete files within the two limits.

NOTE: *You need to append the **GoSubFolders**, **DelFile**, and **GetFolder** routines, listed earlier in this chapter, to this script in order for it to run.*

Deleting Files Depending on Date

A common administrative task is deleting old files from public shares. To delete all files within a root folder and its subfolders depending on last modified date, create and execute a WSH script containing the following:

```
Set FSO = CreateObject("Scripting.FileSystemObject")
sDIR = "directory"
lDATE = "lowerdate"
uDATE = "upperdate"

lDATE = CDate(lDATE)
uDATE = CDate(uDATE)
Set objDIR = GetFolder(sDIR)
GoSubFolders objDIR
Sub MainSub (objDIR)
  For Each efile in objDIR.Files
    If lDATE = Null and uDATE = Null Then
```

73

```
            If efile.DateLastModified = Date Then
               DelFile efile
            End If
         ElseIf lDATE <> Null and uDATE = Null Then
            If efile.DateLastModified < lDATE Then
               DelFile efile
            End If
         ElseIf lDATE = Null and uDATE <> Null Then
            If efile.DateLastModified > uDATE Then
               DelFile efile
            End If
         ElseIf lDATE = uDATE Then
            If efile.DateLastModified = lDATE Then
               DelFile efile
            End If
         Else
            If efile.DateLastModified > lDATE and _
               efile.DateLastModified < uDATE Then
               DelFile efile
            End If
         End If
      Next
   End Sub
```

Here, ***directory*** is the folder containing the files to delete, ***lowerdate*** is the lower date limit, and ***upperdate*** is the upper date limit. If both limits are null, the script will delete files last modified today. If just the upper limit is null, the script will delete files smaller than the lower limit. If just the lower limit is null, the script will delete files larger than the upper limit. If both limits are not null but equal, the script will delete files equal to the limit. If both limits are not null and not equal, the script will delete files within the two limits.

NOTE: You need to append the **GoSubFolders**, **DelFile**, and **GetFolder** routines, listed earlier in this chapter, to this script in order for it to run.

Deleting Files Depending on Name

From hacker tools to new viruses, deleting files with a specific name is a common administrative task. To delete all files with a specific name within a root folder and its subfolders, create and execute a WSH script containing the following:

```
Set FSO = CreateObject("Scripting.FileSystemObject")
sDIR = "directory"
sFILE = "filename"
```

```
Set objDIR = GetFolder(sDIR)
GoSubFolders objDIR

Sub MainSub(objDIR)
  For Each efile in objDIR.Files
    If LCase(efile.Name) = LCase(sFILE) Then
      DelFile efile
    End If
  Next
End Sub
```

Here, ***directory*** is the folder containing the files to delete, and ***filename*** is the name of the file to search for.

---

*NOTE: You need to append the **GoSubFolders**, **DelFile**, and **GetFolder** routines, listed earlier in this chapter, to this script in order for it to run.*

Deleting Files Depending on Extension

Cleaning a system of specific file types, such as TMP (Temporary), MP3 (Motion Picture Experts Group Layer 3 Audio), AVI (Audio Video Interleave), and other file types, is a very common administrative task. To delete all files with a specific extension within a root folder and its subfolders, create and execute a WSH script containing the following:

```
Set FSO = CreateObject("Scripting.FileSystemObject")
sDIR = "directory"
sEXT = "EXT"

Set objDIR = GetFolder(sDIR)
GoSubFolders objDIR

Sub MainSub(objDIR)
  For Each efile in objDIR.Files
    fEXT = FSO.GetExtensionName(efile.Path)
    If LCase(fEXT) = LCase(sEXT) Then
      DelFile efile
    End If
  Next
End Sub
```

Here, ***directory*** is the folder containing the files to delete, and ***EXT*** is the file extension to search for. The sub procedure **MainSub** rotates through every file within the current directory, checks the file extension, and deletes the file if specified.

NOTE: You need to append the GoSubFolders, DelFile, and GetFolder routines, listed earlier in this chapter, to this script in order for it to run.

---

4. File Management

Deleting a Folder

To delete a folder with WSH, you can use the **DeleteFolder** method. Here is a subroutine to delete a folder:

```
Sub DelFolder(sFOLDER)
  On Error Resume Next
  FSO.DeleteFolder sFOLDER, True
  If Err.Number <> 0 Then
    Wscript.Echo "Error deleting folder: " & sFOLDER
  End If
End Sub
```

Deleting All Subfolders

To delete all subfolders within a directory, create and execute a WSH script containing the following:

```
Set FSO = CreateObject("Scripting.FileSystemObject")
sDIR = "directory"
Set objDIR = GetFolder(sDIR)
GoSubFolders objDIR

Sub GoSubFolders (objDIR)
  If objDIR <> "\System Volume Information" Then
    For Each eFolder in objDIR.SubFolders
      DelFolder eFolder
    Next
  End If
End Sub
```

Here, *directory* is the folder containing the subfolders to delete.

NOTE: You need to append the **GoSubFolders**, **DelFile**, and **GetFolder** routines, listed earlier in this chapter, to this script in order for it to run.

Deleting Folders Depending on Size

By maintaining public shares, you get to notice all the bad habits of a typical user. One of these habits includes leaving empty folders spread throughout the public share. To delete all folders depending on size within a root folder and its subfolders, create and execute a WSH script containing the following:

```
Set FSO = CreateObject("Scripting.FileSystemObject")
sDIR = "directory"
lSIZE = lowersize
uSIZE = uppersize

Set objDIR = GetFolder(sDIR)
```

```
GoSubFolders objDIR

Sub MainSub(objDIR)
  If objDIR <> "\System Volume Information" Then
    For Each eFolder in objDIR.SubFolders
      If lSIZE = Null and uSIZE = Null Then
        If efolder.Size = 0 Then
          DelFolder efolder
        End If
      ElseIf lSIZE <> Null and uSIZE = Null Then
        If efolder.Size < lSIZE Then
          DelFolder efolder
        End If
      ElseIf lSIZE = Null and uSIZE <> Null Then
        If efolder.Size > uSIZE Then
          DelFolder efolder
        End If
      ElseIf lSIZE = uSIZE Then
        If efolder.Size = lSIZE Then
          DelFolder efolder
        End If
      Else
        If efolder.Size > lSIZE and _
        efolder.Size < uSIZE Then
          DelFolder efolder
        End If
      End If
    Next
  End If
End Sub
```

Here, ***directory*** is the root folder containing the subfolders to delete, ***lowersize*** is the lower size limit, and ***uppersize*** is the upper size limit. If both limits are null, the script will delete all subfolders with a size of 0. If just the upper limit is null, the script will delete subfolders smaller than the lower limit. If just the lower limit is null, the script will delete subfolders larger than the upper limit. If both limits are not null but equal, the script will delete subfolders equal to the limit. If both limits are not empty and not null, the script will delete subfolders within the two limits.

NOTE: *You need to append the **GoSubFolders**, **DelFile**, and **GetFolder** routines, listed earlier in this chapter, to this script in order for it to run.*

Deleting Folders Depending on Date
If you let them, users will leave files and folders forever on a public share. To delete all folders depending on last modified date within a

root folder and its subfolders, create and execute a WSH script containing the following:

```
Set FSO = CreateObject("Scripting.FileSystemObject")
sDIR = "directory"
lDATE = "lowerdate"
uDATE = "upperdate"

lDATE = CDate(lDATE)
uDATE = CDate(uDATE)
Set objDIR = GetFolder(sDIR)
GoSubFolders objDIR
Sub MainSub(objDIR)
   If objDIR <> "\System Volume Information" Then
     For Each eFolder in objDIR.SubFolders
        If lDATE = Null and uDATE = Null Then
          If efolder.DateLastModified = 0 Then
            DelFolder efolder
          End If
        ElseIf lDATE <> Null and uDATE = Null Then
          If efolder.DateLastModified < lDATE Then
            DelFolder efolder
          End If
        ElseIf lDATE = Null and uDATE <> Null Then
          If efolder.DateLastModified > uDATE Then
            DelFolder efolder
          End If
        ElseIf lDATE = uDATE Then
          If efolder.DateLastModified = lDATE Then
            DelFolder efolder
          End If
        Else
          If efolder.DateLastModified > lDATE and _
             efolder.DateLastModified < uDATE Then
            DelFolder efolder
          End If
        End If
     Next
   End If
End Sub
```

Here, **directory** is the root folder containing the subfolders to delete, **lowerdate** is the lower date limit, and **upperdate** is the upper date limit. If both limits are null, the script will delete subfolders last modified today. If just the upper limit is null, the script will delete subfolders smaller than the lower limit. If just the lower limit is null, the script will delete subfolders larger than the upper limit. If both limits are not null but equal, the script will delete subfolders equal to the limit. If both limits are not null and not equal, the script will delete subfolders within the two limits.

---

*NOTE: You need to append the **GoSubFolders**, **DelFile**, and **GetFolder** routines, listed earlier in this chapter, to this script in order for it to run.*

Deleting Folders Depending on Name

Any user public folder called GAMES or QUAKE is most likely not work-related, unless you have a better job than I do. To delete all folders with a specific name within a root folder and its subfolders, create and execute a WSH script containing the following:

```
Set FSO = CreateObject("Scripting.FileSystemObject")
sDIR = "directory"
sFOLDER = "foldername"

Set objDIR = GetFolder(sDIR)
GoSubFolders objDIR

Sub MainSub(objDIR)
  If objDIR <> "\System Volume Information" Then
    For Each eFolder in objDIR.SubFolders
      If LCase(eFolder.Name) = LCase(sFOLDER) Then
        DelFolder efolder
      End If
    Next
  End If
End Sub
```

---

*NOTE: You need to append the **GoSubFolders** and **GetFolder** routines, listed earlier in this chapter, to this script in order for it to run.*

Copying a File

To copy a file with WSH, you can use the **CopyFile** method. Here is a subroutine to copy a file:

```
Sub CopyFile(sFILE, sDIR)
  If Right(sDIR,1) <> "\" Then sDIR = sDIR & "\"
  On Error Resume Next
  FSO.CopyFile sFILE, sDIR, True
  If Err.Number <> 0 Then
    Wscript.Echo "Error copying file: " & sFILE
  End If
End Sub
```

Here, *sFILE* is the file to copy, and *sDIR* is the location to copy the file to.

Copying a Folder

To copy a folder with WSH, you can use the **CopyFolder** method. Here is a subroutine to copy a folder:

```
Sub CopyFolder(sFOLDER, sDIR)
  If Right(sFOLDER,1) = "\" Then
    sFOLDER = Left(sFOLDER,(Len(sFOLDER)-1))
  End If
  If Right(sDIR,1) <> "\" Then sDIR = sDIR & "\"
  On Error Resume Next
  FSO.CopyFolder sFOLDER, sDIR, True
  If Err.Number <> 0 Then
    Wscript.Echo "Error copying folder: " & sFOLDER
  End If
End Sub
```

Here, **sFOLDER** is the folder to copy, and **sDIR** is the location to copy the folder to.

Moving a File

To move a file with WSH, you can use the **MoveFile** method. Here is a subroutine to move a file:

```
Sub MoveFile(sFILE, sDIR)
  On Error Resume Next
  FSO.MoveFile sFILE, sDIR
  If Err.Number <> 0 Then
    Wscript.Echo "Error moving file: " & sFILE
  End If
End Sub
```

Here, **sFILE** is the file to move, and **sDIR** is the location to move the file to.

Moving Files with Specific Extensions to a Central Directory

Although certain file types, such as MP3s, do not belong in the public share, you may want to keep them for your own purposes. To move files with a specific extension to a central directory, create and execute a WSH script containing the following:

```
Set FSO = CreateObject("Scripting.FileSystemObject")
sEXT = "extension"
sDIR = "startdir"
sNEW = "enddir"

Set objDIR = GetFolder(sDIR)
GoSubFolders objDIR
```

```
Sub MainSub(objDIR)
    For Each efile in objDIR.Files
      fNAME = efile
      fEXT = FSO.GetExtensionName(efile.Path)
      If LCase(fEXT) = LCase(sEXT) Then
    sEXIST = sNEW & efile.Name
        If ((FSO.FileExists(sEXIST)) AND _
      (efile <> sEXIST)) Then
          DelFile sEXIST
        End If
        On Error Resume Next
        MoveFile efile, sNEW
      End If
    Next
End Sub
```

Here, **extension** is the name of the extension to search for, **startdir** is the name of the directory to start the search, and **enddir** is the directory to store all files.

*NOTE: You need to append the **GoSubFolders**, **DelFile**, **MoveFile**, and **GetFolder** routines, listed earlier in this chapter, to this script in order for it to run.*

Moving a Folder

To move a folder with WSH, you can use the **MoveFolder** method. Here is a subroutine to move a folder:

```
Sub MoveFolder(sFOLDER, sDIR)
  If Right(sFOLDER,1) = "\" Then
    sFOLDER = Left(sFOLDER,(Len(sFOLDER)-1))
  End If
  If Right(sDIR,1) <> "\" Then sDIR = sDIR & "\"
  On Error Resume Next
  FSO.MoveFolder sFOLDER, sDIR
  If Err.Number <> 0 Then
    Wscript.Echo "Error moving folder: " & sFOLDER
  End If
End Sub
```

Here, **sFOLDER** is the folder to move, and **sDIR** is the location to move the folder to.

Renaming a File

To rename a file, create and execute a WSH script containing the following:

```
MoveFile "filename", "newname"
```

Here, *filename* is the name of the file to rename, and *sname* is the name to rename the file.

NOTE: *You need to append the **MoveFile** routine, listed earlier in this chapter, to this script in order for it to run.*

Renaming Specific File Extensions

I don't know what planet of bad habits this came from, but some users like to name files with their own personal extensions. Although this might be beneficial to them when searching for their files, it becomes an administrator's nightmare when these files are being shared. Unfortunately, the DOS RENAME command does not have the ability to act through subdirectories. To rename files with specific extensions with a new extension, create and execute a WSH script containing the following:

```
Set FSO = CreateObject("Scripting.FileSystemObject")
sEXT = "oldext"
sNEW = "newext"
sDIR = "directory"

Set objDIR = GetFolder(sDIR)
GoSubFolders objDIR

Sub MainSub(objDIR)
  For Each efile in objDIR.Files
    fEXT = FSO.GetExtensionName(efile.Path)
    If LCase(fEXT) = LCase(sEXT) Then
      fNAME=Left(efile.name,(Len(efile.Name)-Len(fEXT)))+sNEW
      efile.name = fNAME
    End If
  Next
End Sub
```

Here, *oldext* is the name of the extension to search for, *newext* is the name of the extension to replace with, and *directory* is the name of the directory to start the search.

NOTE: *You need to append the **GetFolder** and **GoSubFolders** routines, listed earlier in this chapter, to this script in order for it to run.*

Renaming Files with Short File Names

To rename a file with its short DOS 8.3 name, create and execute a WSH script containing the following:

```
sFILE = "filename"
Set gFILE = GetFile sFILE

ShortName = gFILE.shortname
MoveFile sFile, ShortName
```

Here, *filename* is the name of the file to rename. An important thing to know is that you can't rename a file from a long file name to its short name directly because Windows sees long and short file names collectively, and you can't name a file the same name as another file in the current directory. In this example, we first append an SN to the file name and then change the file name to its short name.

NOTE: *You need to append the **GetFile** and **MoveFile** routines, listed earlier in this chapter, to this script in order for it to run.*

Updating Program Files Depending on the Version

To update a program file with a newer version, create and execute a WSH script containing the following:

```
Set FSO = CreateObject("Scripting.FileSystemObject")
sDIR = "directory"
sFILE = "filename"

Set nFILE = GetFile(sFILE)
Set objDIR = GetFolder(sDIR)
GoSubFolders objDIR

Sub MainSub(objDIR)
  For Each efile in objDIR.Files
    fVER = FSO.GetFileVersion(efile)
    nVER = FSO.GetFileVersion(sFILE)
    If LCase(efile.Name) = LCase(nFILE.Name) Then
      If fVER = nVER Then
        CopyFile nFILE, efile.ParentFolder
      End If
    End If
  Next
End Sub
```

Here, *directory* is the folder containing the files to update, and *filename* is the file used to update the older file versions.

NOTE: *You need to append the **GetFile**, **GetFolder**, **GoSubFolders**, and **CopyFile** routines, listed earlier in this chapter, to this script in order for it to run. Remember, only program files have versions.*

---

4. File Management

Getting File Attributes

To display the attributes of a file, create and execute a WSH script containing the following:

```
Set FSO = CreateObject("Scripting.FileSystemObject")
fNAME = "filename"


Set gFILE = GetFile(fNAME)
gATTRIB = gFILE.Attributes


If gATTRIB and 1 Then ReadOnly = 1 Else ReadOnly = 0
If gATTRIB and 2 Then Hidden = 1 Else Hidden = 0
If gATTRIB and 4 Then System = 1 Else System = 0
If gATTRIB and 5 Then Volume = 1 Else Volume = 0
If gATTRIB and 16 Then Directory = 1 Else Directory = 0
If gATTRIB and 32 Then Archive = 1 Else Archive = 0
If gATTRIB and 64 Then Alias = 1 Else Alias = 0
If gATTRIB and 128 Then Compressed = 1 Else Compressed = 0


Wscript.Echo "FILE: " & UCase(fNAME) & vblf & vblf & _
  "Readonly:   " & vbtab & ReadOnly & vblf & _
  "Hidden:     " & vbtab & Hidden & vblf & _
  "System:     " & vbtab & System & vblf & _
  "Volume:     " & vbtab & Volume & vblf & _
  "Directory: " & vbtab & Directory & vblf & _
  "Archive:    " & vbtab & Archive & vblf & _
  "Alias:      " & vbtab & vbtab & Alias & vblf & _
  "Compressed:" & vbtab & Compressed
```

Here, *filename* is the file that contains the attributes you want to get.

NOTE: You need to append the **GetFile** routine, listed earlier in this chapter, to this script in order for it to run.

Setting File Attributes

To set the attributes of a file, create and execute a WSH script containing the following:

```
Set FSO = CreateObject("Scripting.FileSystemObject")
fNAME = "filename"
ReadOnly= 0
Hidden= 0
System= 0
Archive = 0
Set gFILE = GetFile(fNAME)
gFILE.Attributes = 0
Attribs = 0
```

```
If ReadOnly = 1 Then Attribs =  Attribs + 1
If Hidden = 1 Then Attribs =  Attribs + 2
If System = 1 Then Attribs =  Attribs + 4
If Archive = 1 Then Attribs =  Attribs + 32
gFILE.Attributes = Attribs
```

Here, *filename* is the file that contains the attributes you want to set. To modify *filename*'s attributes, change the value of the corresponding variable names (**ReadOnly**, **Hidden**, **System**, **Archive**) to 1 to enable, or 0 to disable.

NOTE: *You need to append the **GetFile** routine, listed earlier in this chapter, to this script in order for it to run.*

Setting Attributes to All Files within Folders

To set the attributes of all files within a folder and its subfolders, create and execute a WSH script containing the following:

```
Set FSO = CreateObject("Scripting.FileSystemObject")
sDIR = "directory"
sReadOnly = 0
sHidden = 0
sSystem = 0
sArchive = 0

Set objDIR = GetFolder(sDIR)
GoSubFolders objDIR

Sub MainSub(objDIR)
  For Each efile in objDIR.Files
    Set gFILE = GetFile(efile)
    gFILE.Attributes = 0
    Attribs = 0
    If sReadOnly = 1 Then Attribs = Attribs + 1
    If sHidden = 1 Then Attribs = Attribs + 2
    If sSystem = 1 Then Attribs = Attribs + 4
    If sArchive = 1 Then Attribs = Attribs + 32
    gFILE.Attributes = Attribs
  Next
End Sub
```

Here, *directory* contains the files whose attributes you want to set. To modify the attributes, change the values of the corresponding variable names (**ReadOnly**, **Hidden**, **System**, **Archive**) to 1 to enable, or 0 to disable.

NOTE: *You need to append the* **GetFile** *routine, the* **GetFolder** *routine, and the GoSubFolders routine listed earlier in this chapter to this script in order for it to run.*

Appending Text Files

To append the contents of one text file to another, create and execute a WSH script containing the following:

```
Set FSO = CreateObject("Scripting.FileSystemObject")
File1 = "1stfile"
File2 = "2ndfile"

Set txtFile1 = FSO.OpenTextFile(File1, 1)
Set txtFile2 = FSO.OpenTextFile(File2, 8)

Do While txtFile1.AtEndOfline <> True
   txtFile2.WriteLine(txtFile1.Readline & vbcr)
Loop

txtFile1.close
txtFile2.close
```

Here, *1stfile* is the file whose contents you want to append to *2ndfile*.

4. File Management

Chapter 5

Automating Windows and Applications

In Brief

In this chapter, you will first learn how to script applications, Control Panel applets, and Windows and Wizards from the command line. You will then learn about automation and how to script the Windows shell and most common applications (for example, Word, Excel, Internet Explorer). Finally, you will learn how to use send-keys to automate applications that do not easily support conventional scripting methods. In later chapters, you will learn how to automate Windows and applications to perform more specific tasks (such as adding shares, controlling services, or performing backups).

Automation

Automation was originally created as a method for applications to easily access and control one another. Application automation originally developed from Dynamic Data Exchange (DDE), grew to Object Linking and Embedding (OLE), developed into OLE automation, and eventually turned into just Automation. Automation interfaces with applications through Component Object Model (COM) objects. COM objects are ActiveX controls that contain isolated sections of reusable code. Through automation, you can create documents, save files, play sounds, and even control the operating system, depending on whether it has an object model.

Visual Basic for Applications

Microsoft Office applications support a scripting language called Visual Basic for Applications (VBA). VBA, which is based on Visual Basic, is the standard programming language to control Microsoft Office application functions remotely. Application developers can use VBA to call other application functions from within their projects.

NOTE: Applications that support VBA are known as "customizable applications."

A common method to produce easy VBA code is to record a macro and edit it in the built-in Visual Basic editor. To record a new macro, start an Office application and select Tools|Macro|Record New Macro. After you have started recording, perform the functions you would like to code and then stop the macro recording. Next, start the Visual Basic Editor by selecting Tools|Macro|Visual Basic Editor. After the editor opens, select Tools|Macro, highlight your macro, and click Edit. In Figure 5.1, you can see the VBA code of all the functions you have just recorded.

Through Windows Script Host, you can use VBScript to call many VBA functions to automate Office applications. There are three steps to controlling an application through automation: accessing the application object, controlling the application, and closing the application object.

Accessing the Application Object

The application object is the top-level object, which allows you to send data to an application object and manipulate a program through it. As you learned in Chapter 1, in order to gain access to an object, you must first use the **CreateObject** method and set it to a variable:

```
Set variable = CreateObject("object.Application")
```

Once the instance is created, you can use this variable throughout your script to access all the methods within the object. Here is a list of the most common automation identifiers:

- **Access.Application**—Used to automate Microsoft Access
- **Excel.Application**—Used to automate Microsoft Excel
- **InternetExplorer.Application**—Used to automate Microsoft Internet Explorer
- **Outlook.Application**—Used to automate Microsoft Outlook
- **PowerPoint.Application**—Used to automate Microsoft PowerPoint
- **Shell.Application**—Used to automate Microsoft Windows
- **Word.Application**—Used to automate Microsoft Word

Microsoft Office contains help files on how to use automation with the various Microsoft Office applications. To view these files, run the

```
Microsoft Visual Basic - Normal - [NewMacros (Code)]
File  Edit  View  Insert  Format  Debug  Run  Tools  Add-Ins  Window  Help

(General)                                    Macro1

Sub Macro1()
    Selection.Font.Bold = wdToggle
    Selection.TypeText Text:="Hello There"
    Selection.TypeParagraph
    ActiveDocument.Shapes.AddLine(72#, 90#, 549#, 90#).Select
    Selection.ShapeRange.IncrementTop 9#
    Selection.ShapeRange.IncrementTop -9#
    Selection.MoveDown Unit:=wdLine, Count:=2
    Selection.TypeParagraph
    Selection.MoveUp Unit:=wdLine, Count:=1
    Selection.Delete Unit:=wdCharacter, Count:=1
    Selection.MoveDown Unit:=wdLine, Count:=1
    Selection.EndKey Unit:=wdLine
    Selection.TypeParagraph
    Selection.Font.Bold = wdToggle
    Selection.TypeText Text:="This is our sample report"
End Sub
```

Figure 5.1   Editing a recorded Office macro.

Office setup and install the help files for Visual Basic. Run the application's help feature and search for "VBA HELP."

Changing the Application Visibility

After you've instantiated an application object, most of the objects start in hidden mode. This allows you to manipulate the object and perform various tasks before making the object visible. To make the object visible, set the object's visible state to true:

```
Variable.Visible = True
```

Similarly, you can hide the object by setting the visible state to **False**.

Closing the Application Object

After you are finished with the application object, you should close it to free up system resources. To close an application object, proceed as follows:

```
Variable.Quit
```

If an application object is not closed properly, that application will remain in memory regardless of its visibility or use. You should leave objects open only if you plan to use them at a later moment, such as using Microsoft Outlook to send admin alerts.

The Scripting Advantage

Since most of this chapter revolves around Automation and COM objects, Windows Script Host and KiXtart have the clear advantage. While both can access COM objects, due to the size limitations of this book and the popularity of the scripting language, this chapter will provide examples in Windows Script Host only. (It should be extremely simple to convert one of the scripts to KiXtart.) AutoIt offers one advantage with its ability to script Windows directly or exposed through its COM object. While useful for FTP automation and command line scripting, shell scripting isn't as useful here due to its inability to access COM objects.

A Word of Caution

This chapter contains many scripting examples on automating objects, applications, and Windows. A wrong click here and an extra tab there, and you may turn a script designed to return details into a script that incorrectly sets details. As with all scripts, you should first test in an isolated testing environment to ensure the script produces the desired results before using the script in a production environment.

Immediate Solutions

Automating Applications from the Command Line

Most Windows applications support some level of shell scripting. This was originally intended for backward compatibility with DOS batch files, but is slowly dying with the birth of automation objects. Controlling applications from the command line is extremely useful when you need to perform simple tasks from within DOS batch files or Windows shortcuts.

Scripting Windows XP/2003 Defrag

When a file or folder is created or modified, pieces of that file or folder arc scattered throughout the hard disk. This is known as disk fragmentation. Although this behavior occurs naturally, fragmentation does slow down data access time. Reorganizing these files or folders contiguously improves performance and is known as defragmentation. Microsoft XP/2003 includes a scriptable defragmentation utility, defrag.exe. The command-line options are:

- **/A**—Analyzes the drive and displays a report
- **/F**—Forces defragmentation, event when space is low
- **/ V**—Displays complete reports

Scripting a Windows XP/2003 System Defrag

The following command defrags the C: drive and displays a report when complete:

```
DEFRAG C: /V
```

Scripting Norton Antivirus 2006

Although Norton Antivirus 2006 is a Windows graphical antivirus scanner, it does provide support for being scripted from the command line. The basic syntax for command-line scripting is as follows:

```
NAVW32.EXE path options
```

5. Automating Windows and Applications

Here, **path** is any drive, folder, file, or combination of these to be scanned; and **options** are any valid command-line switches passed to NAVW32.EXE. Here is a list of the available switches:

- **/A**—Scan all drives except drives A and B. Network drives will be scanned if the Allow Network Scanning option is selected.

- **/L**—Scan all local drives except drives A and B.

- **/S**—Scan all subfolders specified in the path.

- **/Moption**—Enable or disable memory scanning. Here, **option** is + for enabling, and - for disabling.

- **/MEM**—Scan only memory.

- **/Boption**—Enable or disable boot sector scanning. Here, **option** is + for enabling, and - for disabling.

- **/BOOT**—Scan only boot sectors.

- **/NORESULTS**—Do not display scan results.

- **/DEFAULT**—Reset settings to default.

- **/HEUR:option**—Sets the heuristic scanning sensitivity. Here, **option** can be values 0–4 where 4 is the highest and 0 is disabled.

Scripting FTP

FTP (File Transfer Protocol) is a common method for transferring files between two locations. Although you could use a third-party FTP client (such as FlashFXP), Microsoft FTP is a more than adequate file transfer tool that supports command-line switches, commands, and script files. FTP command line switches control how the FTP client starts. The most common command line switches are:

- **-i**—Interactive mode, turns off interactive prompting during multiple file transfers

- **-n**—Prevents automatic logon

- **-s: script**—Specifies an FTP **script** to run

- **-v**—Verbose mode, turns on transfer data statistics and responses

To start an FTP client in verbose and interactive more, start a command prompt and enter the following:

```
ftp -v -i
```

Once the FTP client is active, you can enter various commands to list, delete, put, retrieve and files. The most common FTP commands are:

- **ascii**—Selected by default, sets the file transfer type to ASCII (shar, uu)

- **binary**—Sets the file transfer site to binary (z, arc, tar, zip)
- **bye**—Terminates the current FTP session and exits the FTP program
- **cd** *directory*—Changes the *directory* on the remote system
- **close**—Terminates the current FTP session
- **delete** *file*—Deletes a remote *file*
- **get** *file*—Retrieves a single *file* from the remote system
- **lcd** *directory*—Changes the *directory* on the local system
- **mdelete** *files*—Deletes remote *files*
- **mget** *files*—Retrieves multiple *files* from the remote system
- **mput** *files*—Uploads local *files* to a remote system
- **open** *host*—Establishes a connection to the *host* name specified
- **password** *password*—Specifies the *password* for the account name specified
- **prompt**—Toggles interactive prompting
- **put** *file*—Uploads a local *file* to a remote system
- **user** *name*—Specifies the account *name* to connect to the remote system

---

TIP: *To see the available FTP switches, enter "FTP -?" at the command line.*

Scripting an FTP Upload

A common administrative task is uploading daily files to an FTP server. To script an FTP upload, select Start|Run and enter "FTP -I -S:*scriptfile*."

Here, **-I** turns off prompting during multiple file copies; **-S:** specifies a script file to use; and *scriptfile* is the full path and file name of a script file that contains the following:

```
OPEN
ftpserver
Username
Password
CD ftpdirectory
LCD filedirectory
MPUT files
BYE
```

Here, *ftpserver* is the server to connect to; *username* and *password* are the logon credentials; *ftpdirectory* is the directory to upload the files to on the FTP server; *filedirectory* is the local directory where the files reside; and *files* are the multiple files to upload (such as *.*, ***.txt, daily**.*).

TIP: To upload a single file, change the MPUT command to PUT.

Scripting an FTP Download

A common administrative task is downloading files from an FTP server. To script an FTP download, select Start|Run and enter "FTP -I -S:*scriptfile.*"

Here, **-I** turns off prompting during multiple file copies; **-S:** specifies a script file to use; and **scriptfile** is the full path and file name of a script file that contains the following:

```
OPEN
ftpserver
Username
Password
CD ftpdirectory
LCD filedirectory
MGET *.*
BYE
```

Here, **ftpserver** is the server to connect to; **username** and **password** are the logon credentials; **ftpdirectory** is the directory to download files from an FTP server; and **filedirectory** is the local directory where the files reside.

Scripting an FTP Download of Norton Antivirus Update Files

Many administrators maintain a share that stores the latest version of antivirus updates and then point their user's antivirus program to the share. This ensures that the administrator can first test the update, as opposed to simply directing the user's antivirus to the vendor. To download Norton antivirus update files to a central share using FTP and shell scripting, proceed as follows:

1. Create a new directory to store all files included in this example.

2. Select Start|Run and enter "*scriptfile*.bat."

Here, **scriptfile** is the full path and file name of a script file that contains the following:

```
@Echo Off
Net Use Z: \\server\share
```

```
ftp -n -s:ftpscript >> logfile
Net Use Z: /Delete
```

Here, **server** is the system containing the network share to store the antivirus update files; **logfile** is the full path and file name of a text file to log the FTP transfer, and **ftpscript** is the full path and file name of a script file containing the following:

```
open ftp.symantec.com
user anonymous
youremail@yourdomain.com
lcd Z:\
cd \public\english_us_Canada\antivirus_definitions\
norton_antivirus\static
bin
mget *
bye
```

NOTE: *The highlighted code above must be entered on one line.*

Scripting an FTP Download of McAfee Antivirus Update Files

To download McAfee antivirus update files to a central share using FTP and shell scripting, proceed as follows:

1. Create a new directory to store all files included in this example.

2. Select Start|Run and enter "*scriptfile*.bat."

Here, **scriptfile** is the full path and file name of a script file that contains the following:

```
@Echo Off
Net Use Z: \\server\share
ftp -n -s:ftpscript >> logfile
Net Use Z: /Delete
```

Here, **server** is the system containing the network share to store the antivirus update files; **logfile** is the full path and file name of a text file to log the FTP transfer, and **ftpscript** is the full path and file name of a script file containing the following:

```
open ftp.nai.com
user anonymous
youremail@yourdomain.com
lcd Z:\dats
cd \pub\antivirus\datfiles\4.x
```

```
prompt
bin
mget *
bye
```

NOTE: *The script above obtains antivirus updates for McAfee VirusScan 4.x. You can change the highlighted code above to obtain updates for your specific version.*

Scripting Control Panel Applets

CONTROL.EXE, located in your Windows directory, is essentially the Windows Control Panel. To open the Control Panel, select Start|Run and enter "control." Using this executable, you can start any Control Panel applet.

Control Panel applets are stored as CPL (Control Panel) files. To call an applet, select Start|Run and enter "control *applet*." One CPL file can actually store multiple applets. To call various applets within one CPL file, select Start|Run and enter "control *applet*, @#". Here, **#** is the number of the applet to call. If you do not specify an applet number, CONTROL.EXE will automatically open the first one (0).

For applets that contain multiple tabs, you can open the exact tab you want by selecting Start|Run and entering "control *applet*, , #". Here, **#** is the number of the tab to open. If you do not specify a tab number, CONTROL.EXE will automatically open the first one (0).

So, what's the big deal about starting a Control Panel applet? After you start an applet, you can use a send-keys utility to perform the task you want.

NOTE: *To find all the applets and functions on your system, search for CPL files and experiment opening the different applets and tabs.*

Changing the Desktop Theme

Here is a quick example to show the use of scripting Control Panel applets combined with using send-keys. To change the desktop theme, create and then execute the following AutoIt script containing these statements:

```
RUN("CONTROL desk.cpl")
WinWaitActive("Display")
Send("{DOWN}{ENTER}")
```

Scripting Wizards and Dialog Boxes

RUNDLL32.EXE is a 32-bit command-line utility that allows you to call functions from DLL files designed to accept calls from it. You can incorporate these calls in your scripts and combine them with send-keys to complete specific tasks. Table 5.1 shows the most common RUNDLL32 calls.

Table 5.1   Wizards and dialog boxes.

Task	RUNDLL32 calls
Cascade windows	RUNDLL32.EXE USER.DLL,cascadechildwindows
Copy a floppy disk	RUNDLL32.EXE DISKCOPY.DLL,DiskCopyRunDll
Create new briefcase	RUNDLL32.EXE SYNCUI.DLL,Briefcase_Create
Create new dialup connection	RUNDLL32.EXE RNAUI.DLL,RnaWizard @1
Create new share	RUNDLL32.EXE NTLANUI.DLL,ShareCreate
Disable keyboard	RUNDLL32.EXE KEYBOARD,disable
Disable mouse	RUNDLL32.EXE MOUSE,disable
Disconnect network drive	RUNDLL32.EXE USER.DLL,wnetdisconnectdialog
Format a disk	RUNDLL32.EXE SHELL32.DLL,SHFormatDrive
Install new modem	RUNDLL32.EXE SHELL32.DLL,Control_RunDLL modem.cpl, ,add
Logoff Windows	RUNDLL32.EXE SHELL32.DLL,SHExitWindowsEx 0
Manage a share	RUNDLL32.EXE NTLANUI.DLL,ShareManage
Map network drive	RUNDLL32.EXE USER.DLL,wnetconnectdialog
Open fonts folder	RUNDLL32.EXE SHELL32.DLL, SHHelpShortcuts_RunDLL FontsFolder
Open printers folder	RUNDLL32.EXE SHELL32.DLL, SHHelpShortcuts_RunDLL PrintersFolder
Open with …	RUNDLL32.EXE SHELL32.DLL,OpenAs_RunDLL *extension*
Print Test Page	RUNDLL32.EXE SHELL32.DLL, SHHelpShortcuts_RunDLL PrintTestPage
Reboot	RUNDLL32.EXE SHELL32.DLL,SHExitWindowsEx 2
Refresh	RUNDLL32.EXE USER.DLL,repaintscreen
Shut down Windows	RUNDLL32.EXE USER.DLL,ExitWindows
Shut down Windows	RUNDLL32.EXE SHELL32.DLL,SHExitWindowsEx 1
Shut down Windows (Force)	RUNDLL32.EXE KRNL386.EXE,exitkernel
Swap mouse buttons	RUNDLL32.EXE USER.DLL,swapmousebutton
Tile windows	RUNDLL32.EXE USER.DLL,tilechildwindows
Add new printer	RUNDLL32.EXE SHELL32.DLL, SHHelpShortcuts_RunDLL AddPrinter

5. Automating Windows and Applications

Automating Applications through an Application Object

Most new applications include a scriptable automation object model, allowing user and other applications to script them.

Using Microsoft Internet Explorer as a Display Tool

Other than dialog boxes and a DOS window, Windows Script Host really doesn't have a method to display output to the user. You can use Microsoft Internet Explorer to display information to the user or to generate HTML documents. To display the contents of C:\TEMP in Microsoft Internet Explorer, create and then execute this WSH script containing the following statements:

```
Set FSO = CreateObject("Scripting.FileSystemObject")
Set MSIE = CreateObject("InternetExplorer.Application")
sDIR = "C:\TEMP"
sTITLE = "Generating Directory List ..."


Set objDIR = GetFolder(sDIR)
SetupMSIE
MSIE.Document.Write "<HTML><TITLE>" & sTitle & _
  "</TITLE><BODY bgcolor=#C0C0C0><FONT FACE=ARIAL>"
MSIE.Document.Write "<B>Displaying the contents of " & _
  'sDIR & ":</B><BR><BR><table border=0 width=100% " & _
  "cellspacing=0 cellpadding=0>"
GoSubFolders objDIR
MSIE.Document.Write "</table><BR><B>End of List</B>" & _
  "</FONT></BODY>"


Sub SetupMSIE()


MSIE.Navigate "About:Blank"
  MSIE.ToolBar = False
  MSIE.StatusBar = False
  MSIE.Resizable = False

  Do
  Loop While MSIE.Busy

  SWidth = MSIE.Document.ParentWindow.Screen.AvailWidth
  SHeight = MSIE.Document.ParentWindow.Screen.AvailHeight
  MSIE.Width = SWidth/2
  MSIE.Height = SHeight/2
  MSIE.Left = (SWidth - MSIE.Width)/2
  MSIE.Top = (SHeight - MSIE.Height)/2
```

```
    MSIE.Visible = True
End Sub

Sub ListFiles(objDIR)
    For Each efile in objDIR.Files
        MSIE.Document.Write "<tr><td>" & efile & "</td>" & _
        "<td> </td><td align=right>" & efile.size & _
        "</td></tr>"
    Next
End Sub

Sub GoSubFolders(objDIR)
  If objDIR <> "\System Volume Information" Then
    ListFiles objDIR
    For Each eFolder in objDIR.SubFolders
        MSIE.Document.Write "<tr><td>" & _
        efolder & "</td><td>&lt;DIR&gt;</td><td " & _
        "align=right>" & efolder.size & "</td></tr>"
      GoSubFolders eFolder
    Next
  End If
End Sub
```

NOTE: *You need to append the **GetFolder** routine, listed earlier in Chapter 4, to this script in order for it to run. In this example, the window will not be updated until the directory listing is complete.*

Creating Detailed Reports in Microsoft Word

You can script Microsoft Word to create logs and reports through Windows Script Host. To delete all temp files from your system and record the actions in a Microsoft Word document, create and then execute this WSH script containing the following statements:

```
Set FSO = CreateObject("Scripting.FileSystemObject")
Set WordApp = CreateObject("Word.Application")
sDIR = "C:\"
sEXT = "TMP"
sTITLE = "Deleting Files"

WordApp.Documents.Add
WordApp.Visible = True
WordApp.Caption = sTITLE
WordApp.Selection.Font.Bold = True
WordApp.Selection.TypeText "Deletion Log:" & sEXT & _
    " Files: "
WordApp.Selection.InsertDateTime
WordApp.Selection.Font.Bold = False
WordApp.Selection.TypeText vblf & vblf
```

5. Automating Windows and Applications

```
Set objDIR = GetFolder(sDIR)
GoSubFolders objDIR
WordApp.Selection.Font.Bold = True
WordApp.Selection.TypeText vblf & "**END OF LOG**"

Sub MainSub(objDIR)
  For Each efile in objDIR.Files
    fEXT = FSO.GetExtensionName(efile.Path)
    If LCase(fEXT) = LCase(sEXT) Then
      DelFile efile
    End If
  Next
End Sub

Sub DelFile(sFILE)
  On Error Resume Next
  FSO.DeleteFile sFILE, True
  If Err.Number <> 0 Then
    WordApp.Selection.TypeText "Error deleting: " & _
      sFILE & vblf
  Else
    WordApp.Selection.TypeText "Deleted: " & sFILE & vblf
  End If
End Sub
```

NOTE: *You need to append the **GetFolder** routine, listed in Chapter 4, to this script in order for it to run.*

Creating Detailed Spreadsheets in Microsoft Excel

You can script Microsoft Excel to create spreadsheets through Windows Script Host. To delete all temp files from your system and record the actions in a Microsoft Excel spreadsheet, create and then execute this WSH script containing the following statements:

```
Set FSO = CreateObject("Scripting.FileSystemObject")
Set ExcelApp = CreateObject("Excel.Application")
Row = 1
Column = 1
ExcelApp.Workbooks.Add
ExcelApp.Visible = True

sDIR = "C:\"
sEXT = "TMP"
sTITLE = "Deleting Files"

ExcelApp.caption = sTITLE
ExcelApp.Range("A1").Select
ExcelApp.Selection.Font.Bold = True
```

```
ExcelApp.Cells(Row,Column).Value = "Deletion Log:" & sEXT & _
  " Files"
Row = Row + 1
Set objDIR = GetFolder(sDIR)
GoSubFolders objDIR
ExcelApp.Selection.Font.Bold = True
Row = Row + 1
ExcelApp.Cells(Row,Column).Value = "**END OF LOG**"

Sub MainSub(objDIR)
  For Each efile in objDIR.Files
    fEXT = FSO.GetExtensionName(efile.Path)
    If LCase(fEXT) = LCase(sEXT) Then
      DelFile efile
    End If
  Next
End Sub

Sub GoSubFolders(objDIR)
  If objDIR <> "\System Volume Information" Then
    MainSub objDIR
    For Each eFolder in objDIR.SubFolders
      GoSubFolders eFolder
    Next
  End If
End Sub
Sub DelFile(sFILE)
  On Error Resume Next
  FSO.DeleteFile sFILE, True
  If Err.Number <> 0 Then
  ExcelApp.Cells(Row,Column).Value = "Error deleting: " & _
    sFILE
  Else
    ExcelApp.Cells(Row,Column).Value = "Deleted: " & sFILE
  End If
  Row = Row + 1
End Sub
```

NOTE: *You need to append the **GetFolder** routine, listed in Chapter 4, to this script in order for it to run.*

Scripting the Windows Shell

Windows has its own automation object called **shell.automation**. Although you might assume that you can completely automate every Windows function, in reality you can control only a limited set of objects available to scripting. To access the Windows shell, you must instantiate the shell object as follows:

```
Set variable = CreateObject("Shell.Application")
```

Controlling System Windows

When an item is opened in Microsoft Windows, it is opened in a system window. The standard window controls include minimize and maximize functions. You can script these Windows commands and more through the Windows shell object. The following is a list of the window objects and their functions:

- **CascadeWindows**—Cascade open windows

- **MinimizeAll**—Minimize open windows

- **TileHorizontally**—Tile open windows horizontally

- **TileVertically**—Tile open windows vertically

- **UndoMinimizeAll**—Restore minimized windows

To call any of these methods, proceed as follows:

```
Set Shell = CreateObject("Shell.Application")
Shell.Method
```

Browsing for Folders

Using the **BrowseForFolder** method, you can incorporate the common Browse For Folder Windows dialog box used in most Windows applications. To call the dialog box, create and then execute this WSH script containing the following statements:

```
Set Shell = CreateObject("Shell.Application")
Set Folder = Shell.BrowseForFolder (handle, "Title", options,_
    RootFolder)
Wscript.Echo "FOLDER: " & Folder.Title & vblf & _
    "PARENT: " & Folder.ParentFolder
```

Here, ***RootFolder*** can be a directory path or a special folder constant.

Table 5.2 lists the special folder constants.

Table 5.2   Special folder constants.

Constant	Folder or Directory Path
&H0	All Users Desktop
&H2	All Users Program folder
&H3	Control Panel
&H4	Printers Folder
&H5	Personal Folder

(continued)

Table 5.2 Special folder constants *(continued)*.

Constant	Folder or Directory Path
&H6	Favorites Folder
&H7	Startup Folder
&H8	Recent Folder
&H9	SendTo Folder
&Ha	Recycle Bin
&Hb	Start Menu
&H10	Desktop Directory
&H11	Drives (My Computer)
&H12	Network Neighborhood
&H13	Fonts Folder
&H14	Templates Folder
&H15	Common Start Menu
&H16	Common Programs Folder
&H17	Common Programs Folder
&H18	Common Startup Folder
&H19	Common Desktop Directory
&H1a	Application Data Folder
&H1b	PrintHood Folder
&H1c	Local Application Data Folder
&H1d	Alt Startup Folder
&H1e	Common Alt Startup Folder
&H1f	Common Favorites Folder
&H20	Common Internet Cache Folder
&H21	Common Cookies Folder
&H22	History Folder
&H23	Common Application Data Folder
&H24	Windows Folder
&H25	System Folder
&H26	Program Files Folder
&H27	My Pictures Folder
&H28	Profile Folder

5. Automating Windows and Applications

Exploring a Folder

To explore a folder through the shell automation object, proceed as follows:

```
Set Shell = CreateObject("Shell.Application")
Shell.Explore RootFolder
```

Here, ***RootFolder*** can be a directory path or a special folder constant.

Opening a Folder

To open a folder through the shell automation object, proceed as follows:

```
Set Shell = CreateObject("Shell.Application")
Shell.Open RootFolder
```

Here, ***RootFolder*** can be a directory path or a special folder constant.

Running a Control Panel Applet

The Control Panel contains various applets you can use to perform various tasks. These applets have .cpl extensions and reside in your system directory. To call a Control Panel applet through the shell automation object, proceed as follows:

```
Set Shell = CreateObject("Shell.Application")
Shell.ControlPanelItem "applet.cpl"
```

Calling System Dialog Boxes

System dialog boxes are windows that require user input, such as the Find Files or Run dialog box. You can call one of these dialog boxes within your script, and combine it with send-keys to perform regular user tasks. To call a system dialog box through the shell automation object, proceed as follows:

```
Set Shell = CreateObject("Shell.Application")
Shell.SysDialog
```

Here, **SysDialog** consists of the following methods:

- **FileRun**—Calls the Start|Run dialog box
- **FindComputer**—Calls the Start|Find/Search|Computer dialog box
- **FindFiles**—Calls the Start|Find/Search|File or Folders dialog box
- **SetTime**—Calls the Date/Time dialog box
- **ShutdownWindows**—Calls the Start|Shutdown dialog box
- **TrayProperties**—Calls the Tray Properties dialog box

Refreshing the Start Menu

To refresh the contents of the Start menu, proceed as follows:

```
Set Shell = CreateObject("Shell.Application")
Shell.RefreshMenu
```

Accessing the Taskbar and Start Menu Properties Page

To access the Taskbar and Start Menu properties page through the shell automation object, proceed as follows:

```
Set Shell = CreateObject("Shell.Application")
Shell.TrayProperties
```

Accessing the Date and Time Properties Page

To access the Date and Time properties page through the shell automation object, proceed as follows:

```
Set Shell = CreateObject("Shell.Application")
Shell.SetTime
```

Accessing the Find Files Properties Page

To access the Find Files properties page through the shell automation object, proceed as follows:

```
Set Shell = CreateObject("Shell.Application")
Shell.FindFiles
```

Ejecting a PC

To undock a notebook through the shell automation object, proceed as follows:

```
Set Shell = CreateObject("Shell.Application")
Shell.EjectPC
```

Suspending a Computer

Most laptops have a feature called suspend, used to place the computer in lower power mode when not in use. To suspend a computer through the shell automation object, proceed as follows:

```
Set Shell = CreateObject("Shell.Application")
Shell.Suspend
```

Setting a Drive Description

By default, Windows Explorer displays the type name (i.e., Local Disk) next to the drive letters. A more helpful description would be "(SQL Data Drive) D:" instead of "(Logical Disk) D:". To set a drive description using the shell automation object, proceed as follows:

5. Automating Windows and Applications

```
Set Shell = CreateObject("Shell.Application")
Shell.NameSpace(Drive).Self.Name = Description
```

Here, *Drive* is the target drive (i.e., C:) and *Description* is the description to set.

Connecting to a Folder Name Space

In Chapter 4, you learned how to connect to a folder using the **GetFolder FileSystemObject** method. To connect to a folder through shell automation, use the **NameSpace** method and proceed as follows:

```
Set Shell = CreateObject("Shell.Application")
Set Folder = Shell.NameSpace(RootFolder)
```

Getting File or Folder Details

Although Windows NT/9*x* only stores basic file and folder information, Windows 2000/XP/2003 store many more pieces of information. You can use the folder object's **GetDetailsOf** method on either operating system to obtain information about the file or folder specified. To connect to a folder through shell automation, use the **NameSpace** method and proceed as follows:

```
Set Shell = CreateObject("Shell.Application")
Set Folder = Shell.NameSpace(RootFolder)
For Each Item in Folder.Items
   Summary = "Name: " & Item.Name & vblf
  For Count = 1 to 37
    On Error Resume Next
    Detail = Folder.GetDetailsOf(Item,Count)
    If Detail <> "" Then
      Summary = Summary & Folder.GetDetailsOf(0,Count) & _
            ": " & Folder.GetDetailsOf(Item,Count) & vblf
    End If
  Next
  Wscript.Echo Summary
Next
```

Here, ***RootFolder*** can be a directory path or a special folder constant. The output of the script may appear similar to Figure 5.2.

Copying and Moving Files and Folders

Whenever you copy or move a file in Windows, graphical dialog boxes appear displaying progress meters and confirmation windows (see Figure 5.3).

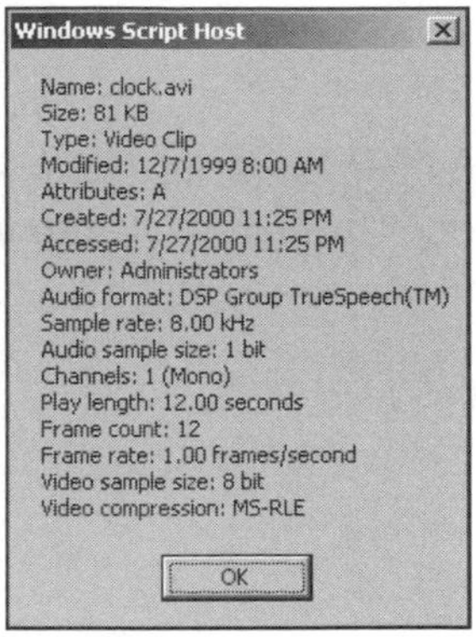

Figure 5.2   The **GetDetailsOf** file and folder output.

Although the **FileSystemObject** can perform file management operations, it does not display any of these dialog boxes. To use these dialog boxes in your scripts, you can use the shell automation object. To copy or move files and folders to another folder, proceed as follows:

```
Set Shell = CreateObject("Shell.Application")
Set Folder = Shell.NameSpace(RootFolder)
Folder.Method "Files", Flags
```

Here, **RootFolder** can be a directory path or a special folder constant; **Method** is the **CopyHere** or **MoveHere** folder method; **Files** are the files or folders to copy or move; and **Flags** are the optional parameters that control the file operation. You can concatenate multiple parameters using the + character.

NOTE: You can use the FOF_SILENT flag to suppress the progress dialog box. For more information on the file operation flags, search Microsoft's Web site for SHFILEOPSTRUCT.

Accessing the Context Menu
Every time you right-click on a file (on a right-handed mouse), you call the context menu. This menu is full of tasks added to the menu

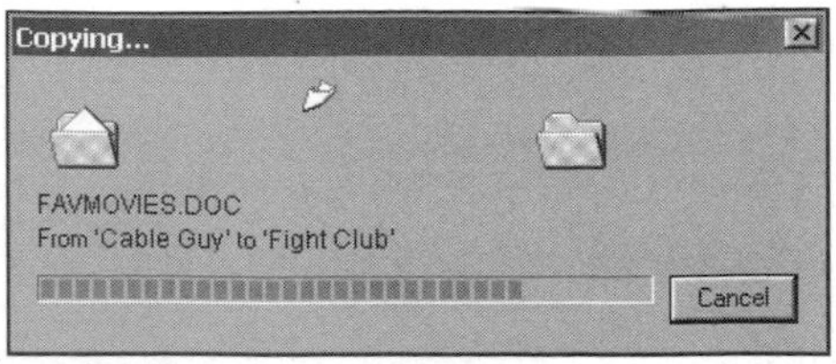

Figure 5.3   Windows file operating dialog box.

by the system, the media, and any programs you may have installed (see Figure 5.4).

You can access these tasks by clicking on them or entering the quick key combination (ALT+the underlined letter). Through shell automation, you activate any of these tasks:

```
Set Shell = CreateObject("Shell.Application")
Set Folder = Shell.NameSpace("RootFolder")
Set File = Folder.ParseName("File")
File.InvokeVerb("Task")
```

Here, **RootFolder** can be a directory path or a special folder constant; **File** is any file within the **RootFolder**; and **Task** is any task listed in the context menu.

There are two important things to note about the **InvokeVerb Task**. The first is that if the task contains a quick key, you must precede that letter with an ampersand (&). For example, to run the Open task for Figure 5.4, you would enter "&Open." The second is that if the command pulls up a system window (such as a properties window), that window will close as soon as the script ends.

Automating Applications through Send-Keys

Some applications have been specifically designed without command-line options or automation object models. Without a scriptable back door to send commands to, another alternative to scripting the unscriptable is by using send-keys.

Figure 5.4 Windows context menu.

Scripting a Windows 2000 Drive Defrag

Windows 2000 includes a special, slimmed-down version of Executive Software's Diskeeper, made specifically for Windows 2000. Unlike Windows XP/2003 defrag, the Windows 2000 defrag utility does not include the scripting capabilities. To script a Windows 2000 drive defrag, create and then execute this AutoIt script containing the following statements:

```
AdlibEnable("AdlibHandler")


Run("c:\WINDOWS\system32\mmc.exe c:\WINDOWS\system32\DFRG.MSC")
Winwaitactive("Disk Defrag")
Send("{ALTDOWN}A{ALTUP}D")
Winwaitactive("Defragmentation Complete")
Send("{TAB}{ENTER}")
Winwaitactive("Disk Defrag")
Send("{ALTDOWN}{F4}{ALTUP}")


Func AdlibHandler()
   If WinActive("Disk Defrag", "Do you want to run Disk Defragmenter") Then
      WinActivate("Disk Defrag", "Do you want to run Disk Defragmenter")
      Send("!Y")
   EndIf
EndFunc
```

Here, *defragmmc* is the full path to MMC.exe and DFRG.msc (ex. "C:\WINDOWS\system32\mmc.exeC:\WINDOWS\system32 \DFRG.MSC").

Changing Internet Explorer's Default Start Page

To change the default start page for Internet Explorer, create and then execute this AutoIt script containing the following statements:

```
Run("control.exe inetcpl.cpl")
WinWaitActive("Internet Properties")
Send("http://www.jesseweb.com{Enter}")
```

Browsing the Internet

Whether you have an Internet provider that consistently disconnects you or a program that feeds off active Internet connections, you may need to have continually active Internet activity. To repeatedly browse Internet sites, create and then execute this AutoIt script containing the following statements:

```
Opt("WinTitleMatchMode", 2)
Run("C:\\Program Files\\Internet Explorer\\Iexplore.exe")
WinWaitActive("Microsoft Internet Explorer")
For $i = 1 to 2 Step 0
  Send("{ALTDOWN}D{ALTUP}www.jesseweb.com{Enter}")
    Sleep("10000")
  Send("{ALTDOWN}D{ALTUP}www.fightclub.com{Enter}")
    Sleep("10000")
  Send("{ALTDOWN}D{ALTUP}www.tylerandjacks.com{Enter}")
    Sleep("10000")
  Send("{ALTDOWN}D{ALTUP}www.customtweaks.com{Enter}")
    Sleep("10000")
  Send("{ALTDOWN}D{ALTUP} www.paraglyphpress.com{Enter}")
    Sleep("10000")
Next
```

Clearing the Microsoft Internet Explorer Cache

Internet Explorer caches Web pages and previously entered user-names, passwords, and form entries. To delete these items using the AutoIt ActiveX control, create and then execute this WSH script containing the following statements:

```
Set Shell = WScript.CreateObject("WScript.Shell")
Set AIT = WScript.CreateObject("AutoItX3.Control")

Shell.Run "control.exe inetcpl.cpl", 1, FALSE
AIT.WinWaitActive "Internet Properties", ""
AIT.Send "{ALTDOWN}F{ALTUP}"
AIT.WinWaitActive "Delete Files", ""
AIT.Send "{TAB}{ENTER}"
AIT.WinWaitActive "Internet Properties", ""
AIT.WinClose "Internet Properties", ""
Shell.Run "control.exe inetcpl.cpl, ,2", 1, FALSE
AIT.WinWaitActive "Internet Properties", ""
AIT.Send "{ALTDOWN}U{ALTUP}"
AIT.WinWaitActive "AutoComplete Settings", ""
AIT.Send "{ALTDOWN}C{ALTUP}"
AIT.WinWaitActive "Internet Options", ""
AIT.Send "{ENTER}"
AIT.WinWaitActive "AutoComplete Settings", ""
AIT.Send "{ALTDOWN}L{ALTUP}"
AIT.WinWaitActive "Internet Options", ""
AIT.Send "{ENTER}{ESC}"
AIT.WinWaitActive "Internet Properties", ""
AIT.Send "{ESC}"

WScript.Quit
```

Chapter 6

Inside the Registry

In Brief

Most administrators go out of their way to avoid working with the registry, and I don't blame them. The registry is one of those aspects of Windows you are constantly being warned not to mess with. With the frequent threats of virtual nuclear destruction combined with the lack of documentation, the registry is a dark and scary place. In this chapter, you will learn the basics of the registry, how to modify it safely, and the hidden tricks and goodies the registry has to offer.

Holy INI Files, Batman!

In the old days of 16-bit Windows, all settings were stored in initialization files. The two main files for storing settings were the SYSTEM.INI and WIN.INI files. As each application was installed, it stored its settings in these two files. Unfortunately, these applications could store only a limited set of entries because of the restrictive 64K size of INI files. To counteract this, application developers started using their own INI files. Although this might have seemed a good idea at first, as the number of applications grew, so did the number of INI files; and as each INI file grew, the system would often slow down.

And Then Came the Registry

The registry was born simultaneously with the birth of Windows NT in 1993 and is the answer to Windows INI files. The registry is a hierarchal, relational database that holds system information, OLE (Object Link Embedding) and Automation information, application settings, operating system configuration data, and more. The information stored includes everything from your display settings to your hardware configuration. To speed access time, the registry is stored in binary format and is composed of multiple files.

Windows 2000/XP/2003 Registry Files

Under Windows 2000/XP/2003, user-related settings are stored in a file called ntuser.dat. This file is stored in the user's profile directory located in the *%USERPROFILE%* directory. System settings are stored in the SYSTEM32\CONFIG directory and consist of the following five files:

- *Default* (HKEY_USERS\DEFAULT)—Stores default settings for new users
- *SAM* (HKEY_LOCAL_MACHINE\SAM)—Stores system security information
- *Security* (HKEY_LOCAL_MACHINE\Security)—Stores network security information
- *Software* (HKEY_LOCAL_MACHINE\Software)—Stores specific application and operating system information
- *System* (HKEY_LOCAL_MACHINE\System)—Stores device driver and system information

The Registry Hierarchy

The registry consists of top-level keys called hives:

- HKEY_CLASSES_ROOT
- HKEY_CURRENT_USER
- HKEY_LOCAL_MACHINE
- HKEY_USERS
- HKEY_CURRENT_CONFIG

These hives store all the keys (subfolders) that make up the registry. These keys store all the values (entries), which specify all the individual system settings.

HKEY_LOCAL_MACHINE

HKEY_LOCAL_MACHINE (HKLM) stores all software, hardware, network, security, and Windows system information. This hive is the largest registry hive and stores two of the main registry hives.

HKEY_CLASSES_ROOT

HKEY_CLASSES_ROOT (HKCR) is actually a virtual link to HKLM\Software\Classes. This hive stores information about all file extensions, descriptions, icons, associations, shortcuts, automation, class IDs, and more.

HKEY_USERS

HKEY_USERS (HKU) stores information about all users of the system and their individual settings. These individual settings include environment variables, color schemes, fonts, icons, desktop configuration, Start menu items, network, and more. Each time a new user logs on, a new key is created based on a default key.

HKEY_CURRENT_USER

HKEY_CURRENT_USER (HKCU) is actually a link to the currently logged-in user's key stored in HKEY_USERS. This hive is named by the user's SID (Security Identifier) value and not by the user's name. This key is rebuilt each time the system reboots.

HKEY_CURRENT_CONFIG

HKEY_CURRENT_CONFIG (HKCC) is actually a link to the currently selected hardware profile stored in HKEY_LOCAL_MACHINE. Hardware profiles allow you to specify which device drivers are to be loaded for a given Windows session. Hardware profiles are commonly used with laptops to distinguish RAS, network, and local Windows sessions.

Registry Data Types

Like any other database, the registry contains various data types to store different types of values. Table 6.1, from *Windows 2000 Registry Little Black Book* (**www.paraglyphpress.com**) lists the various registry data types.

Table 6.1   Registry data types.

Data Type	Raw Type	Function
REG_NONE	Unknown	Encrypted data
REG_SZ	String	Text characters
REG_EXPAND_SZ	String	Text with variables
REG_BINARY	Binary	Binary data
REG_DWORD	Number	Numerical data
REG_DWORD_BIG_ENDIAN	Number	Non-Intel numbers
REG_LINK	String	Path to a file
REG_MULTI_SZ	Multistring	String arrays
REG_RESOURCE_LIST	String	Hardware resource list
REG_FULL_RESOURCE_DESCRIPTOR	String	Hardware resource ID
REG_RESOURCE_REQUIREMENTS_LIST	String	Hardware resource ID

REGEDIT vs. REGEDT32

Because the registry is stored in multiple binary files, it cannot be viewed with a regular text editor. Windows 2000/XP/2003 include two registry editing tools: REGEDIT and REGEDT32. Both of these tools contain various functions, and it's best to know when to use which one.

Using REGEDIT

REGEDIT is the registry-editing tool that comes included in all of Microsoft's 32-bit operating systems. Using this tool, you can add, delete, modify, back up, and restore registry keys and values from a local or remote machine. REGEDIT displays all the registry hives, even the aliased ones (see Figure 6.1). It also has the capability to search for registry keys and values. The most important thing to remember about REGEDIT is that changes happen immediately. There is no Apply, Cancel, or OK button here. The moment you make a change, the change is implemented—so be careful.

TIP: REGEDIT includes additional features such as a registry Favorites menu and the capability to remember the last key viewed before closing REGEDIT.

WARNING! REGEDIT does not recognize all the registry data types. If you edit an unrecognized data type, it will be converted to a type that REGEDIT can recognize.

Using REGEDT32

REGEDT32 is a registry-editing tool that comes included in Windows 2000/XP/2003 (see Figure 6.2). REGEDT32 displays each hive in a separate window, and only displays the HKEY_LOCAL_MACHINE and HKEY_USERS hives when accessing a registry remotely. REGEDT32 includes all the editing features of REGEDIT, but has only a simple find key function. Unlike REGEDIT, REGEDT32 does not apply changes immediately. It applies changes

6. Inside the Registry

Figure 6.1   The Windows REGEDIT screen.

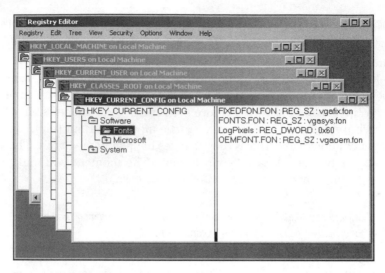

Figure 6.2   The Windows REGEDT32 screen.

only as you close the application. Some additional features include auto-refresh, read-only mode, and the ability to set registry permissions.

NOTE: *Although remote registry access through REGEDT32 only displays two hives, from within these two hives you can still access all the aliased hives that REGEDIT normally displays.*

Registry Editing Safety Tips

You've heard it a thousand times, but here it is again: editing the registry is dangerous. An incorrect registry setting can leave your system in shambles (trust me, I know). Here are some helpful registry editing tips:

• Back up the entire registry or key you intend to modify. If your system starts acting up, you'll be glad you did.

• Update your emergency repair disk (ERD) before you make any registry changes. This proves to be a valuable asset if your machine refuses to boot up properly.

• Do not blindly make changes to the registry. Know what your intended registry change does. Research it.

• Make one change at a time. This makes it easier to narrow down the cause of any problems you may have after editing the registry.

- Always use REGEDT32 when you can. REGEDT32 does not apply changes until you exit the application and can work in read-only mode.

The Scripting Advantage

Through built-in and add-on utilities, shell scripting has even more registry scripting power than the other scripting methods. KiXtart includes both the basic methods (reading, writing, and so on) while also providing backup and restore methods. AutoIt and Windows Script Host provide the basic methods of working with the registry while allowing you to call out to shell scripting when more powerful functionality is needed.

A Word of Caution

This chapter includes many scripting examples on how to modify the registry. Incorrectly changing a registry value can cause applications or the entire system to not work properly. As with all scripts, you should first test each script in an isolated testing environment to ensure the script produces the desired results before using it in a production environment.

Immediate Solutions

Backing Up and Restoring the Registry

Before modifying the registry, you should perform a backup that you can revert to in case of any system failures. Knowing the different methods to back up and restore the entire registry properly can save you hours of unnecessary data recovery and troubleshooting.

Understanding Windows 2000/XP/2003 Registry Backup/Restore Misconceptions

Backing up the registry is a tricky subject. Here is a list of some common misconceptions about backing up the registry:

- You can back up the entire registry by simply making a copy of the registry files. Unlike Windows 9*x*, Windows 2000/XP/2003 accesses many sections of the registry directly. These files are open, so you cannot back them up because they are already in use.

- You can back up the entire registry by running RDISK /S. The RDISK (Repair Disk) utility backs up important system files and parts of the registry to an ERD (Emergency Repair Disk). This disk is used in conjunction with the setup disks to restore critical parts of the operating system that may be damaged. It cannot and was never intended to be used as a registry backup utility.

- You can use REGEDIT to back up and restore the entire registry. REGEDIT for Windows 2000/XP/2003 does not support the same switches as the Windows 9*x* version. Although you may be able to back up the registry manually into one large REG file, you will not be able to restore it. The registry has special security settings on certain keys that prevent restoring or modifying.

Backing Up the Windows 2000/XP/2003 Registry

There are two methods to back up the entire Windows 2000/XP/2003 registry. The first method is to use the built-in backup utility to perform a complete backup of the registry. This will be discussed in more detail in Chapter 14. The second method is to use a resource kit utility called REGBACK. To perform a complete backup of the registry using REGBACK, proceed as follows:

1. Create a new directory to store all files included in this example.

2. Obtain the latest version of REGBACK.EXE from the resource kit and copy it to the new directory.

3. Select Start|Run and enter "*scriptfile*.bat."

Here, **scriptfile** is the full path and file name of a script file that contains the following:

```
@Echo Off
REGBACK C:\REGBACKUP.RBU
if errorlevel 1 echo Error during backup
if errorlevel 0 echo Successfully backed up
```

Restoring the Windows 2000/XP/2003 Registry

The resource kit utility REGREST is used to restore registry backups created by REGBACK. To restore a registry backup created by REGREST, proceed as follows:

1. Create a new directory to store all files included in this example.

2. Obtain the latest version of REGREST.EXE from the resource kit and copy it to the new directory.

3. Select Start|Run and enter "*scriptfile*.bat."

Here, **scriptfile** is the full path and file name of a script file that contains the following:

```
@Echo Off
REGREST C:\REGBACKUP.RBU C:\REGSAVE.RBU
if errorlevel 1 echo Error during restore
if errorlevel 0 echo Successfully restored
```

Here, **C:\REGSAVE.RBU** is an arbitrary name to which your current registry is backed up before restoring your backup.

Modifying the Registry with Shell Scripting

Because shell scripting was created before the birth of the registry, it does not contain any functions to modify the registry. To manipulate the registry through shell scripting, you can use REG.EXE, included in WindowsXP/2003 and in the Windows 2000 Resource Kit. REG.EXE supports the following parameters:

- **Add**—Adds keys or values

- **Backup**—Identical to the Save parameter
- **Compare**—Compares a registry key or value to another or to a string
- **Copy**—Copies a registry key or value from one machine to another
- **Delete**—Deletes keys and values
- **Export**—Saves keys and values to a REG file
- **Find**—Finds and replaces keys or values
- **Import**—Loads registry keys and values from a REG file
- **Load**—Loads hive files to the registry
- **Query**—Displays the contents of keys and values
- **Restore**—Restores registry keys from hive files
- **Save**—Stores registry keys to hive files
- **Unload**—Removes hive files from the registry
- **Update**—Replaces information in a key or value

Backing Up a Registry Key

To back up a registry key using REG.EXE, start a command prompt and enter the following:

```
REG SAVE key file
```

Here, **key** is the registry key to back up, and **file** is the hive file to back up the registry key.

Restoring a Registry Key

To restore a registry key using REG.EXE, start a command prompt and enter the following:

```
REG LOAD file key
```

Here, **file** is the hive file to restore; and **key** is the registry key to which to restore the hive.

Querying the Registry

To display registry keys or values from the command line using REG.EXE, start a command prompt and enter the following:

```
REG QUERY keyval
```

Here, **keyval** is the registry key or value you want to display. For example, to display the current cursor blink rate, start a command prompt and enter the following:

```
REG QUERY "HKCU\Control Panel\Desktop\CursorBlinkRate"
```

NOTE: *If a registry entry contains a space, you must surround it with quotation marks.*

Searching the Registry

Sometimes the registry stores information you wish it didn't, such as usernames and passwords. You can use the resource kit utility SCANREG.EXE to search the registry for these values. To search the registry for a key containing a specific phrase, proceed as follows:

```
SCANREG string start -k
```

Here, **string** is the phrase to search for, and **start** is where to start searching in the registry.

Customizing Windows

With the introduction of a new operating system come new features, and with new features come new annoyances. To remove these annoyances, you simply need to make a few registry changes.

Disabling Start Menu Scrolling

When the Start menu grows larger than one column, Windows will simply scroll the column rather than creating a new column. This can become quite annoying when you have a large Start menu. To disable the Start menu scrolling and have Windows create a new column to fit the additional Start menu items, start a command prompt and enter the following:

```
REG UPDATE HKCU\Software\Microsoft\Windows\CurrentVersion\
Explorer\Advanced\StartMenuScrollPrograms=NO
```

NOTE: *The code above must be placed on one line.*

Disabling Pop-up Descriptions

An initially helpful but quickly annoying feature are the pop-up descriptions that appear when the mouse pointer remains above certain objects for a short period of time. To disable the pop-up descriptions using REG.EXE, start a command prompt and enter the following:

```
REG UPDATE HKCU\Software\Microsoft\Windows\CurrentVersion\
Explorer\Advanced\ShowInfoTip=0
```

NOTE: *The code above must be placed on one line.*

Disabling Balloon Tips

Windows XP balloon tips are another helpful feature that is annoying more often than not. To disable balloon tips using REG.EXE, start a command prompt and enter the following:

```
REG ADD
HKCU\Software\Microsoft\Windows\CurrentVersion\Explorer
     \Advanced\EnableBalloonTips=0
```

NOTE: *The code above must be placed on one line.*

Deleting Registry Keys Using REGEDIT

Although you can use REG.EXE to delete registry keys, you can also use REGEDIT. To delete registry keys using REGEDIT, select Start|Run and enter "regedit *regfile*." Here, ***regfile*** is a registry file that contains the following:

```
REGEDIT4
[-COMPLETEKEY]
```

Here, ***COMPLETEKEY*** is the complete registry key to delete, such as HKEY_LOCAL_MACHINE\SOFTWARE\APPLE.

NOTE:*The minus sign in front of* **COMPLETEKEY** *causes the key to be deleted.*

Clearing the Run Dialog List

Every time you run a command through the Start|Run dialog box, that command is stored in a Most Recently Used (MRU) list within the registry. To delete this list from the registry, select Start|Run and enter "regedit *regfile*." Here, ***regfile*** is a registry file that contains the following:

```
REGEDIT4
[-HKEY_CURRENT_USER\Software\Microsoft\Windows\
CurrentVersion\Explorer\RunMRU]
```

NOTE: *The highlighted code above must be placed on one line.*

Deleting Persistent Drive Mappings

Whenever you map a drive to "reconnect at logon" or map it persistently through the NET USE command, the settings for this drive mapping are stored within the registry. To remove persistent drive mappings for the current user, select Start|Run and enter "regedit *regfile.*" Here, *regfile* is a registry file that contains the following:

```
REGEDIT4
[-HKEY_CURRENT_USER\Software\Microsoft\Windows NT\
CurrentVersion\Network\Persistent Connections]
```

NOTE: The highlighted code above must be placed on one line.

Deleting Registry Values Using REGEDIT

Deleting registry values using REGEDIT is similar to deleting registry keys using REGEDIT. Select Start|Run and enter "regedit *regfile.*"'Here, *regfile* is a registry file that contains the following:

```
REGEDIT4
[COMPLETEKEY]
VALUENAMF=-
```

NOTE: The minus sign after VALUENAME causes it to be deleted.

Exporting Registry Keys Using REGEDIT

To export/backup a registry key, its subkeys, and values to a file from the command line using REGEDIT, start a command prompt and enter the following:

```
REGEDIT /E "filepath" "key"
```

Here, *filepath* is the full path of the file to contain the exported registry key, and *key* is the registry key to export. For example, to export the current users printer connections, start a command prompt and enter the following:

```
REGEDIT /E "c:\printers.reg" "HKEY_CURRENT_USER\Printers"
```

NOTE: If the file path or registry key contains spaces, you must surround them with quotation marks.

Querying Registry Values Using REGEDIT

While REGEDIT does not have built-in query functionality, we can combine its export feature with other shell scripting commands to query registry values. To query a registry value using REGEDIT, create and execute a shell script containing the following:

```
CALL :GetRegValue "Key" "ValueName"
ECHO %GetRegValue%
GOTO:EOF

:GetRegValue
 SETLOCAL ENABLEEXTENSIONS

 SET TEMPFILE=%Random%.txt
 REGEDIT /E %TEMPFILE% %1
 FOR /F "tokens=2 delims=,=" %%a IN ('TYPE %TEMPFILE% ^| FIND /I
     %2') DO SET RegValue=%%a
 DEL %TEMPFILE%

 :: Remove quotes
 SET RegValue=%RegValue:"=%
ENDLOCAL&SET GetRegValue=%RegValue%&GOTO:EOF
```

NOTE: *The highlighted code above must be places on one line.*

Here, **key** is the registry key to query and **valuename** is value name that contains the value to obtain. For example, to see what the screensaver the current user is using, set **key** = "HKEY_ CURRENT_USER\Control Panel\Desktop" and **valuename** = "SCRNSAVE.EXE".

Modifying the Registry with REGINI.EXE

REGINI.EXE, included in Windows XP/2003 and the Windows 2000 Resource Kit, is a powerful utility designed to manipulate the registry through a batch file. It can add or update registry values as well as set registry key permissions. REGINI.EXE interprets registry hives differently because it only works with kernel mode. See Table 6.2.

Disabling Dr. Watson

Dr. Watson is an annoying debugging utility that appears every so often during application or system crashes. To disable Dr. Watson, proceed as follows:

1. Create a new directory to store all files included in this example.

Table 6.2   Regular mode versus kernel mode.

Regular Mode	Kernel Mode
HKEY_LOCAL_MACHINE	\Registry\Machine
HKEY_USERS	\Registry\User

2. For Windows 2000 only, obtain the latest version of REGINI.EXE from the Windows 2000 Resource Kit and copy it to the new directory.

3. Select Start|Run and enter "REGINI *scriptfile.*"

Here, ***scriptfile*** is the full path of the new directory from step 1 and file name of a script file that contains the following:

```
\Registry\Machine
     SOFTWARE
            Microsoft
                  Windows NT
                        CurrentVersion
                              AeDebug
                                    AUTO = REG_SZ 0
```

TIP: To re-enable Dr. Watson, run **DRWTSN32 -I** from the command prompt.

Securing Recycle Bin Properties
To restrict users from modifying the Recycle Bin properties, proceed as follows:

1. Create a new directory to store all files included in this example.

2. For Windows 2000 only, obtain the latest version of REGINI.EXE from the Windows 2000 Resource Kit and copy it to the new directory.

3. Select Start|Run and enter "REGINI *scriptfile.*"

Here, ***scriptfile*** is the full path of the new directory from step 1 and file name of a script file that contains the following:

```
\Registry\Machine
     SOFTWARE
            Microsoft
                  Windows
                        CurrentVersion
                              Explorer
                                    BitBucket [1 17 8]
```

6. Inside the Registry

Modifying the Registry with AutoIt

AutoIt provides several methods to manipulate the registry very similar to Windows Script Host. The most commonly used methods are:

- RegDelete—Deletes registry keys and values
- RegRead—Reads registry keys or values
- RegWrite—Writes registry keys or values

NOTE: *AutoIt does not include any methods to back up or restore registry keys or values.*

Determining the Windows Service Pack Level with AutoIt

To determine the Windows service pack level using AutoIt, create and execute an AutoIt script containing the following:

```
$SP = RegRead("HKEY_LOCAL_MACHINE\SOFTWARE\Microsoft\Windows
NT\CurrentVersion", "CSDVersion")
MsgBox(0, "Service Pack", $SP)
```

Without reading the registry, you can also view the service pack with the built-in AutoIt macro **@OSServicePack**:

```
MsgBox(0, "Service Pack", @OSServicePack)
```

Switching to the Classic Desktop

Call me an old timer, but I like the class Windows desktop look. It had icons, a clean start menu, and no surprises (like start menu items appearing and disappearing). To switch to the classic desktop for the current user, create and execute an AutoIt script containing the following:

```
RegWrite("HKEY_CURRENT_USER\Software\Microsoft\Windows\Current
    Version\Policies\explorer", "ClassicShell", "REG_DWORD", 1)
```

NOTE: *The highlighted code above must be places on one line.*

Modifying the Registry with KiXtart

KiXtart provides many functions to manipulate the registry:

- **AddKey**—Adds a subkey to the regsitry
- **DelKey**—Deletes a subkey from the registry

- **Deltree**—Deletes a key and all its subkeys
- **DelValue**—Deletes a value from the registry
- **EnumKey**—Lists the keys within a key or subkey
- **EnumValue**—Lists the values within a key or subkey
- **ExistKey**—Checks for the existence of a subkey
- **LoadHive**—Loads HKEY_LOCAL_MACHINE or HKEY_USER hive information from a REG file
- **LoadKey**—Loads a registry key from a hive file
- **ReadType**—Determines the value type
- **ReadValue**—Reads the data within a registry value
- **SaveKey**—Saves a key to a hive file
- **WriteValue**—Writes data to or creates a registry value

NOTE: *For complete usage details, see the KiXtart manual.*

Backing Up a Registry Key

To back up a registry key using KiXtart, create and run a script file containing the following:

```
$ReturnCode = SaveKey("key", "file")
```

NOTE: *The SaveKey method saves the contents of registry keys to a file in binary format. You will not be able to clearly see or edit this file. You will need to use the LoadKey method to restore any file created by the SaveKey method.*

Backing up the Current User's Mapped Drives

Whenever you map a network drive, the drive letter, path, and settings are stored in the registry. To back up the current user's mapped drives to c:\mapped.reg using KiXtart, create and run a script file containing the following:

```
$ReturnCode = SaveKey("HKEY_CURRENT_USER\Network",
"c:\mapped.reg")
```

NOTE: *The highlighted code above must be places on one line.*

Restoring a Registry Key

To restore a registry key from a hive file, create and execute a KiXtart script containing the following:

6. Inside the Registry

```
$RegKey = "key"
$RegFile = "file"
LoadKey($RegKey, $RegFile)
```

Here, **key** is the registry key to restore, and *file* is the hive file to restore from.

Disabling the Welcome Screen

Microsoft has made it a habit to greet every new user to a machine running its operating system through the Welcome screen. Although this greeting seems like a good idea, it can quickly become annoying to users as they travel from machine to machine. To disable the Welcome screen, create and execute a KiXtart script containing the following:

```
$RegKey
= "HKEY_LOCAL_MACHINE\SOFTWARE\Microsoft\Windows\
CurrentVersion\Policies\Explorer"
WriteValue($RegKey, "NoWelcomeScreen", "1", "REG_DWORD")
```

NOTE: *The highlighted code above must be placed on one line.*

Working with Icons

Microsoft Windows includes many default icons on the desktop for your convenience. You can easily delete or hide these icons or modify their properties by manipulating the registry.

Removing the My Computer Icon from the Desktop

To remove the My Computer icon from the desktop, create and execute a KiXtart script containing the following:

```
$RegKey
= "HKEY_CLASSES_ROOT\CLSID\
{20D04FE0-3AEA-1069-A2D8-08002B30309D}"
Deltree($RegKey)
```

NOTE: *The highlighted code above must be placed on one line.*

Removing the Dial-Up Networking Icon from My Computer

To remove the Windows 2000 Dial-Up Networking icon from My Computer, create and execute a KiXtart script containing the following:

```
$RegKey
= "HKEY_LOCAL_MACHINE\SOFTWARE\Microsoft\Windows\
```

```
CurrentVersion\ Explorer\MyComputer\NameSpace\
{a4d92740-67cd-11cf-96f2-00aa00a11dd9}"
Deltree($RegKey)
```

NOTE: *The highlighted code above must be placed on one line.*

Removing the Scheduled Tasks Icon from My Computer

To remove the Windows 2000 Scheduled Tasks icon from My Computer, create and execute a KiXtart script containing the following:

```
$RegKey
= "HKEY_LOCAL_MACHINE\SOFTWARE\Microsoft\Windows\
CurrentVersion\ Explorer\MyComputer\NameSpace\
{D6277990-4C6A-11CF-8D87-00AA0060F5BF}"
Deltree($RegKey)
```

NOTE: *The highlighted code above must be placed on one line.*

Hiding the Windows 2000 Network Neighborhood Icon

To hide the Windows 2000 Network Neighborhood icon from the desktop for the current user, create and execute a KiXtart script containing the following:

```
$RegKey
= "SOFTWARE\Microsoft\Windows\CurrentVersion\
Policies\Explorer"
WriteValue($RegKey, "NoNetHood", "1", "REG_DWORD")
```

NOTE: *The highlighted code above must be placed on one line.*

Hiding All Windows 2000 Desktop Icons

To hide all Windows 2000 desktop icons for the current user, create and execute a KiXtart script containing the following:

```
$RegKey
= "SOFTWARE\Microsoft\Windows\CurrentVersion\
Policies\Explorer"
WriteValue($RegKey, "NoDesktop", "1", "REG_DWORD")
```

NOTE: *The highlighted code above must be placed on one line.*

Modifying the Registry with Windows Script Host

Windows Script Host provides the easiest way to manipulate the registry. You can modify the registry using the WScript object. This object contains three simple registry methods:

- **RegDelete**—Deletes registry keys and values
- **RegRead**—Reads registry keys or values
- **RegWrite**—Writes registry keys or values

NOTE: Windows Script Host does not include any methods to back up or restore registry keys or values.

Disabling Windows Security Menu Options

Once Windows is up and running, you can press Ctrl+Alt+Del to call up the Windows security menu to perform common tasks. Although this is convenient for users, you may want to selectively disable these options for guest or kiosk stations.

Disabling the Lock Workstation Button

To disable the Lock Workstation button, create and execute a WSH script containing the following:

```
On Error Resume Next
Set SHELL = CreateObject("WScript.Shell")
RegValue = "HKCU\Software\Microsoft\Windows\" & _
"CurrentVersion\Policies\System\DisableLockWorkstation"
SHELL.RegWrite RegValue, 1, "REG_DWORD"
```

Disabling the Change Password Button

To disable the Change Password button, create and execute a WSH script containing the following:

```
On Error Resume Next
Set SHELL = CreateObject("WScript.Shell")
RegValue = "HKCU\Software\Microsoft\Windows\" & _
"CurrentVersion\Policies\System\DisableChangePassword"
SHELL.RegWrite
RegValue, 1, "REG_DWORD"
```

Disabling the Logoff Button

To disable the Logoff button, create and execute a WSH script containing the following:

```
On Error Resume Next
Set SHELL = CreateObject("WScript.Shell")
RegValue = "HKCU\Software\Microsoft\Windows\" & _
"CurrentVersion\Policies\System\NoLogOff"
SHELL.RegWrite RegValue, 1, "REG_DWORD"
```

Modifying NTFS Properties

NTFS includes many benefits over the regular FAT file system. The price of these benefits is the extra overhead and access time of the file system. You can modify the registry to disable some of these features.

Disabling 8.3 File Naming

When a file is created, it retains both long and short (DOS 8.3) file names. If you do not use DOS programs, you can disable 8.3 file naming to increase performance. To disable 8.3 file naming, create and execute a WSH script containing the following:

```
On Error Resume Next
Set SHELL = CreateObject("WScript.Shell")
RegValue = "HKLM\System\CurrentControlSet\Control\FileSystem\" & _
"NTFSDisable8dot3NameCreation"
SHELL.RegWrite
RegValue, 1, "REG_DWORD"
```

Related solution:	Found on page:
Renaming Files with Short File Names	82

Disabling the Last Access Time Stamp

When a file is accessed, a time stamp is placed on that file. If you do not need this information, you can disable the last access time stamp to increase performance. To disable the last access time stamp, create and execute a WSH script containing the following:

```
On Error Resume Next
Set SHELL = CreateObject("WScript.Shell")
RegValue = "HKLM\System\CurrentControlSet\Control\FileSystem\" & _
    "NTFSDisableLastAccessUpdate"
SHELL.RegWrite RegValue, 1, "REG_DWORD"
```

6. Inside the Registry

Modifying the Context Menu

A context menu is the menu that appears when you right click on almost anything in Windows (file, folder, URL, and so on). Some typical context menu items are "Open," "Print," and "Properties." Context menu items and their associated commands are stored in the registry. You can modify the registry to add your own, modify, or remove existing context menu items.

Adding a Windows XP/2003 "Defrag" Context Menu Item

To add a context menu item used to defrag a partition, create and execute a WSH script containing the following:

```
On Error Resume Next
Set objShell = CreateObject("WScript.Shell")

Command = "DEFRAG.EXE %1"

objShell.RegWrite "HKCR\Drive\Shell\Defrag\Command\", Command
objShell.RegWrite "HKCR\Drive\Shell\Defrag\", "Defrag"
```

After running this script, you can right click on any partition and a "Defrag" item should appear in the context menu. Selecting this item will defrag the partition you right clicked on.

Adding an "Email Attachment" Context Menu Item

Microsoft Outlook includes various command line options to create, open, and print email messages. To add a context menu item which uses Outlook to attach a file to a new email message, create and execute a WSH script containing the following:

```
On Error Resume Next
Set objShell = CreateObject("WScript.Shell")

'Get Outlook's default open command
Command = objShell.RegRead("HKCR\outlook\shell\open\command\")

'Now modify the command to attach a file
Command = REPLACE(Command,CHR(34) & " " & CHR(34),CHR(34) & _
" /a " & CHR(34))

objShell.RegWrite "HKCR\*\Shell\EmailAttachment\Command\", Command
objShell.RegWrite "HKCR\*\Shell\EmailAttachment\", _
"Email Attachment"
```

After running this script, you can right click on any file and an "Email Attachment" item should appear in the context menu. Selecting this item will create a new email message and attach the file you right clicked on.

TIP: *See Microsoft Knowledge Base Article Q296192 to learn about Outlook's additional command line switches.*

Adding an "Open with Notepad" Context Menu Item

When you attempt to open a file an unknown or missing file extension, Windows will prompt you to select a program to open the file and or associate with it. To add a context menu item to open any file with notepad, create and execute a WSH script containing the following:

```
On Error Resume Next
Set objShell = CreateObject("WScript.Shell")

Command = "NOTEPAD.EXE %1"

objShell.RegWrite "HKCR\*\Shell\OpenWithNotepad\Command\", Command
objShell.RegWrite "HKCR\*\Shell\OpenWithNotepad\"_
"Open With Notepad"
```

After running this script, you can right click on any file and a "Open with Notepad" item should appear in the context menu. Selecting this item will open the file you right clicked on in Notepad.

6. Inside the Registry

Chapter 7

Local System Management

(continued)

In Brief

It's such a shame. You spend months creating the perfect system image for your company, only to have users and fellow administrators destroy it little by little through installing new applications, deleting files, and disorganizing the file system. Almost brings a tear to your eye. In this chapter, you will learn how to reorganize the disorganized, secure your systems, and perform updates to keep your imaged systems and servers healthy and clean.

Common Locations

Microsoft uses a common organized structure to store user data. If you know the locations of these directories and the quickest way to access them, you can easily modify their contents within your scripts. Table 7.1 lists common locations for Windows.

Table 7.1   Common data storage paths in Windows.

Data Type	Path
All Users Desktop	%ALLUSERSPROFILE%\Desktop
All Users Start Menu	%ALLUSERSPROFILE%\Start Menu
Desktop	%USERPROFILE%\Desktop
Favorites	%USERPROFILE%\Favorites
NetHood	%USERPROFILE%\NetHood
PrintHood	%USERPROFILE%\PrintHood
Quick Launch	%USERPROFILE%\Application Data\Microsoft\Internet Explorer\Quick Launch
Start Menu	%USERPROFILE%\Start Menu

Accessing SpecialFolders with Windows Script Host

The WshShell object contains a property called SpecialFolders used to access these common locations. To access the SpecialFolders property, proceed as follows:

```
Set SHELL = CreateObject("WScript.Shell")
Set SF = SHELL.SpecialFolders
```

Here is a list of the folders available to the SpecialFolder property:

- AllUsersDesktop
- AllUsersStartMenu
- AllUsersPrograms
- AllUsersStartup
- AppData
- Desktop
- Favorites
- Fonts
- MyDocuments
- NetHood
- PrintHood
- Programs
- Recent
- SendTo
- StartMenu
- Startup
- Templates

Here is an example of how to access these special folders in Windows Script Host:

```
Set SHELL = CreateObject("WScript.Shell")
Set SF = SHELL.SpecialFolders
Wscript.Echo "Desktop: " & SF ("Desktop")
```

NOTE: *Access to these folders is dependent on your version of Windows. For example, there is no AllUsersDesktop folder for Windows 9x.*

Sharing

Sharing is the basic principle to networking: making resources easily available to multiple users. Windows allows you to share files, folders, and even devices to allow others to access your resources over the network.

NOTE: *Because Windows 2000 Professional and Windows XP only allow 10 concurrent network connections, this is the maximum number of simultaneous users that can access a share. The limit for a Windows 2000/2003 Server is dependent on the number of concurrent licenses you have for each server.*

To share a resource, right-click the resource and choose "Sharing" for Windows 2000 or "Sharing and Security" for Windows XP. Select "Share This Folder" and specify a share name. Resources are shared by their share names. Share names do not need to be the same name as the actual resource. For example, a folder called FILES can have a share name called MYFILES. To remain compatible with the DOS naming convention, your share names should not exceed eight characters.

Once a resource is shared, you can control access to it by modifying its share permissions. When a resource is shared, the default settings are to share that object with everyone. You can set varying access levels for your shared resources, and the process is identical to modifying NTFS permissions. Although NTFS is not required to set share permissions, you can increase security and functionality by using it.

NTFS Overview

The NTFS (NT File System) file system contains significant improvements over the previous Windows file systems (FAT and FAT32). Some of these improvements include:

- Maximum size: 16 exabytes
- Long file name support
- File, folder, and volume security
- Compression
- Bad cluster recovery
- *Disk quotas*—Disk usage limits you can set on a per-user basis
- *Encryption*—A method to make data unreadable for unauthorized viewers using the 56 Bit DES (Data Encryption Standard)
- *Reparse points*—An enhancement to file objects that allows developers to extend file system functionality
- *Sparse files*—Files that can be created at any size, but which grow only as needed
- *Change Journal*—Originally called the Update Sequence Number (USN) journal, a hidden journal that records changes to the file system

NTFS Security

NTFS stores extra information such as file ownership and uses access control lists (ACLs) to secure its files and folders from users and groups. The ACL contains access control entries (ACEs) that determine which type of access will be given. NTFS provides different ACEs for files and folders. To view the different ACEs you can set, open Windows Explorer and select Properties|Security|Permissions for a specific file or folder (see Figure 7.1).

In addition to the default NTFS permissions, you can specifically set individual permissions through the Type of Access|Special Access selection, as shown in Figure 7.2.

WARNING! Setting "No Access" to the group Everyone will prevent even administrators from accessing the affected resources.

The Scripting Advantage

Due to the diversity of the content in this chapter, the various scripting methods almost break even. Shell scripting proves its worth by providing an easy way to execute services, shortcuts, and the shutdown/logoff process from the command line. AutoIt pulls through with its unique ability to mask passwords and display tooltips, traytips, and progress bars. KIXtart hangs in there with its ability to manage shortcuts, the desktop, start menu, and dialog/input boxes. Finally, Windows Script Host's survives with its built-in ability to display dialog/input boxes and manage shortcuts and its COM ability to leverage on the power of the FileSystemObject object.

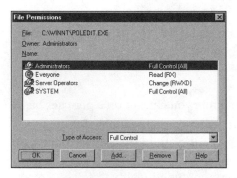

Figure 7.1   Editing NTFS general permissions.

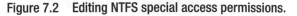

Figure 7.2   Editing NTFS special access permissions.

A Word of Caution

This chapter contains many scripting examples on modifying files, stopping services, shutting down computers, and logging off users. Obviously, accidentally shutting down an Exchange server, stopping the services on a SQL server, or deleting critical documents on a file server would be bad (if you're caught). As with all scripts, you should first test a script in an isolated testing environment to ensure the script produces the desired results before using the script in a production environment.

Immediate Solutions

Interacting with the User

When scripting, you might often need the ability to prompt or ask the user for input. This is useful when you need to inform the user that the script has ended, display error messages, ask for the location of a directory, and more.

Using Dialog Boxes with Shell Scripting

Shell scripting does not contain any built-in method to create dialog boxes from the command line. Msgbox.exe is a freeware utility that you can use to create dialog boxes from the command line. The basic syntax of msgbox is as follows:

```
Msgbox /commands "title" text
```

Here, *title* is the dialog box window title. Any characters after *title* will display *text* in the body of the dialog box. Multiple quoted phrases of *text* will result in multiple body lines of text. The available *commands* are as follows:

- **/BARI**—Displays Abort, Retry, and Ignore buttons
- **/BO**—Displays the OK button
- **/BOC**—Displays the OK and Cancel buttons
- **/BRC**—Displays the Retry and Cancel buttons
- **/BYN**—Displays the Yes and No buttons
- **/BYNC**—Displays the Yes, No, and Cancel buttons
- **/Dx**—Selects a default button where x is the button number, from left to right
- **/F1**—Sets the dialog box to the foreground before input
- **/F2**—Sets the dialog box to the foreground after input
- **/H**—Hides the console window during the prompt
- **/I!**—Displays the exclamation icon

- **/II**—Displays the information icon
- **/IQ**—Displays the question icon
- **/IS**—Displays the stop icon
- **/MA**—Normal display (Application Modal)
- **/MS**—On top display (System Modal)
- **/MT**—Normal display, includes title icon (Task Modal)
- **/T*x***—Times out after *x* seconds

To create a batch file example to illustrate the use of msgbox.exe, proceed as follows:

1. Create a new directory to store all files included in this example.
2. Download msgbox.exe from **www.jsiinc.com** to the new directory.
3. Start a command prompt and enter "*scriptfile*.bat."

Here, *scriptfile* is the full path of the new directory from step 1 and file name of a script file that contains the following:

```
@Echo Off
:Start

MSGBOX /H /MT /BO /I! "MSGBOX Example"
   "This example illustrates how to make"
   "dialog boxes from the command line."

MSGBOX /H /MT /BARI /IS "Fake Error"
   "Non critical program error."
   "Pressing a button will continue the example."

MSGBOX /H /MT /BYN /D2 /IQ "Repeat Example?"
   "Would you like to repeat this example?"

If errorlevel 5 goto End
If errorlevel 2 goto Start

:End
```

NOTE: *The highlighted code above must be placed on one line.*

Using Dialog Boxes with AutoIt

The AutoIt command **MessageBox** allows you to display a dialog box to the user with icons, button controls, and an optional window timeout (in seconds). To display a dialog box and have it timeout after 10 seconds using AutoIt, create and then execute an AutoIt script containing the following statement:

```
MsgBox(4096, "Window Title", "Window Message", 10)
```

NOTE: *The MsgBox command supports many functions, such as allowing for different buttons and icons. See the AutoIt help file to learn more about the included features.*

Using Dialog Boxes with KiXtart

The KiXtart command **MessageBox** allows you to display a dialog box to the user. To display a dialog box using KiXtart, create and then execute a KiXtart script containing the following statement:

```
MessageBox("This is a dialog box.", "DIALOG BOX", 0)
```

NOTE: *The **MessageBox** command supports many functions, such as allowing for different buttons and icons. See the KiXtart manual for all the included features.*

Using Dialog Boxes with Windows Script Host

Windows Script Host provides several methods to display dialog boxes. In the previous chapters, you have seen the Wscript.Echo used to display command prompt lines of text to the user when invoked using CSCRIPT.EXE, the command-line Windows Script Host engine. If you start your scripts with WSCRIPT.EXE, the line of text will be displayed in a message box:

```
WScript.Echo "This is a dialog box."
```

Another method of displaying dialog boxes is using WshShell's **PopUp**:

```
Set SHELL = CreateObject("WScript.Shell")
SHELL.PopUp "Window Text", 0, "Window Title", 0
```

Finally, you can use the MsgBox method to display a dialog box:

```
MsgBox "Window Text", vbOKCancel, "Window Title"
```

NOTE: *PopUp and MsgBox are very similar to KiXtart's **MessageBox**. See the WSH documentation for all the included features.*

Displaying a ToolTip with AutoIt

ToolTip's are the helpful little and yellow-boxed text messages that are displayed whenever you hover over certain items (usually toolbar buttons). The AutoIt **ToolTip** command allows you to create your own tool tip anywhere on the screen. To display a tool tip using AutoIt, create and then execute an AutoIt script containing the following:

```
ToolTip("Take a break!", x, y)
Sleep(5000)
```

Here, x and y are the corresponding X and Y coordinates of where the tooltip will be displayed. Note the sleep command, which uses milliseconds. This command is used to prevent the script from ending so quickly that you would not be able to see the tooltip.

Displaying a Tray Tip with AutoIt

Tray tips are the balloon messages that display from the system tray area. The AutoIt **TrayTip** command allows you to create your own tray tip. To display a tray tip using AutoIt, create and then execute an AutoIt script containing the following:

```
TrayTip("Help Me!", _
  "My disk  is full!", 5, 2)
Sleep(5000)
```

Here, 5 is the amount of seconds to display the tip, and 2 is any one of the icon values (0=None, 1=Info, 2=Warning, 3=Error) to use. Note the sleep command which uses milliseconds. This command is used to prevent the script from ending so quickly that you would not be able to see the tray tip.

Accepting User Input with Shell Scripting

Shell scripting does not include any method to accept user input, aside from creating temporary files and then parsing the files. Included in Windows 2003 server and available in the NT, 2000, and XP resource kits is a utility called CHOICE.EXE that allows you to accept user choices (one key press) from the command line:

```
CHOICE /C:ABC
IF ERRORLEVEL 1 ECHO You pressed A
IF ERRORLEVEL 2 ECHO You pressed B
IF ERRORLEVEL 3 ECHO You pressed C
```

7. Local System Management

Here, the **/C** switch states which keys are allowed for input (for example, **/C:ABC**). You can determine which key has been pressed by checking the appropriate errorlevel. The first key allowed, in this example A, is associated with the first errorlevel (errorlevel 1), and so on.

Accepting User Input with AutoIt

The AutoIt command **InputBox** allows you to store a line of user input to a variable. To accept user input using AutoIt, create and then execute an AutoIt script containing the following:

```
$Computer = InputBox("Computer Name", _
  "Enter the name of the computer", _
  "localhost")
MsgBox(4096, "Your Choice", _
"You entered: " & $Computer, 10)
```

TIP: *The AutoIt InputBox command also accepts parameters that allow you to set the width, height, location, and more.*

Accepting User Input with KiXtart

The KiXtart command **GETS** allows you to store a line of user input to a variable. To accept user input using KiXtart, create and then execute a KiXtart script containing the following:

```
GETS $variable
FLUSHKB
```

Here, ***variable*** is the variable to store the user input. The **FLUSHKB** command clears the keyboard buffer.

TIP: *You can use the KiXtart command **Get** to accept a single key of input.*

Accepting User Input with Windows Script Host

The Windows Script Host command **InputBox** allows you to store a line of user input to a variable. To accept user input using Windows Script Host, create and then execute a WSH script containing the following:

```
Name = InputBox("Please type enter your name:", _
"YOUR NAME REQUIRED", "JOHN BREYAN")
Wscript.Echo "Hello " +
Name
```

Accepting a Password with AutoIt

While most prompts for passwords mask the input with a *, Shell Scripting, KiXtart, and Windows Script Host input methods cannot. Fortunately, the AutoIt command **InputBox** allows you to mask input with the character of your choosing. To accept a password (or any masked input) using AutoIt, create and then execute an AutoIt script containing the following:

```
$Password = InputBox("Password Required", _
  "Enter a password", _
  "", "*")
MsgBox(4096, "Your Password", _
"You entered: " & $Password, 10)
```

Displaying a Progressbar with AutoIt

Progressbars are used everywhere, from loading files in Windows to copying files to saving games. Because they are so common, you probably want to use them with your own scripts. With a progressbar, not only can you let the user know how far a certain process is at before completion, but which step of the process is being completed. AutoIt is the only scripting method that includes the ability to display a progressbar. To display a progressbar using AutoIt, create and then execute an AutoIt script containing the following:

```
ProgressOn("Please wait", _
  "We are doing stuff", _
  "0% Complete")
Sleep(1000)

ProgressSet(10, _
    "10% Complete", _
    "Initializing")
Sleep(1000)

ProgressSet(20, _
    "20% Complete", _
    "Finalizing")

For $i = 21 to 100 step 1
  Sleep(100)
  ProgressSet( $i, _
    $i & "% Complete")
Next
```

```
ProgressSet(100 , _
  "Done", "100% Complete")
Sleep(2000)
ProgressOff()
```

Changing the Desktop Wallpaper

KiXtart includes a command called **SETWALLPAPER** to change the desktop wallpaper for the current user. To change the desktop wallpaper using KiXtart, create and then execute a KiXtart script containing the following:

```
SETWALLPAPER("wallpaper")
```

Here, *wallpaper* is the complete path and file name of the bitmap to use.

Working with Shortcuts

Shortcuts are merely pointers to the files and folders you use most often. Shortcuts are easily identified by their .LNK extension and are the building blocks of the Start menu. Most users live and breathe shortcuts, and would be lost without them. Through shell scripting and Windows Script Host, you can easily modify or create shortcuts anywhere on a system.

Creating Shortcuts Using Shell Scripting

SHORTCUT.EXE is a freeware utility you can use to create shortcuts from the command line. To create a shortcut using SHORTCUT.EXE, proceed as follows:

1. Create a new directory to store all files included in this example.

2. Download shortcut.exe from **www.jsiinc.com** to the new directory.

3. Start a command prompt and enter "*scriptfile*.bat."

Here, *scriptfile* is the full path of the new directory from step 1 and file name of a script file that contains the following:

```
SHORTCUT /F:"name" /A:Create /T:"target" /W:"directory" /D:"description"
```

NOTE: *Here, name is the full path and name of the shortcut; target is the full path and name of the item to create a shortcut to; directory is the full directory path to start the target in; and description is the comment for the shortcut.*

TIP: *SHORTCUT.EXE supports many command-line parameters. Type "shortcut.exe /?" for more information.*

Creating Shortcuts Using KiXtart

KiXtart does not have the ability to create shortcuts, other than within the Start menu. If you want to create a shortcut somewhere else, you can create a Start menu shortcut, copy the shortcut to the desired location, and then delete the original shortcut. To create a shortcut using KiXtart, create and then execute a KiXtart script containing the following:

```
$SName = "name"
$STarget = "target"
$SDir = "directory"
$SDest = "destination"
$RCODE = AddProgramItem($STarget,$SName,"",0,$SDir,0,0)
Copy "SMPDIR\$SName.lnk" $SDest
$RCODE = DelProgramItem($SName)
```

Here, **name** is the name of the shortcut without the extension or path; **target** is the full path and name of the item to create a shortcut to; **directory** is the full directory path to start the target in; **smpdir** is the full path of the Start Menu\Programs directory; and **destination** is where to store the shortcut.

TIP: *If you just want to create a shortcut in the Start menu, simply use the **AddProgramItem** command.*

Creating Shortcuts Using Windows Script Host

To create a shortcut using Windows Script Host, create and then execute a WSH script containing the following:

```
Set Shell = CreateObject("WScript.Shell")
sNAME = "name"
sTARGET = "target"
sDIR = "directory"
sICON = "icon"
sHKEY = "hotkey"
```

```
Set Scut = Shell.CreateShortcut(sNAME)
Scut.TargetPath = Shell.ExpandEnvironmentStrings(sTARGET)
Scut.WorkingDirectory = Shell.ExpandEnvironmentStrings(sDIR)
Scut.WindowStyle = 4
Scut.IconLocation = Shell.ExpandEnvironmentStrings(sICON)
Scut.HotKey = sHKEY
Scut.Save
```

Here, **name** is the complete path and name of the shortcut; **target** is the item to place a shortcut to; **directory** is the item's working directory; **icon** is the shortcut icon to use; and **hotkey** is the quick key combination to activate the shortcut (for example, ALT+SHIFT+Q).

Deleting Broken Shortcuts

Shortcuts are merely pointers to a file or folder on your system, and when those target items get moved or deleted, those shortcuts are useless. To delete a broken shortcut using Windows Script Host, create and then execute a WSH script containing the following:

```
Set FSO = CreateObject("Scripting.FileSystemObject")
Set Shell = CreateObject("Wscript.Shell")
sDIR = directory

Set objDIR = GetFolder(sDIR)
GoSubFolders objDIR

Sub MainSub(objDIR)
  For Each efile in objDIR.Files
    fEXT = FSO.GetExtensionName(efile.Path)
    If LCase(fEXT) = LCase("lnk") Then
      Set Shortcut = Shell.CreateShortcut(efile)
      If NOT FSO.FileExists(Shortcut.TargetPath) Then
          If NOT FSO.FolderExists(Shortcut.TargetPath) Then
            DelFile efile
          End If
      End If
    End If
  Next
End Sub
```

Here, **directory** is the location to start searching for broken shortcuts.

NOTE: You need to append the **GoSubFolders**, **DelFile**, and **GetFolder** routines, listed in Chapter 4, to this script in order for it to run.

TIP: *You can use the resource kit utility CHKLNKS.EXE to perform the same task manually.*

Controlling the Start Menu

The Start menu is the central point for organizing application and system shortcuts. For every new application installed, more than likely an associated shortcut or two is installed in the Start menu. Users can spend a good portion of their day navigating through this menu to get to the application or data they want, so it is important to organize this data effectively.

Adding a Program Group with KiXtart

As you learned in the previous section, you can create Start menu shortcuts using the command **AddProgramItem**. KiXtart also includes a function called **AddProgramGroup** to create folders in the Start menu:

```
AddProgramGroup("Folder", Location)
```

Here, *folder* is the name of the group to create, and ***location*** specifies whether to place the group in the common or user Start menu. A value of 0 specifies the user Start menu, whereas a value of 1 specifies the common Start menu.

Moving All Uninstall Shortcuts to a Central Directory

When an application installer places its shortcuts in the Start menu, an uninstall icon is normally included to uninstall this product quickly and easily. Unfortunately, a user quickly browsing through the Start menu might click on an uninstall icon and accidentally remove or damage application or system files. To move the uninstall shortcuts from the Start menu to a central directory, create and then execute a WSH script containing the following:

```
Set FSO = CreateObject("Scripting.FileSystemObject")
Set Shell = CreateObject("Wscript.Shell")
sMENU = Shell.SpecialFolders("Programs")
sDIR = "C:\UNINSTALL"
If Not FSO.FolderExists(sDIR) Then
    FSO.CreateFolder sDIR
End If

Set objDIR = GetFolder(sMENU)
GoSubFolders objDIR
```

```
Sub MainSub (objDIR)
For Each efile in objDIR.Files
  fEXT = FSO.GetExtensionName(efile.Path)
  fNAME = LCase(FSO.GetBaseName(efile.Path))
  Folder = FSO.GetBaseName(objDIR)
  If LCase(fEXT) = LCase("lnk") Then
    If InStr(fNAME, "uninstall") <> 0 Then
        If fNAME = "uninstall" Then
          efile.Name = fNAME & " " & Folder & "." & fEXT
        End If
      MoveFile efile, sDIR
    End If
  End If
Next
End Sub
```

NOTE: *You need to append the **GoSubFolders**, **MoveFile**, and **GetFolder** routines, listed in Chapter 4, to this script in order for it to run.*

Deleting Old User Profiles

Whenever a new user logs on, a user profile is created. User profiles consist of the user's own personal Start menu, shortcuts, and user registry. As time progresses, profiles can take up a good portion of hard drive space. DELPROF.EXE is a Windows 2000 resource kit utility that allows you to delete old profiles that haven't been used for a while. To delete old user profiles, proceed as follows:

```
DELPROF /Q /I /D:days
```

Here, **/Q** disables prompting during profile deletion; **/I** instructs DELPROF to ignore errors and continue deletion; and **/D** indicates to delete profiles inactive more than the specified number of *days*.

NOTE: *If a specific user profile cannot be deleted by DELPROF, it might be in use. This includes the current user profile and profiles belonging to accounts associated with running services. You will need administrative privileges to delete other user's profiles.*

Managing Services from the Command Line

Services are processes that run in the background, independent of a user logon. Normally, these services are managed manually through the Control Panel|Services applet, but in this section you will learn how to manage services from the command line.

Installing a Service

INSTSRV.EXE is a resource kit utility to install a service from the command line. To install a service, start a command prompt and enter the following:

```
INSTSRV name exe -a account -p password
```

Here, **name** is the name to give the service; **exe** is the path and name of the executable to run; **account** is the name of the account to run the service under; and **password** is the password of the account.

NOTE: *After you install a service with INSTRV.EXE, the service is not automatically started. See the following section on starting services from the command line.*

Uninstalling a Service

To uninstall a service, start a command prompt and enter the following:

```
INSTSRV name Remove
```

Here, **name** is the name of the service to uninstall. The keyword **remove** instructs INSTSRV to uninstall the service.

Related solution:	Found on page:
Deleting a Service	185

Starting a Service

You can use the NET command to control services from the command line. To start a service from the command line, start a command prompt and enter the following:

```
NET START "service"
```

Here, **service** is the name of the service to start.

Related solution:	Found on page:
Starting Services	183

7. Local System Management

Pausing a Service

To pause a started service from the command line, start a command prompt and enter the following:

```
NET PAUSE "service"
```

Here, *service* is the name of the started service to pause.

Related solution:	*Found on page:*
Pausing Services	184

Resuming a Service

To resume a paused service from the command line, start a command prompt and enter the following:

```
NET CONTINUE "service"
```

Here, *service* is the name of the paused service to resume.

Related solution:	*Found on page:*
Resuming Services	185

Stopping a Service

To stop a started service from the command line, start a command prompt and enter the following:

```
NET STOP "service"
```

Here, *service* is the name of the started service to stop.

Related solution:	*Found on page:*
Stopping Services	184

Managing NTFS from the Command Line

In Chapter 4, you learned how to modify file and folder properties. NTFS adds additional properties that you can modify through scripting.

Modifying NTFS Permissions

The Windows 2000 resource kit utility XCACLS.EXE allows you to change NTFS permissions from the command line. Most administrators use this utility in a batch file to lock down their desktops and servers. To secure the *%WINDIR%*\Repair directory access to just administrators, start a command prompt and enter the following:

```
XCACLS C:\%WINDIR%\REPAIR\*.* /G administrators:F
```

TIP: *XCACLS contains many command-line parameters. Enter "XCACLS /?" for more information.*

Changing a File Owner

The resource kit utility SUBINACL.EXE allows you to view or modify file, registry, and service security properties. You can use this utility to change the NTFS owner of a file. To set a new owner using SUBINACL.EXE, start a command prompt and enter the following:

```
SUBINACL /FILE/filename/SETOWNER=ownername
```

Here, *filename* is the full path and name of the file whose ownership is to be changed.

Managing NTFS Encryption

Although NTFS permissions allow you to secure your files and folders from other users, several methods are available to bypass this security (for example, NTFSDOS). Windows 2000/XP/2003 uses an encrypting file system (EFS) to secure your files.

TIP: *The Microsoft Knowledge Base article Q255742 explains several methods to recover data from encrypted files, even if the private key is lost.*

Encrypting Files from the Command Line

CIPHER.EXE is a utility that allows you to encrypt/decrypt your files from the command line. This utility supports the following parameters:

- **/A**—Specifies to act on files and folders
- **/D**—Decrypts files and folders
- **/E**—Encrypts files and folders

- **/F**—Forces encryption, even on files already encrypted
- **/H**—Includes system and hidden files
- **/I**—Ignores errors
- **/K**—Creates a new encryption key for the current user
- **/Q**—Runs in silent mode
- **/S**—Performs action on the current folder and all subfolders

WARNING! *Encrypted files cannot be read during the boot process. Encrypting files that the system needs to access while booting will cause your system not to boot.*

To silently encrypt all the files and folders within a directory, start a command prompt and enter the following:

```
CIPHER /E /A /S /F /Q /H "directory"
```

Here, *directory* is the folder to encrypt.

Decrypting Files from the Command Line

To decrypt all the files within a directory, start a command prompt and enter the following:

```
CIPHER /D /A /S /Q "directory"
```

Here, *directory* is the folder to encrypt.

Managing Shares from the Command Line

Shares allow users to access resources from one common source on the network. As more and more systems and devices are added and shared on your network, managing shares can become an intensive chore.

Listing Shares

You can list shares from the command line using the built-in **NET** command. To list all shares from the command line, start a command prompt and enter the following:

```
NET SHARE
```

Adding Shares

Sharing a resource makes that object available on the network. To share a resource from the command line, start a command prompt and enter the following:

```
NET SHARE name=path /USERS:maxnum /REMARK:"comment"
```

Here, **name** is the name of the share; **path** is the path to create the share to; **maxnum** is the maximum number of users allowed to simultaneously access the share; and **comment** is the comment to give the share.

TIP: *If you want to allow an unlimited number of users to access the share simultaneously, replace the /users:**maxnum** switch with the /**unlimited** switch.*

Related solution:	Found on page:
Creating a Share	177

Removing Shares

To delete a share from the command line, start a command prompt and enter the following:

```
NET name /DELETE
```

Here, **name** is the name of the share.

TIP: */D is the abbreviated form of the /**DELETE** switch. When you delete a share, you are only disabling sharing for that resource, not deleting that resource.*

Related solution:	Found on page:
Deleting a Share	178

Copying Share Permissions

Currently, there is no Microsoft method to set share permissions from the command line. However, you can use the resource kit utility PERMCOPY.EXE to copy permissions from one share to another. To use PERMCOPY.EXE to copy permissions from one share to another, start a command prompt and enter the following:

```
PERMCOPY \\source sname \\destination dname
```

Here, ***source*** is the computer containing the share (***sname***) with proper permissions; and ***destination*** is the computer containing the share (***dname***) to copy permissions to.

TIP: *Supplying both the **source** and **destination** with the local computer name will copy permissions from one local share to another.*

WARNING! *Do not use PERMCOPY.EXE to copy permissions on administrative shares (for example, C$). This will cause SERVICES.EXE to crash.*

Creating Shares with Permissions

Currently, there is no Microsoft method to create shares with permissions from the command line. RMTSHARE.EXE is a Windows 2000 resource kit utility to create shares with permissions on remote stations. You can provide this utility with the local computer name to create shares with permissions on the local station. To use RMTSHARE.EXE to create shares with permissions, start a command prompt and enter the following:

```
RMTSHARE \\computer\name=path /GRANT guser:permission
/REMOVE ruser
```

NOTE: *The code above must be placed on one line. Here, **computer** is the computer name to create the share on; **name** is the name of the share; **path** is the path to create the share to; **guser** is the username to grant **permissions** to; and **ruser** is the username to deny share access to.*

TIP: *RMTSHARE.EXE also supports the same switches as the **NET SHARE** command.*

Calling System Events

In Chapter 5, you learned how to call system events (for example, shutdown, restart) using DLL calls. In this section, you will learn how to call these events without using DLL calls.

Shutting Down/Restarting the Computer in Windows 2000

The resource kit utility SHUTDOWN.EXE allows you to shut down or restart Windows. The basic syntax of the SHUTDOWN command is:

```
SHUTDOWN parameters
```

The available parameters for SHUTDOWN.EXE are as follows:

- *"message"* —Displays a message prior to shutdown
- **/A**—Used to abort a shutdown performed with the **/T** switch
- **/C**—Force-closes all running applications
- **/L**—Specifies to work with the local computer
- **/R**—Restarts the computer after shutdown
- **/T:seconds**—Performs a shutdown after the number of seconds specified
- **/Y**—Answers YES to any dialog box prompts

WARNING! *Using the /C switch will close all applications without saving and might result in losing data. Use this switch only when you are certain that the local machine does not have any open unsaved files.*

Related solution:	Found on page:
Shutting Down a System	186

Logging Off a User

The resource kit utility LOGOFF.EXE allows you to log off a user from a current Windows session. The basic syntax of the LOGOFF command is:

```
LOGOFF /F /N
```

Here, **/F** force-closes all running applications and **/N** removes any user prompts.

WARNING! *Using the /F switch will close all applications without saving and may result in losing data. Use this switch only when you are certain that the local machine does not have any open unsaved files.*

Shutting Down/Restarting the Computer in Windows XP/2003

Windows XP/2003 includes the SHUTDOWN command, which you can use to shut down or restart Windows. The basic syntax of the SHUTDOWN command is:

```
SHUTDOWN parameters
```

The available parameters for SHUTDOWN.EXE are as follows:

- **-A**—Used to abort a shutdown
- **-C**—Used to display a message prior to shutdown
- **-D *code***—Reason code for the shutdown
- **-F**—Force-closes all running applications
- **-I**—Displays a GUI Interface
- **-L**—Logs off the current user
- **-M *computername***—Specifies the remote computer name
- **-R**—Restarts the computer after shutdown
- **-T:*seconds***—Performs a shutdown after the number of seconds specified

WARNING! *Using the -F switch will close all applications without saving and might result in losing data. Use this switch only when you are certain that the local machine does not have any open unsaved files.*

Related solution:	Found on page:
Shutting Down a System	186

Logging Off a User in Windows XP/2003

To log off the current user session using the SHUTDOWN command, start a command prompt and enter the following:

```
SHUTDOWN -L
```

Windows XP/2003 also provides the LOGOFF command to log off a user from a Windows session. To log off the current user session using the LOGOFF command, start a command prompt and enter the following:

```
LOGOFF
```

7. Local System Management

Remote System Management

(continued)

In Brief

Remote management is essential to becoming a good administrator. When you're working at a site with 300 or more systems, visiting and updating every single system becomes an impossible task. In this chapter, you will learn how to manage remote systems from the command line and through Windows Management Instrumentation.

Administrative Shares

By default, Windows creates special shares so that administrators can perform various tasks remotely. These special shares are called *administrative shares* and are automatically created when you install the operating system and whenever you add a nonremovable drive or partition. Administrative shares are hidden shares that only administrators can access. The permissions, names, and settings for these shares cannot be modified, and these shares can only be removed by making special registry entries. The most common administrative shares are:

- ADMIN$—Shares the directory Windows was installed in (for example, C:\WINNT)
- *DRIVE*$—Shares all available drives, where *drive* is the specific drive letter
- IPC$—Share that represents the named pipes communication mechanism
- PRINT$—Share for shared printer drivers
- REPL$—Shares replication directory on a server

Attaching to Shares

Many remote administrative tasks can be performed through network share access. Once you attach to a share, you can perform tasks on these shares as if they were local resources. The process of attaching to a network share and assigning that connection a drive letter is called *mapping*. Mapping a drive requires that you specify the complete Universal Naming Convention (UNC) path of the share and the available drive letter to which you want to map it.

Once you map a drive to a share, you will be able to perform many of the tasks you perform on your drives locally. To map a drive from within Windows, right-click Network Neighborhood and select Map Drive. The Map Network Drive dialog box will appear (see Figure 8.1).

To map a drive from the command line, start a command prompt and enter the following:

```
NET USE DRIVE: \\COMPUTER\SHARE
```

Here, **DRIVE** is the drive letter you want to map the **SHARE** name to, and **COMPUTER** is the system holding the shared resource.

You can also map a drive as a different user:

```
NET USE DRIVE: \\COMPUTER\SHARE /USER:DOMAIN\USERNAME PASSWORD
```

Performing Tasks through a Share

Once a remote share has been mapped, you can perform command-line tasks on it as if it were a local drive. Here is an example to delete all the files within a directory on a remote system:

```
NET USE DRIVE: \\COMPUTER\SHARE
DEL DRIVE:\*.*
```

Once a drive is successfully mapped, you can utilize any of the file management methods that were detailed in Chapter 4.

Figure 8.1   Mapping a network drive.

Disconnecting Mapped Shares

When you no longer need to access the resources of a mapped share, you can disconnect it to free up available drives. To disconnect a mapped drive from within Windows, right-click Network Neighborhood and select Disconnect Drive. When the Disconnect Network Drive dialog box appears (see Figure 8.2), select the drive and click OK.

To disconnect a mapped share from the command line, start a command prompt and enter the following:

```
NET USE DRIVE: /DELETE
```

Here, **DRIVE** is the drive letter mapped to the share that you want to disconnect.

TIP: */D is the abbreviated form of the /DELETE switch.*

Windows Management Instrumentation

As enterprises grow larger, they become more difficult to manage. Web-Based Enterprise Management (WBEM) is an initiative to provide an environment-independent solution to manage data and devices. WBEM was developed by the Desktop Management Task Force (DMTF), a collective organization consisting of Microsoft, Compaq, and other large corporations. Windows Management Instrumentation (WMI) is Microsoft's Windows implementation of the WBEM initiative.

What Is WMI?

WMI, formerly called WBEM, provides scripters and developers with a standardized method to monitor and manage local and remote resources. It comes included in Windows 98 and Windows 2000/XP/2003, and is available as a download for Windows 95 and Windows

8. Remote System Management

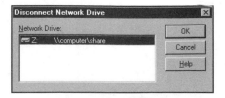

Figure 8.2   Disconnecting a mapped drive.

NT (Service Pack 5 or higher). WMI provides a standard, scriptable interface to various resources. The devices and applications controlled by WMI are known as *managed objects*. Managed objects can be anything from hardware, such as a hub or motherboard, to software, such as the operating system or an application.

The WMI Process

The executable that provides all the functionality of WMI is called WINMGMT.EXE. WINMGMT.EXE runs as a standard executable on Windows 9x (because Windows 9x does not support services) and as a service on Windows NT/2000/XP/2003 systems. When a script or application (known as a consumer) issues calls to the WMI namespace, the executable awakes and passes these calls to the CIM Object Manager (CIMOM). The CIMOM is the entrance to the WMI infrastructure. It allows for the initial object creation and provides a uniform method to access managed objects. When CIMOM receives a request to control a managed object, it first checks the CIMOM object repository.

The CIMOM object repository is a storage area for the Common Information Model (CIM). The CIM contains the WMI object models and a description of all the available managed objects, called the *management schema*. This repository is full of all the different access methods and properties of manageable objects, known as static management data. If the information requested cannot be found in the repository, the repository passes the request down to the object provider.

A *provider* is the interface between the device to be managed and the CIMOM. The provider collects the information from a device and makes it available to the CIMOM. This information is known as dynamic management data. Developers create providers when the CIM does not contain methods to access a managed resource. Several providers come packaged with WMI:

- Active Directory provider
- Event Log provider
- Performance Counter provider
- Registry provider
- SNMP provider
- View provider
- WDM provider
- Win32 provider
- Windows Installer provider.

Once the provider has completed processing the request, it sends all results back to the originating script or application.

Scripting WMI

In Chapter 1, you learned how to connect to a WSH object. The process of connecting to the WMI object model is similar to connecting to the WSH object model. To gain access to an object, you use the **GetObject** function and set it to a variable. This is called *instantiating* an object, as in the following example:

```
Set variable = GetObject("winmgmts:{" & _
  "impersonationLevel=impersonate}!\\" & _
  Computer & "\root\namespace").ExecQuery _
  (WQL)
```

Here, **variable** is the variable used throughout your script to access all the properties and methods within the object, **Computer** is the name of the target system to run the script on, and **\ROOT\namespace** specifies which namespace to connect to within the CIMOM object repository. The **winmgmts** namespace specifies a call to the WMI service.

Impersonation

{Impersonationlevel=impersonate}! instructs WMI to execute the script with the credentials of the caller (person who executed the script) and not the credentials of the currently logged-on user of the targeted system. This instruction is extremely useful when administrators are running remote scripts on systems and the logged on user does not have sufficient privileges to perform all the specified requests.

TIP: *{Impersonationlevel=impersonate}! is the default impersonation level on Windows 2000/ XP/2003, and therefore can be omitted from your scripts if you are running any of these operating systems. It is included in the scripts in this book only for completeness and Windows NT compatibility. Impersonations are not supported by Windows 9x because the operating system does not support user privileges.*

Namespaces

Namespaces are organized containers of information within a schema. Namespace hierarchy runs from left to right and is separated with backslashes. ROOT is the parent namespace for WMI and contains all the child namespaces. WMI includes three child namespaces:

- *Cimv2*—Stores Win32 system classes
- *Default*—Stores system classes
- *Security*—Stores WMI security classes

Most of your WMI scripting will include the Cimv2 namespace, because it holds many classes and instances for a Win32 system.

WMI Query Language

WMI uses a rich query language called the WMI Query Language (WQL). This language, similar to SQL (Structured Query Language), allows you to query WMI information. The basic syntax for a WQL statement is as follows:

```
.ExecQuery("select propmeth from class")
```

TIP: *In addition to the select and from statements above, you can use many statements and keywords based on SQL.*

ExecQuery runs the WQL statement, which is stored in quotes and surrounded by parentheses. *PropertyName* specifies the name of the property to retrieve from the specified *class*. Classes are organized containers for properties and methods of a manageable device. For example, the **Win32_TapeDrive** class contains all the properties and methods to manage tape drives.

In addition to the **ExecQuery**, you can also use the **ExecNotification-Query** to perform WQL queries. The **ExecNotificationQuery** method is used to detect when instances of a class are modified. In plain English, this method allows you to poll for events. Combined with WQL, you can use this method to monitor the event log, CPU, memory, and more based on a specified interval.

Displaying WMI Instance Property Names and Values

A WMI instance (e.g, a Share, Process, Service) can have many properties (e.g., status, name, description). The following subroutine can be used to display all of the property names and values of a WMI instance with a single call:

```
Sub DisplayWMIProperties(WMIInstances)
  On Error Resume Next
  For Each WMIObject In WMIInstances
    For Each Property In WMIObject.Properties_
      Wscript.Echo Property.Name & ":" & _
        Property.Value
    Next
    Wscript.Echo VBCRLF
  Next
End Sub
```

NOTE: *Notice the use of On Error Resume Next. This allows the script to skip over complex value types that would normally cause an error.*

The WMI SDK: Worth Its Weight in Gold

Microsoft creates software developer kits (SDKs) to assist third-party application developers in creating Windows applications. The WMI SDK includes the core WMI installation, documentation, utilities, and examples. You can obtain the WMI SDK free from **msdn.microsoft.com**.

WMI Object Browser

The WMI Object Browser (see Figure 8.3) is a Web application to explore WMI namespaces. Through it, you can view and manipulate all the classes and their properties and methods. The application runs within a Web browser and allows you to connect to any namespace on a local or remote system.

NOTE: *The WMI Object Browser is an intensive Web application. If it seems to be frozen when navigating through the various classes, it may actually be loading the properties, methods, and subclasses into memory.*

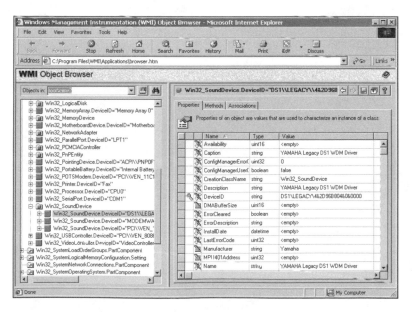

Figure 8.3   The WMI Object Browser.

The Scripting Advantage

Since this chapter is largely focused around WMI, Windows Script Host and KiXtart have the clear advantage. While both scripting tools can access WMI through COM, due to size limitations of the book and popularity of the scripting language, this chapter will provide WMI examples in Windows Script Host only. (It should be simple to convert any of the scripts to KiXtart.) Shell scripting offers one advantage with its ability to easily run command a line script for MMC snap-ins and utilities. Finally, AutoIt is not appropriate and is not discussed in this chapter.

A Word of Caution

This chapter contains many scripting examples on remotely controlling and managing systems. Accidentally stopping a critical service or uninstalling a critical application on a production server could be your last mistake on the job. As with all scripts, you should first test the script in an isolated testing environment to ensure the script produces the desired results before using it in a production environment.

Immediate Solutions

Working with the MMC

Microsoft Management Console (MMC) is a multi-document interface (MDI) shell that hosts applications called snapins. Windows comes with many snapins, from Device Management to User Management. While by default most snapins connect to the local system, you can use the command line to connect a snapin to a remote system.

Opening the "Computer Management" MMC Snapin

To open the computer management MMC snapin for a remote system, start a command prompt and enter the following:

```
mmc %windir%\system32\compmgmt.msc -s /computer:\\computer
```

Here, *computer* is the name of the remote system.

Opening the "Event Viewer" MMC Snapin

To open the event viewer MMC snapin for a remote system, start a command prompt and enter the following:

```
mmc %windir%\system32\eventvwr.msc /computer=\\computer
```

Here, *computer* is the name of the remote system.

TIP: *The Local Users and Computers (lusrmgr.msc) and Services (services.msc) snapins also support the /computer= option.*

Remote Management from the Command Line

Most local system management is performed through the MMC or the Control Panel on Windows 2000/XP/2003 systems. Although most of these tools include remote management capability, you can also use command-line utilities to create scripts for remote management.

Installing the Remote Console

Remote Console is a Windows 2000 resource kit utility that allows you to run a client/server command-prompt session between two systems, similar to a telnet session. To install the Remote Console, start a command prompt and enter the following:

```
RSETUP \\computer
```

Installing the Remote Command

Remote Command is a resource kit utility that allows you to run a program and a command prompt session on a remote computer from your local station. In essence, you call up a command prompt window on your machine that will run commands on the remote machine. To install the remote command service, start a command prompt and enter the following:

```
RCMDSVC -INSTALL
NET START "Remote Command Service"
```

Executing Commands on a Remote System

You can start commands on a remote system using either the remote command (RCMD) or Remote Console utilities. The remote command utility allows you to start either a batch file or a program on a remote system. To start a command on a remote system using the remote command, start a command prompt and enter the following:

```
RCMD \\computer program
```

The Remote Console utility allows you to start a batch file on a remote system. To start a batch file on a remote system using Remote Console, start a command prompt and enter the following:

```
RCLIENT \\computer /RUNBATCH program
```

Here, **computer** is the remote system to run the *program* on.

Listing Shares and Permissions

SRVCHECK.EXE is a resource kit utility to list shares and permissions on a remote system. To view the shares and permission on a remote system, start a command prompt and enter the following:

```
SRVCHECK \\computer
```

Here, **computer** is the name of the remote system.

Related solution:	Found on page:
Listing Shares	176

Creating Shares with Permissions

RMTSHARE.EXE is a resource kit utility to create shares with permissions on remote stations. To use RMTSHARE.EXE to create shares with permissions, start a command prompt and enter the following:

```
RMTSHARE \\computer\name=path/GRANT
guser:permission/REMOVE ruser
```

NOTE: *The code above must be placed on one line.*

Here, **computer** is the computer name to create the share on; **name** is the name of the share; path is the path to create the share to; **guser** is the username to grant permissions to; and **ruser** is the username to deny share access to.

TIP: *RMTSHARE.EXE also supports the same switches as the **NET SHARE** command.*

Related solution:	Found on page:
Creating Shares with Permissions	173

Listing Processes

PULIST.EXE is a Windows 2000 resource kit utility that allows you to list running processes and their associated IDs on a remote system. To display remote processes, start a command prompt and enter the following:

```
PULIST \\COMPUTER
```

Terminating Processes

The Windows 2000 resource kit provides a service called RKILLSRV.EXE that allows you to view and terminate processes on a remote PC. Unfortunately, not all of us are lucky enough to have the time or authority to install any services we like. PSKILL.EXE is a free utility from Sysinternals (**www.sysinternals.com**) that allows you to terminate a process or a remote station without having to add any additional services or configuration. To terminate a process on a remote system, start a command prompt and enter the following:

```
PSKILL \\computer -U username -P password process
```

Here, **computer** is the name of the remote system, **username** and **password** are the administrative credentials for the remote system, and **process** is the name or process ID to terminate. Here is a quick example to terminate a user running Notepad:

```
PSKILL \\computer -U username -P password notepad
```

Listing Services

SCLIST.EXE is a Windows 2000 resource kit utility that allows you to list running services on a remote system. To display remote services, start a command prompt and enter the following:

```
SCLIST \\computer parameters
```

Here, **computer** is the name of the remote system to display services. The available **parameters** for SCLIST are as follows:

- /M—Displays all services
- /R—Displays running services
- /S—Displays stopped services

Alternatively, you can use the resource kit utility NETSVC to list services:

```
NETSVC /LIST
```

Managing Services

NETSVC is a Windows 2000 resource kit utility that allows you to manage services on remote systems. The basic syntax for NETSVC is:

```
NETSVC parameter service \\computer
```

Here, *parameter* is the action to perform; *service* is the specific service to work with; and *computer* is the remote system to manage. Here is a list of available NETSVC parameters:

- **/CONTINUE**—Restarts a service
- **/LIST**—Lists services, do not specify a service name
- **/PAUSE**—Pauses a service
- **/QUERY**—Displays the status of a service
- **/START**—Starts a service
- **/STOP**—Stops a service

Related solution:	*Found on page:*
Managing Services from the Command Line	152

Connecting to a Remote System through "Remote Desktop"

Remote Desktop allows you to access and control a remote Windows 2000 Server/XP Professional/2003 system. To connect to a remote system through remote desktop, proceed as follows:

1. For Windows 2000 only, download and install the latest version of Remote Desktop Connection Software from **www.microsoft.com**.

2. Start a command prompt and enter the following:

```
%windir%\system32\mstsc.exe /F /V:computer
```

Here, the */F* option specifies fullscreen mode and the */V* option is used to connect to a remote system, *computer*.

NOTE: *You must enable remote control functionality on the remote system before connecting with remote desktop. See the Microsoft Knowledge Base article Q306624 for Windows 2000/2003 server and Q315328 for Windows XP Professional.*

Connecting to a Remote System through VNC

VNC (Virtual Network Computing) is a free, remote control software, similar to pcAnywhere. To connect to a remote system through VNC, proceed as follows:

1. Create a new directory to store all files included in this example.

2. Download the latest version of VNC from **www.realvnc.com**, to the new directory.

8. Remote System Management

3. Install and configure VNC on the local and remote system.

4. Start a command prompt and enter the following:

```
installdir\vncviewer.exe -FULLSCREEN computer
```

Here, *installdir* is the full path where VNC was installed on the local system. The *FULLSCREEN* option specifies fullscreen mode and *computer* is the name of the remote system.

Related solution:	Found on page:
Scripting a Silent RealVNC Installation	49

Remote Management through WMI

WMI provides a standard scriptable interface to your local and network resources. Using WMI, you can monitor and manipulate many settings on any resource on your network.

Listing Shares

The **Win32_Share** class manages all shared resources on a system. These devices include directories, drives, printers, removable media, or any other shareable resource. To list all shares on a system using WMI, create and then execute a WSH script containing the following:

```
On Error Resume Next
Computer = InputBox("Enter the computer name", _
  "List Shares", "localhost")

Set Shares = GetObject("winmgmts:{" & _
  "impersonationLevel=impersonate}!\\" & _
  Computer & "\root\cimv2").ExecQuery _
  ("select * from Win32_Share")

For each Share in Shares
  SList = SList & Share.Caption & " = " & _
    Share.Path & vbLf
Next

WScript.Echo "Shares:" & VBlf & VBlf & SList
```

Related solution:	Found on page:
Listing Shares	176

Display Share Properties

To display all the properties of a share using WMI, create and then execute a WSH script containing the following:

```
On Error Resume Next
Computer = InputBox("Enter the computer name", _
"Share Properties", "localhost")

SName = InputBox("Enter the name of the share", _
"Share Properties")

Set Shares = GetObject("winmgmts:{" & _
  "impersonationLevel=impersonate}!\\" & _
  Computer & "\root\cimv2").ExecQuery _
  ("select * from Win32_Share where Name = '" & _
  SName & "'")

DisplayWMIProperties Shares
```

NOTE: You need to append the DisplayWMIProperties routine, listed earlier in this chapter, to this script in order for it to run.

Creating a Share

The **Create** method for **Win32_Share** allows you to share a resource. To create a share using WMI, create and then execute a WSH script containing the following:

```
On Error Resume Next
Computer = InputBox("Enter the computer name", "Create Share",
"localhost")

SName = InputBox("Enter the name of the share", "Share Name",
"Temp")

SPath = InputBox("Enter the path of the share", "Share Path",
"C:\Temp")

TypeMenu = "Choose a share type:" & VBlf & VBlf & _
  "0 - Disk Drive" & VBlf & _
  "1 - Print Queue" & VBlf & _
  "2 - Device" & VBlf & _
```

```
"3 - IPC" & VB1f & _
"2147483648 - Disk Drive Admin" & VB1f & _
"2147483649 - Print Queue Admin" & VB1f & _
"2147483650 - Device Admin" & VB1f & _
"2147483651 - IPC Admin"
SType = InputBox(TypeMenu, "Share Type", 0)
SMax = InputBox("Enter the maximum number of users",
"Maximum Users", 10)

SDescribe = InputBox("Enter the description of the share",
"Share Description", "Temp Share")

SPass = InputBox("Enter the password to access the share",
"Share Password", "Temp Password")

Set Security = GetObject("winmgmts:{impersonationLevel=
impersonate,(Security)}!\\" & Computer & "\root\cimv2")

Set Share = Security.Get("Win32_Share")
Set Methods = Share.Methods_("Create").
InParameters.SpawnInstance_()
   Methods.Properties_.Item("Description") = SDescribe
   Methods.Properties_.Item("MaximumAllowed") = SMax
   Methods.Properties_.Item("Name") = SName
   Methods.Properties_.Item("Password") = SPass
   Methods.Properties_.Item("Path") = SPath
   Methods.Properties_.Item("Type") = SType
Set Complete = Share.ExecMethod_("Create", Methods)
```

NOTE: *The highlighted code above must be placed on one line. The (Security) statement is necessary because this script modifies share access.*

Related solution:	Found on page:
Adding Shares	157

Deleting a Share

The **Delete** method for **Win32_Share** allows you to delete a share from a manageable system. To delete a share using WMI, create and then execute a WSH script containing the following:

```
On Error Resume Next
Computer = InputBox("Enter the computer name", _
   "Delete Share", "localhost")
```

```
SName = InputBox("Enter the name of the share", _
  "Delete Share")

Set Shares = GetObject("winmgmts:{" & _
  "impersonationLevel=impersonate}!\\" & _
  Computer & "\root\cimv2").ExecQuery _
  ("select * from Win32_Share where " & _
  "Name =
'" & SName & "'")

For each Share in Shares
  Share.Delete()
Next
```

Related solution:	Found on page:
Removing Shares	157

Listing Processes

The **Win32_Process** class manages all running processes on a system. These processes include all running applications, background tasks, and hidden system processes. To list all running processes using WMI, create and then execute a WSH script containing the following:

```
On Error Resume Next
Computer = InputBox("Enter the computer name", _
"List Processes", "localhost")

Set Processes = GetObject("winmgmts:{" & _
  "impersonationLevel=impersonate}!\\" & _
  Computer & "\root\cimv2").ExecQuery _
  ("select * from Win32_Process")

For each Process in Processes
  PList = PList & Process.Name & VBlf
Next

WScript.Echo "Processes:" & VBlf & vbLf & UCase(PList)
```

Displaying Process Properties

To display the properties of a process using WMI, create and then execute a WSH script containing the following:

```
On Error Resume Next
Computer = InputBox("Enter the computer name", _
  "Process Properties", "localhost")
```

8. Remote System Management

179

```
PName = InputBox("Enter the name of the process", _
"Process Properties")

Set Processes = GetObject("winmgmts:{" & _
  "impersonationLevel=impersonate}!\\" & _
  Computer & "\root\cimv2").ExecQuery _
  ("select * from Win32_Process where " & _
  "Name = '" & PName & "'")

DisplayWMIProperties Processes
```

NOTE: *You need to append the DisplayWMIProperties routine, listed earlier in this chapter, to this script in order for it to run.*

Creating a Process

The **Create** method for **Win32_Process** allows you to create a new process. The key benefit of this method is the ability to launch an application, such as a virus scanner or an application update, on a remote system. To create a process using WMI, create and then execute a WSH script containing the following:

```
On Error Resume Next
Computer = InputBox("Enter the computer name",
"Start Process", "localhost")

AName = InputBox("Enter the executable to run",
"Start Process", "explorer")

Set Process = GetObject("winmgmts:{impersonationLevel=
impersonate}!\\" &
Computer & "\root\cimv2:Win32_Process")

Process.Create AName,null,null,null
```

NOTE: *The highlighted code above must be placed on one line.*

Changing Process Priority

The **SetPriority** method for **Win32_Process** allows you to change the execution priority of a running process. Table 8.1 lists the available priorities and their corresponding values.

Table 8.1 Process priority values.

Value	Name
256	Realtime
128	High
32768	Above Normal
32	Normal
16384	Below Normal
64	Low/Idle

To change the priority of a process using WMI, create and then execute a WSH script containing the following:

```
On Error Resume Next
Computer = InputBox("Enter the computer name",
"Process Priority", "localhost")

PName = InputBox("Enter the name of the process",
"Process Priority")

Set Processes = GetObject("winmgmts:{impersonationLevel=
impersonate}!\\" & Computer & "\root\cimv2").ExecQuery
("select * from Win32_Process where Name = '" & PName & "'")

For each Process in Processes
   Process.SetPriority(PriorityValue)
Next
```

Here, **priorityvalue** is the value from table 8.1 to assign to the process **Pname**.

NOTE: *The highlighted code above must be placed on one line.*

Terminating a Process

The **Terminate** method for **Win32_Process** allows you to end a process and all its threads. The key benefit of this method is the ability to forcibly close a running application, such as an unauthorized port scanner or a corrupted program, on a remote system. To terminate a process using WMI, create and then execute a WSH script containing the following:

```
On Error Resume Next
Computer = InputBox("Enter the computer name",
"Terminate Process", "localhost")
```

```
PName = InputBox("Enter the name of the process",
"Terminate Process")

Set Processes = GetObject("winmgmts:{impersonationLevel=
impersonate}!\\" & Computer & "\root\cimv2").ExecQuery
("select * from Win32_Process where Name = '" & PName & "'")

For each Process in Processes
    Process.Terminate
Next
```

NOTE: *The highlighted code above must be placed on one line.*

Listing Services

The **Win32_Service** class manages all services installed on a system. This class does not apply to Windows $9x$, because Windows $9x$ does not support services. To list all installed services using WMI, create and then execute a WSH script containing the following:

```
On Error Resume Next
Computer = InputBox("Enter the computer name", _
    "List Services", "localhost")

Set Services = GetObject("winmgmts:{" & _
    "impersonationLevel=impersonate}!\\" & _
    Computer & "\root\cimv2").ExecQuery _
    ("select * from Win32_Service")

For each Service in Services
    If Service.State = "Paused" Then
        PList = PList & Service.Name & VBlf
    End If
    If Service.State = "Running" Then
        RList = RList & Service.Name & VBlf
    End If
    If Service.State = "Stopped" Then
        SList = SList & Service.Name & VBlf
    End If
Next

WScript.Echo "Paused Services: " & VBlf & VBlf & PList
WScript.Echo "Running Services: " & VBlf & VBlf & RList
WScript.Echo "Stopped Services: " & VBlf & VBlf & SList
```

Displaying Service Properties

To display the properties of a service using WMI, create and then execute a WSH script containing the following:

```
On Error Resume Next
Computer = InputBox("Enter the computer name", _
  "Service Properties", "localhost")

SName = InputBox("Enter the name of the service", _
"Service Properties")

Set Services = GetObject("winmgmts:{" & _
  "impersonationLevel=impersonate}!\\" & _
  Computer & "\root\cimv2").ExecQuery _
  ("select * from Win32_Service where " & _
  "Name = '" & SName & "'")

DisplayWMIProperties Services
```

NOTE: *You need to append the DisplayWMIProperties routine, listed earlier in this chapter, to this script in order for it to run.*

Starting Services

The **StartService** method for **Win32_Service** allows you to start a stopped service. This method applies only to stopped services; paused services have their own method for resumption. To start a stopped service using WMI, create and then execute a WSH script containing the following:

```
On Error Resume Next
Computer = InputBox("Enter the computer name", _
  "Start Service", "localhost")

SName = InputBox("Enter the name of the service", _
  "Start Service")

Set Services = GetObject("winmgmts:{" & _
  "impersonationLevel=impersonate}!\\" & _
  Computer & "\root\cimv2").ExecQuery _
  ("select * from Win32_Service where " & _
  "Name = '" & SName & "'")

For each Service in Services
  Service.StartService()
Next
```

Related solution:	Found on page:
Starting a Service	153

Stopping Services

The **StopService** method for **Win32_Service** allows you to stop a service. Through this method, you can stop a running or paused service. To stop a service using WMI, create and then execute a WSH script containing the following:

```
On Error Resume Next
Computer = InputBox("Enter the computer name", _
  "Stop Service", "localhost")

SName = InputBox("Enter the name of the service", _
  "Stop Service")

Set Services = GetObject("winmgmts:{" & _
  "impersonationLevel=impersonate}!\\" & _
  Computer & "\root\cimv2").ExecQuery _
  ("select * from Win32_Service where " & _
  "Name = '" & SName & "'")

For each Service in Services
  Service.StopService()
Next
```

Related solution:	Found on page:
Stopping a Service	154

Pausing Services

The **PauseService** method for **Win32_Service** allows you to pause a running service. This method will not place a stopped service into paused mode. To pause a running service using WMI, create and then execute a WSH script containing the following:

```
On Error Resume Next
Computer = InputBox("Enter the computer name", _
  "Pause Service", "localhost")

SName = InputBox("Enter the name of the service", _
  "Pause Service")

Set Services = GetObject("winmgmts:{" & _
  "impersonationLevel=impersonate}!\\" & _
```

```
Computer & "\root\cimv2").ExecQuery _
("select * from Win32_Service where " & _
"Name = '" & SName & "'")

For each Service in Services
  Service.PauseService()
Next
```

Resuming Services

The **ResumeService** method for **Win32_Service** allows you to re-sume a paused service. This method will not start a stopped service. To create a process using WMI, create and then execute a WSH script containing the following:

```
On Error Resume Next
Computer = InputBox("Enter the computer name", _
  "Resume Service", "localhost")

SName = InputBox("Enter the name of the service", _
  "Resume Service")

Set Services = GetObject("winmgmts:{" & _
  "impersonationLevel=impersonate}!\\" & _
  Computer & "\root\cimv2").ExecQuery _
  ("select * from Win32_Service where " & _
  "Name = '" & SName & "'")

For each 'Service in Services
  Service.ResumeService()
Next
```

Deleting a Service

The **Delete** method for **Win32_Services** allows you to remove a service from your system. This method will happen immediately, regard-less of whether a service is running. To delete a service using WMI, create and then execute a WSH script containing the following:

```
On Error Resume Next
Computer = InputBox("Enter the computer name", _
  "Delete Service", "localhost")

SName = InputBox("Enter the name of the service", _
  "Delete Service")

Set Services = GetObject("winmgmts:{" & _
  "impersonationLevel=impersonate}!\\" & _
```

8. Remote System Management

```
    Computer & "\root\cimv2").ExecQuery _
    ("select * from Win32_Service where " & _
    "Name = '" & SName & "'")

For each Service in Services
    Service.Delete()
Next
```

Related solution:	Found on page:
Uninstalling a Service	153

Rebooting a System

The **Win32_OperatingSystem** class manages many aspects of the Windows operating system, from the serial number to the service pack. The **Reboot** method for **Win32_OperatingSystem** allows you to shut down and restart a manageable system. To reboot a system using WMI, create and then execute a WSH script containing the following:

```
On Error Resume Next
Computer = InputBox("Enter the computer name",
"Reboot System", "localhost")

Set OS = GetObject("winmgmts:{impersonationLevel=
impersonate}!\\" &
Computer & "\root\cimv2").ExecQuery
("select * from Win32_ OperatingSystem where Primary=true")

For each System in OS
    System.Reboot()
Next
```

Here, **Primary=True** is a check to ensure that Windows is the primary operating system currently running.

NOTE: *The highlighted code above must be placed on one line.*

Related solution:	Found on page:
Shutting Down/Restarting the Computer	186

Shutting Down a System

The **ShutDown** method for **Win32_OperatingSystem** allows you to shut down a computer to the prompt "It is now safe to turn off your computer." To shut down a system using WMI, create and then execute a WSH script containing the following:

```
On Error Resume Next
Computer = InputBox("Enter the computer name",
"Reboot System", "localhost")

Set OS = GetObject("winmgmts:{impersonationLevel=
impersonate}!\\" & Computer & "\root\cimv2").ExecQuery
("select * from Win32_ OperatingSystem where Primary=true")

For each System in OS
  System.Shutdown()
Next
```

NOTE: *The highlighted code above must be placed on one line.*

Related solution:	Found on page:
Shutting Down/Restarting the Computer	160

Monitoring CPU Utilization

To monitor CPU utilization using the WMI ExecNotificationQuery method, create and then execute a WSH script containing the following:

```
On Error Resume Next
Computer = InputBox("Enter the computer name",
"CPU Monitor", "localhost")

CPULoad = InputBox("Enter the CPU overload threshold",
"CPU Threshold", "75")

Poll = InputBox("Enter the polling interval",
"Poll Interval", "5")
If Computer = "" Then Computer = "Localhost"
If CPULoad = "" Then CPULoad = 75
If Poll = "" Then Poll = 5
Set ProLoad = GetObject("winmgmts:{impersonationLevel=
impersonate}!\\" &
Computer & "\root\cimv2").
ExecNotificationQuery("SELECT * FROM __
InstanceModificationEvent WITHIN " & Poll & " WHERE
TargetInstance ISA 'Win32_Processor' and
TargetInstance .LoadPercentage > " & CPULoad)
```

```
If Err.Number <> 0 then
  WScript.Echo Err.Description, Err.Number, Err.Source
End If

Do
  SetILoad = ProLoad.nextevent
  If Err.Number <> 0 then
    WScript.Echo Err.Number, Err.Description, Err.Source
    Exit Do
  Else
    AMessage = ILoad.TargetInstance.DeviceID & _
    " is overloaded at " & _
    & ILoad.TargetInstance.LoadPercentage & "%!"
    Wscript.Echo "Event Alert: " & AMessage
  End If
Loop
```

NOTE: *The highlighted code above must be placed on one line.*

Here, **computer** is the name of the system to monitor; **CPULoad** is the CPU utilization threshold to monitor for (1–100); and **poll** is the amount of seconds to check for events.

Assigning a Static IP Address

To assign a static IP address to a remote system's network cards using WMI, create and then execute a WSH script containing the following:

```
On Error Resume Next
Computer =
InputBox("Enter the computer name", "Assign Static", "localhost")
IPAddress=InputBox("Enter the IP Address","IP Address", "192.168.1.50")
SubnetMask=InputBox("Enter the Subnet Mask","Subnet Mask", "255.255.255.0")
Gateway=InputBox("Enter the Gateway","Gateway", "192.168.1.1")
DNS1=InputBox("Enter the Primary DNS Server","Primary DNS", "192.168.1.2")
DNS2=InputBox("Enter the Secondary DNS","Secondary DNS", "192.168.1.3")

Set Adapters=GetObject("winmgmts:{impersonationLevel=impersonate}!\\" &_
    Computer & "\root\cimv2").ExecQuery("select * from
Win32_NetworkAdapterConfiguration where IPEnabled=true")

IPArray = Array(IPAddress)
MaskArray = Array(SubnetMask)
GatewayArray = Array(Gateway)
GatewayMetric = Array(1)
```

```
DNSArray = Array (DNS1,DNS2)

For each NIC in Adapters
    NIC.EnableStatic IPArray, MaskArray
    NIC.SetGateways GatewayArray, Gatewaymetric
    NIC.SetDNSServerSearchOrder DNSArray
Next
```

NOTE: *The highlighted code above must be placed on one line.*

Switching to DHCP

To change a remote system's network cards from a Static IP to DHCP using WMI, create and then execute a WSH script containing the following:

```
On Error Resume Next
Computer = InputBox("Enter the computer name",
"Enable DHCP", "localhost")
Set Adapters = GetObject("winmgmts:{impersonationLevel=
impersonate}!\\" & Computer & "\root\cimv2").ExecQuery
("select * from Win32_NetworkAdapterConfiguration where IPEnabled=true")

For each NIC in Adapters
  NIC.EnableDHCP()
Next
```

NOTE: *The highlighted code above must be placed on one line.*

Renewing DHCP Leases

To renew the DHCP leases of a remote system's network cards using WMI, create and then execute a WSH script containing the following:

```
On Error Resume Next
Computer = InputBox("Enter the computer name",
"Renew DHCP", "localhost")

Set Adapters = GetObject("winmgmts:{impersonationLevel=
impersonate}!\\" & Computer & "\root\cimv2").ExecQuery
("select * from Win32_NetworkAdapterConfiguration where IPEnabled=true")
For each NIC in Adapters
  NIC.RenewDHCPLease()
Next
```

8. Remote System Management

189

NOTE: *The highlighted code above must be placed on one line.*

Listing Software

The **Win32_Product** class manages all products installed by the Windows Installer. To list all Windows Installer software installed on a system using WMI, create and then execute a WSH script containing the following:

```
On Error Resume Next
Computer = InputBox("Enter the computer name", _
"List Software", "localhost")

Set Software = GetObject("winmgmts:{" & _
  "impersonationLevel=impersonate}!\\" & _
  Computer & "\root\cimv2").ExecQuery _
  ("select * from Win32_Product")

For each Product in Software
  PList = PList & Product.Name & VBlf
Next

WScript.Echo "Software:" & VBlf & vbLf & UCase(PList)
```

Display Software Properties

To display all the properties of a software product using WMI, create and then execute a WSH script containing the following:

```
On Error Resume Next
Computer = InputBox("Enter the computer name", _
  "Product Properties", "localhost")

PName = InputBox("Enter the name of the Product", _
"Product Properties")

Set Products = GetObject("winmgmts:{" & _
  "impersonationLevel=impersonate}!\\" & _
  Computer & "\root\cimv2").ExecQuery _
  ("select * from Win32_Product where " & _
  "Name = '" & PName & "'")

DisplayWMIProperties Products
```

NOTE: *You need to append the DisplayWMIProperties routine, listed earlier in this chapter, to this script in order for it to run.*

Installing Software

The **Install** method for **Win32_Product** allows you to install a Windows Installer package. To install a Windows Installer package using WMI, create and then execute a WSH script containing the following:

```
On Error Resume Next
Computer = InputBox("Enter the computer name",
"Install Software", "localhost")

InstallPath = InputBox("Enter the complete software path",
"Install Software", "")

Set Products = GetObject("winmgmts:{impersonationLevel=
impersonate}!\\" & Computer & "\root\cimv2 ")

Set Software = Products.Get("Win32_Product")
Software.Install InstallPath, ,True
```

NOTE: The highlighted code above must be placed on one line.

Uninstalling Software

To uninstall a Windows Installer package using WMI, create and then execute a WSH script containing the following:

```
On Error Resume Next
Computer = InputBox("Enter the computer name",
"Uninstall Software", "localhost")

sName=InputBox ("Enter the name of the software", "uninstall
software", "")
Set Products = GetObject("winmgmts:{impersonationLevel=
impersonate}!\\" & Computer & "\root\cimv2").ExecQuery
("select * from Win32_Product  where Name = '" & SName & "'")
For each Software in Products
    Software.Uninstall()
Next
```

NOTE: The highlighted code above must be placed on one line.

Enterprise Management

(continued)

In Brief

Corporations spend millions of dollars a year on packaged applications and manpower to keep their computing environments running like finely tuned engines. Although most third-party solutions provide the tools to assist in enterprise management, they often come overloaded with fancy reporting features and are limited in actual functionality. And when you finally find a package that is really helpful in your administrative tasks, you'd be lucky to get the budget approval passed in this lifetime.

In this chapter, you will learn about all the important aspects of managing an enterprise environment, and how to maintain it without expensive third-party solutions. You will also learn how to accomplish most of your administrative tasks with simple scripts.

Understanding a Windows Network

The biggest advantage of a Windows 2000/2003 network as opposed to Windows NT is its restructuring and use of directory services. Windows 2000/2003 gives you several new ways to organize and centrally manage your network.

Trees and Forests

Windows 2000/2003 allows you to organize your domains into hierarchical groups called trees. Trees share a common schema, global catalog, replication information, and DNS namespace (for example, **www.jesseweb.com**). Once trees are established, you can organize your trees into hierarchical groups called forests. Forests also share a common schema, global catalog, and replication information, but do not share a common DNS namespace. This allows you to combine the resources of two completely separate Internet domains (for example, **www.mydomain.com** and **www.yourdomain.com**). Through trees and forests, Windows 2000 automatically establishes two-way trusts between all domains.

Objects

Windows 2000/2003 treats all resources as objects. These objects can consist of any of the various resources on a network, such as users, computers, printers, and shares. Each object contains its own set of attributes, functions, and properties as set by the schema. Whenever

9. Enterprise Management

you access a resource, the schema sets which properties and features are presentable. For example, a user account has a lockout property but a share does not, as instructed by the schema.

Organizational Units

Windows 2000/2003 allows you to organize network objects into logical containers called Organizational Units (OUs). OUs can contain any network resource, such as accounts, groups, queues, shares, and even other OUs. Through OUs, you can delegate administration and assign permissions to the OU or the individual objects within. The most common use of organizational units is to organize company resources by department.

Global Catalog

Windows 2000/2003 stores information about the objects in a tree or forest in a common database, called a global catalog. Global catalog servers reduce network searches and object query time by processing these requests directly. The first domain controller within a forest stores the global catalog, and is called a global catalog server. You can assign additional global catalog servers to help network queries.

WARNING! Global catalog servers synchronize their information through replication. A large quantity of catalog servers can cripple a network with replication traffic.

ADSI

Active Directory Services Interfaces (ADSI), previously OLE Directory Services, is Microsoft's implementation of a directory service that organizes an enterprise into a tree-like structure. A directory service provides a standard, consistent method to manage and locate network resources. Directory services are actually databases that store information about all the resources on your network. Whenever a request for a network resource is made, the directory service interprets and processes the request. ADSI comes packaged with Windows 2000/XP/2003 and is available as a free, separate download from Microsoft for Windows 9x/NT.

The ADSI Process

When a script or application issues a call to ADSI, the call is first sent to the ADSI client, as shown in Figure 9.1. The ADSI client is included in all versions of Windows 2000/XP/2003 and is available as a download for Windows 9x/NT systems. Do not confuse the ADSI client with the Active Directory Services Interface. The client is used to access a

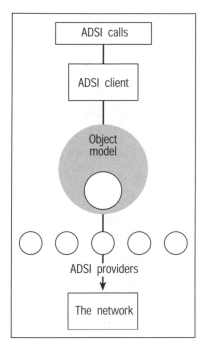

Figure 9.1   The ADSI process.

directory service, whereas the Active Directory Services Interface is the directory service itself.

NOTE: *Windows 2000/2003 Server contains both the Active Directory Services Interfaces and the ADSI client.*

Once the client receives the call, it passes it to the object model, called a router. The router interprets the request and passes it to the appropriate provider. The provider is then responsible to take the appropriate action based on the request.

Providers

ADSI provides a common interface to manage the network, regardless of directory service type. ADSI uses components called providers to communicate with other directory services. These providers are stored in DLL files and are loaded when ADSI is installed. The various providers included with ADSI are as follows:

- IIS (Adsiis.dll)—Provider for Internet Information Server

- LDAP (Adsldp.dll, Adsldpc.dll, and Adsmext.dll)—Provider for Windows 2000/2003 Server and other LDAP-compliant applications

9. Enterprise Management

- NWCompat (Adsnw.dll)—Provider to Netware Bindery servers

- NDS (Adsnds.dll)—Provider for Novell NDS servers

- WinNT (Adsnt.dll)—Provider for Windows NT domains and Windows 2000/2003 local resources

---

NOTE: *The provider names, specified in parentheses above, are case-sensitive.*

The next section will give you a brief overview of the two main Windows providers: LDAP and WinNT.

The LDAP Provider

Lightweight Directory Access Protocol (LDAP) was developed in 1990 as a simple alternative to the complex X.500 directory standard. The LDAP provider is used to manage Windows 2000/2003 Active Directory servers, Exchange 5.5 or higher servers, Lotus Notes servers, Netscape directory servers, and other LDAP-compliant applications or servers. The basic syntax to bind to the LDAP provider is:

```
Set variable = GetObject("LDAP:OU=orgunit, DC=Domain")
```

Here, ***variable*** is an arbitrary variable that you can use to access the LDAP provider; ***orgunit*** is the name of the organizational unit; and ***domain*** is the name of the domain you want to connect to.

Windows 2000/2003 uses Internet domain names, such as **marketing. jesseweb.com**. Each of the domain levels must be separated by commas and in descending hierarchy, as follows:

```
Set variable = GetObject("LDAP:OU=orgunit, DC=marketing,
DC=jesseweb, DC=com")
```

NOTE: *The highlighted code above must be placed on one line.*

With LDAP, you can avoid specifying domain names by binding to the directory tree directly:

```
Set variable = GetObject("LDAP://rootDSE")
```

The WinNT Provider

The WinNT provider is used to manage Windows NT domain resources and Windows 2000/2003 local resources. This provider is provided for backward compatibility with Windows NT domains and cannot access Windows 2000/2003 Internet domain names. The basic syntax to bind to the WinNT provider is:

```
Set variable = GetObject("WinNT://Domain/Computer/
Object,Class")
```

NOTE: *The highlighted code above must be placed on one line.*

Here, *variable* is an arbitrary variable that you can use to access the WinNT provider; *domain* is the name of the domain you want to connect to; *computer* is the name of the system to connect to; *object* is the object that you want to connect to; and *class* is the class type you want to connect to (for example, user, group, computer). Any parameters specified after the provider name, in this case **WinNT:**, are optional.

If you are working outside your domain or need to use a different account to access the domain, you must use the **OpenDSObject** function:

```
Set NTObj = GetObject("WinNT:")
Set variable = NTObj.OpenDSObject("WinNT://Domain/Server/
Object, username, password
```

NOTE: *The highlighted code above must be placed on one line.*

Here, *password* is the password of the *username* to connect with.

The Scripting Advantage

Microsoft has included (either with Windows or made available for download) many tools to shell script almost all domain and Active Directory tasks. This allows us to create quick, easy, and to-the-point shell scripts. Microsoft has also provided WinNT and LDAP providers that can be accessed through COM. While both KiXtart and WSH can access these providers through COM, due to size limitations of this book and the popularity of the scripting language, this chapter will provide the scripting examples in Windows Script Host only. (It should be simple to convert the scripts to KiXtart.) Finally, AutoIt is not appropriate and is not discussed in this chapter.

9. Enterprise Management

A Word of Caution

This chapter contains many powerful scripting examples on managing a domain and Active Directory. Accidentally targeting the wrong object or running the wrong script can cause some serious problems (like deleting 300 computer accounts at a time, right Rick!). As with all scripts, you should first test your script in an isolated testing environment to ensure the script produces the desired results before using it in a production environment.

Immediate Solutions

Managing Computer Accounts with Shell Scripting

Computer accounts, like user accounts, allow the system to be part of the domain and access its resources. When a computer joins a domain, a computer account is created establishing a one-way trust and allowing the computer to access the domain. Although computer account management is usually done through the administrative tools of the operating system, computer account management can be scripted from the command line.

Managing Computer Accounts with the NET Command

The built-in NET.EXE command allows you to manage computer accounts from the command line on any domain controller. The basic syntax of the NET command to add computer accounts is:

```
NET COMPUTER \\compname/commands
```

Here, **compname** is the computer account to manage, and the available **commands** are:

- **/ADD**—Adds a computer account to the domain
- **/DELETE**—Removes a computer account from the domain

TIP: *You can use one of the remote management methods discussed in Chapter 8 to run this command on a remote domain controller.*

Managing Computer Accounts with the NETDOM Utility

NETDOM is a Windows 2000 Resource Kit Utility/Windows XP Support Tool used to manage computer accounts from the command line. The basic syntax of NETDOM is:

```
NETDOM MEMBER \\computer /D:domain /U:domain\user
/P:password /commands
```

> **NOTE:** *The highlighted code on the previous page must be placed on one line.*

Here, **computer** is the computer account to manage; **password** is the password of the **domain\user** account with privileges to manage computer accounts on the specified **domain**; and the available **commands** are as follows:

- **/ADD**—Adds a computer account to the domain
- **/DELETE**—Removes a computer account from the domain
- **/JOINDOMAIN**—Joins the computer to the domain
- **/QUERY**—Retrieves information on an existing computer account

To connect to the domain and add a computer account, you would enter:

```
NETDOM MEMBER \\computer /D:domain /U:domain\user
/P:password /JOINDOMAIN

NETDOM MEMBER \\computer /D:domain /U:domain\user
/P:password /ADD
```

> **NOTE:** *The highlighted code above must be placed on one line.*

To connect to the domain and remove a computer account, you would enter:

```
NETDOM MEMBER \\computer /D:domain /U:domain\user
/P:password /JOINDOMAIN

NETDOM MEMBER \\computer /D:domain /U:domain\user
/P:password /DELETE
```

> **NOTE:** *The highlighted code above must be placed on one line.*

Managing User Accounts with Shell Scripting

User accounts allow users to access domain and local system resources with a valid username and password. Although user management is mostly done through the administrative tools of the operating system, scripting user account management from the command line is significantly faster when dealing with remote systems and multiple modifications.

Managing User Accounts with the NET Command

One of the most unused command-line utilities to manage user accounts is the NET command. The basic syntax of the NET command to manage user accounts is:

```
NET USER USERNAME PASSWORD /commands
```

Here, **username** is the user account to manage; **password** is either the password of the account or an asterisk (*) to be prompted for a password; and the available **commands** are as follows:

- **/ACTIVE:***X*—Controls the activation of an account where *X* is YES or NO.

- **/ADD**—Adds a user account.

- **/DELETE**—Removes a user account.

- **/DOMAIN**—Creates the account in the currently active domain (see warning below).

- **/COMMENT**: "*X*" —Sets the account description where *X* is the comment.

- **/COUNTRYCODE:***X*—Sets the account's country code.

- **/USERCOMMENT**: "*X*"—Sets the user comment where *X* is the comment.

- **/EXPIRES:***X*—Sets the expiration date of the account where *X* is either **NEVER** or a date in the format of MM/DD/YY. This format may differ depending on your country code.

- **/FULLNAME**: "*X*"—Sets the full account name where *X* is the name.

- **/HOMEDIR:***X*—Sets the home directory where *X* is the path.

- **/PASSWORDCHG:***X*—Controls the user's ability to change the password where *X* is **YES** or **NO**.

- **/PASSWORDREQ:***X*—Sets whether a password is required where *X* is **YES** or **NO**.

- **/PROFILEPATH:***X*—Sets the profile directory where *X* is the path.

- **/SCRIPTPATH:***X*—Sets the logon script directory where *X* is the path.

- **/TIMES:***X*—Sets the hours a user may log on where *X* is either **ALL** or days and times separated by commas.

WARNING! You should only use the NET USER command with the /DOMAIN switch to create domain accounts if you have a Windows NT domain. Attempting creation in a Windows 2000/2003 domain will result in incomplete, unusable user accounts.

9. Enterprise Management

Here is an example showing how to add an account using the NET command:

```
NET USER "Tyler" TEMPPASSWORD /ADD /COMMENT:"Project Account"
/ACTIVE:NO /EXPIRES:12/31/03 /FULLNAME:"Tyler Durden"
/HOMEDIR:C:\ /PASSWORDCHG:NO /PASSWORDREQ:YES
/PROFILEPATH:C:\PROFILES\TD /USERCOMMENT:"Corporate Sponsor"
/WORKSTATIONS:STATION1 /SCRIPTPATH:SOMEWHERE\OUTTHERE
/TIMES:MONDAY-THURSDAY,8AM-5PM
```

NOTE: *The highlighted code above must be placed on one line.*

Adding User Accounts with DSADD

DSADD.EXE is a Windows 2003 administration utility and is the preferred shell scripting method for creating Windows 2000/2003 domain user accounts. The basic syntax for using DSADD to create a user is:

```
DSADD USER UserDN -samid Username -pwd Password
```

Here, **UserDSN** is the Windows 2000/2003 active directory distinguished name; **Username** is the pre-Windows 2000 logon name, and **Password** is the default password to assign to the user. Here is an example of how to add a user account:

```
DSADD USER CN=John.Doe,CN=Users,DC=internal,DC=initech,DC=com -
samid John.Doe -pwd SomePassword
```

NOTE: *If you have a Windows 2000 domain, your domain controllers must be running at least Windows 2000 service pack 3.*

Managing User Accounts with the ADDUSERS Utility

ADDUSERS.EXE is a Windows 2000 resource kit utility to manage user accounts from the command line. This utility reads command-delimited text files and can create or delete user accounts. The basic syntax of ADDUSERS to manage user accounts is:

```
ADDUSERS \\compdomain commands file
```

Here, **compdomain** is either the target computer (for adding a local account) or domain name (for adding domain accounts); **file** is the name of the comma-delimited text file to use; and the available **commands** are as follows:

9. Enterprise Management

- **/C**—Creates user accounts or groups specified in the *file*
- **/D**—Dumps the user account or group information to the *file*
- **/E**—Deletes user account specified in the *file*
- **/P:***X*—If combined with **/C**, specifies the creating parameters where *X* is:
  - **C**—User cannot change password
  - **D**—Account disabled
  - **E**—Password never expires
  - **L**—Do not change password at next logon

TIP: *To add a user account to the local computer, omit the computer name from the command line.*

The basic syntax of the comma-delimited *file* is:

```
[User]
UserName,FullName,Password,Comment,Home,Profile,Script,
```

Here, **Comment** is the account description; **Home** is the path to the user home directory; **Profile** is the path to the user's profile; **Script** is the name of the logon script to use; and **UserNames** are the user names (separated by commas) to add to the groups.

The following example adds a user called JFROST to the computer BOB:

```
ADDUSERS \\BOB/C file
```

Here, *file* is the full path and file name of a text file that contains the following:

```
[User]
JFROST,Jack E. Frost,Password,Project Manager,\\SERVER\HOME\
JFROST,\\SERVER\PROFILE\JFROST,LOGON.KIX,
```

NOTE: *The highlighted code above must be placed on one line.*

Managing User Accounts with the CURSMGR Utility

CURSMGR.EXE is a Windows 2000 resource kit utility to modify current account or group properties. This utility supports many switches, all of which are case-sensitive. The basic syntax of CURSMGR is:

```
CURSMGR -u username -m \\computer commands
```

Here, ***username*** is the user account to manage; ***computer*** is the computer name on which to perform management; and the available ***commands*** are as follows:

- **-C**—Sets user comment
- **-D**—Deletes a user account
- **-F**—Sets user full name
- **-h**—Sets the path to the user's home directory
- **-H**—Sets the drive letter to map the user's home directory
- **-n**—Sets the path to the logon script's directory
- **-p**—Sets a random password
- **-P**—Sets the password to Password
- **+-S**—Use the **+S** or **-S** to set or reset the following properties
    - **AccountLockout**—Locks/unlocks a user account
    - **MustChangePassword**—Sets/resets the User Must Change Password At Next Logon option
    - **CanNotChangePassword**—Sets/resets the User Cannot Change Password option
    - **PasswordNeverExpires** —Sets/resets the Password Never Expires option
    - **AccountDisabled**—Disables/enables an account
    - **RASUser**—Enables/disables remote access dial-in
- **-U**—Sets the path to the user's profile directory

Here is an example of how to modify a user account:

```
CUSRMGR -u
name -m \\computer -h \\server\homeshare -f
"fullname" -c "description" -H Q
```

NOTE: *The highlighted code above must be placed on one line.*

Here, ***name*** is the user name; ***computer*** is the system that holds the account; ***\\server\homeshare*** is where the user's home directory resides; ***fullname*** is the user's fullname; and ***description*** is the account description.

TIP: *For domain accounts, supply the PDC or PDC Emulator name where the **computer** name is required.*

Managing Groups with Shell Scripting

Groups allow administrators a method of organizing and assigning user account privileges. Groups are also helpful when attempting to identify a collection of users with a common trait (for example, temporary employees). You can script group management from the command line to automate your daily tasks.

Managing Groups with the NET Command

The built-in NET.EXE command allows you to manage local and global groups from the command line. The basic syntax of the NET command to manage global groups is:

```
NET type name commands
```

Here, **type** is the keyword **GROUP** for global or **LOCALGROUP** for local group management; **name** is the group to manage, and the available **commands** are as follows:

- **/ADD**—Adds user accounts to the specified group where multiple user accounts are separated by spaces

- **/COMMENT: "X"**—Sets the group comment

- **/DELETE**—Deletes a group or removes the user account from the specified group

- **/DOMAIN**—Performs the operation on the primary domain controller

- **username**—Specifies a user account to add or remove from the group

Adding Groups with DSADD

DSADD.EXE is a Windows 2003 administration tools utility and is the preferred shell scripting method for creating Windows 2000/2003 domain groups. The basic syntax of DSADD for creatng a group is:

```
DSADD GROUP "LDAPPath" -secgrp yesno -scope grouptype
```

Here, **LDAPPath** is the full LDAP path of the new group (e.g., LDAP://cn=My New Group, cn=Users, dc=jesseweb, dc=com), **yesno** is either **yes** or **no** to make the new group a security group (otherwise the group is created as a distribution group), and **groupytpe** is either l, g, or u to set the new group type to either Local, Global, or Universal.

9 Enterprise Management

NOTE: *If you have a Windows 2000 domain, your domain controllers must be running at least Windows 2000 service pack 3.*

Managing Groups with the ADDUSERS Utility

Earlier in this chapter, you learned how to use the resource kit utility
ADDUSERS.EXE to manage user accounts from the command line.
This utility can also be used to add groups and group members from
the command line. The basic syntax of ADDUSERS to add groups is:

```
ADDUSERS \\computer /C file
```

Here, **computer** is the computer account to manage, and **file** is the
name of the comma-delimited text file to use. The basic syntax of the
comma-delimited **file** is:

```
[Global]
Name,Comment,UserNames,
[Local]
Name,Comment,UserNames,
```

Here, the **[GLOBAL]** sections add global groups; **name** is the name
of the group to add; **comment** is the group description; and
usernames are the users, separated by commas, to add to the group.

Managing Groups with the USRTOGRP Utility

USRTOGRP.EXE is an NT resource kit utility to add user accounts to
groups from the command line. The basic syntax of the USRTOGRP
utility is:

```
USRTOGRP file
```

Here, **file** is a text file with the following format:

```
DOMAIN: computer grouptype: group users
```

Here, **computer** is the name of the system or domain that contains
the specified group; **grouptype** specifies the group type as either
LOCALGROUP or **GLOBALGROUP**; **group** is the name of the group;
and **users** are the usernames, separated by spaces, to add to the group.

Here is a quick example to add two users to the Domain Admins group
in the PROJECT domain:

```
USRTOGRP file
```

Here, **file** is the full path and file name of a text file that contains the
following:

```
DOMAIN: PROJECT GLOBALGROUP: Domain Admins JACK TYLER
```

Managing the Enterprise with ADSI

Prior to ADSI, your only alternatives to manage network resources were command-line utilities and administrative tools. Through ADSI, you can create simple scripts to control all the resources of your network.

Listing Shares

To list shares using ADSI, create and then execute a WSH script containing the following:

```
On Error Resume Next
Set DomObj = GetObject("WinNT://Domain/Computer/lanmanserver,
FileService")

For each Share in DomObj
  List = List & Share.Name & VB1F
Next
Wscript.Echo List
```

NOTE: The highlighted code above must be placed on one line.

Here, **domain** is the name of the domain, and **computer** is the computer name containing the shares to list.

Related solution:	Found on page:
Listing Shares	173

Creating a Share

To create a share using ADSI, create and then execute a WSH script containing the following:

```
On Error Resume Next
Set DomObj = GetObject("WinNT://Domain/Computer/
lanmanserver")
Set Share = DomObj.Create("fileshare", "ShareName")
Share.Path = "SharePath"
Share.Description = "ShareDescribe"
Share.MaxUserCount = maxnum
Share.SetInfo
```

NOTE: The highlighted code above must be placed on one line.

Here, **domain** is the name of the domain; **computer** is the computer name on which you want to create shares; **sharename** is the name of the share to create; **sharepath** is the path to the new share; **sharedescribe** is the share comment; and **maxnum** is the maximum number of simultaneous connections to the share.

Related solution:	Found on page:
Listing Shares	156

Deleting a Share

To delete a share using ADSI, create and then execute a WSH script containing the following:

```
On Error Resume Next
Set DomObj = GetObject("WinNT://Domain/Computer/lanmanserver")
DomObj.Delete "fileshare", "ShareName"
```

Here, **domain** is the name of the domain; **computer** is the computer name on which you want to create shares; and **sharename** is the name of the share to delete.

Related solution:	Found on page:
Removing Shares	157

Listing Computer Accounts

To list computer accounts using ADSI, create and then execute a WSH script containing the following:

```
On Error Resume Next
Set DomObj = GetObject("WinNT://" & Domain)
DomObj.Filter = Array("computer")

For Each Computer In DomObj
     wscript.echo Computer.name
Next
```

Here, **domain** is the name of the domain to query.

Creating a Computer Account

To create a computer account using ADSI, create and then execute a WSH script containing the following:

```
On Error Resume Next
Set DomObj = GetObject("WinNT://Domain")
Set Computer = DomObj.Create("Computer", "name")
Computer.SetInfo
```

Here, **domain** is the name of the domain, and **name** is the computer name to assign to the computer account.

Deleting a Computer Account

To delete a computer account, create and then execute a WSH script containing the following:

```
On Error Resume Next
Set DomObj = GetObject("WinNT://Domain")
DomObj.Delete "Computer", "name"
```

Here, **domain** is the name of the domain, and **name** is the name of the computer account to delete.

Setting a User's Domain Password

To set a user's domain password using ADSI, create and then execute a WSH script containing the following:

```
On Error Resume Next
Set DomObj = GetObject("WinNT://Domain/Name,user")
DomObj.SetPassword "pswd"
```

Here, **domain** is the name of the domain; **name** is the user account to modify; and **pswd** is the new password to assign.

Changing the Local Administrator Password

A common administrative task is to change the local administrator password on a system. To change the local administrator password using ADSI, create and then execute a WSH script containing the following:

```
On Frror Resume Next
Set DomObj = GetObject("WinNT://Domain/Computer/
Administrator,user")
DomObj.SetPassword "pswd"
```

NOTE: *The highlighted code above must be placed on one line.*

Here, *domain* is the name of the domain; *computer* is the computer containing the local administrator account; *Administrator* is the name of the local administrator account; and *pswd* is the new password to assign.

Listing User Accounts

To list user accounts using ADSI, create and then execute a WSH script containing the following:

```
On Error Resume Next
Set DomObj = GetObject("WinNT://" & Domain)
DomObj.Filter = Array("user")

For Each User In DomObj
       Wscript.Echo User.name
Next
```

Here, *domain* is the name of the domain to query.

Creating a User Account

To create a user account using ADSI, create and then execute a WSH script containing the following:

```
On Error Resume Next
Set DomObj = GetObject("WinNT://Domain")
Set User = DomObj.Create("User", "Name")
User.SetPassword("pswd")
User.FullName = "fullname"
User.HomeDirectory = "homedir"
User.Profile = "profiledir"
User.LoginScript = "script"
User.Description = "describe"
User.SetInfo
```

Here, *domain* is the name of the domain; *name* is the name of the user account to create; *pswd* is the password to assign to the new account; *fullname* is the user's full name; *homedir* is the path of the user's home directory; *profiledir* is the path of the user's profile; *script* is the name of the logon script; and *describe* is the user description.

TIP: *You can create new users with initial blank passwords by omitting the highlighted line in the script above.*

Deleting a User Account

To delete a user account using ADSI, create and then execute a WSH script containing the following:

```
On Error Resume Next
Set DomObj = GetObject("WinNT://Domain")
DomObj.Delete "User", "name"
```

Here, **domain** is the name of the domain, and **name** is the name of the user account to delete.

Displaying User Account Locked Out Status

The **IsAccountLocked** user property returns true or false if a user account is locked out. To determine if a user account is locked out using ADSI, create and then execute a WSH script containing the following:

```
On Error Resume Next
Set User = GetObject("WinNT://Domain/Name,User")
Wscript.Echo User.IsAccountLocked
```

Here, **domain** is the name of the domain and **name** is the name of the user account.

Unlocking a User Account

To unlock a user account using ADSI, create and then execute a WSH script containing the following:

```
On Error Resume Next
Set User = GetObject("WinNT://Domain/Name,User")
User.IsAccountLocked = False
User.SetInfo
```

Here, **domain** is the name of the domain, and **name** is the name of the user account to unlock.

NOTE: Although ADSI can unlock a user account, it cannot lock an account.

Disabling/Enabling a User Account

To disable an active user account using ADSI, create and then execute a WSH script containing the following:

```
DisableUser "Domain", "Name"
```

```
Sub DisableUser(DomainName, UserName)
```

```
On Error Resume Next
Set User = GetObject("WinNT://" & _
  DomainName & "/" & _
  UserName & ",User")
If User.AccountDisabled = False Then
  User.AccountDisabled = True
  User.SetInfo
End If
End Sub
```

Here, ***domain*** is the name of the domain, and ***name*** is the name of the user account to unlock. Similarly, to enable a disabled user account using ADSI, create and then execute a WSH script containing the following:

```
EnableUser "Domain", "Name"

Sub EnableUser(DomainName, UserName)
  On Error Resume Next
  Set User = GetObject("WinNT://" & _
    DomainName & "/" & _
    UserName & ",User")
  If User.AccountDisabled = True Then
    User.AccountDisabled = False
    User.SetInfo
  End If
End Sub
```

Listing a User's Groups

To list the groups a user belongs to using ADSI, create and then execute a WSH script containing the following:

```
On Error Resume Next
Set User = GetObject("WinNT://" & Domain & "/" & Name & ",user")
For Each Group in User.Groups
  Wscript.Echo Group.Name
Next
```

Here, ***domain*** is the name of the domain, and ***name*** is the name of the user account.

Listing Groups

To list user accounts using ADSI, create and then execute a WSH script containing the following:

```
On Error Resume Next
Set DomObj = GetObject("WinNT://" & Domain)
DomObj.Filter = Array("group")
```

```
For Each User In DomObj
        Wscript.Eecho User.name
Next
```

Here, ***domain*** is the name of the domain to query.

Creating Groups

To create a global group using ADSI, create and then execute a WSH script containing the following:

```
On Error Resume Next
Set DomObj = GetObject("WinNT://Domain")
Set Group = DomObj.Create("group", "name")
Group.GroupType = 4
Group.Description = "describe"
Group.SetInfo
```

Here, ***domain*** is the name of the domain; ***name*** is the name of the group to create; and ***describe*** is the group description.

TIP: *To create a local group, omit the highlighted line in the script above.*

Deleting Groups

To delete a group using ADSI, create and then execute a WSH script containing the following:

```
On Error Resume Next
Set DomObj = GetObject("WinNT://Domain")
DomObj.Delete "group", "name"
```

Here, ***domain*** is the name of the domain, and ***name*** is the name of the group to delete.

Adding a User Account to a Group

To add a user account to a group using ADSI, create and then execute a WSH script containing the following:

```
On Error Resume Next
Set Group = GetObject("WinNT://Gdomain/groupname,group")
Group.Add "WinNT://UDomain/useraccount,User"
```

Here, ***gdomain*** is the name of the domain containing the specified ***groupname***, and ***udomain*** is the domain containing the ***useraccount*** to add to the specified group.

Removing a User Account from a Group

To remove a user account from a group using ADSI, create and then execute a WSH script containing the following:

```
On Error Resume Next
Set Group = GetObject("WinNT://gdomain/groupname,group")
Group.Remove "WinNT://udomain/useraccount,User"
```

Here, ***gdomain*** is the name of the domain containing the specified ***groupname***, and ***udomain*** is the domain containing the ***useraccount*** to remove from the specified group.

Listing Groups Members

To list the user accounts that belong to a particular group using ADSI, create and then execute a WSH script containing the following:

```
On Error Resume Next
Set DomObj = GetObject("WinNT://" & Domain & "/" & Group)

For Each User In DomObj.Members
     wscript.echo User.name
Next
```

Here, ***domain*** is the name of the domain and ***group*** is the name of the group.

Managing Windows 2000/2003 through LDAP

Most of the previous ADSI examples merely need the binding statement changed in order to convert a WinNT provider script to an LDAP provider script. This section will illustrate a few of the changes you need to make to use these scripts in a Windows 2000/2003 domain.

NOTE: *Remember, you can still use the WinNT provider to manage a Windows 2000/2003 domain. Using the LDAP provider is slightly harder than the WinNT provider because you'll need to know the target's full LDAP path.*

Creating OUs under Windows 2000/2003

To create an organizational unit under Windows 2000/2003, create and then execute a WSH script containing the following:

```
On Error Resume Next
Set Root = GetObject("LDAP://RootDSE")
Set DomObj = GetObject( "LDAP://" & Root.Get ("defaultNamingContext"))
Set OU = DomObj.Create("organizationalUnit", "OU=name")
```

```
OU.Description = "describe"
OU.SetInfo
```

Here, **name** is the name of the organizational unit to create, and **describe** is the OU description.

Deleting OUs under Windows 2000/2003

To delete an organizational unit under Windows 2000/2003, create and then execute a WSH script containing the following:

```
On Error Resume Next
Set Root = GetObject("LDAP://RootDSE")
Set DomObj = GetObject( "LDAP://" &
Root.Get("defaultNamingContext"))
DomObj.Delete "organizationalUnit", "OU=name"
```

Here, **name** is the name of the organizational unit to delete.

Listing Computer Accounts under Windows 2000/2003

To list computer accounts using LDAP, create and then execute a WSH script containing the following:

```
On Error Resume Next
Set Root = GetObject("LDAP://RootDSE")
DomObj = Root.Get("DefaultNamingContext")

Set Conn = CreateObject("ADODB.Connection")
Conn.Provider = "ADsDSOObject"
Conn.Open "Active Directory Provider"

Set CMD = CreateObject("ADODB.Command")
CMD.ActiveConnection = Conn
CMD.CommandText = "<LDAP://" &
DomObj & ">;(objectCategory=computer);name;subtree"
CMD.Properties("Page Size") = 1000
CMD.Properties("Timeout") = 30
CMD.Properties("Cache Results") = False

Set RS =
CMD.Execute
RS.MoveFirst
```

```
While Not RS.EOF
    Wscript.Echo RS.Fields("name")
    RS.MoveNext
Wend
```

Creating Computer Accounts under Windows 2000/2003

To create a computer account using LDAP, create and then execute a WSH script containing the following:

```
On Error Resume Next
Set Root = GetObject("LDAP://RootDSE")
Set DomObj = GetObject( "LDAP://" & Root.Get
("defaultNamingContext"))
Set Computer = DomObj.Create("computer", "CN=name")
Computer.samAccountName = "name"
Computer.SetInfo
```

Here, **name** is the name of the computer account to create.

NOTE: *The highlighted code above must be placed on one line.*

Deleting Computer Accounts under Windows 2000/2003

To delete a computer account using LDAP, create and then execute a WSH script containing the following:

```
On Error Resume Next
Set Root = GetObject("LDAP://RootDSE")
Set DomObj = GetObject( "LDAP://" & Root.Get
("defaultNamingContext"))
Set Computer = DomObj.Create("computer", "CN=name")
Computer.samAccountName = "name"
Computer.SetInfo
```

NOTE: *The highlighted code above must be placed on one line.*

Here, **name** is the name of the computer account to delete.

Setting a User's Domain Password under Windows 2000/2003

To set a user's domain password using LDAP, create and then execute a WSH script containing the following:

```
On Error Resume Next
Set User = GetObject("LDAPPath")
User.SetPassword("pswd")
```

Here, **LDAPPath** is the full LDAP path of the target user (ex. LDAP:/
/cn=Adam.Sessler, cn=XPlay, dc=G4TV, dc=com) and **pswd** is the
password to assign.

Unlocking a User Account under Windows 2000/2003

To unlock a user account using LDAP, create and then execute a WSH
script containing the following:

```
Set User = GetObject("LDAP://
cn=Han.Solo,ou=marketing,dc=jesseweb,dc=com")
User.IsAccountLocked = False
User.SetInfo
```

Here, **LDAPPath** is the full LDAP path of the target user (ex. LDAP:/
/cn=Morgan.Webb, cn=XPlay, dc=G4TV, dc=com).

Listing User Accounts under Windows 2000/2003

To list computer accounts using LDAP, create and then execute a WSH
script containing the following:

```
On Error Resume Next
Set Root = GetObject("LDAP://RootDSE")
DomObj = Root.Get("DefaultNamingContext")

Set Conn = CreateObject("ADODB.Connection")
Conn.Provider = "ADsDSOObject"
Conn.Open "Active Directory Provider"
Set CMD = CreateObject("ADODB.Command")
CMD.ActiveConnection = Conn
CMD.CommandText = "<LDAP://" &
DomObj & ">;
(&(objectClass=user)(objectCategory=person));name;subtree"
CMD.Properties("Page Size") = 1000
CMD.Properties("Timeout") = 30
CMD.Properties("Cache Results") = False

Set RS =
CMD.Execute
RS.MoveFirst
While Not RS.EOF
    Wscript.Echo RS.Fields("name")
    RS.MoveNext
Wend
```

NOTE: *The highlighted code above must be placed on one line.*

NOTE: *The **LDAP** ObjectClass contains both user and computer accounts. To query for only user accounts, we must use "(&(objectClass=user)(objectCategory=person))" as in the example above.*

Creating User Accounts under Windows 2000/2003

To create a user account using LDAP, create and then execute a WSH script containing the following:

```
On Error Resume Next
Set Root = GetObject("LDAP://RootDSE")
Set DomObj = GetObject( "LDAP://" & Root.Get ("defaultNamingContext"))
Set User = DomObj.Create("user", "CN=fullname")
User.samAccountName = "name"
User.SetInfo
```

Here, ***name*** is the name of the user account to create, and ***fullname*** is the user's full name.

Deleting User Accounts under Windows 2000/2003

To delete a user account using LDAP, create and then execute a WSH script containing the following:

```
On Error Resume Next
Set Root = GetObject("LDAP://RootDSE")
Set DomObj = GetObject( "LDAP://" & Root.Get ("defaultNamingContext"))
DomObj.Delete "user", "CN=name"
```

NOTE: *The highlighted code above must be placed on one line.*

Here, ***name*** is the name of the user account to delete.

Displaying a Group's Type under Windows 2000/2003

To display the type of a group using LDAP, create and then execute a WSH script containing the following:

```
Wscript.Echo GetGroupType( _
  "LdapPath")


Function GetGroupType(GroupPath)
  Set Group = GetObject(GroupPath)
  Select Case Group.GroupType
    Case 2
      GetGroupType = "Global Distribution"
    Case 4
      GetGroupType = "Local Distribution"
    Case 8
```

```
        GetGroupType = "Universal Distribution"
    Case -2147483640
        GetGroupType = "Universal Security"
    Case -2147483644
        GetGroupType = "Local Security"
    Case -2147483646
        GetGroupType = "Global Security"
  End Select
End Function
```

Here, **LDAPPath** is the full LDAP path of the target group (ex. LDAP:/
/cn=Domain Admins, cn=Users, dc=jesseweb, dc=com).

Listing Groups under Windows 2000/2003

To list computer accounts using LDAP, create and then execute a WSH
script containing the following:

```
On Error Resume Next
Set Root = GetObject("LDAP://RootDSE")
DomObj = Root.Get("DefaultNamingContext")

Set Conn = CreateObject("ADODB.Connection")
Conn.Provider = "ADsDSOObject"
Conn.Open "Active Directory Provider"

Set CMD = CreateObject("ADODB.Command")
CMD.ActiveConnection = Conn
CMD.CommandText = "<LDAP://" &
DomObj & ">;(objectCategory=group);name;subtree"
CMD.Properties("Page Size") = 1000
CMD.Properties("Timeout") = 30
CMD.Properties("Cache Results") = False

Set RS = CMD.Execute
RS.MoveFirst
While Not RS.EOF
    Wscript.Echo RS.Fields("name")
    RS.MoveNext
Wend
```

NOTE: *The highlighted code above must be placed on one line.*

---

9 Enterprise
Management

Listing Group Members under Windows 2000/2003

To list the user accounts that belong to a particular group using LDAP, create and then execute a WSH script containing the following:

```
On Error Resume Next
Set Root = GetObject("LDAP://RootDSE")
DomObj = Root.Get("DefaultNamingContext")

Set Group = GetObject("LDAP://CN=Domain Admins,CN=Users," & _
DomObj)
For each objMember in Group.Members
     Wscript.Echo Replace(objMember.Name,"CN=","")
Next
```

The example above lists the members of the Domain Admins group.

Managing Inventory

In Brief

Managing inventory in an enterprise is an extremely involved task. Although several expensive inventory management packages are available, many companies cannot afford to purchase these systems and train employees to implement them. In this chapter, you will learn how to inventory your enterprise with simple, customizable scripts. In the previous chapters, you learned how to collect information about various items such as files, folders, shares, and services. In this chapter, you will learn how to collect information from various system and device components, such as a battery, mouse, monitor, sound card, printer, and more.

Windows System Tools

Microsoft Windows contains many tools you can use to view and modify system resource information. Each tool provides a central location to easily identify resources and conflicts, and modify device settings and drivers.

Microsoft System Information

Windows 98 included a utility called Microsoft System Information (MSI). MSI was first introduced with Microsoft Office 97 and can be started by clicking Start|Run and entering **MSINFO32**. This utility included quick links to other diagnostic tools (Dr. Watson and ScanDisk) under the Tools menu. One of the most valuable features of this tool was the History page. Under this page you would find a history of system changes that you could use to diagnose system malfunctions.

Windows 2000/XP/2003 follows Windows 98 and uses an updated version of Microsoft System Information. MSI is an invaluable system tool that uses WMI to provide an easy method to locate drivers, resources, components, and sources of system errors, to print reports, and more. Some advanced features include remote system connectivity and report generation. You can start this utility by clicking Start|Run and entering MSINFO32 or by entering WINMSD. MSI is actually a Microsoft Management Console (MMC) snap-in, stored as C:\Program Files\Common Files\Microsoft Shared\MSInfo\MSInfo32.msc.

Within the same directory is a file called MSINFO32.EXE, used to run MSI from the command line. You can use MSINFO32 to connect to a remote computer or store system information to an NFO (Information) file. The basic syntax of the MSINFO32 command is:

```
MSINFO32 /commands
```

Here, the available *commands* are:

- **/CATEGORIES +/- *name***—Displays (+) or does not display (-) the category name specified. Supplying the name ALL will display all categories.
- **/CATEGORY *name***—Specifies the category to open at launch.
- **/COMPUTER *name***—Connects to the specified computer name.
- **/MSINFO_FILE=*file***—Opens an NFO or CAB file.
- **/NFO *file***—Sends output to an NFO file.
- **/REPORT *file***—Generates a report to the specified file.

WARNING! *MSInfo32 is a memory-intensive application and might use up valuable system resources.*

Device Manager

Windows 2000/XP/2003 include a graphical utility called Device Manager (see Figure 10.1) to manipulate the various devices on your system. From within this utility, you can view or modify system settings, device properties, device drivers, and more. Device Manager displays its items in a tree-like structure, allowing you to easily view dependencies. This utility is most commonly used among administrators to determine resource conflicts (noted by yellow exclamation points) and update device drivers.

Microsoft Systems Management Server

Microsoft Systems Management Server (SMS) is a complete enterprise inventory and management package. Some of the advanced features include remote control, software licensing, and electronic software distribution (ESD). Although this product is extremely helpful, many companies cannot afford to pay for the training or licensing of SMS (about $1800 for 25 users). As related to this chapter, SMS

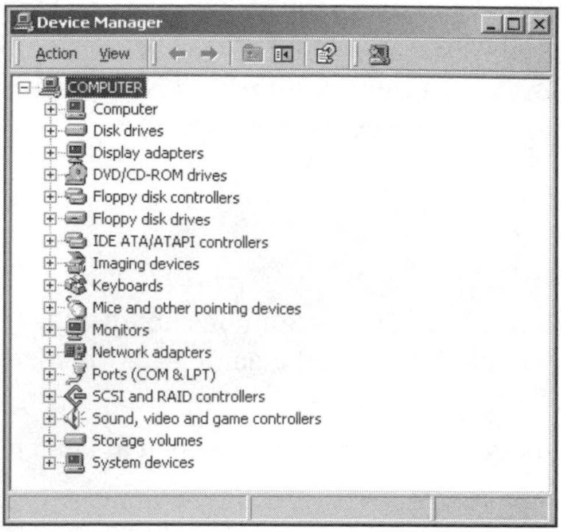

Figure 10.1   The Windows 2000 Device Manager.

performs system inventory using Windows Management Instrumentation. In this chapter, you will learn how to perform similar WMI queries to gather the system information you need—for free.

The Scripting Advantage

Through WMI, we can collect tons of inventory information to create reports and alerts. While both KiXtart and Windows Script Host can access WMI through COM, due to size limitations of this book and the popularity of the scripting language, this chapter will provide WMI examples in Windows Script Host only. (It should be simple to convert any of the scripts to KiXtart.) KiXtart does include a few variables to provide a quick and easy way to get the values of a few key properties (like OS type, CPU type, CPU speed, and so on). There are a few utilities to collect inventory information through shell scripting, although this information is limited in comparison to WMI. Finally, AutoIt is not appropriate and is not discussed in this chapter.

A Word of Caution

This chapter contains many scripting examples on collecting and reporting inventory. As with all scripts, you should first test each script in an isolated testing environment to ensure the script produces the desired results before using it in a production environment.

Immediate Solutions

Gathering Information with Shell Scripting

Shell scripting is very limited when it comes to gathering system resource information. Most new devices are designed specifically to work with Windows, not DOS, and most resource configuration tools are GUI-controlled and not command-line controllable. However, there are still several tools and methods you can utilize to collect and report resource information through shell scripting.

Collecting Information Using SRVINFO

SRVINFO is a resource kit utility to display various system information from the command line. The basic syntax of the SRVINFO command is:

```
SRVINFO /commands \\computer
```

Here, **computer** is the name of the computer to collect information from, and the available **commands** are:

- **-D**—Displays service drivers
- **-NS**—Does not display service information
- **-S**—Displays shares
- **-V**—Displays Exchange and SQL version information

Here is an example to display all the information SRVINFO can report:

```
SRVINFO -S -V -D
```

Collecting BIOS Information

To collect BIOS (Basic Input/Output System) information from the command line, you can use REG.EXE to extract the appropriate information. To display processor information using shell scripting, proceed as follows:

1. Create a new directory to store all files included in this example.

2. For Windows 2000 only, obtain REG.EXE from the Windows 2000 Resource Kit and copy it to the new directory.

3. Start a command prompt and enter "*scriptfile*.bat."

Here, **scriptfile** is the full path of the new directory from step 1 and file name of a script file that contains the following:

```
@ECHO OFF
Reg Query HKLM\HARDWARE\DESCRIPTION\System\
SystemBiosVersion > BIOS.TXT
Set Count=3
:Count
For /f "tokens=%Count%" %%I in ('TYPE BIOS.TXT'
) Do Set Version=%Version% %%I
Set /A Count+=1
If %Count% LSS 10 Goto Count
Echo BIOS Version: %Version%

Reg Query HKLM\HARDWARE\DESCRIPTION\System\
SystemBiosDate > BIOS.TXT

For /f "tokens=3" %%I in ('TYPE BIOS.TXT'
) Do Echo BIOS Date: %%I
Del BIOS.txt > Nul
Set Count=
Set Version=
```

NOTE: *The highlighted code above must be placed on one line.*

Related solution:	Found on page:
Modifying the Registry with Shell Scripting	119

Collecting Memory Information

PSTAT is a Windows 2000 resource kit utility used to display running threads from the command line. You can use this tool to display memory information. To display memory information using shell scripting, proceed as follows:

1. Create a new directory to store all files included in this example.

2. Obtain PSTAT.EXE from the Resource Kit and copy it to the new directory.

3. Start a command prompt and enter "*scriptfile*.bat."

Here, **scriptfile** is the full path of the new directory from step 1 and file name of a script file that contains the following:

```
PSTAT | Find " Memory: " > MEM.TXT
For /F "tokens=2" %%M In ('Type MEM.txt') Do Echo Memory: %%M
Del MEM.txt > Nul
```

Collecting Processor Information

To collect processor information from the command line, you can use REG.EXE to extract the appropriate information. To display processor information using shell scripting, proceed as follows:

1. Create a new directory to store all files included in this example.

2. For Windows 2000 only, obtain REG.EXE from the Windows 2000 Resource Kit and copy it to the new directory.

3. Start a command prompt and enter "*scriptfile*.bat."

Here, **scriptfile** is the full path of the new directory from step 1 and file name of a script file that contains the following:

```
@ECHO OFF
for /f "Tokens=4,5" %%i in ('reg QUERY "HKLM\HARDWARE\_
DESCRIPTION\System\CentralProcessor\0" /v Identifier') do set_
family=%%j

for /f "Tokens=6,7" %%i in ('reg QUERY "HKLM\HARDWARE\_
DESCRIPTION\System\CentralProcessor\0" /v Identifier') do set_
model=%%j

for /f "Tokens=8,9" %%i in ('reg QUERY "HKLM\HARDWARE\_
DESCRIPTION\System\CentralProcessor\0" /v Identifier') do set_
step=%%j

for /f "Tokens=2*" %%i in ('reg QUERY "HKLM\HARDWARE\_
DESCRIPTION\System\CentralProcessor\0" /v ~MHZ') do set _
speed=%%j
SET /a speed=%speed%

SET PType=Unknown

IF %family% EQU 5 (
   IF %model% LSS 4 SET PType=Pentium
   IF %model% GEQ 4 SET PType=Pentium MMX
)
IF %family% EQU 6 (
   IF %model% LSS 3 SET PType=Pentium Pro
   IF %model% GEQ 3 (
```

```
            IF %model% LSS 5 (
              SET PType=Pentium II
            )
            IF %model% EQU 5 (
              If %Step% EQU 0 Set PTYPE=Pentium II or Celeron
              If %Step% EQU 1 Set PTYPE=Pentium II or Celeron
              If %Step% EQU 2 Set PTYPE=Pentium II or Pentium II Xeon
              If %Step% EQU 3 Set PTYPE=Pentium II or Pentium II Xeon
            )
            IF %model% EQU 6 SET PType=Celeron
            IF %model% GTR 6 SET PType=Pentium III or Pentium III Xeon
            IF %model% EQU A SET PType=Pentium III Xeon
          )
        )
        IF %family% EQU 15 (
          IF %model% GEQ 0 SET PType=Pentium 4
        )

        ECHO Processor Type: %PType%
        ECHO Processor Speed: %SPEED% MHZ
```

NOTE: *The highlighted code on the previous page must be placed on one line. The routine to determine the processor type was derived from various Intel processor spec sheets.*

Gathering Information with KiXtart

KiXtart provides many macros to retrieve user information, but only a few of these macros can be used to retrieve resource information. By combining KiXtart macros and registry commands, you can collect and report various resource information through simple scripts.

Collecting BIOS Information

KiXtart does not provide any direct method to collect BIOS information. Alternatively, you can query the registry and extract the BIOS information you want using KiXtart. To collect printer information using KiXtart, create and then execute a KiXtart script containing the following:

```
; Get the system BIOS type
$SBiosType = READVALUE("HKEY_LOCAL_MACHINE\HARDWARE\
DESCRIPTION\System","SystemBiosVersion")
```

```
;  Get the system BIOS date
$SBiosDate = READVALUE("HKEY_LOCAL_MACHINE\HARDWARE\
DESCRIPTION\System","SystemBiosDate")

? "BIOS Type:      $SBiosType"
? "BIOS Date:      $SBiosDate"
SLEEP 10
```

NOTE: *The highlighted code above must be placed on one line.*

Related solution:	Found on page:
Modifying the Registry with KiXtart	126

Collecting Drive Information

Although KiXtart provides no built-in method to determine all system drives and their total size, you can perform checks for available drives and free disk space. An available drive is considered to be any drive with media present. For example, a drive without a floppy or CD-ROM is an unavailable drive. To collect information on available drives using KiXtart, create and then execute a KiXtart script containing the following:

```
$DLetter = 67
While $DLetter < 91
  $Drive = CHR($DLetter) + ":"
  If Exist ($Drive)
    $DiskSpace = GETDISKSPACE($Drive)
    SELECT
      CASE $DiskSpace = 0
        $DiskSpace = "0 Bytes"
      CASE $DiskSpace < 1024
        $DiskSpace = $DiskSpace * 100
        $DiskSpace = "$DiskSpace KB"
      CASE $DiskSpace => 1024 and $DiskSpace < 1048576
        $DiskSpace = ($DiskSpace * 100) / 1024
        $DiskSpace = "$DiskSpace MB"
      CASE $DiskSpace => 1048576
        $DiskSpace = $DiskSpace / 10486
        $DiskSpace = "$DiskSpace GB"
    ENDSELECT
      $DiskSpace = SUBSTR($DiskSpace, 1, LEN($DiskSpace) - 5)
      + "." + SUBSTR($DiskSpace,LEN($DiskSpace)- 4, 5)
    ?"Drive $Drive Free Space: $DiskSpace"
  EndIf
```

```
    $DLetter = $DLetter + 1
Loop
Sleep 5
```

NOTE: *The highlighted code above must be placed on one line.*

Notice that the drive letter count (**$Dletter**) starts at 67 and runs until 91. These numbers represent ASCII characters C to Z. If you start **$Dletter** with 65 (A), your script might pause and you might be prompted for a floppy disk if none is present.

Collecting Operating System Information

To collect OS information using KiXtart, create and then execute a KiXtart script containing the following:

```
; Initialize variables
$SUITE = ""

SELECT ; Product Suite?
  CASE @PRODUCTSUITE = 1
    $SUITE = "Small Business"
  CASE @PRODUCTSUITE = 2
    $SUITE = "Enterprise"
  CASE @PRODUCTSUITE = 4
    $SUITE = "Back Office"
  CASE @PRODUCTSUITE = 8
    $SUITE = "Communication Server"
  CASE @PRODUCTSUITE = 16
    $SUITE = "Terminal Server"
  CASE @PRODUCTSUITE = 32
    $SUITE = "Small Business (Restricted)"
  CASE @PRODUCTSUITE = 64
    $SUITE = "Embedded NT"
  CASE @PRODUCTSUITE = 128
    $SUITE = "Data Center"
  CASE @PRODUCTSUITE = "256"
    $SUITE = "Single User Terminal Server"
  CASE @PRODUCTSUITE = 512
    $SUITE = "Home Edition"
  CASE @PRODUCTSUITE = 1024
    $SUITE = "Blade Server"
  CASE @PRODUCTSUITE = 2048
    $SUITE = "Embedded (Restricted)"
  CASE @PRODUCTSUITE = 4096
    $SUITE = "Security Appliance"
  CASE @PRODUCTSUITE = 8192
    $SUITE = "Storage Server"
```

```
      CASE @PRODUCTSUITE = 16384
        $SUITE = "Compute Cluster Server"
      CASE 1
        $SUITE = "UNDETERMINED"
ENDSELECT

? "Operating System: @PRODUCTTYPE" ; Display OS type
? "Build:           @BUILD" ; Display the build number
? "Suite:           " + $SUITE ; Display the product suite
? "Service Pack:    @CSD" ; Display the service pack
SLEEP 10
```

Collecting Printer Information

KiXtart does not provide any direct method to collect information about all the printers installed on a system. Alternatively, you can query the registry and extract the printer information you want using KiXtart. To collect printer information using KiXtart, create and then execute a KiXtart script containing the following:

```
$Printers="HKEY_LOCAL_MACHINE\SYSTEM\CurrentControlSet\
Control\Print\Printers\"
$Index=0

:GatherInfo
$Printer=enumkey("$Printers",$Index)
If @Error=0
  $Desc = Readvalue("$Printers\$Printer","Description")
  $Loc = Readvalue("$Printers\$Printer","Location")
  $Port = Readvalue("$Printers\$Printer","Port")
  $Share = Readvalue("$Printers\$Printer","Share Name")
  ? "Printer: $Printer"
  ? "Description: $Desc"
  ? "Location: $Loc"
  ? "Port: $Port"
  ? "Share: $Share"
  ?
  ?$Index = $Index + 1
  Goto GatherInfo
EndIf
Sleep 10
```

NOTE: *The highlighted code above must be placed on one line.*

Collecting Processor Information

KiXtart includes the @CPU and @MHZ macros to provide the name and speed of the primary processor installed on a system. Additionally, you can query the registry and extract the processor count using KiXtart. To collect processor information using KiXtart, create and then execute a KiXtart script containing the following:

1. Create a new directory to store all files included in this example.

2. Download and extract the latest version of KiXtart, from **www.kixtart.org**, to the new directory.

3. Select Start|Run and enter "kix32 *scriptfile.*"

Here, *scriptfile* is the full path of the new directory from step 1 and file name of a script file that contains the following:

```
;  Get the number of processors
$ProCount = 0
$Count = 0
WHILE $Count < 65
  $ProTemp = EXISTKEY("HKEY_LOCAL_MACHINE\HARDWARE\
  DESCRIPTION\System\CentralProcessor\$ProCount")
  IF $ProTemp = 0
    $ProCount = $ProCount + 1
  ENDIF
  $Count = $Count + 1
LOOP

; The code below is to simply display the final results
? "Processor Count:  $ProCount"
? "Processor Name: " + TRIM(@CPU)
? "Processor Speed:  @MHZ MHZ"
SLEEP 10
```

NOTE: *The highlighted code above must be placed on one line.*

Gathering Information with WMI

Windows Management Instrumentation provides a centralized management system for almost all the resources on your system. Through various WMI classes and Windows Script Host, you can collect and report various resource information through simple scripts. Remember, this chapter shows you how to collect inventory information using WMI on a local system as follows:

```
Set SomeVar = GetObject("winmgmts:")_
  .InstancesOf("WMIClass")
```

You can collect inventory information using WMI from remote systems using this method presented in Chapter 8:

```
Set SomeVar = GetObject("winmgmts:{" & _
  "impersonationLevel=impersonate}!\\" & _
  Computer & "\root\cimv2").InstancesOf _
  ("WMIClass")
```

TIP: *The examples in the following sections illustrate only a few of the classes and class properties that WMI has to offer. Consult the WMI SDK documentation for a complete list of classes and their properties.*

Collecting Battery Information

The **Win32_Battery** class allows you to query laptop battery and Uninterruptible Power Supply (UPS) information through WMI. To collect battery information on a system using WMI, create and then execute a WSH script containing the following:

```
Set BatterySet = GetObject("winmgmts:").InstancesOf
("Win32_Battery")
For each Battery in BatterySet
 Select Case Battery.Chemistry
  Case 1
   BType = "Other"
  Case 2
   BType = "Unknown"
  Case 3
   BType = "Lead Acid"
  Case 4
   BType = "Nickel Cadmium"
  Case 5
   BType = "Nickel Metal Hydride"
  Case 6
   BType = "Lithium-ion"
  Case 7
   BType = "Zinc air"
  Case 8
   BType = "Lithium Polymer"
 End Select
 Select Case Battery.BatteryStatus
  Case 1
   BStatus = "Other"
```

```
      Case 2
        BStatus = "Unknown"
      Case 3
        BStatus = "Fully Charged"
      Case 4
        BStatus = "Low"
      Case 5
        BStatus = "Critical"
      Case 6
        BStatus = "Charging"
      Case 7
        BStatus = "Charging and High"
      Case 8
        BStatus = "Charging and Low"
      Case 9
        BStatus = "Charging and Critical"
      Case 10
        BStatus = "Undefined"
      Case 11
        BStatus = "Partially Charged"
    End Select
    WScript.Echo "Name: " & Battery.Description & VBlf & _
      "Type: " & BType & VBlf & _
      "% Left: " & Battery.EstimatedChargeRemaining & VBlf & _
      "Minutes Left: " & Battery.ExpectedLife & VBlf & _
      "Status: " & BStatus
    Next
```

NOTE: *The highlighted code above must be placed on one line.*

Collecting BIOS Information

The **Win32_BIOS** class allows you to query BIOS information through WMI. To collect BIOS information on a system using WMI, create and then execute a WSH script containing the following:

```
Set BIOSSet = GetObject("winmgmts:").InstancesOf
("Win32_BIOS")
For each BIOS in BIOSSet
  BDate = Left(BIOS.ReleaseDate,8)
  BDate = Mid(BDate,5,2) & "/" & Mid(BDate,7,2) & "/" & _
  Mid(BDate,1,4)
  WScript.Echo "Name: " & BIOS.Name & VBlf & _
    "Manufacturer: " & BIOS.Manufacturer & VBlf & _
    "Date: " & BDate & VBlf & _
    "Version: " & BIOS.Version & VBlf & _
    "Status: " & BIOS.Status
Next
```

Collecting CD-ROM Information

The **Win32_CDROMDrive** class allows you to query CD-ROM information through WMI. To collect CD-ROM information on a system using WMI, create and then execute a WSH script containing the following:

```
Set CDSet = GetObject("winmgmts:")_
  .InstancesOf("Win32_CDROMDrive")

DisplayWMIProperties CDSet
```

NOTE: *You need to append the DisplayWMIProperties routine, listed in Chapter 8, to this script in order for it to run.*

Collecting Chassis Information

The **Win32_SystemEnclosure** class allows you to query system enclosure information through WMI. To collect system enclosure information on a system using WMI, create and then execute a WSH script containing the following:

```
Set SystemSet = GetObject("winmgmts:")_
  .InstancesOf ("Win32_SystemEnclosure")

For each
Chassis in SystemSet
  For Each ChassisType in Chassis.ChassisTypes
    Select Case ChassisType
      Case 1
        Wscript.Echo "Other"
      Case 2
        Wscript.Echo "Unknown"
      Case 3
        Wscript.Echo "Desktop"
      Case 4
        Wscript.Echo "Low Profile Desktop"
      Case 5
        Wscript.Echo "Pizza Box"
      Case 6
        Wscript.Echo "Mini Tower"
      Case 7
        Wscript.Echo "Tower"
      Case 8
        Wscript.Echo "Portable"
      Case 9
```

```
          Wscript.Echo "Laptop"
        Case 10
          Wscript.Echo "Notebook"
        Case 11
          Wscript.Echo "Hand Held"
        Case 12
          Wscript.Echo "Docking Station"
        Case 13
          Wscript.Echo "All in One"
        Case 14
          Wscript.Echo "Sub Notebook"
        Case 15
          Wscript.Echo "Space-Saving"
        Case 16
          Wscript.Echo "Lunch Box"
        Case 17
          Wscript.Echo "Main System Chassis"
        Case 18
          Wscript.Echo "Expansion Chassis"
        Case 19
          Wscript.Echo "SubChassis"
        Case 20
          Wscript.Echo "Bus Expansion Chassis"
        Case 21
          Wscript.Echo "Peripheral Chassis"
        Case 22
          Wscript.Echo "Storage Chassis"
        Case 23
          Wscript.Echo "Rack Mount Chassis"
        Case 24
          Wscript.Echo "Sealed-Case PC"
      End Select
    Next
Next
```

Collecting Drive Information

The **Win32_LogicalDisk** class allows you to query disk information
through WMI. To inventory disks on a system using WMI, create and
then execute a WSH script containing the following:

```
Set DiskSet = GetObject("winmgmts:")_
  .InstancesOf ("Win32_LogicalDisk")

For each Disk in DiskSet
 Select Case Disk.DriveType
  Case 0
    DType = "Unknown"
```

```
Case 1
  DType = "No Root Directory"
Case 2
  DType = "Removable Disk"
Case 3
  DType = "Local Disk"
Case 4
  DType = "Network Drive"
Case 5
  DType = "Compact Disc"
Case 6
  DType = "RAM Disk"
End Select
WScript.Echo "Drive: " & Disk.DeviceID & VBlf & _
"Name: " & Disk.Description & VBlf & _
"Type: " & DType & VBlf & _
"File System: " & Disk.FileSystem & VBlf & _
"Size: " & Disk.Size & VBlf & _
"Free Space: " & Disk.FreeSpace & VBlf & _
"Compressed: " & Disk.Compressed
Next
```

Collecting Memory Information

The **Win32_LogicalMemoryConfiguration** class allows you to query memory information through WMI. To collect memory information on a system using WMI, create and then execute a WSH script containing the following:

```
Set MemorySet = GetObject("winmgmts:")_
.InstancesOf ("Win32_LogicalMemoryConfiguration")

For each Memory in MemorySet
  WScript.Echo "Total: " & _
  Memory.TotalPhysicalMemory/1024 & VBlf & _
  "Virtual: " & Memory.TotalVirtualMemory/1024 & VBlf & _
  "Page: " & Memory.TotalPageFileSpace/1024
Next
```

Collecting Modem Information

The **Win32_POTSModem** class allows you to query modem information through WMI. To collect modem information on a system using WMI, create and then execute a WSH script containing the following:

```
Set Modems = GetObject("winmgmts:")_
  .InstancesOf ("Win32_POTSModem")

DisplayWMIProperties Modems
```

> **NOTE:** *You need to append the DisplayWMIProperties routine, listed in chapter 8, to this script in order for it to run.*

Collecting Monitor Information

The **Win32_DesktopMonitor** class allows you to query information on computer monitors through WMI. To collect monitor information on a system using WMI, create and then execute a WSH script containing the following:

```
Set Monitors = GetObject("winmgmts:")_
  .InstancesOf ("Win32_DesktopMonitor")

DisplayWMIProperties Monitors
```

> **NOTE:** *You need to append the DisplayWMIProperties routine, listed in Chapter 8, to this script in order for it to run.*

Collecting Mouse Information

The **Win32_PointingDevice** class allows you to query mouse, track-ball, touch screen, touch pad, and other pointing device information through WMI. To collect pointing device information on a system using WMI, create and then execute a WSH script containing the following:

```
Set Pointers = GetObject("winmgmts:")_
  .InstancesOf ("Win32_PointingDevice")

DisplayWMIProperties Pointers
```

> **NOTE:** *You need to append the DisplayWMIProperties routine, listed in Chapter 8, to this script in order for it to run.*

Collecting Network Adapter Information

The **Win32_NetworkAdapter** class allows you to query information on network adapters through WMI. To collect Network Interface Card (NIC) information on a system using WMI, create and then execute a WSH script containing the following:

```
Set NICs = GetObject("winmgmts:")_
  .InstancesOf ("Win32_NetworkAdapter")

DisplayWMIProperties NICs
```

NOTE: *You need to append the DisplayWMIProperties routine, listed in Chapter 8, to this script in order for it to run.*

Collecting Operating System Information

The **Win32_OperatingSystem** class allows you to query various operating system information through WMI. To collect operating system information on a system using WMI, create and then execute a WSH script containing the following:

```
Set OSs = GetObject("winmgmts:")_
  .InstancesOf ("Win32_OperatingSystem")

DisplayWMIProperties OSs
```

NOTE: *You need to append the DisplayWMIProperties routine, listed in chapter 8, to this script in order for it to run.*

Collecting Printer Information

The **Win32_Printer** class allows you to query printer information through WMI. This includes both local and network printers. To collect printer information on a system using WMI, create and then execute a WSH script containing the following:

```
Set Printers = GetObject("winmgmts:")_
  .InstancesOf ("Win32_Printer")

DisplayWMIProperties Printers
```

NOTE: *You need to append the DisplayWMIProperties routine, listed in Chapter 8, to this script in order for it to run.*

Collecting Processor Information

The **Win32_Processor** class allows you to query processor information through WMI. To collect processor information on a system using WMI, create and then execute a WSH script containing the following:

```
Set Processors = GetObject("winmgmts:")_
  .InstancesOf ("Win32_Processor")

DisplayWMIProperties Processors
```

NOTE: *You need to append the DisplayWMIProperties routine, listed in Chapter 8, to this script in order for it to run.*

Collecting Sound Card Information

The **Win32_SoundDevice** class allows you to query sound card information through WMI. To collect sound card information on a system using WMI, create and then execute a WSH script containing the following:

```
Set SoundDevices = GetObject("winmgmts:")_
  .InstancesOf ("Win32_SoundDevice")

DisplayWMIProperties SoundDevices
```

NOTE: *You need to append the DisplayWMIProperties routine, listed in Chapter 8, to this script in order for it to run.*

Collecting Tape Drive Information

The **Win32_TapeDrive** class allows you to query tape drive information through WMI. To collect tape drive information on a system using WMI, create and then execute a WSH script containing the following:

```
Set TapeDrives = GetObject("winmgmts:")_
  .InstancesOf ("Win32_TapeDrive")

DisplayWMIProperties TapeDrives
```

NOTE: You need to append the DisplayWMIProperties routine, listed in Chapter 8, to this script in order for it to run.

Collecting Plug and Play Information

The **Win32_PnPEntity** class allows you to query plug and play device information through WMI. This is useful to inventory externally-connected devices (USB, FireWire, Serial, and so on). Remember, this class returns any device (internal and external) that receives a plug and play ID, so you may need to do some filtering to return reports like external USB connected devices, and so on. To collect plug and play device information on a system using WMI, create and then execute a WSH script containing the following:

```
Set PNPDevices = GetObject("winmgmts:")_
  .InstancesOf ("Win32_PnPEntity")

DisplayWMIProperties PNPDevices
```

NOTE: You need to append the DisplayWMIProperties routine, listed in Chapter 8, to this script in order for it to run.

Collecting Video Card Information

The **Win32_VideoController** class allows you to query video card information through WMI. To collect video card information on a system using WMI, create and then execute a WSH script containing the following:

```
Set Videos = GetObject("winmgmts:")_
  .InstancesOf ("Win32_VideoController")

DisplayWMIProperties Videos
```

NOTE: You need to append the DisplayWMIProperties routine, listed in Chapter 8, to this script in order for it to run.

Listing Installed Software

The **Win32_Product** class allows you to query installed software information through WMI. This class can only retrieve information on products installed with the Windows installer. To collect Installed software information on a system using WMI, create and then execute a WSH script containing the following:

```
Set Software= GetObject("winmgmts:")_
  .InstancesOf ("Win32_Product")
For each Application in Software
  Wscript.Echo "Name: " & Application.Name & VBCRLF & _
  "Vendor: " & Application.Vendor & VBCRLF & _
  "Install Date: " & Mid(Application.InstallDate2, 5, 2) & "/" & _
  Mid(Application.InstallDate2, 7, 2) & "/" & _
  Mid(Application.InstallDate2, 1, 4)
Next
```

Listing Hotfixes

The **Win32_QuickFixEngineering** class allows you to query installed hotfix and update information through WMI. To collect installed software information on a system using WMI, create and then execute a WSH script containing the following:

```
Set HotFixes = GetObject("winmgmts:")_
  .InstancesOf
("Win32_QuickFixEngineering")

DisplayWMIProperties HotFixes
```

NOTE: *You need to append the DisplayWMIProperties routine, listed in Chapter 8, to this script in order for it to run.*

Security

In Brief

As sad as I am to admit this, the attitude of most administrators is "security through obscurity." This expression means that the best way of dealing with security holes is ignoring them, hoping no one will find them, and praying they will go away. Unfortunately, this attitude never works. It seems nowadays there is a new virus or security hole being publicized daily. The days of merely running **FDISK /MBR** or deleting PWL files are over. Viruses and intruders are more sophisticated than ever. In this chapter, you will learn about the Windows security architecture and how to decrease the chances of unauthorized entry.

Hackers and Crackers

If you can think of system security as a war, then hackers and crackers are your opponents. Before you go into battle, it's always good to know a little about your opponents. Here is the truth about a common myth: Hackers never intentionally damage data. Hackers are knowledgeable computer users whose pure goal is to solve problems and continually learn about the inner workings of operating systems, applications, and transmission methods. Although their methods of obtaining information may be questionable, they tend to create tools to identify or improve upon system weaknesses. Hackers like to document and publicly share their information with all who are willing to learn. Hackers usually receive bad press because people don't understand the difference between the terms "hackers" and "crackers."

Crackers are knowledgeable computer users whose goal is to break into systems and damage or steal data. They tend to reverse-engineer programs and illegally use them for even more illicit purposes. Cracking techniques usually do not involve skillful or complicated methods, but rather crude methods such as stealing files from trash bins or tricking other users into handing them information. Examples of crackers are users who sniff the network for passwords, pirate software, write Trojan horse programs or viruses, or crash the network with broadcasts or email bombs.

TIP: *For more information about hackers and crackers, visit www.hackers.com.*

Security Configuration and Analysis Tool

The Microsoft Security Configuration and Analysis tool (MSSCE) provides a centralized method to analyze or modify a system's security settings. Figure 11.1 shows this tool. MSSCE is a Microsoft Management Console (MMC) snap-in that allows you to create or use security templates to apply to your environment. These security settings are stored in configuration files and can be applied to all the machines in your environment.

Predefined Security Templates

The MSSCE includes several predefined templates in the %WINDIR%\Security\Templates directory. The security templates included with the MSSCE are:

- *Basicdc.inf*—Default domain controller

- *Basicsv.inf*—Default server

- *Basicwk.inf*—Default workstation

These three basic security templates contain the standard security settings for each system.

- *Compatws.inf*—Compatible workstation or server

The compatibility template contains lower security settings to allow regular users maximum control of installed applications. Applying the compatibility template will remove all users from the power users group.

Figure 11.1   The Security Configuration and Analysis tool.

- *Dedicadc.inf*—Dedicated domain controller

The dedicated template contains security settings for domain controllers that will not be running server-based applications.

- *Hisecdc.inf*—Highly secure domain controller
- *Hisecws.inf*—Highly secure workstation or server

The high security templates provide the maximum security settings for the system. Applying this template on a Windows 2000 system will prevent that system from communicating with other Windows NT systems.

- *Securedc.inf*—Secure domain controller
- *Securews.inf*—Secure workstation or server

The secure templates are the recommended security settings.

Important Security Practices

Here is a list of several security practices to help protect your environment:

- Administrators should always lock their system when not in use. This should be a top priority for administrators. It takes only a few seconds of distraction for an intruder to go to work under your logged-on account.

- Do not allow other accounts to access or log on to an administrator's system. If another user can access your system (even if you are not logged on), he or she can potentially extract passwords, grab your files, and more.

- Always use the latest security patches and service pack. It seems Microsoft is always releasing security patches and service packs to combat system exploits. These patches don't do any good unless they are actually loaded onto your system.

- Increase the minimum password length. To slow down brute-force password utilities, you can force users to use longer passwords by increasing the minimum password length.

- Passwords should be a mix of upper- and lowercase, letters, and numbers. The more complex your passwords are, the longer it takes for a password-cracking program to guess a password.

- Do not use dictionary-based passwords (for example, MyKids). Dictionary-based passwords are the easiest and usually the first passwords determined through password-guessing utilities.

- Use the New Technology File System (NTFS). In addition to increased reliability, NTFS provides dramatically increased security compared to the other Windows file systems.

- Set your system BIOS to boot from the hard drive only. Even if you use NTFS, a hacker can access all your protected files by booting from removable media.

The Scripting Advantage

Microsoft has included quite a few COM objects that can be used to manage security. We have seen some of them in other chapters (like WinNT, LDAP, and WMI) and others will be introduced in this chapter for the first time. While both KiXtart and WSH can access these objects through COM, due to size limitations of this book and the popularity of the scripting language, this chapter will provide these examples in Windows Script Host only. (It should be simple to convert the scripts to KiXtart.) Microsoft also includes a few security command line tools, which can easily be controlled through shell scripting. While KiXtart is briefly covered in this chapter, you should be able to use it to run any of this chapter's shell or WSH scripts. Finally, AutoIt is not appropriate and is not discussed in this chapter.

A Word of Caution

This chapter contains many powerful scripting examples on securing Windows systems and domains. While your intention may be to secure objects, incorrectly configured or executed scripts can end up making your systems even more vulnerable. As with all scripts, you should first test each script in an isolated testing environment to ensure that the script produces the desired results before using it in a production environment.

Immediate Solutions

Setting the Boot Timeout

Allowing users to choose other operating systems (OS) at bootup is a security risk because the other operating systems can be used to bypass or defeat Windows security.

Setting the Boot Timeout Using Bootcfg

To set the boot timeout using Bootcfg from a Windows XP/2003 system, start a command prompt and enter the following:

```
Bootcfg /timeout 0
```

Related solution:	Found on page:
Displaying the Boot.ini using Bootcfg	36

Setting the Boot Timeout Using KiXtart

To set the boot timeout using KiXtart, create and then execute a KiXtart script containing the following:

```
$File = "C:\boot.ini"

$RCode = SetFileAttr($File,128)
WriteProfileString($File, "boot loader", "timeout", "0")
$RCode = SetFileAttr($File,1)
```

This script first clears any file attributes on BOOT.INI, modifies the boot timeout, and then marks the file as read-only.

Related solution:	Found on page:
Setting File or Folder Attributes	63

Setting the Boot Timeout Using WMI

To set the boot timeout to zero using WMI, create and then execute a WSH script containing the following:

```
On Error Resume Next
Computer = InputBox("Enter the computer name", "Boot Timeout",
"localhost")

Set Boot = GetObject("winmgmts:{impersonationLevel=
impersonate}!\\" &
Computer & "\root\cimv2").
ExecQuery("select * from Win32_ComputerSystem")

For each Item in Boot
  Item.SystemStartupDelay = 0
  Item.Put_()
Next
```

NOTE: *The highlighted code above must be placed on one line.*

Removing POSIX and OS/2 Subsystems

By default, Windows 2000 includes three environment subsystems:
OS/2, POSIX, and Win32 subsystems. Originally developed by
Microsoft, OS/2 is IBM's operating system for the personal computer.
POSIX stands for Portable Operating System Interface for Unix and
is a set of interface standards used by developers to design applica-
tions and operating systems.

Win32 is the main subsystem used by Windows, whereas the others
are merely present for compatibility with other operating systems
and applications. To remove the POSIX and OS/2 subsystems from
the command line, proceed as follows, create and then execute a
shell script containing the following:

```
@ECHO OFF
RMDIR /Q /S "%WINDIR%\System32\OS2"
DEL /F /Q "%WINDIR%\SYSTEM32\PSXDLL.DLL"
DEL /F /Q "%WINDIR%\SYSTEM32\PSXSS.EXE"
DEL /F /Q "%WINDIR%\SYSTEM32\POSIX.EXE"
DEL /F /Q "%WINDIR%\SYSTEM32\PSXSS.EXE"
DEL /F /Q "%WINDIR%\SYSTEM32\OS2.EXE"
DEL /F /Q "%WINDIR%\SYSTEM32\OS2SRV.EXE"
DEL /F /Q "%WINDIR%\SYSTEM32\OS2SS.EXE"

ECHO REGEDIT4 > C:\OS2.REG
ECHO [-HKEY_LOCAL_MACHINE\SOFTWARE\Microsoft\
```

```
OS/2 Subsystem for NT] >>
C:\OS2.REG
REGEDIT /S C:\OS2.REG
DEL  /F /Q C:\OS2.REG
```

NOTE: *The highlighted code above must be placed on one line.*

Removing Administrative Shares

Administrative shares are hidden shares created by the system to allow administrators to access files remotely. Although these shares are hidden, they are no secret to the savvy user and should be removed for maximum security. To remove administrative shares, create and then execute a WSH script containing the following:

```
On Error Resume Next
Set SHELL = CreateObject("WScript.Shell")
Set Drives = FSO.Drives

For Each Drive in Drives
   SHELL.Run "NET SHARE " & Drive & "\ /D", 0, False
   SHELL.Run "NET SHARE " & Drive & "\WINNT /D", 0, False
Next
```

WARNING! *Certain programs use administrative shares and might not work if they are removed.*

Related solution:	Found on page:
Removing Shares	157

Locking Down Administrative Tools

Administrative tools, such as User Manager and REGEDT32, should be locked down for administrative access only. To lock down various administrative tools, proceed as follows:

1. Create a new directory to store all files included in this example.

2. Copy XCACLS.EXE from the Windows 2000 resource kit to the new directory.

3. Start a command prompt and enter "*scriptfile*.bat."

Here, **scriptfile** is the full path of the new directory from step 1 and file name of a script file that contains the following:

```
@ECHO OFF
XCACLS "%WINDIR%\POLEDIT.EXE" /G Administrators:F;F /Y
XCACLS "%WINDIR%\REGEDIT.EXE" /G Administrators:F;F /Y
XCACLS "%WINDIR%\SYSTEM32\CACLS.EXE" /G Administrators:F;F /Y
XCACLS "%WINDIR%\SYSTEM32\CLIPBRD.EXE" /G
Administrators:F;F /Y

XCACLS "%WINDIR%\SYSTEM32\NCADMIN.EXE" /G
Administrators:F;F /Y

XCACLS "%WINDIR%\SYSTEM32\NTBACKUP.EXE" /G
Administrators:F;F /Y

XCACLS "%WINDIR%\SYSTEM32\REGEDT32.EXE" /G
Administrators:F;F /Y

XCACLS "%WINDIR%\SYSTEM32\RASADMIN.EXE" /G
Administrators:F;F /Y
XCACLS "%WINDIR%\SYSTEM32\RDISK.EXE" /G Administrators:F;F /Y
XCACLS "%WINDIR%\SYSTEM32\SYSKEY.EXE" /G
Administrators:F;F /Y

XCACLS "%WINDIR%\SYSTEM32\USRMGR.EXE" /G
Administrators:F;F /Y

XCACLS "%WINDIR%\SYSTEM32\WINDISK.EXE" /G
Administrators:F;F /Y
```

NOTE: *The highlighted code above must be placed on one line. Although this script prevents an ordinary user from accessing these tools, they could always bring them in and run them from an alternate source, such as a floppy disk.*

Related solution:	Found on page:
Modifying NTFS Permissions	155

Running Commands under Different Security Contexts

Every time someone logs on to the network with an administrator account, it creates a big security risk. Malicious ActiveX components from the Web, Trojan horses, or even a hidden batch file can wipe out an entire server, database, and more when run under administrative privileges. If you think about it, you don't really need administrative privileges when you are checking your mail or surfing the Net. A common solution to this security problem is to log on with a regular user account and use a utility to run trusted applications under the security context of an administrative account.

A security context specifies all the rights and privileges granted to a user. For administrators, this security context allows them to manage users, groups, trusts, and domains. The process of switching to the security context of another user is known as impersonation. Impersonation is mostly used by system services.

Using the RunAs Command

Windows 2000/XP/2003 includes the utility RUNAS.EXE, which allows users to run applications under the security context of a different user. This utility is integrated into the Windows shell, which allows you to set up shortcuts to utilize the RUNAS utility. The basic syntax of the RUNAS utility is:

```
RUNAS /commands program
```

Here, **program** is the shortcut, Control Panel applet, MMC console, or application to run. The available **commands** are:

- **/ENV**—Keep the current environment

- **/NETONLY**—Specifies for remote access only

- **/PROFILE**—Loads the specified user's profile

- **/USER:***username*—Specifies the **username** to run application as. Valid name formats are *domain\user* or *user@domain*

NOTE: *Once you have entered the command, you will be prompted for the password associated with the account.*

To start an instance of User Manager using an administrator account called ADMIN@MYDOMAIN.COM, enter the following:

```
RUNAS /USERNAME:ADMIN@MYDOMAIN.COM USRMGR
```

Using the SECEDIT Utility

The SECEDIT.EXE utility is the command-line version of the Microsoft security configuration editor that allows you to run security configuration and analysis from the command line.

Running a Security Analysis

The basic syntax to run an analysis using SECEDIT is as follows:

```
secedit /analyze /commands
```

Here, the available **commands** are:

- **/DB** *filename*—Required, specifies the database to compare against

- **/CFG** *filename*—Valid with **/DB**, specifies the security template to be imported

- **/LOG** *logpath*—Specifies the log file to use

- **/VERBOSE**—Specifies to include more detail to the log or output

- **/QUIET**—Runs the analysis with no screen or log output

Here is an example to run a system analysis against the high security template for a domain controller:

```
Secedit /analyze /DB "%WINDIR%\Security\Database\hisecdc.sdb"
/CFG "%WINDIR%\Security\Templates\hisecdc.inf"
/LOG "%WINDIR%\Security\Logs\hisecdc.log" /VERBOSE
```

NOTE: The code above must be placed on one line.

Reapplying a Group Policy

To reapply a local or user policy, start a command prompt and enter the following:

```
SECEDIT /REFRESHPOLICY policy/ENFORCE
```

Here, **/ENFORCE** forces the policy to be reapplied, even if no security changes were found.

NOTE: For Windows XP/2003, the GPUpdate command is the preferred method to reapply a group policy.

Applying a Security Template

The basic syntax to apply a security template using SECEDIT is as follows:

```
secedit /configure /commands
```

Here, the available *commands* are:

- **/AREAS** *name*—Specifies the specific security areas to apply, where *name* is:
  - **FILESTORE**—Local file security
  - **GROUP_MGMT**—Group settings
  - **REGKEYS**—Local registry security
  - **SECURITYPOLICY**—Local or domain policy
  - **SERVICES**—Local services security
  - **USER_RIGHTS**—User's rights and privileges
- **/CFG** *filename*—Valid with **/DB**; specifies the security template to be imported
- **/DB** *filename*—Required; specifies the database containing the template to be applied
- **/OVERWRITE**—Valid with **/CFG**; specifies to overwrite templates in the database
- **/LOG** *logpath*—Specifies the log file to use
- **/VERBOSE**—Specifies to include more detail to the log or output
- **/QUIET**—Runs the analysis with no screen or log output

Fixing Security on a Windows NT

When you upgrade from Windows NT to Windows 2000, the security settings on the system are not modified. This means none of the intended Windows 2000 security settings are implemented. To apply the Windows 2000 basic security settings, start a command prompt and enter the following:

```
Secedit /configure
/db "%WINDIR%\Security\Database\basicwk.sdb"
/cfg "%WINDIR%\Security\Templates\basicwk.inf"
/log "%WINDIR%\Security\Logs\basicwk.log"
/verbose
```

NOTE: *The code above must be placed on one line.*

Exporting Security Settings

The basic syntax to export security settings using SECEDIT is as follows:

```
secedit /export /commands
```

Here, the available **commands** are:

- **/AREAS** *name*—Specifies the specific security areas to export, where *name* is:
    - **FILESTORE**—Local file security
    - **GROUP_MGMT**—Group settings
    - **REGKEYS**—Local registry security
    - **SECURITYPOLICY**—Local or domain policy
    - **SERVICES**—Local services security
    - **USER_RIGHTS**—User's rights and privileges
- **/DB** *filename*—Required; specifies the database containing the template to be exported
- **/CFG** *filename*—Valid with **/DB**; specifies the security template to export to
- **/MERGEDPOLICY**—Valid with **/CFG**; specifies to overwrite templates in the database
- **/LOG** *logpath*—Specifies the log file to use
- **/VERBOSE**—Specifies to include more detail to the log or output
- **/QUIET**—Runs the analysis with no screen or log output

Here is an example of how to export the local registry security area to the registry template:

```
Secedit /export /mergedpolicy
/db "%WINDIR%\Security\Database\security.sdb"
/cfg "%WINDIR%\Security\Templates\registry.inf"
/log "%WINDIR%\Security\Logs\registry.log"
/verbose
```

Using the NET ACCOUNTS Command

The built-in NET command has an ACCOUNTS parameter to modify the password and logon requirements for the local computer or a specified domain. The basic syntax of the NET ACCOUNTS utility is:

```
NET ACCOUNTS /commands
```

Here, the available *commands* are:

- **/DOMAIN**—If used, performs the specified operations on the primary domain controller of the current domain; otherwise, performs the operations on the local computer.

- **/FORCELOGOFF:***min*—Sets the number of minutes before a user session is terminated where *min* is either the number of minutes or **NO** to specify no forced logoff.

- **/MAXPWAGE:***days*—Specifies the maximum duration a password is valid where *days* is either the number of days (1 through 49,710) or **UNLIMITED** to set no maximum time.

- **/MINPWAGE:***days*—Specifies the minimum duration before a user can change his or her password, where *days* is either the number of days (1 through 49,710) or **UNLIMITED** to set no time limit. This value must be less than the **MAXPWAGE**.

- **/MINPWLEN:***length*—Specifies the minimum password length.

- **/SYNC**—Forces backup domain controllers to synchronize their password and logon requirements with those set on the primary domain controller.

- **/UNIQUEPW:***changes*—Specifies that users cannot repeat the same password for the specified amount of password changes (0 through 24).

For example, to modify the logon and password requirements using the NET ACCOUNTS command, you would enter the following command:

```
NET ACCOUNTS /DOMAIN /MAXPWAGE:30 /MINPWAGE:UNLIMITED
/MINPWLEN:14
```

NOTE: *The highlighted code above must be placed on one line.*

TIP: *When the administrator has specified a forced logoff, the user receives a warning that a domain controller will force a logoff shortly.*

Managing Security through ADSI

Active Directory Services Interfaces provides another medium to control security. In Chapter 9, you learned how to manage shares, groups, and user accounts through ADSI. In the following section, you will learn how to manage security through ADSI.

Setting the Minimum Password Length

For maximum security under a Windows NT Domain, you should set your domain password minimum length to the maximum value, 14. Under a Windows 2000/2003 domain, passwords should be longer than 15 characters. To set the minimum password length for the domain using ADSI, create and then execute a WSH script containing the following:

```
On Error Resume Next
Set objDomain = GetObject("WinNT://Domain")
objDomain.Put "MinPasswordLength", max
objDomain.SetInfo
```

Here, **domain** is the name of the domain, and **max** is the maximum password length to set.

Setting the Password Age

For maximum security, you should implement a policy to force users to change their password regularly. To set the password age for the domain using ADSI, create and then execute a WSH script containing the following:

```
On Error Resume Next
Set objDomain = GetObject("WinNT://Domain")
objDomain.Put "MinPasswordAge", Min * (60*60*24)
objDomain.Put "MaxPasswordAge", Max * (60*60*24)
objDomain.SetInfo
```

Here, **domain** is the name of the domain; **min** is the minimum duration in days before a user can change his or her password; and **max** is the maximum duration in days a password is valid. The formula 60 x 60 x 24 is the calculation from seconds to days (60 seconds x 60 minutes x 24 hours).

Setting Unique Password Changes

For maximum security, you should implement a policy to force users to select passwords different from their previous passwords. To set the unique password duration for the domain using ADSI, create and then execute a WSH script containing the following:

```
On Error Resume Next
Set objDomain = GetObject("WinNT://Domain")
objDomain.Put "PasswordHistoryLength",
min objDomain.SetInfo
```

Here, ***domain*** is the name of the domain, and ***min*** is the minimum number of passwords used before a user can repeat that previous password. The formula 60 x 60 x 24 is the calculation from seconds to days (60 seconds x 60 minutes x 24 hours).

Setting the Account Lockout Policy

For maximum security, you should implement a policy to lock out accounts after a certain number of bad attempts. To implement an account lockout policy using ADSI, create and then execute a WSH script containing the following:

```
On Error Resume Next
Set objDomain = GetObject("WinNT://Domain")
objDomain.Put "MaxBadPasswordAllowed", Max
objDomain.SetInfo
```

Here, ***domain*** is the name of the domain. The formula 60 x 60 x 24 is the calculation from seconds to days (60 seconds x 60 minutes x 24 hours).

Searching for Locked-Out Accounts

It's good practice to regularly search the domain for locked-out accounts. To search for locked-out accounts using ADSI, create and then execute a WSH script containing the following:

```
On Error Resume Next
Set objDomain = GetObject("WinNT://Domain")

For Each Item in objDomain
  If Item.Class = "User" Then
   If Item.IsAccountLocked = "True" Then
     Wscript.Echo "Name: " & Item.Name & VBlf & _
     "Bad Password Attempts: " & _
     Item.BadPasswordAttempts & VBlf & _
     "Last Login: " & Item.LastLogin
   End If
  End If
Next
```

Here, ***domain*** is the name of the domain.

Related solution:	Found on page:
Unlocking a User Account	213

Renaming the Administrator Account

Windows creates a default administrative account called "Administrator" to be the master account for that system. This account cannot be deleted, but should be renamed to foil hackers attempting to gain access through this account. To rename the administrator account using ADSI, create and then execute a WSH script containing the following:

```
On Error Resume Next

Set objDomain = GetObject("WinNT://Computer")
Set objUser = ObjDomain.GetObject("User", "Administrator")
objDomain.MoveHere objUser.AdsPath, Name
```

Here, **computer** is the name of the computer holding the account, and **name** is the new name to give the account.

TIP: *You can use this script to rename any account simply by replacing the word ADMINISTRATOR with the user account name desired.*

Searching for Unused Accounts

It's good practice to regularly search the domain for accounts that have either been logged on for a long duration of time or have not logged on in a long time. To search for unused accounts using ADSI, create and then execute a WSH script containing the following:

```
On Error Resume Next
Days = amount
Set objDomain = GetObject("WinNT://Domain")

For Each Item in objDomain
  If Item.Class="User" Then
    DUR = DateDiff("D", Item.LastLogin, Date)
    If DUR > Days Then
      Wscript.Echo "Name: " & Item.Name & VBlf & _
      "Account Disabled: " & Item.AccountDisabled & VBlf & _
      "Last Login: " & Item.LastLogin & VBlf & _
      "Amount of days: " & DUR
    End If
  End If
Next
```

Here, **domain** is the name of the domain to search, and **amount** is the least number of days since the last logon.

Enabling the Windows Firewall

Windows XP Service Pack 2 introduced the Windows firewall. This software component prevents others from talking to your computer unless you talked to them first. The purpose is to allow you to communicate with any site and computer you wish, but to prevent uninvited, malicious activity directed at your computer. To enable the Windows firewall, create and then execute a WSH script containing the following:

```
Enabled = EnableFirewall(FALSE)
Wscript.Echo "Firewall Enabled: " & Enabled

Function EnableFirewall(Enable)
   On Error Resume Next
   Set Firewall = CreateObject("HNetCfg.FwMgr")
   Set Policy = Firewall.LocalPolicy.CurrentProfile
   Policy.FirewallEnabled = Enable

   EnableFirewall = Policy.FirewallEnabled
End Function
```

Enabling Automatic Windows Updates

Keeping systems up to date is a commonly forgotten aspect of security. Outdated systems may be running exploitable code that can allow others to steal data or corrupt, crash, or even control your system. Through a Windows policy, we can set Windows to automatically download and install Windows updates while also preventing users from changing these settings. To enable automatic Windows updates, create and then execute a WSH script containing the following:

```
Set WSHShell = CreateObject("wscript.Shell")
RegKey = "HKEY_LOCAL_MACHINE\SOFTWARE\Policies\" & _
   "Microsoft\Windows\WindowsUpdate\AU\"

WSHShell.RegWrite RegKey & _
   "NoAutoUpdate", 0, "REG_DWORD"
WSHShell.RegWrite RegKey & _
   "AUOptions", 4, "REG_DWORD"
WSHShell.RegWrite RegKey & _
   "ScheduledInstallDay", 7, "REG_DWORD"
WSHShell.RegWrite RegKey & _
   "ScheduledInstallTime", 3, "REG_DWORD"
```

11. Security

Here, we have enabled updates (NoAutoUpdate=0) to automatically download and install (AUOptions=4) every Saturday (Scheduled InstallDay=7) at 3 AM (ScheduledInstallTime=3). The full options for the script above are as follows:

- **NoAutoUpdate**—0 to enable or 1 to disable automatic updates

- **AUOptions**—Determines how updates should be downloaded and installed depending on the selected value:
  - **1**—Automatic Updates are disabled
  - **2**—Notify to download and install
  - **3**—Automatically download but notify to install
  - **4**—Automatically download and install

- **ScheduledInstallDate**—The day to install updates depending on the selected value:
  - **1**—Sunday
  - **2**—Monday
  - **3**—Tuesday
  - **4**—Wednesday
  - **5**—Thursday
  - **6**—Friday
  - **7**—Saturday

- **ScheduledInstallTime**—Hour of the day (0-23) to install updates (0 = Midnight, 5 = 5AM, and 14 = 2PM)

Using the Microsoft Script Encoder

The Microsoft Script Encoder allows you to protect your scripts using a simple encoding scheme. This encoding scheme is not intended to prevent advanced cracking techniques, but to merely make your scripts unreadable to the average user. The default supported file types are asa, asp, cdx, htm, html, js, sct, and vbs. The basic syntax of the script encoder is as follows:

```
SCRENC inputfile outputfile
```

Here, ***inputfile*** is the file to encode and ***outputfile*** is the encoded result. Microsoft Script Encoder supports many command-line parameters, as shown in Table 11.1.

WARNING! *Always back up your scripts before encoding them. Once a script is overwritten with an encoded version, there is no way to return it to its original state.*

Table 11.1   Microsoft Script Encoder parameters.

Parameter	Description
/E *extension*	Specifies a known extension for unrecognized input file types
/F	Specifies to overwrite the input file with the encoded version
/L *language*	Specifies to use the scripting language Jscript or VBScript
/S	Specifies to work in silent mode
/X1	Specifies not to include to @language directive to ASP files

Previous Security Scripts

Some of the scripts included in previous chapters can increase your system security. These scripts are shown in Table 11.2.

Table 11.2   Security scripts.

Chapter	Script
Chapter 6	Disabling 8.3 File Naming
Chapter 6	Disabling the Lock Workstation Button
Chapter 6	Disabling the Change Password Button
Chapter 6	Disabling the Logoff Button
Chapter 6	Modifying the Registry with REGINI.EXE
Chapter 7	Managing NTFS Encryption
Chapter 7	Modifying NTFS Permissions
Chapter 9	Changing the Local Administrator Password

11. Security

Chapter 12

Logging and Alerting

(continued)

In Brief

The purpose of logging is to record the status of an operation generated by the system or an application. Along with many scripts and applications, Windows 2000/XP/2003 has a built-in method to log events and errors. Managing event logs across an enterprise can become an involved process. Third-party utilities such as Dorian Software's Event Archiver allow you to read, write, modify, and archive event logs and entries. Although these utilities are available at a modest price, this chapter will show you how to access and control the event log through simple scripts, for free.

Logs provide a good method of recording events, but they are only as good as the time and frequency with which you check them. Alerting is the method of notifying a user when an event occurs. In this chapter, you will learn the various methods to create alerts to keep you informed of the many events that occur in your environment.

Inside The Event Log

Windows 2000/XP/2003 includes a built-in event-logging system known as the event log. Before an interaction with the event log is performed, a request is sent to the Service Control Manager (SCM). SCM is controlled by *%WINDIR%*\System32\SERVICES.EXE. When the system first boots up, the event log service is started and the event log files are opened. Once the service receives the request, it processes it by storing or modifying an event in the proper event log.

Types of Logs

The event log is divided into three categories:

- *Application Log (AppEvent.Evt)*—Stores application and system events, such as application errors

- *Security Log (SecEvent.Evt)*—Stores audited security events, such as clearing the event log

- *System Log (SysEvent.Evt)*—Stores operating-system-related events, such as creating a new user

These logs are stored in a proprietary binary format and reside in the *%WINDIR%*\System32\Config directory. Although all users can view the application and system logs, only administrators can view and clear the security event log.

NOTE: *The event log files cannot merely be copied and opened on another system. When the system opens the event logs, it modifies the file headers and doesn't reset the header until the file is closed. To copy the event log, use the Save Log As option from the File menu of the Event Viewer.*

The Event Viewer

The Event Viewer is a built-in Windows 2000/XP/2003 tool to easily view the three separate event log files (see Figure 12.1). The Event Viewer executable (EVENTVWR.EXE) resides in the *%WINDIR%*\System32 directory. To start the Event Viewer, open Administrative Tools and run the Event Viewer. From within the Event Viewer, you can view, delete, archive, or import an entire event log or entry. The most common use of the event log is to troubleshoot system errors, such as service failures.

NOTE: *The executable called EVENTVWR.EXE is actually just a pointer to the MMC snap-in EVENTVWR.MSC.*

Event Log Entries

Event log entries consist of an event ID that categorizes the type of event, and an event description that is the actual error or event text. The event type specifies the following classification of recorded events:

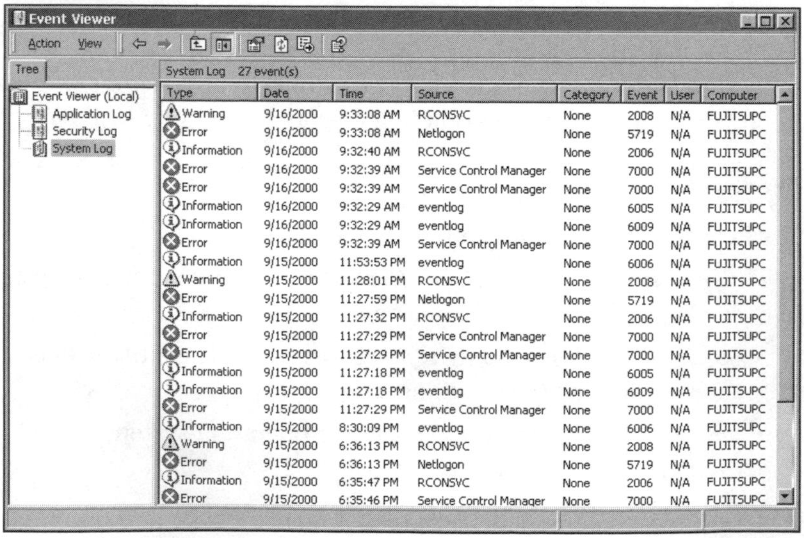

Figure 12.1   The Windows 2000 Event viewer.

- *Error*—Indicates critical errors and corruption of data
- *Failure Audit*—Combined with auditing, indicates a failed security event, such as a bad password
- *Information*—Indicates a successful operation, such as a successful driver load
- *Success Audit*—Combined with auditing, indicates a successful security event, such as a successful logon
- *Warning*—Indicates a non-critical warning, such as a failed attempt to obtain a browse list

Other items logged with each event are:

- *Computer*—The name of the target computer
- *Date*—Date the event was written
- *Source Type*—The source of the event
- *Time*—Time the event was written
- *User Name*—The currently logged-on user

Event Log Etiquette

The event log is a logging system that stores critical and important system and application events. The original intent of this log system was only for the system and applications to write events. Some systems might be set up to overwrite events or to crash the system when the event log is full. Storing routine messages like "Logon script completed successfully" might overwrite critical events or cause a system to crash because the event log is full.

Understanding NetBIOS

Logging provides a method to record events, and alerting provides a method to send event messages to users. A common method of sending messages over a network is to use Network Basic Input Output System (NetBIOS). NetBIOS is a non-routable interface that allows various types of computers to communicate over the local area network (LAN). NetBIOS was created by IBM and Sytek during the mid-1980s and has since become an industry standard for network communication. Microsoft Windows currently implements NetBIOS on the following protocols: NetBIOS Enhanced User Interface (NetBEUI), Internetwork Packet Exchange/Sequenced Packet Exchange (IPX/SPX), and Transmission Control Protocol/Internet Protocol (TCP/IP).

12. Logging and Alerting

NOTE: *A common use of NetBIOS is the Network Neighborhood.*

NetBIOS Communication Modes

NetBIOS contains two modes of communication: session or datagram. Session mode establishes a reliable channel between two systems, and uses error checking to ensure proper data transfer. Datagram mode is a one-way communication method that transmits small messages without error checking. This type of communication is commonly referred to as connectionless communication. A datagram is a container used to transmit data across a network.

NOTE: *The term* datagram *is interchangeable with the term* packet.

Windows includes the ability to send command-line messages to other users or computers through NetBIOS using a utility called NET.EXE. These messages are sent in datagrams to other NetBIOS computer or user names. NetBIOS messages have a restricted size of 128 characters, whereas NetBIOS names are restricted to 15 characters (with a 16th hidden character used by the operating system).

TIP: *Windows 2000/XP/2003 monitors these messages through the Messenger Service. If the system experiences errors while transmitting or receiving NetBIOS messages, you should first check the Messenger Service.*

NOTE: *Windows XP Service Pack 2 disables the messenger service which prevents the sending and receiving of messages via the NET.EXE utility. This is designed to prevent "messenger spam," where outsiders will bombard your machine with messages. If you are properly protected from "messenger spam" (i.e., you have an external firewall), you can enable this service.*

Understanding MAPI

MAPI (Messaging Application Program Interface) is an interface that provides a standard method for applications to send email. MAPI includes a standard set of functions (such as logging on, creating new messages, reading messages, etc.) that developers can call directly in their applications using C or C++. MAPI is a built-in part of Windows 2000/XP/2003. Simple MAPI is a slimmed-down version of MAPI that can be accessed using C, C++, Visual Basic, or Visual Basic for Applications (VBA).

The Scripting Advantage

All the scripting methods (except for AutoIt) have an almost balanced advantage in handling the tasks for this chapter. Through included or downloadable utilities, shell scripting has full access to logging and messaging. KiXtart includes a few built in methods that allow you to manage event logs, text logs, and even send messages. Windows Script Host also has its fair share of logging and event log methods. Through COM, WSH can also send out messages using Outlook or MAPI. While Windows Script Host and KiXtart can access WMI through COM, due to size limitations of this book and the popularity of the scripting language, this chapter will provide COM examples in Windows Script Host only. (It should be simple to convert the scripts to KiXtart.) Finally, AutoIt is not appropriate and is not discussed in this chapter.

A Word of Caution

This chapter contains many scripting examples to control logs and send messages. You should take caution in arbitrarily clearing logs as you may need the information in the future (such as from a Security log). It may even be a violation of your company's technology policy to clear logs without prior consent. In addition, accidentally spamming your company with one of these scripts could be detrimental to your career path. As with all scripts, you should first test each script in an isolated testing environment to ensure that the script produces the desired results before using it in a production environment.

Immediate Solutions

Using Logs with Shell Scripting

Currently, shell scripting contains no built-in methods to access the event log. Fortunately, you can create your own text logs or use resource kit utilities to access the event log.

Writing to Text Logs

The simplest way to log events in shell scripting is to append text to a text log. The basic syntax to append text to a text log is as follows:

```
Command >> textlog
```

Here, ***command*** is either an echoed statement or the output of a command, and ***textlog*** is the complete path and file name of the log file. Here is a quick example to send a message to a log file called log.txt:

```
@Echo Off
Echo This is a test to log an event. >> log.txt
```

TIP: *To clear the log, simply delete the file (**DEL textlog**).*

Related solution:	*Found on page:*
Appending Text Files	67

Writing to Text Logs with the Date and Time

Recording the date and time within a log is essential to determine the exact moment of a particular event. To place the date and time into an environment variable, create and then execute a shell script containing the following:

```
@Echo Off
For /F "Delims= Tokens=1" %%I in ('Date /T')
Do Set Dtime=%%I
```

```
For /F "Delims= Tokens=1" %%I in ('Time /T')
Do Set Dtime=%Dtime%%%I
```

NOTE: *The highlighted code above must be placed on one line.*

To log an event using the date and time, create and then execute a shell script containing the following:

```
Call setdtime.bat
Echo %Dtime% message >> textlog
```

Here, **message** is the alert message to log, and **textlog** is the complete path and file name of the log file.

TIP: *To clear the date and time variable (**dtime**), add the following line at the end of your entire script:* SET %Dtime%=.

Using LOGEVENT to Write to the Event Log

LOGEVENT.EXE is a Windows 2000 resource kit utility to write events to the event log from the command line. The basic syntax of LOGEVENT.EXE is as follows:

```
logevent -m \\computer -s
type -c category -r source -e id -t time "message"
```

NOTE: *The highlighted code above must be placed on one line.*

Here, **computer** is the name of a remote system to connect to; **source** specifies the origin of the event; **id** indicates the entry ID number (0-65535); **category** is the number for the desired category; **message** is the text to include in the entry; **time** is the amount of seconds the system waits before an exit; and **type** specifies one of the following event types:

- **E**—Error
- **F**—Failure
- **I**—Information
- **S**—Success
- **W**—Warning

12. Logging and Alerting

TIP: *LogEvent will accept either the full name or the first letter of the event type. Example, you can specify **-S ERROR** or **-S E**.*

Here is an example of how to write an event to the event log:

```
logevent -S ERROR -C 3 -E 10 -R ShellScript "Some Event Text"
```

Using EVENTCREATE to Write to the Event Log

EVENTCREATE.EXE is a built-in Windows XP/2003 utility to write events to the event log from the command line. The basic syntax of EVENTCREATE.EXE is as follows:

```
eventcreate /s computer /u domain\username /p password /t type /l
logname /so source /Id eventid /d "message"
```

NOTE: *The highlighted code above must be placed on one line.*

Here, **computer** is the name of a remote system to connect to; **domain\username** and **password** specifies the credentials to use when writing the event; **source** specifies the origin of the event; **eventid** indicates the entry ID number (0-65535); **logname** is the name of the event log to write to; **message** is the text to include in the entry; and **type** specifies one of the following event types:

- Error
- Information
- Warning

Here is an example of how to write an event to the event log:

```
eventcreate /t ERROR /l application /so SHELLSCRIPT /Id 10 /d
"Some Event Text"
```

Using Dumpel to Back Up the Event Log

Dumpel is a Windows 2000 resource kit utility that allows you to back up an event log in text format from the command line. The basic syntax for using Dumpel is as follows:

```
Dumpel -F textfile -L logtype commands
```

Here, **textfile** is the complete path and file name to back up the event log to; **logtype** is the type of log to back up (Application, System, or Security); and **commands** are any of the following optional commands:

- **-D** *days*—Displays only the last number of *days* specified where *days* must be larger than zero

- **-E** *ID*—Displays only the specified event *ID*s where *ID* may be up to ten various event IDs

- **-M** *name*—Displays only the events with the *name* specified

- **-R**—Specifies to filter by sources of records

- **-S** *computer*—Specifies the *computer* to connect to

- **-T**—Separates values using tabs as opposed to spaces

To back up security log events from the past ten days using Dumpel, start a command prompt and enter the following:

```
Dumpel -F "C:\DUMP.TXT" -L "Security" -D 10
```

Using Logs with KiXtart

KiXtart provides several methods to write text logs and to access the event log. Through KiXtart, you can write to, back up, and clear the event logs.

Writing to Text Logs

Text logs allow all users, regardless of operating system, to write, modify, and read logged events. To log an event to a text log, create and then execute a KiXtart script containing the following:

```
$RCODE = Open(1, "textlog", 5)
$RCODE = WriteLine(1, @Date + " " + @Time
+ "message" + Chr(13) + Chr(10))
$RCODE = Close(1)
```

NOTE: *The highlighted code above must be placed on one line.*

Here, *message* is the alert message to log, and *textlog* is the complete path and file name of the log file. Notice that the first line opens and sets the text log to file number 1, the next line writes to file number 1, and then the final line closes file number 1. All three steps are necessary to write to a text file. Failure to include the **close** statement will result in wasted memory space.

TIP: *To clear the log, simply delete the file (**DEL textlog**).*

Related solution:	Found on page:
Appending Text Files	67

Writing an Event to the Event Log

LogEvent is a KiXtart command that allows you to write entries to the event log. The basic syntax for using the **LogEvent** command is as follows:

```
LOGEVENT (type, ID, event, computer, source)
```

NOTE: *All events are stored in the application log and cannot be redirected to the system or security logs.*

Here, **ID** is the entry ID number to assign; **event** is the text event entry; **computer** is an optional parameter specifying the name of a remote system to write events to; **source** specifies the event source; and **type** specifies one of the following event types:

- **0**—SUCCESS
- **1**—ERROR
- **2**—WARNING
- **4**—INFORMATION
- **8**—AUDIT_SUCCESS
- **16**—AUDIT_FAILURE

To write an event to the event log using KiXtart, proceed as follows:

1. Create a new directory to store all files included in this example.
2. Download and extract the latest version of KiXtart, from **www.kixtart.org**, to the new directory.
3. Select Start|Run and enter "kix32 *scriptfile*."

Here, **scriptfile** is the full path of the new directory from step 1 and file name of a script file that contains the following:

```
$RCODE = LogEvent(0, 10, "This stuff is easy!",
"", "New Event")
If @ERROR <> 0 or $RCODE <> 0
```

```
    ? "Error writing event"
EndIf
```

NOTE: *The highlighted code above must be placed on one line.*

Backing Up the Event Log

BackUpEventLog is a KiXtart command that allows you to back up the event log in the standard event log binary format. The basic syntax for using the **BackUpEventLog** command is as follows:

```
BackUpEventLog ("logtype", "textfile")
```

Here, **logtype** is the type of log to back up (Application, System, or Security), and **textfile** is the complete path and file name to back up the event log to. To back up the security log to a file called Backup.evt, create and then execute a KiXtart script containing the following:

```
$RCODE = BackUpEventLog ("Security", "C:\BACKUP.EVT")
If @ERROR <> 0 or $RCODE <> 0
    ? "Error backing up log"
EndIf
```

Clearing the Event Log

ClearEventLog is a KiXtart command that allows you to clear the contents of an event log. The basic syntax for using the **ClearEventLog** command is as follows:

```
ClearEventLog ("logtype")
```

TIP: *You can clear the event log of a remote computer by including the UNC path before the log type, for example:* `ClearEventLog ("\\computer\Security")`.

Here, **logtype** is the type of log to clear (Application, System, or Security). To clear the event log, create and then execute a KiXtart script containing the following:

```
$RCODE = ClearEventLog ("Security")
If @ERROR <> 0 or $RCODE <> 0
    ? "Error clearing the event log"
EndIf
```

Using Logs with Windows Script Host

Windows Script Host allows you to write events to a text log and the event log using simple script files. This allows you to store critical events in the event log, while storing less severe events to a text log.

NOTE: *Windows Script Host does not contain any methods to read or modify events in the event log.*

Writing to Text Logs

Text logs provide an easy way to record events and share the file with others, regardless of operating system. To log an event to a text log, create and then execute a KiXtart script containing the following:

```
On Error Resume Next
Set FSO = CreateObject("Scripting.FileSystemObject")
txtlog = "textlog"

If FSO.FileExists(txtlog) Then
   Set LogFile = FSO.OpenTextFile(txtlog, 8)
Else
   Set LogFile = FSO.CreateTextFile(txtlog, True)
End If

LogFile.WriteLine Date & " " & Time & " message"
LogFile.Close
```

Here, *message* is the alert message to log, and *textlog* is the complete path and file name of the log file.

Related solution:	*Found on page:*
Appending Text Files	67

Writing an Event to the Event Log

You can use Wscript.Shell's **LogEvent** method to write events to the event log. The basic syntax for using the **LogEvent** method is as follows:

```
LogEvent(type,event,computer)
```

NOTE: *All events are stored in the application log, and cannot be redirected to the system or security logs.*

Here, *event* is the text event entry; *computer* is an optional parameter specifying the name of a remote system to write events to; and *type* specifies one of the following event types:

- **SUCCESS (0)**
- **ERROR (1)**
- **WARNING (2)**
- **INFORMATION (4)**
- **AUDIT_SUCCESS (8)**
- **AUDIT_FAILURE (16)**

TIP: You can use the corresponding numbers, as opposed to key words, to specify event types.

When you use **LogEvent** to create an event log entry, the following is recorded:

- **Category**—Logged as None
- **Computer**—The name of the target computer
- **Date**—Date the event was written
- **Event**—Logged as 0
- **Source Type**—Logged as WSH
- **Time**—Time the event was written
- **Type**—Type of event entry
- **User Name**—Logged as N/A

Here is a subroutine to write an event:

```
Sub WriteLog(Ltype, Ldesc)
  On Error Resume Next
  Set SHELL = CreateObject("WScript.Shell")

  LEvent = SHELL.LogEvent(Ltype, Ldesc)
  If Err.Number <> 0 Or LEvent = False Then
    Wscript.Echo "Error writing event"
  End If
End Sub
```

NOTE: Because Windows 9x does not contain an event log, all written events will be stored in %WINDIR%\wsh.log.

Here, ***ltype*** is the type of event, and ***ldesc*** is the event text to write. Using the following command combined with the subroutine above will write a success event to the event log:

```
WriteLog 0, "This stuff is cool!"
```

Accessing the Event Log Using WMI

The **Win32_NTLogEvent** class manages the event logs on Windows 2000/XP/2003 systems. Through this class, you can view, write, modify, delete, and back up the event log through simple scripts.

Backing Up an Event Log in Binary Mode

The **BackupEventLog** method allows you to back up an event log to a file in standard event log binary format. To create a backup of the event log in standard event log binary format using WMI, create and then execute a WSH script containing the following:

```
On Error Resume Next
Set FSO = CreateObject("Scripting.FileSystemObject")
LogType = InputBox("Enter the log to backup", "Log Type"
, "application")

BFile = InputBox("Enter file to backup to", "Backup File"
, "C:\BACKUP.LOG")
    If FSO.FileExists(BFile) Then
        FSO.DeleteFile BFile
    End If
Set EventLog = GetObject("winmgmts:{impersonationLevel=
impersonate,(Backup)}").ExecQuery("select * from
Win32_NTEventLogFile where LogfileName='" & LogType & "'")
For each Entry in EventLog
  Entry.BackupEventLog BFile
Next
Wscript.Echo "Done"
```

NOTE: *The highlighted code above must be placed on one line. The **(Backup)** privilege is explicitly included in the example above to allow you to use the **BackUpEventLog** method.*

Here, ***LogType*** is the event log to back up (application, security, or system), and ***Bfile*** is the complete path and filename to back up to.

Backing Up the Entire Event Log in Text Mode

In the previous sections, you learned that the **BackUpEventLog** method and the Dumpel utility back up the event log to a text file in binary format. Although this format conforms to the standard event log storage format, it does not allow you to easily view the contents of the backup. To create a backup of the event log in plain-text, tab-delimited format using WMI, create and then execute a WSH script containing the following:

```
On Error Resume Next
Set EventLog = GetObject("winmgmts:{impersonationLevel=
impersonate}").ExecQuery("select * from Win32_NTLogEvent")

Set FSO = CreateObject("Scripting.FileSystemObject")
Set txt = FSO.CreateTextFile("textfile", True)
For each Entry in EventLog
  If Len(Entry.Message) > 0 Then
    For x = 1 to Len(Entry.Message)
      Char = Mid(Entry.Message,x,1)
      If Asc(Char) = 10 Then
        MSG = MSG & " "
      ElseIf Asc(Char) <> 13 Then
        MSG = MSG & Char
      End If
    Next

    EDate = Mid(Entry.TimeGenerated,5,2) & "/" & _
      Mid(Entry.TimeGenerated,7,2) & "/" &  _
      Mid(Entry.TimeGenerated,1,4)
    ETime = Mid(Entry.TimeGenerated,9,2) & ":" & _
      Mid(Entry.TimeGenerated,11,2) & ":" & _
      Mid(Entry.TimeGenerated,13,2)
    ETime = FormatDateTime(ETime,3)

    IfIsNull(Entry.User) Then
      User = "N/A"
    Else
      User = Entry.User
    End If

    IfIsNull(Entry.CategoryString) Then
      Category = "none"
    Else
      Category =Entry.CategoryString
    End If
```

```
      EVT = Entry.LogFile & VBtab & _
      Entry.Type & VBtab & _
      EDate & VBtab & _
      ETime & VBtab & _
      Entry.SourceName & VBtab & _
      Category & VBtab & _
      Entry.EventCode & VBtab & _
      User & VBtab & _
      Entry.ComputerName & VBtab & _
      MSG
      txt.writeline EVT

      EVT = Null
      Char = Null
      MSG = Null
   End If
Next
txt.close
Wscript.echo "Done"
```

NOTE: *The highlighted code above must be placed on one line.*

Here, ***textfile*** is the complete path and file name to back up the event log to.

Clearing an Event Log

The **ClearEventLog** method allows you to clear individual event log entries. To clear the entire contents of an event log using WMI, create and then execute a WSH script containing the following:

```
On Error Resume Next
LogType = InputBox("Enter the log to clear", "Clear Log"
, "application")

Set EventLog = GetObject("winmgmts:{impersonationLevel=
impersonate}").ExecQuery("select * from
Win32_NTEventLogFile where LogfileName='" & LogType & "'")
For each Entry in EventLog
   Entry.ClearEventlog()
Next
Wscript.Echo "Done"
```

NOTE: *The highlighted code above must be placed on one line.*

Here, ***LogType*** is the event log to clear (Application, Security, or System).

Sending Alerts Using Shell Scripting

Shell scripting does not include a method to send alerts from the command line. Microsoft Windows includes the NET.EXE utility to allow you to send messages to users or computers over the network.

Sending Alerts to a Single User or Computer

To send a message over the network, start a command prompt and enter the following:

```
NET SEND name message
```

NOTE: *NetBIOS messages have a maximum limit of 128 characters.*

Here, ***message*** is the message to send, and ***name*** is the NetBIOS name of a computer or user ID.

Sending Alerts to Multiple Users and Computers

You can also use the asterisk symbol (*) to send messages to all computers on the local network:

```
Net Send * message
```

Here, ***message*** is the message to send. As opposed to specifying a name or asterisk, you can use one of the following commands to send messages to multiple users or computers:

- **/DOMAIN**—Sends a message to the local domain

- **/DOMAIN:*name***—Sends a message to a specified domain

- **/USERS**—Sends messages to users connected to the server

Here is an example to send a ***message*** to the JESSEWEB domain:

```
Net Send /DOMAIN:JESSEWEB message
```

NOTE: *Sending messages to the entire network or domain will not only utilize a good portion of your network's bandwidth but it is also annoying to all the other users.*

Sending Alerts to Specific Multiple Users and Computers

Although the **Net Send** command contains methods to send messages to multiple users, it does not contain a method to send messages to specific user and computer names. To send an alert to an exact list of user or computer names using shell scripting, create and then execute a shell script containing the following:

```
@Echo Off
For /F %%N in (textfile) Do (Echo Sending Message to
%%N... & Net Send %%N Message)
```

NOTE: The highlighted code above must be placed on one line.

Here, **textfile** is the name of a text file with each line containing a user or computer name, and **message** is the message to send.

Sending Alerts Using KiXtart

KiXtart includes a command called **SendMessage** that allows you to send NetBIOS messages to users or computers over the network. This command transports messages in a similar fashion to the Microsoft NET.EXE utility.

Sending Alerts to a Single User or Computer

To send an alert to a single user, create and then execute a KiXtart script containing the following:

```
$RCODE = SENDMESSAGE ("name", "message")
If @ERROR <> 0 or $RCODE <> 0
  ? "Error sending message"
EndIf
```

Here, **name** is the user or computer name to send a **message** to.

Sending Alerts to Multiple Users or Computers

To send an alert to multiple users, create and then execute a KiXtart script containing the following:

```
$COUNT = 4 ; User Array Count
DIM $NAME[$COUNT] ; User Array
$NAME[0] = "name1"
$NAME[1] = "computer1"
$NAME[2] = "computer2"
$NAME[3] = "name2"

$NETMESSAGE = "This is a test message."

$Index = 0
WHILE $Index <> $COUNT
  $RCODE = SENDMESSAGE ($NAME[$Index], $NETMESSAGE)
  If @ERROR <> 0 or $RCODE <> 0
    ? "Error sending message"
  EndIf
  $Index = $Index + 1
LOOP
```

Here, **$count** is the size of the array. This is the number of users you want to send messages to. This number must exactly match the number of users that you send messages to, or an error will result. **$name** is the array that holds the user or computer names to send messages to, and **$netmessage** is the message to send.

NOTE: *The array size is limited to the amount of memory the system has. Remember, the contents of an array start at 0, not at 1. Using versions older than KiXtart 3.62 will cause a script error when attempting to create an array.*

Sending Alerts Using Windows Script Host

Windows Script Host does not include any methods to send messages to users or computers. Through Windows Script Host, you can call upon the NET.EXE utility or use automation to send messages.

Sending an Alert to a Single User or Computer

To send an alert to a single user or computer, create and then execute a WSH script containing the following:

```
On Error Resume Next
Set Shell = CreateObject("Wscript.Shell")

RCV = "name"
MSG = "message"
```

```
SHELL.Run "Net Send " & Name & " " & MSG, 0, False
```

Here, **RCV** is the user or computer **name** to send a message to, and **MSG** is the **message** to send.

Sending Alerts to Multiple Users or Computers

To send an alert to multiple user or computer names, create and then execute a WSH script containing the following:

```
On Error Resume Next
Set Shell = CreateObject("Wscript.Shell")

Dim Name(2)
Name(0) = "name1"
Name(1) = "name2"

MSG = "message"

For X = 0 to UBound(Name)
    SHELL.Run "Net Send " & Name(X) & " " & MSG, 0, False
Next
```

Here, **Name** is the array that holds the user or computer names to send messages to. The size of this array should be equal to the number of users or computers you want to send messages to. **MSG** is the **message** to send.

Sending an Email Using Outlook Automation

To send an email using Outlook automation, create and then execute a WSH script containing the following:

```
On Error Resume Next
RCP = "emailaddress"
SUB = "subject"
MSG = "message"

Set Outlook = CreateObject("Outlook.Application")
Set MAPI = Outlook.GetNameSpace("MAPI")
Set NewMail = Outlook.CreateItem(0)
NewMail.Subject = SUB
NewMail.Body = MSG
NewMail.Recipients.Add RCP

MAPI.Logon "profile", "password"
```

```
NewMail.Send
MAPI.Logoff
```

Here, **RCP** stores the **email address** to email; **SUB** is the email **subject**; **MSG** is the **message** to send; and **profile** and **password** are the logon credentials to send the email.

TIP: *You can omit the highlighted lines above if you do not need to log on to a mail server or if your information is cached.*

Sending an Email with Attachments Using Outlook Automation

To send an email to multiple users with attachments using Outlook, create and then execute a WSH script containing the following:

```
On Error Resume Next
RCP = "emailaddress"

Dim File(2)
File(0) = "file1"
File(1) = "file2"

SUB = "subject"
MSG = "message"

Set Outlook = CreateObject("Outlook.Application")
Set MAPI = Outlook.GetNameSpace("MAPI")
Set NewMail = Outlook.CreateItem(0)
NewMail.Subject = SUB
NewMail.Body = MSG
NewMail.Recipients.Add RCP

For X = 0 to (UBound(File)-1)
  NewMail.Attachments.Add(file(X))
Next

MAPI.Logon "profile", "password"
NewMail.Send
MAPI.Logoff
```

Here, **file** is the array that holds the file names to attach to the message; **RCP** stores the **email address** to email; **SUB** is the email **subject**; **MSG** is the **message** to send; and **profile** and **password** are the logon credentials to send the email.

TIP: *You can omit the highlighted lines above if you do not need to log on to a mail server or if your information is cached.*

Sending Emails and Attachments to Multiple Recipients Using Outlook Automation

To send an email to multiple users with attachments using Outlook, create and then execute a WSH script containing the following:

```
On Error Resume Next
Dim Name(2)
Name(0) = "emailaddress1"
Name(1) = "emailaddress2"

Dim File(2)
File(0) = "file1"
File(1) = "file2"

SUB = "subject"
MSG = "message"

Set Outlook = CreateObject("Outlook.Application")
Set MAPI = Outlook.GetNameSpace("MAPI")
Set NewMail = Outlook.CreateItem(0)
NewMail.Subject = SUB
NewMail.Body = MSG

For X = 0 to (UBound(Name)-1)
   NewMail.Recipients.Add Name(X)
Next

For X = 0 to (UBound(File)-1)
   NewMail.Attachments.Add(file(X))
Next

MAPI.Logon "profile", "password"
NewMail.Send
MAPI.Logoff
```

Here, *name* is the array that holds the *email addresses* to email; *file* is the array that holds the file names to attach to the message; *SUB* is the email *subject*; *MSG* is the *message* to send; and *profile* and *password* are the logon credentials to send the email.

TIP: *You can omit the highlighted lines above if you do not need to log on to a mail server or if your information is cached.*

Sending an Email Using CDOSYS

Collaboration Data Objects for Windows (CDOSYS) is a built-in messaging object library (CDOSYS.dll) which allows developers and scripters to send email on Windows 2000/XP/2003 without having Outlook or any other email client installed. To send an email using CDOSYS, create and then execute a WSH script containing the following:

```
On Error Resume Next
RCP = "emailaddress"
FROM = "myemailaddress"
SUB = "subject"
MSG= "message"

Set NewMail = CreateObject("CDO.Message")
NewMail.Subject = SUB
NewMail.Sender = FROM
NewMail.To = RCP
NewMail.TextBody = MSG

NewMail.Configuration.Fields.Item _
("http://schemas.microsoft.com/cdo/configuration/sendusing") = 2

NewMail.Configuration.Fields.Item _
("http://schemas.microsoft.com/cdo/configuration/smtpserver") =
"mailserver"

NewMail.Configuration.Fields.Item _
("http://schemas.microsoft.com/cdo/configuration/authenticate") = 1

NewMail.Configuration.Fields.Item _
("http://schemas.microsoft.com/cdo/configuration/sendusername") =
"username"

NewMail.Configuration.Fields.Item _
("http://schemas.microsoft.com/cdo/configuration/sendpassword") =
"password"
```

12. Logging and Alerting

```
NewMail.Configuration.Fields.Item _
("http://schemas.microsoft.com/cdo/configuration
smtpconnectiontimeout") = 60

NewMail.Configuration.Fields.Update

NewMail.Send
```

NOTE: *The highlighted code above must be placed on one line.*

Here, **FROM** stores the **email address** of the sender; **RCP** stores the **email address** to email; **SUB** is the email **subject**; **MSG** is the **message** to send; **mailserver** is the name or IP address of your email server; and **username** and **password** are the logon credentials to send the email.

Sending an Email with Attachment Using CDOSYS

To send an email with attachment using CDOSYS, create and then execute a WSH script containing the following:

```
On Error Resume Next
RCP = "emailaddress"
FROM = "myemailaddress"
SUB = "subject"
MSG= "message"
ATCH="attachmentfilepath"

Set NewMail = CreateObject("CDO.Message")
NewMail.Subject = SUB
NewMail.Sender = FROM
NewMail.To = RCP

NewMail.TextBody = MSG
NewMail.AddAttachment = ATCH

NewMail.Configuration.Fields.Item _
("http://schemas.microsoft.com/cdo/configuration/sendusing") = 2

NewMail.Configuration.Fields.Item _
("http://schemas.microsoft.com/cdo/configuration/smtpserver") =
"mailserver"

NewMail.Configuration.Fields.Item _
("http://schemas.microsoft.com/cdo/configuration/authenticate") = 1
```

```
NewMail.Configuration.Fields.Item _
("http://schemas.microsoft.com/cdo/configuration/sendusername") =
"username"

NewMail.Configuration.Fields.Item _
("http://schemas.microsoft.com/cdo/configuration/sendpassword") =
"password"

NewMail.Configuration.Fields.Item _
("http://schemas.microsoft.com/cdo/configuration
smtpconnectiontimeout") = 60

NewMail.Configuration.Fields.Update

NewMail.Send
```

NOTE: *The highlighted code above must be placed on one line.*

Here, **FROM** stores the **email address** of the sender; **RCP** stores the **email address** to email; **SUB** is the email **subject**; **MSG** is the **message** to send; **ATCH** stores the file path of the attachment to send; **mailserver** is the name or IP address of your email server; and **username** and **password** are the logon credentials to send the email.

12. Logging and Alerting

Chapter 13

Logon Scripts

In Brief

A logon script is a script that runs automatically each time a user logs on to the network. This script can contain various commands or programs that process on the local station, such as mapping printers or updating the local system time. In this chapter, you will learn how to create logon scripts to easily standardize and update your environment automatically.

TIP: *Although this chapter discusses tasks specifically geared toward logon scripts, you can use any of the scripts within this book in a logon script.*

Common Logon Script Tasks

The difference between a regular script and a logon script is that a logon script performs its functions when the user logs on. Logon scripts are not limited in functionality, but actually contain the same functionality as any other script. Although logon scripts can perform many different tasks, several tasks are commonly performed in logon scripts:

- Synchronize the local time
- Manage network printers and drives
- Update drivers or settings
- Access or modify the registry
- Perform hardware or software inventory
- Set or modify environment variables
- Update antivirus files

Synchronizing the Local Time

Time synchronization is essential when planning to perform enterprise-wide tasks simultaneously, such as remote updates. Windows 2000/XP/2003 uses a service called time synchronization to update the local system time with that of a network time source. A time source is any object providing the time to another object.

Time Source Hierarchy

Time synchronization is performed in a hierarchal format (see Figure 13.1). At the top of the hierarchy is the top-level time source that contains the accurate, universal time, such as the Atomic Clock. Primary

13. Logon Scripts

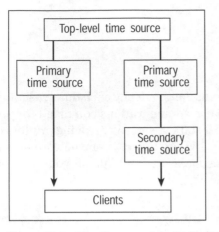

Figure 13.1   The time synchronization hierarchy.

time sources, usually a domain controller, synchronize their local time with the top-level time source. Below the primary time sources are secondary time sources and clients. Secondary time sources are basically backup primary time sources that obtain their time from a primary time source. Secondary time sources are typically resource domain controllers that obtain their time from the master domain. Underneath the time sources are the clients that synchronize their local time with a secondary or primary time source.

Environment Variables

Environment variables are basically keyword shortcuts that the system and users use to easily access files, directories, and values. You can use these variables in your logon scripts to easily identify the operating system, computer name, domain name, and more. Generally there are two types of environment variables: user and system. User environment variables are set per user, whereas system environment variables are set to the system level and affect all users who log on to the system. These variables are called static variables and are actually stored as registry entries: HKEY_CURRENT_USER\ Environment for user variables and HKEY_LOCAL_MACHINE\ System\CurrentControlSet\Control\Session Manager\Environment for system variables. Dynamic variables, created by the **SET** command, are stored in memory and are applicable for the current command-prompt session. Table 13.1 is a list of common environment variables.

Table 13.1   Registry data types.

Variable Name	Description
ComputerName	Specifies the name of the local system
HomeDrive	Specifies the drive letter to map the user's home directory
HomePath	Specifies the local path to the user's home directory
HomeShare	Specifies the share path to the user's home directory
OS	Specifies the operating system
UserDomain	Specifies the name of the domain the user is currently logged on to
UserName	Specifies the user ID of the currently logged on user
WinDir	Specifies the directory where the operating system is installed

TIP: To see the current environment variables from the command prompt, enter SET.

Norton Antivirus

Although most antivirus products include auto-updating features, updating antivirus files through a logon script provides a backup mechanism to ensure your clients are always up to date. Norton Antivirus is an advanced antivirus utility from Symantec (**www.symantec.com**), designed for both home and corporate use. This utility's antivirus signature files can be easily updated with an executable called Intelligent Updater. This executable supports the following command-line switches:

- **/EXTRACT** *location*—Extracts files from the executable to the *location* specified

- **/Q**—Undocumented switch, specifies to install the update silently

- **/TEMP=***path*—Specifies the temporary directory to use

McAfee VirusScan

McAfee VirusScan is a popular antivirus utility from NAI (**www.nai.com**), for both home and corporate use. NAI releases updates to their antivirus engine and signature files (.DAT extension) in a self-extracting executable (for example, sdat9999.exe) called SuperDAT. They also release a version of the SuperDAT without the engine update (for example, 9999xdat.exe) to reduce the size of the update file and to supply updated signature files simply. These files provide an easy way to update antivirus software because they first stop running antivirus services, update the antivirus files, and then restart the antivirus services.

13. Logon Scripts

The two executables just described support the following command-line switches:

- **/E** *location*—Extracts files from the executable to the specified *location*
- **/F**—Forces an updating of existing files
- **/LOGFILE** *textfile*—Logs the status to a **text file**
- **/PROMPT**—Displays a prompt dialog before reboot
- **/REBOOT**—Reboots if necessary
- **/SILENT**—Runs the executable in silent mode, with no prompting
- **/V**—Displays information about the executable

The Windows 2000/2003 Logon Process

The logon sequence is initiated on a Windows 2000/2003 machine when the user enters the secure command sequence (SCS), better known as Ctrl+Alt+Del. After the user enters the username and password, the Kerberos client encrypts the password through a one-way function (OWF) using the DES-CBC-MD5 algorithm (Data Encryption Standard Cipher Block Channel Message Digest 5). The client then converts the password to an encryption key.

The Kerberos client then sends the encryption key, username, a time stamp, and the authentication request to the Key Distribution Center (KDC), which is a service running on the authenticating server. The user name is then checked for a valid name stored in the active directory database, the password is verified, and the time stamp is checked to ensure the request is not old or falsified.

Once the user account has been validated, the KDC then sends back a Kerberos authentication response. This response is called a ticket granting number (TGT) and includes an encrypted copy of the KDC's encryption key. The client finally stores this ticket into memory and is allowed into the domain.

Windows Replication

Replication helps to easily distribute logon scripts to all your servers based on a regular schedule. The purpose of replication is to synchronize the contents of one file location with the contents of another. Replication is a service that performs one-way transfers, ensuring that all child locations are synchronized with the parent location. This synchronization includes file additions, modifications, and deletions.

NOTE: *The master replication server replicates files to itself, from the export to the import directory.*

File Replication Service

Windows 2000 uses the file replication service (FRS) to perform file replication. FRS is a replication service that is used to replicate system policies and logon scripts to the System Volume directory (SYSVOL). FRS can be used to replicate files in addition to policies and logon scripts. The FRS synchronizes immediately within sites and synchronizes on a schedule between sites. File replication service is a robust replication service that works well for all types of data files.

The Scripting Advantage

KiXtart was originally designed for logon scripting and contains all the macros and methods you would expect and need. Windows Script Host provides the functionality needed, but is not as complete or as easy to work with as KiXtart. AutoIt's true power comes with its ability to generate GUIs. While its general logon scripting capabilities are limited, this unique ability to create a GUI logon script for our users quickly makes up for its lack of functionality. (We can always call out to another scripting method when needed.) Finally, shell scripting combined with some extra utilities provides a quick and easy way to whip up some simple logon scripts.

A Word of Caution

Logon scripts are usually where most users get introduced to the administrators scripting abilities. A logon script that crashes, hangs, or simply takes a long time to run can cause the users to loose faith in the administrator's scripting skills. As with all scripts, you should first test each script in an isolated testing environment to ensure the script produces the desired results before using it in a production environment.

Immediate Solutions

Creating Logon Scripts with Shell Scripting

Shell scripting is the original source of logon scripting for Windows. Although it may lack some of the more complex features of other scripting languages, its main advantage is compatibility. Unlike AutoIt and KiXtart, shell scripting does not require any installed client files to run (other than the operating system). Shell scripting provides a simple, logon script solution for quick and easy deployment.

Setting the Window Title

Windows 2000/XP/2003 supports the **title** command to change the title of a shell prompt window. The basic syntax of the **title** command is as follows:

```
Title name
```

Here, **name** is the name to give the current command-prompt window. Here is an example to change the shell prompt title to "Logon Script":

```
If "%OS%"=="Windows_NT" Title Logon Script
```

Here, %**OS**% is an environment variable that indicates the operating system type.

Changing the Background and Foreground Colors

Windows 2000/XP/2003 supports the **color** command to change the background and foreground in a shell prompt. The basic syntax of the **color** command is as follows:

```
COLOR BF
```

Here, **B** is the background color value and **F** is the foreground color value. The **color** command supports the following color values:

- **0**—Black
- **1**—Blue
- **2**—Green
- **3**—Aqua
- **4**—Red
- **5**—Purple
- **6**—Yellow
- **7**—White
- **8**—Gray
- **9**—Light Blue
- **A**—Light Green
- **B**—Light Aqua
- **C**—Light Red
- **D**—Light Purple
- **E**—Light Yellow
- **F**—Bright White

Here is an example to change the shell prompt colors to bright white text on a blue background:

```
IF "%OS%"=="Windows_NT" COLOR 1F
```

Here, **%OS%** is an environment variable that indicates the operating system type.

Synchronizing the Local System Time

Synchronizing the local system to a central time source allows you to perform enterprise-wide tasks simultaneously. The basic syntax to synchronize the local clock with a specified time source is as follows:

```
Net Time \\server/commands
```

Here, **\\server** is the name of the time source server to sync with. This parameter is only necessary when syncing with a specific server. If this parameter is omitted (**Net Time**), the system will search the local domain for a time source server. **/commands** are any of the following parameters:

13. Logon Scripts

- **/SET**—Sets the local time to the time source server

- **/Y**—Forces to sync the time with the server specified, regardless of whether the server is a time source server or not

- **/DOMAIN:***domainname*—Searches the specified domain for a time source server

The following script attempts to sync the local system time with the server named ***servername***. If this fails, the domain will be searched for a time source to sync with. To execute this script, proceed as follows:

1. Create a new directory to store all files included in this example.

2. Select Start|Run and enter "*scriptfile*.bat."

Here, ***scriptfile*** is the full path and file name of a script file that contains the following:

```
@Echo Off
CLS ; Clears the screen
Set TServer=ServerName

Echo Syncing the time with %TServer%...
Net Time \\%TServer% /set /yes
If %errorlevel% NEQ 0 CLS && Goto Domain
CLS && Echo Sync Successful
Goto End

:Domain
Echo Searching the local domain for a time-server...
Net Time /set /yes
If %errorlevel% EQU 0 CLS && Echo Sync Successful && Goto End
CLS && Echo Time Sync Error

:End
```

Here, ***tserver*** is a variable containing the name of the time source server; **NEQ** is the "not equal to" operator; and **&&** allows you to run a second command after the first has completed.

Mapping Universal Drives

Mapping common drives for all users allows you to present a central resource location for applications or data. In Chapter 8, you learned how to map network drives from within Windows and the command prompt. To map a network drive and display the status from the command prompt, create and then execute a shell script containing the following:

13. Logon Scripts

```
@Echo Off
CLS ; Clears the screen
Set Drive=DriveLetter
Set Share=\\server\sharename

Echo Mapping drive %Drive% to %Share%
Net Use %Drive%: /Delete && CLS
Net Use %Drive%: %Share%
If %errorlevel% EQU 0 CLS && Echo Map Successful && Goto End
CLS && Echo Error mapping drive %Drive% to %Share%

:End
```

Here, *driveletter* is the *drive* letter to map a *share* to, and *server* contains the *sharename* you want to map to.

Mapping Drives by Group

Mapping drives by group membership allows you to control which drives and resources will be available to which users. The resource kit utility IfMember allows you to determine a user's group membership from the command line. The basic syntax of the IfMember utility is as follows:

```
IfMember /Commands Groups
```

Here, *Groups* are any group, separated by spaces, whose membership you want to check. An errorlevel of 1 indicates the user is a member of the specified group. The available *commands* are as follows:

- **/List**—Lists all groups the user belongs to
- **/Verbose**—Displays all group matches

To map a network drive according to group membership and display the status from the command prompt, create and then execute a shell script containing the following:

```
@Echo Off
CLS ; Clears the screen
Fullpath\IfMember GroupName > Nul

If Not %errorlevel% EQU 1 Goto End
Set Drive=DriveLetter
Set Share=\\server\sharename
```

13. Logon Scripts

```
Echo Mapping drive %Drive% to %Share%
Net Use %Drive%: /Delete && CLS
Net Use %Drive%: %Share%
If %errorlevel% EQU 0 CLS && Echo Map Successful && Goto End
CLS && Echo Error mapping drive %Drive% to %Share%

:End
```

Here, *fullpath* is the full path where the IfMember utility is located; *GroupName* is the name of the group to check membership; *driveletter* is the *drive* letter to map a *share* to; **NEQ** is the "not equal to" operator; **EQU** is the "equal to" operator; *server* contains the *sharename* you want to map to; and **&&** allows you to run a second command after the first has completed.

Mapping Printers Using Con2PRT

Mapping printers through a logon script provides an easy method to remotely update printer connections. Con2PRT (Connect To Port) is a Windows 2000 Resource Kit utility used to control printer connections from the command line. The basic syntax of the con2PRT utility is as follows:

```
Con2prt /commands \\server\printer
```

Here, *server* is the name of the printer server containing the shared *printer* to map. The available *commands* are:

- **/F**—Removes all printer connections
- **/C**—Connects to the *printer* specified
- **/CD**—Connects to the *printer* specified and marks it as the default printer

To remove all current printer connections and map a default printer using con2PRT, create and then execute a shell script containing the following:

```
@Echo Off
Set Pserver=server
Set DPrinter=Printer

fullpath\con2prt /F
fullpath\con2prt /CD \\%server%\%printer%
```

Here, *pserver* is the variable holding the printer *server* name; *dprinter* is the variable holding the name of the *printer* share; and *fullpath* is the full path where con2prt is located.

Adding Printers Using the PrintUI DLL

Windows 2000/XP/2003 includes the PrintUI.dll to add and remove printers from the command line. To use the PrintUI.dll, you must call the PrintUIEntry function through the rundll32 command. To add a default printer using the PrintUI DLL, start a command prompt and enter the following:

```
rundll32 printui.dll,PrintUIEntry /in /y /n \\pserver\dprinter
```

Here, *pserver* is the name of the print server and *dprinter* is name of the printer share.

Checking for Remote Access

Determining whether a client is logging in through the network or remote access helps you specify which parts of the script to run. CheckRAS is a command-line, SMS resource kit utility to determine whether a user is using remote access. To determine whether the current user is using remote access during a logon script, create and then execute a shell script containing the following:

```
@Echo Off
CLS ; Clears the screen
Set RAS=NO
fullpath\CheckRAS > Nul
If %errorlevel% EQU 1 Set RAS=YES
```

Here, *fullpath* is the full path where the CheckRAS utility is located, and *RAS* indicates whether the current user is using remote access or not.

Displaying Time-Based Greetings

Although it's not essential, many administrators like to display a greeting to the user depending on the time of day. To display a time-based greeting from the command line, create and then execute a shell script containing the following:

```
@Echo Off
CLS
For /F "Delims=: Tokens=1" %%I in ('Time /T') Do Set Hour=%%I
For /F "Delims=: Tokens=2" %%I in ('Time /T') Do Set Min=%%I
For /F "Delims=0,1,2,3,4,5,6,7,8,9 Tokens=2" %%I in
('Set Min') Do Set AP=%%I
```

13. Logon Scripts

```
If %AP% EQU p Goto PM
Set Greet=Good Morning
Goto End

:PM
If %Hour% EQU 12 Set Hour=0
If %Hour% LSS 12 Set Greet=Good Evening
If %Hour% LSS 6 Set Greet=Good Afternoon

:End
Echo %Greet%
Set Hour=
Set Min=
Set AP=
```

NOTE: *The highlighted code above should be placed on one line.*

Here, the **Time /T** command indicates the local system time.

Updating McAfee Antivirus Files

To update your McAfee antivirus engine and/or signature files, create
and then execute a shell script containing the following:

```
@Echo Off
CLS
Set SDAT="superdat"
Set DAT="datfile"
Set NAILOG="textlog"
Set DDAY="DOTW"

For /F "Tokens=1" %%I in ('Date /T') Do Set Day=%%I

If %DAY% EQU %DDAY% Goto UENGINE
%DAT% /F /PROMPT /REBOOT /SILENT /LOGFILE
%NAILOG%
GOTO END

:UENGINE
%SDAT% /F /PROMPT /REBOOT /SILENT /LOGFILE %NAILOG%
GOTO END

:END
Set SDAT=
Set DAT=
Set NAILOG=
Set DAY=
```

Here, **SDAT** is a variable containing the complete path and file name of the SuperDAT executable; **DAT** is a variable containing the complete path and file name of the DAT executable; **NAILOG** is a variable containing the complete path and file name of the status log text file; and **DDAY** is the day of the week (Mon, Tue, Wed, Thu, Fri, Sat, Sun) to run the SuperDAT as opposed to the daily DAT file.

Updating Norton Antivirus Files

To update your Norton antivirus files, create and then execute a shell script containing the following:

```
@Echo Off
Set IUPDATER=iufile

%IUPDATER% /Q > Nul
```

Here, **IUPDATER** is a variable containing the complete path and file name of the Intelligent Updater executable.

Creating Logon Scripts with AutoIt

While AutoIt does not have as many methods and macros as KiXtart, it provides just enough features to be suitable for logon scripting. In addition, AutoIt provides advanced GUI creation not found in any of the other scripting methods, allowing you to create rich GUI's for your logon scripts.

Synchronizing the Local System Time

AutoIt does not have a time synchronization command to sync the local system time with a network time source. However, we can use the **run** command and the **Net Time** command to sync the time for us. To sync the local system time with a domain source, create and then execute an AutoIt script containing the following:

```
Run("Net Time / Set /Yes", "", @SW_HIDE)
```

Here, @SW_HIDE causes the run window to be hidden.

Mapping Drives

To map a network drive and display the status using AutoIt, create and then execute AutoIt script containing the following:

```
Dim $Drive, $Share, $Return
$Drive="DriveLetter"
$Share="\\server\sharename"

  $Return = DriveMapAdd($Drive, $Share)
  If $Return=1 Then
    MsgBox(0, "Drive Mapping", "OK")
  Else
    MsgBox(0, "Drive Mapping", "ERROR")
  EndIf
```

Here, **driveletter** is the drive letter to map a share to, and **server** contains the **sharename** you want to map to.

Displaying Time-Based Greetings

Although it's not essential, many administrators like to display a greeting to the user depending on the time of day. To display a time-based greeting, create and then execute an AutoIt script containing the following:

```
Dim $Greeting
Select
  Case @Hour > 0 AND @Hour < 12
    $Greeting = "Good Morning"
  Case @Hour > 12 AND @Hour < 18
    $Greeting = "Good Afternoon"
  Case Else
    $Greeting = "Good Evening"
EndSelect
MsgBox(0, "Greeting", $Greeting)
```

Here, the **@HOUR** macro indicates the current hour (0-23).

Displaying a GUI Based Logon Script

One of AutoIt's most powerful features is the ability to create GUI's with buttons, listboxes, progressbars, and more. To display a GUI based logon script, create and then execute an AutoIt script containing the following:

```
#NoTrayIcon
#include <GuiConstants.au3>

;Declare variables
Dim $OSVersion, $LogonServer, $LIstItem, $Return
Dim $Progress, $mem, $ListView1, $ListView2, $Greeting
```

```
;Time based greeting
Select
  Case @Hour > 0 AND @Hour < 12
    $Greeting = "Good Morning"
  Case @Hour > 12 AND @Hour < 18
    $Greeting = "Good Afternoon"
  Case Else
    $Greeting = "Good Evening"
EndSelect

$OSVersion = StringReplace(@OSVersion,"WIN_", "Windows ")
$LogonServer = StringReplace(@LogonServer,"\\", "")
$mem = MemGetStats()

;Create controls
GuiCreate(@LogonDomain & " Logon Script", 640, 480)
GUICtrlCreateLabel ($Greeting & " - Please wait until the logon
script completes", 10, 10, 620, 100)

$listView1 = GuiCtrlCreateListView("Property|Value|", 10, 30, 250, 390)
$listView2 = GuiCtrlCreateListView("Activity|Status|", 270, 30, 360, 390)

$Progress = GuiCtrlCreateProgress(10, 430, 620, 40)
GuiCtrlSetData($Progress, 0)

;Show GUI
GuiSetState()

;Info
GuiCtrlCreateListViewItem("Computer|" & @ComputerName, $listView1)
GuiCtrlCreateListViewItem("User|" & @UserName, $listView1)
GuiCtrlCreateListViewItem("IP|" & @IPAddress1, $listView1)
GuiCtrlCreateListViewItem("Domain|" & @LogonDomain, $listView1)
GuiCtrlCreateListViewItem("DNS|" & @LogonDNSDomain, $listView1)
GuiCtrlCreateListViewItem("Logon Server|" & $LogonServer, $listView1)
GuiCtrlCreateListViewItem("OS Name|" & $OSVersion, $listView1)
GuiCtrlCreateListViewItem("OS Service Pack|" & @OSServicePack, $listView1)
GuiCtrlCreateListViewItem("Total Memory|" & Round($mem[1]/1024,0), $listView1)
GuiCtrlCreateListViewItem("Available Memory|" & Round($mem[2]/1024,0),
   $listView1)
GuiCtrlCreateListViewItem("Total Page Memory|" & Round($mem[3]/
   1024,0), $listView1)
GuiCtrlCreateListViewItem("Available Page Memory|" &
Round($mem[4]/1024,0), $listView1)
GuiCtrlCreateListViewItem("Total Virtual Memory|" & Round($mem[5]
1024,0), $listView1)
GuiCtrlCreateListViewItem("Available Virtual Memory|" &
Round($mem[6]/1024,0), $listView1)
```

```
;Status
SyncTime()
GuiCtrlSetData($Progress, 20)

GuiCtrlCreateListViewItem("Securing System|OK", $listView2)
Sleep(2000) ; Do stuff here
GuiCtrlSetData($Progress, 40)

GuiCtrlCreateListViewItem("Updating System Files|OK", $listView2)
Sleep(2000) ; Do stuff here
GuiCtrlSetData($Progress, 60)

MapDrive("X:","\\first\share")
GuiCtrlSetData($Progress, 80)

MapDrive("Y:","\\second\share")
GuiCtrlSetData($Progress, 90)

GuiCtrlCreateListViewItem("Logon Script Complete|OK", $listView2)
GuiCtrlSetData($Progress, 100)
Sleep(5000)
Exit

Func SyncTime()
  $LIstItem = GuiCtrlCreateListViewItem("Syncing Time|PENDING", $listView2)
  Run("Net Time / Set /Yes", "", @SW_HIDE)
  GUICtrlSetData($ListItem,"|OK",)
EndFunc

Func MapDrive($DriveLetter, $DrivePath)
  Dim $ItemText
  $ItemText =  "Mapping " & $DriveLetter & " to " & $DrivePath & "|PENDING"

  $ListItem = GuiCtrlCreateListViewItem($ItemText, $listView2)

  DriveMapDel($DriveLetter)
  $Return = DriveMapAdd($DriveLetter, $DrivePath)
  If $Return=1 Then
    GUICtrlSetData($ListItem,"|OK",)
  Else
    GUICtrlSetData($ListItem,"|ERROR",)
  EndIf
EndFunc
```

NOTE: *The highlighted code above must be placed on one line.*

Creating Logon Scripts with KiXtart

KiXtart is a powerful scripting tool primarily focused and used for logon scripts. KiXtart contains many built-in methods and macros to retrieve quick information; other scripting languages would require external tools or extensive scripting to retrieve the same information.

Setting Up the Environment

When creating a logon script, it is important to make sure the script looks and feels as it was intended. KiXtart includes several commands to customize the logon script environment. To set up a customized logon script environment, create and then execute a KiXtart script containing the following:

```
CLS ; Clear screen
BREAK OFF ; Logoff user when attempt to close logon box
$RCODE= SETCONSOLE("ALWAYSONTOP") ; Set box on top
$RCODE = SETASCII("ON") ; Turn on ASCII characters
```

This script first clears the screen (CLS) and sets the logon script box to log off the current user if he/she attempts to close the box. The logon script box is then set to be on top of all other windows. The final command turns on ASCII characters. This is a new feature included with KiXtart 3.62 and higher that allows you to change the look of text by turning ASCII on or off.

Changing the Background and Foreground Colors

KiXtart supports the **color** command to change the background and foreground in a shell prompt. The basic syntax of the **color** command is as follows:

```
COLOR Fx/By
```

Here, F is the foreground color value, x is an optional indicator to increase the color intensity if a plus sign (+) is specified, B is the background color value, and y is an optional indicator that causes the background to blink if a plus sign (+) is specified. The **color** command supports the following color values:

- **N**—Black
- **B**—Blue
- **G**—Green
- **C**—Cyan

- **R**—Red
- **M**—Magenta
- **Y**—Yellow/Brown
- **W**—White

Here is an example to change the shell prompt colors to bright white text on a blue background:

```
COLOR W+/B
```

Synchronizing the Local System Time

Synchronizing the local system to a central time source allows you to perform enterprise-wide tasks simultaneously. KiXtart includes the **SetTime** command to synchronize the local system time to a time source. The basic syntax of the **SetTime** command is as follows:

```
SetTime source
```

Here, **source** is any one of the following types:

- **\\Server**—Specifies the name of a time source **server**
- **DomainName**—Searches the specified domain for a time source
- **"*"**—Specifies to search the local domain for a time source

The following script attempts to sync the local system time with the logon server. If this fails, the domain will be searched for a time source to sync with:

```
? "Syncing the time with @LSERVER..."
SETTIME "@LSERVER"
If @ERROR <> 0
  ? "Searching the local domain for a time-server..."
  SETTIME "*"
  If @ERROR <> 0
    ? "Time Sync Error"
  Else
    ? "Sync Successful"
  EndIf
EndIf
```

Mapping Universal Drives

Mapping common drives for all users allows you to present a central resource location for applications or data. In Chapter 8, you learned how to map network drives from within Windows and the command prompt. KiXtart includes the **use** command, similar to the **Net Use** command, to attach a drive letter to a network share. To map a network drive and display the status using KiXtart, create and then execute a KiXtart script containing the following:

```
$Drive="DriveLetter"
$Share="\\server\sharename"

? " Mapping drive $Drive to $Share"
Use " $Drive: " /Delete
Use " $Drive: " $Share
If @Error = 0
  ? " Map Successful"
Else
  ? " Error mapping drive $Drive to $Share"
EndIf
```

Here, *driveletter* is the *drive* letter to map a *share* to, and *server* contains the *sharename* you want to map to.

Mapping Drives by Group

Mapping drives by group membership allows you to control which drives and resources will be available to which users. KiXtart includes the **InGroup** command, similar to the IfMember resource kit utility, to determine group membership. To map a network drive according to group membership and display the status, create and then execute a KiXtart script containing the following:

```
$Drive="DriveLetter"
$Share="\\server\sharename"

If InGroup("GroupName")
  ? "Mapping drive $Drive to $Share"
  Use "$Drive: "/Delete
  Use "$Drive: "$Share
  If @Error = 0
    ? "Map Successful"
  Else
    ? "Error mapping drive $Drive to $Share"
  EndIf
EndIf
```

Here, *GroupName* is the name of the group to check membership; *driveletter* is the *drive* letter to map a *share* to; and *server* contains the *sharename* you want to map to.

Mapping Printers

Mapping printers through a logon script provides an easy method to remotely update printer connections. KiXtart contains several commands to add, remove, and set default printers. To map a printer, create and then execute a KiXtart script containing the following:

```
$Pserver="Server"
$DPrinter="Printer"

If AddPrinterConnection("\\$PServer\$DPrinter") = 0
  ? "Added printer $DPrinter"
Else
  ? "Error adding $DPrinter"
EndIf
```

Here, **pserver** is the variable holding the printer **server** name, and **dprinter** is the variable holding the name of the **printer** share.

Checking for Remote Access

Determining whether a client is logging in through the network or remote access helps you specify which parts of the script to run. KiXtart includes the @RAS macro to the number of remote access connections. To determine whether a user is logging on through remote access, create and then execute a KiXtart script containing the following:

```
If @RAS = 0
  ? " You are logging in through the local network. "
Else
  ? "You are logging on through remote access"
EndIf
```

Displaying Time-Based Greetings

Although it's not essential, many administrators like to display a greeting to the user depending on the time of day. To display a time-based greeting, create and then execute a KiXtart script containing the following:

```
SELECT
  CASE ((@TIME > "00:00:00") AND (@TIME < "12:00:00"))
    ? "Good Morning @FULLNAME"
  CASE ((@TIME > "12:00:00") AND (@TIME < "18:00:00"))
    ? "Good Afternoon @FULLNAME"
  CASE 1
```

```
    ? "Good Evening @FULLNAME"
ENDSELECT
```

Here, the **@TIME** macro indicates the current time, and **@FULLNAME**
indicates the full name of the current user.

Updating McAfee Antivirus Files

To update your McAfee antivirus engine and/or signature files, create
and then execute a KiXtart script containing the following:

```
$SDAT="superdat"
$DAT="datfile"
$NAILOG="textlog"
$DDAY="DOTW"

If @DAY = $DDAY
    SHELL "%COMSPEC% /C $SDAT /F /PROMPT /REBOOT /SILENT
    /LOGFILE $NAILOG"
Else
    SHELL "%COMSPEC% /C $DAT /F /PROMPT /REBOOT /SILENT
    /LOGFILE $NAILOG"
EndIf
```

Here, *SDAT* is a variable containing the complete path and file name
of the SuperDAT executable; *DAT* is a variable containing the complete path and file name of the DAT executable; *NAILOG* is a variable containing the complete path and file name of the status log text
file; and *DDAY* is the day of the week (Monday-Sunday) to run the
SuperDAT as opposed to the daily DAT file.

NOTE: *The highlighted code above must be placed on one line.*

Updating Norton Antivirus Files

To update your Norton antivirus files, create and then execute a KiXtart
script containing the following:

```
$IUPDATER = "iufile"
SHELL "%COMSPEC% /C $IUPDATER /Q"
```

Here, *IUPDATER* is a variable containing the complete path and file
name of the Intelligent Updater executable.

Creating Logon Scripts with Windows Script Host

Windows Script Host is a relatively new scripting language and is rather limited with logon scripts. Although you can call external functions or custom COM objects to perform specific logon script tasks, WSH does not contain many of the standard logon script functions other scripting languages may have, such as a time synchronization command.

Synchronizing the Local System Time

Windows Script Host does not have a time synchronization command to sync the local system time with a network time source. You can use the shell **run** command to call external commands, such as the **Net Time** command, and use a return variable to indicate whether the command was successful. The following script attempts to sync the local system time with the server named ***servername*** using the Net Time command. If this synchronization fails, the domain will be searched for a time source to sync with. To execute this script, create and then execute a WSH script containing the following:

```
On Error Resume Next
Set SHELL = CreateObject("WScript.Shell")
TServer="ServerName"

Wscript.Echo "Syncing the time with " & TServer & "..."
ELevel = Shell.Run("Net Time \\" & TServer & "
/Set /Yes",0,True)

If (ELevel <> 0) Then
  Wscript.Echo "Searching the local domain for a " & _
  "time-server..."
  ELevel = Shell.Run("Net Time / Set /Yes",0,True)
If (ELevel = 0) Then
  Wscript.Echo "Sync Successful"
Else
  Wscript.Echo "Time Sync Error"
 End If
Else
  Wscript.Echo "Sync Successful"
End If
```

NOTE: *The highlighted code above must be placed on one line.*

---

13. Logon Scripts

Mapping Universal Drives

Mapping common drives for all users allows you to present a central resource location for applications or data. In Chapter 8, you learned how to map network drives from within Windows and the command prompt. You can use the Windows Script Host network object to attach a drive letter to a network share. To map a network drive and display the status using Windows Script Host, create and then execute a WSH script containing the following:

```
On Error Resume Next
Set Network = CreateObject("WScript.Network")
Drive = "DriveLetter:"
Share = "\\server\sharename"

Wscript.Echo "Mapping drive " & Drive & " to " & Share
Network.MapNetworkDrive Drive, Share
If Err.Number = 0 Then
  Wscript.Echo "Map Successful"
Else
  Wscript.Echo "Error mapping drive " & Drive & " to " & _
    Share
End If
```

Here, *driveletter* is the *drive* letter to map a *share* to, and *server* contains the *sharename* you want to map to.

Mapping Drives by Group

Mapping drives by group membership allows you to control which drives and resources will be available to which users. Windows Script Host does contain a method to determine group membership. Although you can use the ADSI IfMember method, this method can be slow on larger networks. Alternatively, you can use the WSH shell run command to call external commands, such as the IfMember resource kit utility, and use a return variable to indicate whether the command was successful. To map a network drive according to group membership and display the status using Windows Script Host, create and then execute a WSH script containing the following:

```
On Error Resume Next
Set SHELL = CreateObject("WScript.Shell")
Set Network = CreateObject("WScript.Network")
Drive = "DriveLetter:"
Share = "\\server\sharename"
DGroup = "groupname"
```

13. Logon Scripts

```
ELevel = Shell.Run("fullpath\IfMember " & DGroup,0,True)
If (ELevel = 1) Then
  Wscript.Echo "Mapping drive " & Drive & " to " & Share
  Network.MapNetworkDrive Drive, Share
  If Err.Number = 0 Then
    Wscript.Echo "Map Successful"
  Else
    Wscript.Echo "Error mapping drive " & Drive & " to " & _
    Share
  End If
End If
```

Here, *fullpath* is the full path where the IfMember utility is located; *GroupName* is the name of the group to check membership; *driveletter* is the *drive* letter to map a *share* to; and *server* contains the *sharename* you want to map to.

Mapping Printers

Mapping printers through a logon script provides an easy method to remotely update printer connections. Starting with version 2, Windows Script Host provides several commands to add, remove, and set default printers. To map a printer using Windows Script Host, create and then execute a WSH script containing the following:

```
On Error Resume Next
PServer = "Server"
DPrinter = "Printer"
Port = "LPT1"
Set Network = CreateObject("Wscript.Network")

Network.AddPrinterConnection Port, "\\" & PServer &
"\" &Printer
If Err.Number <> 0 Then
  Wscript.Echo "Added printer " & Printer
Else
  Wscript.Echo "Error adding printer " & Printer
End If
```

NOTE: *The highlighted code above must be placed on one line.*

Here, *pserver* is the variable holding the printer *server* name, and *dprinter* is the variable holding the name of the *printer* share.

TIP: *You can use the **AddWindowsPrinterConnection** method to add printers to Windows NT/2000 systems without having to supply a port.*

Checking for Remote Access

Determining whether a client is logging in through the network or remote access helps you specify which parts of the script to run. Windows Script Host does not contain a method to detect remote access connections. CheckRAS is a command-line, SMS resource kit utility to determine whether a user is using remote access. To determine whether the current user is using remote access during a logon script using Windows Script Host, create and then execute a WSH script containing the following:

```
On Error Resume Next
Set SHELL = CreateObject("WScript.Shell")

ELevel = Shell.Run("fullpath\CheckRAS",0,True)
If (ELevel = 0) Then
 RAS = "YES"
Else
 RAS = "NO"
End If
```

Here, *fullpath* is the full path where the CheckRAS utility is located, and *RAS* indicates whether the current user is using remote access or not.

Displaying Time-Based Greetings

Although it's not essential, many administrators like to display a greeting to the user depending on the time of day. To display a time-based greeting using Windows Script Host, create and then execute a WSH script containing the following:

```
On Error Resume Next
If Hour(Now) < 12 Then
  Wscript.Echo "Good Morning"
ElseIf Hour(Now) < 18 Then
  Wscript.Echo "Good Afternoon"
Else
  Wscript.Echo "Good Evening"
End If
```

Updating McAfee Antivirus Files

To update your McAfee antivirus engine and/or signature files, create and then execute a WSH script containing the following:

```
On Error Resume Next
Set SHELL = CreateObject("WScript.Shell")
```

13. Logon Scripts

```
SDAT="superdat"
DAT="datfile"
NAILOG="textlog"
DDAY="DOTW"

If WeekDayName(WeekDay(Date)) = DDAY
    Shell.Run CHR(34) & SDAT & CHR(34) & " /F /PROMPT /REBOOT
    /SILENT /LOGFILE NAILOG",1,True
Else
    Shell.Run CHR(34) & DAT & CHR(34) & " /F /PROMPT /REBOOT
    /SILENT /LOGFILE NAILOG",1,True
EndIf
```

NOTE: *The highlighted code above must be placed on one line. Chr(34) translates the ASCII code character 34 into a quotation mark ("). This is necessary when using the Shell.Run command with long file names.*

Here, **SDAT** is a variable containing the complete path and file name of the SuperDAT executable; **DAT** is a variable containing the complete path and file name of the DAT executable; **NAILOG** is a variable containing the complete path and file name of the status log text file; and **DDAY** is the day of the week (Monday-Sunday) to run the SuperDAT as opposed to the daily DAT file.

Updating Norton Antivirus Files

To update your Norton antivirus files, create and then execute a WSH script containing the following:

```
On Error Resume Next
Set SHELL = CreateObject("WScript.Shell")

IUPDATER = "iufile"
Shell.Run CHR(34) & IUPDATER & CHR(34) & " /Q",1,True
```

NOTE: *Chr(34) translates the ASCII code character 34 into a quotation ("). This is necessary when using the Shell.Run command with long file names.*

Here, **IUPDATER** is a variable containing the complete path and file name of the Intelligent Updater executable.

Using Microsoft Internet Explorer as a Logon Script Box

Through Automation, you can use Internet Explorer to display logon script status to the user. To use Internet Explorer as a logon script box using the previous WSH logon scripts, create and then execute a WSH script containing the following:

```
On Error Resume Next
Set Network = CreateObject("WScript.Network")
Set MSIE = CreateObject("InternetExplorer.Application")
sTITLE = "Processing Logon Script, please wait..."
Drive = "DriveLetter:"
Share = "\\server\sharename"

SetupMSIE
MSIE.Document.Write "<HTML><TITLE>" & sTitle & _
 "</TITLE><BODY bgcolor=#COCOCO><FONT FACE=ARIAL>"

IfHour(Now) < 12 Then
 MSIE.Document.Write "<B>Good Morning " & _
   Network.UserName & "</B><BR><BR>"
ElseIf Hour(Now) < 18 Then
 MSIE.Document.Write "<B>Good Afternoon " & _
   Network.UserName & "</B><BR><BR>"
Else
 MSIE.Document.Write "<B>Good Evening " & _
   Network.UserName & "</B><BR><BR>"
End If

MSIE.Document.Write "<B>Mapping drive " & Drive & " to " & _
 Share & "...</B><BR>"

Network.MapNetworkDrive Drive, Share
If Err.Number = 0 Then
 MSIE.Document.Write "  Mapping Successful<BR>"
Else
 MSIE.Document.Write "  Error mapping drive " & Drive & _
   " to " & Share & "<BR>"
End If

MSIE.Document.Write "<BR><B>Closing in 3 seconds</B><BR>"
Wscript.Sleep 3000
MSIE.Quit

Sub SetupMSIE
 MSIE.Navigate "About:Blank"
 MSIE.ToolBar = False
 MSIE.StatusBar = False
 MSIE.Resizable = False
 Do
 Loop While MSIE.Busy
 SWidth = MSIE.Document.ParentWindow.Screen.AvailWidth
 SHeight = MSIE.Document.ParentWindow.Screen.AvailHeight
 MSIE.Width = SWidth/2
 MSIE.Height = SHeight/2
```

```
MSIE.Left = (SWidth - MSIE.Width)/2
MSIE.Top = (SHeight - MSIE.Height)/2

MSIE.Visible = True
End Sub
```

Here, ***driveletter*** is the ***drive*** letter to map a ***share*** to, and ***server*** contains the ***sharename*** you want to map to.

Related solution:	Found on page:
Using Microsoft Internet Explorer as a Display Tool	98

Chapter 14

Backups and Scheduling

In Brief

Most companies and people couldn't continue to be in business or do their work if all their data were lost. Backups provide an easy method to restore a system or a set of files after some corruption, deletion, or hardware failure has taken place. Backups are an extremely important part of your task as an administrator—something that no one likes to do, but everyone appreciates when needed. Although many third-party backup tools are available, a limited budget or compatibility issues might prevent you from using them.

In previous chapters, you learned how to back up files and the registry using simple scripts. In this chapter, you will learn how to automate backups and restores. You will also learn how to schedule your backups and scripts to run automatically.

Backups under Windows 2000/XP/2003

NTBackup (New Technology Backup) is a utility that allows you to back up your registry and data files. These backups are stored using the Microsoft Tape Format (MTF). NTBackup can read and restore any backup stored in this format. This includes many of today's third-party backup programs that comply to this format, such as Veritas Backup Exec. Before performing any backup, you should decide which type of backup you would like to perform. NTBackup supports the following backup types:

- *Full*—Also called a normal backup, backs up all the files specified. The archive bit is cleared for all files backed up. This provides the most complete backup but also takes the most time and occupies the greatest amount of storage space on the backup media. This backup type provides the quickest restore method.

- *Incremental*—Only backs up files that have changed since the last full and incremental backup. The archive bit is cleared for all files backed up. This backup type requires marginal time and backup space but provides the longest restore method because the full backup and all other incremental backups must be restored sequentially.

14. Backups and Scheduling

- *Differential*—Only backs up files that have changed since the last full backup. The archive bit is not cleared for any files. This is the most common backup method used and provides an average restore time because the full backup must be restored before a differential backup can be restored.

- *Daily*—Only backs up files modified on the day the backup is performed. The archive bit is not modified.

- *Custom*—Allows you to specify which files to back up. This method is most commonly used on an on-demand basis when a small number of files are to be backed up.

- *Copy*—Copies files to the backup media. The archive bit is not cleared because you are merely copying files. This method is best used when you want to perform backups in combination with other backup utilities, and do not want the archive bit to be modified.

NOTE: *An archive bit is a file attribute that is cleared when a file is modified. This is a signal to all backup programs that this file needs to be backed up.*

New and Improved

Starting with Windows 2000, NTBackup supports many new features, such as scheduling and UNC support. In addition to tape devices, NTBackup can now back up data to removable media, such as a Jaz or Zip drive, using Remote Storage Management (RSM). You can back up to any removable media that RSM supports and that does not require special formatting at the time of backup. RSM cannot back up to CD-R (Compact Disc Recordable), CD-RW (Compact Disc ReWritable), or DVD-RAM (Digital Versatile Disc Random Access Memory) because it sees these devices as read-only. As with both versions of NTBackup, a major drawback to this backup utility is that you can only back up folders, not files.

NOTE: *You cannot restore files from the command line using NTBackup.*

Best Backup Practices

The following list describes the best backup practices to help protect your data:

- *Secure your backups*. Many companies protect their servers and yet leave their backup tapes in an open cabinet. If an intruder can access your backup tapes, he or she can access your data.

- *Perform backup verifies.* Verify compares the contents of the backup media with the targeted files backed up, and reports any corruption or differences.

- *Test your backups and hardware regularly.* Although your backup software may state that your backups are successfully running, there is no real indication of this until you perform a restore.

- *Rotate your backups offsite.* If something happens to your office building or location where you store your backups, you'll be glad you stored more tapes in another location.

- *Store your backups in a fire/water-proof container.* Tapes are very sensitive to corruption, especially heat. Storing your tapes in fire/water-proof containers helps protect your backups from damage.

- *Remember that backups can be subpoenaed.* Only back up files you wouldn't mind discussing in court.

- *Establish a written backup policy and stick to it.* This helps ensure that all the backup practices mentioned here, and many others, are clearly understood and followed daily.

Scheduling Windows NT/2000 Tasks

The **AT** command is a command line utility that allows you to schedule applications to run based on a predetermined schedule. You can use this command to automatically launch your backups, scripts, or any other tasks you can think of. The **AT** command works with the schedule service to monitor the system time, start tasks, and run the programs under the security context of the specified account.

The Evolution of the AT Command

Originally, the **AT** command worked with a service called schedule (ATSVC.EXE) that, by default, was configured as a system service. You could later configure this service to run under a specific administrative domain account, allowing your tasks to run for all users regardless of user privilege.

The New and Improved Task Scheduler

If you have at least Windows 2000 or Microsoft Internet Explorer 4, the schedule service is replaced with the Task Scheduler service (MSTASK.EXE). This service does not need to be configured with a specific account because you can now specify these credentials with each new task you create. For backward compatibility with tasks created by the **AT** command, you can still set the Task Scheduler service to run under a specified account.

The new task scheduler also adds a control panel applet called Scheduled Tasks, that provides a graphical interface to create, view, and modify scheduled tasks created by the **AT** command or task scheduler. These tasks are stored in the *%WINDIR%*\tasks directory. Although you can view and modify tasks under the Scheduled Tasks applet, the **AT** command does not recognize tasks created by the new task scheduler. This is because tasks created by the task scheduler can use additional features and require a specific user account to run. Any task created by the **AT** command will be converted to a task created by the task scheduler if a specific user account is specified or if any of the task scheduler's additional features are used, such as power management.

Introducing SCHTASKS

SCHTASKS is a Windows XP/2003 command line utility that allows you to create, delete, or view scheduled tasks. It is the replacement for the antiquated AT command and allows you to access tasks created with the Windows Scheduled Task Wizard, access tasks by name, and perform other tasks. Since both the AT command and the WMI Win32_ScheduledJob class cannot access tasks created or modified with the new task scheduler, SCHTASKS is your scripting tool of choice for scheduled task management.

The Scripting Advantage

Shell scripting has a slight advantage here because Microsoft and third parties have provided some powerful backup, restore, and scheduled task management utilities. With just a few lines of code (sometimes only 1), you can quickly create powerful shell scripts. Through COM and WMI, you can also automate backups, restores, and scheduled tasks. While both KiXtart and WSH can access these providers, due to size limitations of this book and the popularity of the scripting language, this chapter will provide these examples in Windows Script Host only. (It should be simple to convert the scripts to KiXtart.) Finally, AutoIt is not appropriate and is not discussed in this chapter.

A Word of Caution

This chapter contains many powerful scripting examples on backing up, restoring, and managing scheduled tasks. Accidentally restoring the wrong files, deleting production schedule tasks, or scheduling tasks on the wrong machine can all lead to disaster. As with all scripts, you should first test each script in an isolated testing environment to ensure the script produces the desired results before using it in a production environment.

Immediate Solutions

Managing NTBackup

The NTBackup utility supports multiple switches for performing backups from the command line. Here is a list of the available switches:

- **/A**—Appends backups

- **/D** *"label"*—Specifies a backup set *label*

- **/DS** *"server"*—Backs up the Microsoft Exchange directory service for the specified *server* name

- **/F** *"name"*—Specifies full path and file *name* of the backup file

- **/G** *"tapeID"*—Specifies to overwrite or append to the tape based on the specified *tape id*

- **/HC:***x*—Controls hardware compression where *x* is **ON** or **OFF**

- **/IS** *"server"*—Backs up the Microsoft Exchange information store for the specified *server* name

- **/J** *"job"*—Specifies a descriptive job name to record in the log file

- **/L:***x*—specifies the type of log file where *x* is:
  - **F**—Complete logging
  - **S**—Summary logging
  - **N**—No logging

- **/M:***x*—Specifies the backup type where *x* is:
  - **copy**—Back up files and do not clear their archive flag
  - **daily**—Back up today's changed files and do not clear their archive flag
  - **differential**—Back up changed files and do not clear their archive flag
  - **incremental**—Back up changed files then clear their archive flag

- **normal**—Back up files then clear their archive flag
- **/N** "*name*"—Specifies a new *name* to give the tape
- **/P** "*name*"—Specifies the *name* of the media pool to use
- **/R:*x***—Restricts tape access to the tape owner or administrators, where *x* is **YES** or **NO**
- **/RS *x***—Specifies to back up the removable storage database, where *x* is **YES** or **NO**
- **/T** "*tapename*"—Specifies to overwrite or append to the tape based on the specified *tape name*
- **/UM**—Specifies to find and format the find media available
- **/V:*x***—Performs backup verification, where *x* is **YES** or **NO**

Running NTBackup with Shell Scripting

To automate a full backup using NTBackup and shell scripting, create and execute a shell script that contains the following:

```
@Echo Off
Set BList=folders
Set BFile=backupfile
Set BComment=BackupComment

fullpath\NTBACKUP.EXE Backup %BList% /d "%BComment%" /l:F
/F "%BFile%" /V:YES

Set BList=
Set BFile=
Set BComment=
```

NOTE: *The highlighted code above must be placed on one line.*

Here, *folders* are the folders to back up; *backupfile* is the complete path and file name of the backup file to create (typically stored with a BKS extension); *BackupComment* is the comment to give the backup; and *fullpath* is the complete path to the NTBackup utility.

Running NTBackup with KiXtart

To automate a full backup using NTBackup, create and execute a KiXtart script that contains the following:

```
$BList = "folders"
$BFile = "backupfile"
$BComment = "BackupComment"
```

```
$BCommand = "fullpath\NTBACKUP.EXE Backup $BList /d " +
   chr(34) + "$BComment" + chr(34) + " /l:F /F " +
   chr(34) + "$BFile" + chr(34) + " /V:YES"
Run $Bcommand
```

NOTE: *The highlighted code above must be placed on one line. Chr(34) translates the ASCII code character 34 into a quotation mark ("). This is necessary when you are using the Run command with long file names.*

Here, *folders* are the folders to back up; *backupfile* is the complete path and file name of the backup file to create (typically stored with a BKS extension); *BackupComment* is the comment to give the backup; and *fullpath* is the complete path to the NTBackup utility.

Running NTBackup with Windows Script Host

To automate a full backup using NTBackup, create and execute a WSH script that contains the following:

```
On Error Resume Next
Set Shell = CreateObject("Wscript.Shell")

BList = "folders"
BFile = "backupfile "
BComment = "BackupComment"

BCommand = "fullpath\NTBACKUP.EXE Backup " & _

BList & " /d " & chr(34) & BComment & chr(34) & _
   " /l:F /F " & chr(34) & BFile & chr(34) & " /V:YES"

Shell.Run BCommand, 0, TRUE
```

NOTE: *You cannot completely hide the NTBackup process with Windows Script Host.*

Here, *folders* are the folders to back up; *backupfile* is the complete path and file name of the backup file to create (typically stored with a BKS extension); *BackupComment* is the comment to give the backup; and *fullpath* is the complete path to the NTBackup utility.

Backing Up the IIS 6.0 Metabase Using Shell Scripting

The Internet Information Server Metabase is a database like structure used to store IIS configuration settings. Starting with IIS 6.0, the metabase is stored in a single, easy to read and modify XML file. To automate a backup of the IIS 6.0 metabase, create and execute a shell script that contains the following:

```
xcopy /o /x /h /y /c
"\\computername\c$\WINDOWS\system32\inetsrv\MetaBase.xml"
"backuplocation"
```

Here, ***computername*** is the name of the IIS 6.0 server and ***backuplocation*** is the directory where the metabase XML file will be stored.

Restoring the IIS 6.0 Metabase Using Shell Scripting

To restore the an XML backup of an IIS 6.0 metabase, create and execute a shell script that contains the following:

```
IISRESET computername /STOP
xcopy /o /x /h /y /c "backupfile"
"\\computername\c$\WINDOWS\system32\inetsrv\"
IISRESET computername /START
```

NOTE: *The highlighted code above must be placed on one line.*

Here, ***computername*** is the name of the target IIS server and ***backupfile*** is the complete path where the backed up, IIS 6.0 metabase XML file is stored.

Backing Up the IIS Metabase Using Windows Script Host

While IIS 6.0 stores the metabase in a clear, easy to read XML file, earlier versions are stored in binary format. Through the IIS provider, you can quickly backup and restore the metabase for these earlier versions. To automate a backup of the IIS metabase using Windows Script Host, create and execute a WSH script that contains the following:

```
On Error Resume Next
NextVersion = &HFFFFFFFF
BackupFlags = 0

Set objComputer = GetObject("IIS://" & ComputerName)
objComputer.Backup backupfile, NextVersion, BackupFlags
```

Here, ***computername*** is the name of the IIS server and ***backupflle*** is the name of the backup file to create.

Restoring the IIS Metabase Using Windows Script Host

To restore the most recent backup of the IIS metabase using Windows Script Host, create and execute a WSH script that contains the following:

```
On Error Resume Next
HighestVersion = &HFFFFFFFE
BackupFlags = 0

Set objComputer = GetObject("IIS://" & ComputerName)
objComputer.Restore backuplocation, HighestVersion, BackupFlags
```

Here, ***computername*** is the name of the IIS server and ***backuplocation*** is the complete path where the IIS metabase backup is stored.

Controlling Backup Exec from the Command Line

Backup Exec is a complete backup solution from Veritas (**www.veritas.com**) that includes advanced backup functionality, such as virus scanning. The BackupExec executable (BKUPEXEC.EXE) allows you to run a scheduled job from the command line. The basic syntax of BKUPEXEC is as follows:

```
BkupExec /J:"jobname"
```

Here, **/J** indicates to run BackupExec in command-line mode, and ***jobname*** is the name of the scheduled backup job.

NOTE: *If the BackupExec program is running or the jobname does not exist, the BkupExec command will not work.*

Consolidating BackUp Exec Logs

Whenever BackUp Exec performs a task, it records the progress in an individual log file stored in the program's data directory. Call me lazy, but I hate having to go to the server room, log onto multiple servers, and then check the job status. To remotely consolidate these log files to a central Excel spreadsheet (right from your desk), and execute a WSH script that contains the following:

```
On Error Resume Next
Set FSO = CreateObject("Scripting.FileSystemObject")
Set objXL = CreateObject("Excel.Application")

BEPath = "logpath"
Server = "servername"
```

```
SDays = InputBox("Please enter the number of days to report")
SDays = Int(SDays) - 1

Column = 1
Row = 1
SetupXL 'Setup Excel Sheet

BEFolder = "\\" & Server & "\" & BEPath
ChkBkUp BEFolder

Wscript.Echo "Complete."
Wscript.Quit

Sub SetupXL 'Setup and format Excel Sheet
    objXL.Workbooks.Add
    objXL.Columns(1).ColumnWidth = 20
    objXL.Columns(2).ColumnWidth = 10
    objXL.Columns(3).ColumnWidth = 15
    objXL.Columns(4).ColumnWidth = 10
    objXL.Columns(5).ColumnWidth = 15
    objXL.Columns(6).ColumnWidth = 10

    objXL.Cells(1,Column).Value = "Server"
    objXL.Cells(1,Column+1).Value = "Job"
    objXL.Cells(1,Column+2).Value = "Type"
    objXL.Cells(1,Column+3).Value = "Start Date"
    objXL.Cells(1,Column+4).Value = "Start Time"
    objXL.Cells(1,Column+5).Value = "Status"
    objXL.Cells(1,Column+6).Value = "Size"
    objXL.Range("A1:K1").Select
    objXL.Selection.Font.Bold = True 'Bold top row
    objXL.Selection.Interior.ColorIndex = 1
    objXL.Selection.Interior.Pattern = 1
    objXL.Selection.Font.ColorIndex = 2
End Sub

Sub ChkBkUp(BEFolder) 'Check if log folder exists
    If FSO.FolderExists(BEFolder) Then
        Set objDirectory = FSO.GetFolder(BEFolder)
        Set DirFiles = objDirectory.Files
        ExcelSheet(DirFiles)
    Else
        Wscript.echo "Could not access folder: " & BEFolder
    End If
End Sub

Sub ExcelSheet(DirFiles) 'Enter info to Excel sheet
    For Each objFile in DirFiles
```

```
objXL.Visible = True
FEXT = FSO.GetExtensionName(objFile.Path)
fDate = DateDiff("d", objFile.DateCreated, Date)
'Check if log date is within the search days specified
If (LCase(FEXT) = "txt") AND ((fDate <= SDays) AND _
(fDate > 0)) Then
 Verify = 0
 strSize = 0
 'Open log and transfer data to Excel sheet
 Set ts = FSO.OpenTextFile(objFile, 1)
 Do while ts.AtEndOfStream <> true
 s =ts.ReadLine
 If InStr(s, "Job server: ") <> 0 Then
   Row = Row + 1
   objXL.Cells(Row,Column).Value = Mid(s, 13)
 ElseIf InStr(s, "Job type: ") <> 0 Then
   objXL.Cells(Row,Column+1).Value = Mid(s, 11)
 ElseIf InStr(s, "Job name: ") <> 0 Then
   objXL.Cells(Row,Column+2).Value = Mid(s, 11)
 ElseIf InStr(s, "Job started: ") <> 0 Then
  dTemp = InStr(s, ", ")
  tTemp = InStr(s, " at ")
  dTemp = dTemp + 2
  dEnd = tTemp - dTemp
   objXL.Cells(Row,Column+3).Value = Mid(s, dTemp,dEnd)
  tTemp = tTemp + 4
   objXL.Cells(Row,Column+4).Value = Mid(s, tTemp)
  ElseIfS = "Job Operation - Verify" Then
   Verify = 1
  ElseIf (Verify = 1) AND _
  InStr(s, "Processed ") <> 0 Then
   myarray = Split(s)
   If IsNumeric(myarray(1)) Then
     strSize = strSize + _
     (LEFT((myarray(1)/1073741824),6))/1
  End If
   ElseIf InStr(s, "Job completion status: ") <> 0
   Verify = 0
    objXL.Cells(Row,Column+6).Value = strSize
    objXL.Cells(Row,Column+5).Value = Mid(s, 24)
    'If backup failed, bold and highlight red
   If LCase(Mid(s, 24)) = LCase("Failed") Then
     tRange = "A" & Row & ":G" & Row
   objXL.Range(tRange).Select
   objXL.Selection.Font.Bold = True
   objXL.Selection.Font.ColorIndex = 3
  'If backup not successful, bold
```

```
    ElseIf LCase(Mid(s, 24)) <> LCase("Successful") Then
      tRange = "A" & Row & ":G" & Row
      objXL.Range(tRange).Select
      objXL.Selection.Font.Bold = True
    End If
  End If
    Loop
    ts.Close 'Close log file
    End If
    Next
  End Sub
```

Here, *servername* is the name of the server to connect to, and *logpath* is the administrative share and complete path where the logs are stored (typically c$\Program Files\Veritas\Backup Exec\NT\Data).

Related solution:	Found on page:
Creating Detailed Spreadsheets in Microsoft Excel	100

Controlling ARCserve 2000 from the Command Line

ARCserve 2000 is an advanced backup utility from Computer Associates (**www.cai.com**). ARCbatch, included with ARCserve, is a command-line utility that runs backup script files or templates. The basic syntax of the ARCbatch command is as follows:

```
ARCbatch /H=server /S=script
```

Here, *server* is the name of the server to run the specified *script*. *Script* is the full name and path to the ARCbatch script or template file. ARCbatch scripts have an ASX extension and are created with the ARCserve manager. ARCbatch templates are INI files you can create to perform or schedule backups and restores. To immediately run a full backup using ARCbatch, proceed as follows:

1. Create a new directory to store all files included in this example.

2. Start a command prompt and enter "*fullpath*\ARCbatch H=*server*/S=*template*."

Here, *fullpath* is the full path to the ARCbatch utility; *server* is the name of the server to run the specified *script*; and *template* is the full path and file name of a template file that contains the following:

```
[GENERAL]
HOST=*
JOBTYPE=BACKUP
JOBDESCRIPTION=description

[SOURCE_BACKUP]
NODE_NUM=1
BKMETHOD=1
VERIFICATION=2

[NODE_1]
DOMAINNAME=*
NODENAME=$HOST$
NODETYPE=NTAGENT

[DESTINATION_BACKUP]
TAPENAME=tape
GROUPNAME=group

[MEDIA_OPTIONS]
FIRSTTAPEOPTIONS=2
```

Here, **description** is the comment to add to the job; **tape** is the name of the tape; and **group** is the name of the device group.

Scheduling Tasks with the **AT** Command

The **AT** command allows you to schedule tasks from the command line. The basic syntax of the **AT** command is as follows:

```
AT \\remote ID /COMMANDS "fullpath"
```

TIP: To display a list of schedule tasks from the command line, start a command prompt and enter "AT."

Here, **remote** is an optional name of a remote system of which tasks to control; **ID** specifies a task ID to modify; **fullpath** is the complete path and file name of the item to schedule; and the available **commands** are as follows:

- **/DELETE**—Removes a scheduled job.

- **/YES**—Combined with **/DELETE**, suppresses all jobs cancellation prompt.

- **/INTERACTIVE**—Sets the job to interact with the desktop. This switch must be set if you want the user to have any interactivity with the scheduled task.

- **/EVERY:x**—Recurrently runs the command on the specified day (x).

- **/NEXT:x**—Runs the command on the next specified date (x).

TIP: *You can use the Windows 2000 Resource Kit Utility WINAT to graphically control and view scheduled tasks.*

Creating Tasks with the AT Command

To schedule a script file to run at a specified time every work day, start a command prompt and enter the following:

```
AT  \\remote time /interactive /every:M,T,W,TH,F scriptfile
```

Here, **remote** is the name of the system to store the scheduled task; **time** is the time to run the task; and **scriptfile** is the full path and name of the script to run.

Listing Tasks with the AT Command

To list tasks on a remote system with the AT command, start a command prompt and enter the following:

```
AT \\computer
```

Here, **computer** is the name of the computer to query.

Deleting Tasks with the AT Command

To delete a scheduled task on a remote system with the AT command, start a command prompt and enter the following:

```
AT \\computer id /delete /yes
```

Here, **id** is the identifier of the target task to delete and **computer** is the name of the remote system. To delete all scheduled tasks on a remote system with the AT command, start a command prompt and enter the following:

```
AT \\computer /delete /yes
```

Creating Tasks Using SCHTASKS

To create a scheduled daily task using SCHTASKS, start a command prompt and enter the following:

```
schtasks /create /tn "taskname" /tr fullpath /sc daily /st miltime
```

Here, **taskname** is the name of the task to create; **fullpath** is the full path and file name of the program to execute; and **miltime** is the time to schedule a task to run (in military format).

Listing Tasks Using SCHTASKS

To list tasks on a remote system using SCHTASKS, start a command prompt and enter the following:

```
schtasks /query /s computer
```

Here, **computer** is the name of the computer to query.

Running Tasks Using SCHTASKS

To run a scheduled task on a remote system using SCHTASKS, start a command prompt and enter the following:

```
schtasks /run /tn "taskname" /s computer
```

Here, ***taskname*** is the name of the task to run and ***computer*** is the name of the remote system.

Ending Running Tasks Using SCHTASKS

To end a running scheduled task on a remote system using SCHTASKS, start a command prompt and enter the following:

```
schtasks /end /tn "taskname" /s computer
```

Here, ***taskname*** is the name of the running task to end and ***computer***.

Deleting Tasks Using SCHTASKS

To delete a scheduled task on a remote system using SCHTASKS, start a command prompt and enter the following:

```
schtasks /delete /tn "taskname" /s computer
```

Here, ***taskname*** is the name of the task to delete and ***computer*** is the name of the remote system.

TIP: You can use the /tn * parameter to delete all scheduled tasks.

Creating Tasks with WMI

The **Win32_ScheduledJob** class allows you to create, delete, or view scheduled tasks. This class is extremely limited in functionality, incorrectly documented, and difficult to work with. There is no method to modify an existing task and there are only a few available parameters when creating a task. This class also only recognizes and can create tasks compatible with the **AT** command. Whenever possible, you should use the SCHTASKS command (as discussed above). For whatever reason, to create a scheduled task using WMI, create and execute a WSH script that contains the following:

```
On Error Resume Next
DTime = MilTime

Set TZone = GetObject("winmgmts:{impersonationLevel=
impersonate}!\\computer\root\cimv2").ExecQuery
("select * from Win32_TimeZone")

For each Zone in TZone
  TBias = Zone.bias + 60 'Compensates for daylight savings
Next

STime = "********" & DTime & "00.000000" & TBias

Set ScheduledJob = GetObject("winmgmts:{impersonationLevel=
impersonate}!\\computer\root\cimv2:Win32_ScheduledJob")
  Set method = ScheduledJob.Methods_("Create")
  SetinParam = method.inParameters.SpawnInstance_()
    inParam.Command = "fullpath"
    inParam.StartTime = STime
    inParam.RunRepeatedly = rp
    inParam.DaysOfWeek = dow
  Set outParam = ScheduledJob.ExecMethod_("Create", inParam)
```

NOTE: *The highlighted code above must be placed on one line.*

Here, ***miltime*** is the time to schedule a task to run (in military format); ***fullpath*** is the full path and file name of the program to execute; ***rp*** is a binary entry (0 or 1) that specifies whether to create a reoccurring task; and ***dow*** are the days of the week to run the task. ***Dow*** does not accept abbreviated day names (M,T,W,…), but must be entered in binary format where the days of the week are as follows:

- *Monday*—1
- *Tuesday*—2
- *Wednesday*—4
- *Thursday*—8
- *Friday*—16
- *Saturday*—32
- *Sunday*—64

To schedule a task to run on a specific day, simply add up the day values and enter the total. For example, to run a task on Tuesday, Friday, and Saturday, you would enter 50 (2+16+32).

Listing Tasks in Internet Explorer Using WMI

The **Win32_ScheduledJob** class can retrieve and display information on any task previously created using the **Win32_ScheduledJob** class or **AT** command. To list these scheduled tasks within a formatted Internet Explorer window, create and execute a WSH script that contains the following:

```
On Error Resume Next
Set FSO = CreateObject("Scripting.FileSystemObject")
Set MSIE = CreateObject("InternetExplorer.Application")
Set ScheduledJob = GetObject("winmgmts:{impersonationLevel=
impersonate}!\\computer\root\cimv2").ExecQuery("select *
from Win32_ScheduledJob")

SetupMSIE
MSIE.Document.Write "<HTML><TITLE>Scheduled Jobs" & _
  "</TITLE><BODY bgcolor=#ffffff><FONT FACE=ARIAL>"
MSIE.Document.Write "<B>Displaying tasks created " & _
  "with WMI or the AT command:</B><BR><BR>" & _
  "<table border=0 width=100% cellspacing=0 " & _
  "cellpadding=0>"

For each ejob in ScheduledJob
  IEWrite "Caption", EJob.Caption
  IEWrite "Command", EJob.Command
  IEWrite "Days Of Month", EJob.DaysOfMonth
  IEWrite "Days Of Week", EJob.DaysOfWeek
  IEWrite "Description", EJob.Description
  IEWrite "Install Date" ,EJob.InstallDate
  IEWrite "Interact With Desktop", EJob.InteractWithDesktop
  IEWrite "Job ID", EJob.JobID
  IEWrite "Job Status", EJob.JobStatus
  IEWrite "Name", EJob.Name
  IEWrite "Notify", EJob.Notify
  IEWrite "Owner", EJob.Owner
  IEWrite "Priority", EJob.Priority
  IEWrite "Run Repeatedly", EJob.RunRepeatedly
  IEWrite "Start Time", EJob.StartTime
  IEWrite "Status", EJob.Status
  IEWrite "Time Submitted", EJob.TimeSubmitted
  IEWrite "Until Time", EJob.UntilTime
  IEWrite " ", " "
Next
```

14. Backups and Scheduling

343

```
MSIE.Document.Write "</table><BR><B>End of List</B>" & _
  "</FONT></BODY>"

Sub SetupMSIE
  MSIE.Navigate "About:Blank"
  MSIE.ToolBar = False
  MSIE.StatusBar = False
  MSIE.Resizable = False

  Do
  Loop While MSIE.Busy

  SWidth = MSIE.Document.ParentWindow.Screen.AvailWidth
  SHeight = MSIE.Document.ParentWindow.Screen.AvailHeight
  MSIE.Width = SWidth/2
  MSIE.Height = SHeight/2
  MSIE.Left = (SWidth - MSIE.Width)/2
  MSIE.Top = (SHeight - MSIE.Height)/2

  MSIE.Visible = True
End Sub
Sub IEWrite(Caption,Prop)
    MSIE.Document.Write "<tr><td>" & Caption & "</td>" & _
      "<td> </td><td align=right>" & Prop & _
      "</td></tr>"
End Sub
```

NOTE: *The highlighted code above must be placed on one line.*

Here, **computer** is the name of the computer containing the tasks to list.

Related solution:	Found on page:
Using Microsoft Internet Explorer as a Display Tool	98

Deleting Tasks Using WMI

The **Win32_ScheduledJob** class can delete any task previously created with the **Win32_ScheduledJob** class or **AT** command. To delete all of these scheduled tasks using WMI, create and execute a WSH script that contains the following:

```
On Error Resume Next
Set ScheduledJob = GetObject("winmgmts:" & _
  "{impersonationLevel=impersonate}!\\" & _
  computer & "\root\cimv2")_

.ExecQuery("select * from Win32_ScheduledJob")

For each
ejob in ScheduledJob
  ejob.Delete()
Next
```

NOTE: *The highlighted code above must be placed on one line.*

Here, ***computer*** is the name of the computer containing the tasks to delete.

Chapter 15

SQL Processing and Automation

In Brief

The popularity of Microsoft SQL server has likely grown due to its simplicity and self management, when compared to other database systems. Within 30 minutes, anyone can have SQL server installed and up and running. This simplicity and self management, on the other hand, makes SQL server a nightmare for administrators. As a company falls in love with the simplicity, more and more SQL servers may start popping up. And while it may seem that the servers manage themselves, they will quickly require attention as more data is added and more users are connected. Databases grow out of control, queries run slow, servers crash, and then management turns to you to solve the problem.

Managing one, if not multiple, SQL servers in an enterprise can be a full time job. Without a little help, this can be an overwhelming task. This chapter will give you a brief introduction to SQL server, its objects, and its custom terminology. You will then learn how to take control of SQL server through shell and Windows Script host scripting.

NOTE: This chapter focuses on Microsoft SQL 2000. All of the examples in this chapter have been tested on Microsoft SQL 2000, but they should also work on Microsoft SQL 2005.

The Insides of SQL Server

SQL server is a huge product and fortunately you can practically script every aspect of SQL server. Due to the size of this book, we can't discuss and show you how to script every SQL object. This is why we decided to focus on the most common objects and tasks.

The Services

SQL server is controlled by two services: the SQL server service and the SQL agent service. The SQL server service is the core service that processes, sends, and receives requests. The name of the SQL server service is **MSSQLSERVER** for the default instance and **MSSQL$*InstanceName*** for a named instance. If this service is stopped, SQL is completely useless.

The SQL Agent service is the heart of running SQL jobs. The name of the SQL agent service is **SQLSERVERAGENT** for the default instance and **SQLAGENT$*InstanceName*** for a named instance. If this service is stopped, jobs and job schedules will not be able to start.

Databases

A database is a structure that holds related data with the sole purpose of allowing fast and easy data storage, retrieval, searches, and analysis. In addition to data, a database also contains security information on who can access what data. SQL server can serve one or several databases simultaneously. For example, a company may have a database for each department (Sales, Marketing, HR, and so on).

Tables

A table is a structure that stores data in rows and columns. The columns are given names and types (e.g., string, integer, date, and so on) providing you with an easy way to target the data you want. Rows are how SQL stores entries in a table. The following table shows the contents of an example SQL table:

Table 15.1   Example Customers SQL Table.

CustomerID	FirstName	LastName
1	Peter	Griffin
2	Cleveland	Brown
3	Joe	Swanson
4	Glen	Quagmire

SQL has two types of tables: system and user. System tables are tables created and required by SQL server and all other tables are user tables (created by users). A SQL server database can house one or multiple tables. For example, a sales database may have multiple tables (customers, products, orders, and so on).

Jobs

SQL server includes a job server known as the SQL Agent. The SQL Agent runs as a service, can execute jobs, and can even log and email the job status. SQL server can run one or multiple jobs on multiple schedules. For example, you may have jobs that perform data archiving, database backups, and database maintenance at the same or on different days and times. Every SQL job must have a unique name and every job must have at least one step.

Job Steps

Every SQL job is comprised of steps. These steps individually perform the desired actions of the job. These steps can be a T-SQL script, a replication script, a shell script, and even an SQLDMO VBScript. Each job step is assigned a number which indicates the run order. Every SQL job step must have a unique name.

Linked Servers

If you have multiple servers, you may want those servers to be able to talk to one another. This is where linked servers come in. Linked servers are merely shortcuts to other servers. They contain information like the name of the server, the connection method, and which credentials to use. Each server must have a unique name. Once a linked server is setup, you can query that server using either the server's name or a friendly name. For example, if you are on ServerA and you want to select data from the Customers table in the Sales database on a ServerB, you may run:

```
SELECT * FROM ServerB.dbo.Sales.Customers
```

Stored Procedures

A stored procedure is simply a saved SQL script. It can contain a simple query or complex queries and code to perform just about any operation you can think of. While SQL server comes with tons of built-in queries, you can also create your own. The following example is a very simple example of a stored procedure:

```
CREATE Procedure dbo.GetCustomerOrders
     @CustomerID INT
AS
SELECT *
FROM dbo.Orders
WHERE CustomerID=@CustomerID
```

You then could call the stored procedure as follows:

```
EXEC dbo.GetCustomerOrders 24
```

Here, 24 is the customer ID for which you wish to obtain order information.

Security

SQL server security is two part: authentication and authorization. First, you must authenticate (prove to the server you are who you say you are) the server and then you can access resources with the proper permissions (authorization).

Authentication Modes

SQL server provides two connection modes: Windows and mixed. Windows mode only allows authenticated Windows users to connect to the server. Mixed mode includes Windows mode, but additionally allows for SQL logins.

Logins

A login is a SQL login, Windows group, or Windows user that is allowed to access the SQL server. The purpose of a login is purely authentication and its only job is to allow access (with a valid login) or deny access (without a valid login) to the SQL server. Without a valid login, you cannot connect to the SQL server. It does not allow access to databases, database objects, and so on. SQL logins are logins created in an individual SQL server. While Windows users and groups can be added as logins without supplying passwords, creating a SQL login requires a password of your choosing.

Users

Once you have access to the SQL server via a login, you need access to databases and their objects. The purpose of a user is purely authorization. They are created in a desired database, map to SQL logins, and can either be granted or denied access to objects within that database. Unlike creating a SQL login, SQL users do not require you to create a new password as they map back to a login with an existing password.

NOTE: *While you can create a SQL user with a different name from the corresponding SQL login, this is not recommended practice and is not shown in this book.*

The Terminology

Besides having its own programming language (T-SQL also known as Transact-SQL) and custom objects, SQL server also has its own terminology for very basic concepts. While this chapter attempts to avoid the usage of this specific terminology wherever possible, it is included to give you a better understanding of some of the more advanced topics in this chapter.

Dropping/Deleting

"Dropping" refers to the deletion of an entire object. "dropping a login," "dropping a database," or "dropping a table," simply means to delete the object (data included). Dropping a table will cause the table to be deleted, which means all the data it contained is lost. Dropping a database will cause all the database objects to also be deleted, which means all the data it contained is lost.

Scripting/Exporting

"Scripting" refers to the exporting of an object to a file. Exporting objects only exports the creation and structure of the object and does not export data within objects. This structure is called DDL or Data Definition Language. The following is an example of an exported table's DDL:

```
CREATE TABLE [dbo].[Employees] (
     [EmloyeeID] [int] IDENTITY (1, 1) NOT NULL ,
     [FirstName] [varchar] (50) COLLATE
SQL_Latin1_General_CP1_CI_AS NOT NULL ,
     [LastName] [varchar] (50) COLLATE
SQL_Latin1_General_CP1_CI_AS NOT NULL
) ON [PRIMARY]
GO
```

Once an object is exported, you can restore them, restore them to another SQL server, import them into a SourceSafe, and so on. This chapter includes several examples on how to export individual objects and even how to export all the objects of a SQL database all at once.

Executing/Running

"Executing" refers to the running of a query or stored procedure. This phrase comes from the SQL key word **EXEC** or **EXECUTE,** which instructs the server to run the query or stored procedure.

Selecting

"Selecting" refers to the displaying of data. "Selecting rows from a table" simply means to display the rows from a table. This phrase comes from the SQL key word **SELECT,** which instructs the server to display data.

Results

"Results" are the rows and columns returned when selecting data. SQL stores data and returns data in rows and columns, similar to an Excel spreadsheet. After data is selected, the results are displayed.

Deleting/Truncation

SQL server offers two ways to delete data from a table. You can either delete the data from the table or truncate the table. Deleting the data from the table instructs SQL to go through the table row by row and delete the data. This allows you to target a specific set of data to delete. Here's an example:

```
DELETE FROM TableName WHERE ColumnName=SomeValue
```

Using the **DELETE** command can be extremely slow if you have a large amount of rows. If you simply need to delete all the data, you can use the **TRUNCATE** command. Truncating a table instructs SQL to delete all the data in one shot, thus speeding up the deletion process. Here's an example:

```
TRUNCATE TABLE TableName
```

Queries

Just like a script, a SQL query is merely a command or group of commands. Queries can perform simple tasks like selecting (displaying), updating, deleting, or inserting data as well as executing stored procedures and even performing complex control logic. The following is an example of a simple query that selects data:

```
SELECT * FROM TableName
```

The following is an example of a query that retrieves a value, passes that value to a stored procedure, then executes that stored procedure:

```
DECLARE @CustomerID INT
SET @CustomerID =(SELECT TOP 1 CustomerID
FROM dbo.Customers
WHERE FirstName='Doc'
AND LastName='Brown')
EXEC dbo.GetCustomerOrders @CustomerID
```

OSQL

OSQL is a utility that allows you to run queries on SQL servers from the command line. It comes installed whenever SQL Server or SQL Server client tools are installed. By providing the proper SQL queries, not only can you select, change, and return data but you can also perform administrative tasks like controlling logins, users, linked servers, and more. The OSQL utility is typically located in C:\Program Files\Microsoft SQL Server\80\Tools\Binn.

NOTE: *SQLCMD.exe is an extension of the OSQL utility and is only available in SQL 2005.*

SQLDMO

SQL Enterprise Manager is the SQL 2000 tool to manage SQL servers and instances. If you've ever had to work with a SQL 2000 server, you know this tool and know it well. Unfortunately, while this tool is very powerful, it does not support scripting. Behind the scenes, SQL Enterprise Manager uses SQLDMO (SQL Distributed Management Objects), a central API for SQL management. Fortunately for us scripters, you can connect to this API to create scripts to do just about anything SQL Enterprise Manager can do.

SQLDMO gives you complete access to all SQL objects (databases, tables, views, stored procedures, triggers, indexes, jobs, users, logins, and more). SQLDMO is installed whenever SQL Server or SQL Server client tools are installed.

The Scripting Advantage

Due to the power of SQLDMO, Windows Script Host and KiXtart have the clear advantage. While both can access SQLDMO through COM, due to the size limitations of this book and the popularity of the scripting language, this chapter will provide SQLDMO examples in Windows Script Host only. (It should be simple to convert the scripts to KiXtart.) Through OSQL, shell scripting has a following advantage, but it simply cannot compete with SQLDMO. Finally, AutoIt follows with its inability to nicely interact with SQLDMO and OSQL, although you can use AutoIt to run any of the shell and Windows Script Host scripts in this chapter.

A Word of Caution

This chapter contains many scripting examples on modifying and deleting SQL objects (database, tables, and so on). As with all scripts, you should first test each script in an isolated testing environment to ensure the script produces the desired results before using it in a production environment.

Immediate Solutions

Scripting SQL with Shell Scripting

In all of the examples presented in this section, *ServerName* is the name of the SQL server (or "" to connect to the local server) you wish to target. You will also need to append the ExecSQLQuery routine, listed earlier in this chapter, to all scripts in this section in order for the scripts to run. In all examples, no username and password are passed to the ExecSQLQuery routine, thus using the Windows credentials of the logged on user. You may supply a SQL username and password if needed.

Executing a Query with Results

OSQL provides an easy way to run queries and have results returned from the command line. Unfortunately, those results are not nicely displayed by default. Throughout this chapter, we will use the following function to execute a SQL query and return a result set from the command line:

```
:ExecSQLQuery
SETLOCAL ENABLEEXTENSIONS

Set OutFile=%RANDOM%.txt
Set SQL=SET NOCOUNT ON %5
 ::Remove quotes
Set SQL=%SQL:"=%

Set Server=%1
IF %Server%=="" Set Server="(local)"

IF NOT %2=="" SET Creds=-U %2 -P %3
IF %2=="" Set Creds=-E

OSQL %Creds% -h-1 -w 65536 -S %Server% -d %4 -Q "%SQL%" -o
%OutFile%
For /F "tokens=* delims=" %%A in (%OutFile%) Do Echo. %%A
DEL %OutFile% > NUL

ENDLOCAL&GOTO:EOF
```

For example, to select all the data from the Customers table in the Purchasing database, create and then execute a shell script containing the following:

```
CALL :ExecSQLQuery "ServerName" "" "" "Purchasing" "SELECT * from
Customers"
GOTO:EOF
```

NOTE: *The highlighted code above must be placed on one line.*

Exporting Objects

SCPTXFR is a command line utility that can export a database and its objects to a file. This utility comes with the standard install of SQL server and is usually located at C:\Program Files\Microsoft SQL Server\MSSQL\Upgrade. To export a database and its objects to a file with SCPTXFR, start the command prompt and enter the following:

```
SCPTXFR /s ServerName /I /d DatabaseName /f FilePath
```

Here, ***DatabaseName*** is the name of the job you wish to target and ***FilePath*** is the complete path of a file that will contain the exported database and object structures.

NOTE: *SCPTXFR is not available in SQL 2005.*

Scripting SQL Servers

The following section will introduce you to the basic techniques of shell scripting the core SQL services and returning basic server information like the service pack and server edition.

Listing SQL Servers with OSQL

OSQL provides a simple way to list running SQL server instances on the network. To list SQL servers with OSQL, start the command prompt and enter the following:

```
OSQL -L
```

NOTE: *You do not need to append the ExecSQLQuery routine to the script above.*

Displaying the SQL Edition

To display the edition of a given SQL server, create and then execute a shell script containing the following:

```
CALL :ExecSQLQuery "ServerName" "" "" "MASTER" "SELECT
SERVERPROPERTY ('edition')"
GOTO:EOF
```

Displaying the SQL Product Level

The **ProductLevel** property returns a string describing the installed product level of a SQL server. Once your SQL server has a service pack installed, this property will return a string like "SP4." If your SQL server has no service pack installed, it may display "RTM" (Release to Manufacturing—this is the original product version), "B1" (Beta 1), or something else. To display the service pack for a given SQL server, create and then execute a shell script containing the following:

```
CALL :ExecSQLQuery "ServerName" "" "" "MASTER" "SELECT
SERVERPROPERTY ('productlevel')"
GOTO:EOF
```

Starting/Stopping the SQL Service

To stop or start the SQL service, you can use any of the service control scripts from Chapters 7 and 8. For example, using information we learned in Chapter 8 we could stop the default SQL server instance on a remote machine called **BumbleBee** using the Windows 2000 resource kit utility NETSVC by starting a command prompt and entering the following:

```
NETSVC /STOP MSSQLSERVER \\BumbleBee
```

NOTE: *You do not need to append the ExecSQLQuery routine to the script above.*

Scripting Databases

In all examples in this section, ***DatabaseName*** is the name of the database you wish to target.

Listing Databases

To list databases for a given SQL server, create and then execute a shell script containing the following:

```
CALL :ExecSQLQuery "ServerName" "" "" "Master" "SELECT Name FROM
dbo.SysDatabases"
GOTO:EOF
```

NOTE: *The highlighted code above must be placed on one line.*

Shrinking Databases

If a SQL database is set to automatically grow, it will continue to grow as data is added and will not shrink even if you delete all the data. To shrink a database for a given SQL server, create and then execute a shell script containing the following:

```
CALL :ExecSQLQuery "ServerName" "" "" "Master" "DBCC
SHRINKDATABASE(DatabaseName)"
GOTO:EOF
```

Deleting Databases

To delete a database from a given SQL server, create and then execute a shell script containing the following:

```
CALL :ExecSQLQuery "ServerName" "" "" "Master" "DROP DATABASE
DatabaseName"
GOTO:EOF
```

Scripting Tables

In all examples in this section, ***DatabaseName*** is the name of the database that contains the table (***TableName***) you wish to target.

Listing Tables

To list both user and system tables for a given SQL server database, create and then execute a shell script containing the following:

```
CALL :ExecSQLQuery "ServerName" "" "" "DatabaseName" "SELECT Name
FROM dbo.SysObjects WHERE xtype IN ('U','S') ORDER BY Name"
GOTO:EOF
```

To list only user tables for a given SQL server database, create and then execute a shell script containing the following:

```
CALL :ExecSQLQuery "ServerName" "" "" "DatabaseName" "SELECT Name
FROM dbo.SysObjects WHERE xtype = 'U' ORDER BY Name"
GOTO:EOF
```

Updating Table Statistics

Updated table statistics are vital to fast responding queries. To update the statistics of a table for given SQL server database, create and then execute a shell script containing the following:

```
CALL :ExecSQLQuery "ServerName" "" "" "DatabaseName" "UPDATE
STATISTICS TableName"
GOTO:EOF
```

NOTE: *The highlighted code above must be placed on one line.*

Deleting all Data from a Table

To delete all data from a table for a given SQL server database, create and then execute a shell script containing the following:

```
CALL :ExecSQLQuery "ServerName" "" "" "DatabaseName" "DELETE FROM
TableName"
GOTO:EOF
```

To truncate a table for a given SQL server database, create and then execute a shell script containing the following:

```
CALL :ExecSQLQuery "ServerName" "" "" "DatabaseName" "TRUNCATE
TABLE TableName"
GOTO:EOF
```

NOTE: *The TRUNCATE command cannot be used on tables referenced by foreign keys.*

Deleting Tables

To delete a table for a given SQL server database, create and then execute a shell script containing the following:

```
CALL :ExecSQLQuery "ServerName" "" "" "DatabaseName" "DROP TABLE
TableName"
GOTO:EOF
```

Scripting Stored Procedures

In all of the examples presented in this section, *DatabaseName* is the name of the database you wish to target, *StoredProcedure* is the name of the stored procedure you wish to target, and *Parameters* are the parameters (if any) you wish to pass to the stored procedure.

Listing Stored Procedures

To list both user and system stored procedures in a given SQL server database, create and then execute a shell script containing the following:

```
CALL :ExecSQLQuery "ServerName" "" "" "DatabaseName" "SELECT Name
FROM dbo.SysObjects WHERE xtype='P' ORDER BY Name"
GOTO:EOF
```

NOTE: *The highlighted code above must be placed on one line.*

To only list user stored procedures in a given SQL server database, create and then execute a shell script containing the following:

```
CALL :ExecSQLQuery "ServerName" "" "" "DatabaseName" "SELECT Name
FROM dbo.SysObjects WHERE xtype='P' AND Category=0 ORDER BY Name"
GOTO:EOF
```

Display Stored Procedure Code

To display the code of a stored procedure in a given SQL server database, create and then execute a shell script containing the following:

```
CALL :ExecSQLQuery "ServerName" "" "" "DatabaseName" "EXEC
sp_helptext StoredProcedure"
GOTO:EOF
```

NOTE: *If a stored procedure is encrypted, you will not be able to see or modify the stored procedure.*

Running Stored Procedures

To run a stored procedure in a given SQL server database, create and then execute a shell script containing the following:

```
CALL :ExecSQLQuery "ServerName" "" "" "DatabaseName" "EXEC
StoredProcedure Parameters "
GOTO:EOF
```

For example, if you wanted to run the stored procedure **Delete Customer** to delete customer 24, your script would contain:

```
CALL :ExecSQLQuery "ServerName" "" "" "DatabaseName" "EXEC
DeleteCustomer 24"
GOTO:EOF
```

Deleting Stored Procedures

To delete a stored procedure in a given SQL server database, create and then execute a shell script containing the following:

```
CALL :ExecSQLQuery "ServerName" "" "" "DatabaseName" "DROP
PROCEDURE ProcedureName"
GOTO:EOF
```

NOTE: *The highlighted code above must be placed on one line.*

Scripting Jobs

In all examples in this section, *JobName* is the name of the job you wish to target, and *JobStepNumber* is the number of the job step you wish to target.

Listing Jobs

To list jobs for a given SQL server, create and then execute a shell script containing the following:

```
CALL :ExecSQLQuery "ServerName" "" "" "MSDB" "SELECT Name FROM
dbo.SysJobs ORDER BY Name"
GOTO:EOF
```

Listing Job Steps

To list the steps within a job, create and then execute a shell script containing the following:

```
CALL :ExecSQLQuery "ServerName" "" "" "MSDB" "SELECT step_name
FROM dbo.SysJobs J INNER JOIN dbo.SysJobSteps JS ON
J.job_id=JS.job_id WHERE J.originating_server='ServerName' AND
J.Name='JobName'"
GOTO:EOF
```

Starting/Stopping a Job

While the SQL Agent service is responsible for starting and stopping your SQL jobs when needed, there may be times when you need to start and even stop a SQL job through scripting. To start/stop a SQL job, create and then execute a shell script containing the following:

```
CALL :ExecSQLQuery "ServerName" "" "" "MSDB" " EXEC sp_Action_job
@job_name = 'JobName'"
GOTO:EOF
```

Here, *Action* is either the word "Stop" or "Start," depending on if you want to stop or start the job.

Starting a Job at a Specific Step

To start a SQL job at a specific step, create and then execute a shell script containing the following:

```
CALL :ExecSQLQuery "ServerName" "" "" "MSDB" " EXEC sp_start_job
@job_name = 'JobName', @step_name='JobStepName'"
GOTO:EOF
```

Deleting a Job Step

To delete a step within a SQL job, create and then execute a shell script containing the following:

```
CALL :ExecSQLQuery "ServerName" "" "" "MSDB" " EXEC
sp_delete_jobstep @job_name = 'JobName', @step_id=JobStepNumber"
```

NOTE: The highlighted code above must be placed on one line.

```
GOTO:EOF
```

Deleting a Job

To delete a SQL job, create and then execute a shell script containing the following:

```
CALL :ExecSQLQuery "ServerName" "" "" "MSDB" "EXEC sp_delete_job
@job_name = 'JobName'"
GOTO:EOF
```

Scripting Logins

In all of the examples presented in this section, *LoginName* is the name of the SQL login you wish to target, *Password* is the password to assign to the SQL login, and *DomainName* is the name of the Windows domain that contains the user or group (*DomainObject*) you wish to target.

Listing Logins

To list logins for a given SQL server, create and then execute a shell script containing the following:

```
CALL :ExecSQLQuery "ServerName" "" "" "MASTER" "SELECT Name FROM
dbo.SysXLogins WHERE srvid IS NULL ORDER BY Name"
GOTO:EOF
```

Creating a Login

To create a SQL login, create and then execute a shell script containing the following:

```
CALL :ExecSQLQuery "ServerName" "" "" "MASTER" "EXEC sp_addlogin
'LoginName' 'Password'"
GOTO:EOF
```

To add a Windows login or group, you must use the **sp_grantlogin** stored procedure:

```
CALL :ExecSQLQuery "ServerName" "" "" "MASTER" "EXEC sp_grantlogin
'DOMAINNAME\DomainObject'"
GOTO:EOF
```

NOTE: *The highlighted code above must be placed on one line.*

Deleting a Login

To delete a SQL login, create and then execute a shell script containing the following:

```
CALL :ExecSQLQuery "ServerName" "" "" "MASTER" "EXEC sp_droplogin
'LoginName'"
GOTO:EOF
```

To delete a Windows login, you must use the **sp_revokelogin** stored procedure:

```
CALL :ExecSQLQuery "ServerName" "" "" "MASTER" "EXEC
sp_revokelogin 'DOMAINNAME\DomainObject'"
GOTO:EOF
```

Scripting Users

In all of the examples presented in this section, *DatabaseName* is the name of the target database, *LoginName* is the name of an existing SQL server login, and *UserName* is the name of the SQL user.

Listing Users

To list logins for a given SQL database, create and then execute a shell script containing the following:

```
CALL :ExecSQLQuery "ServerName" "" "" "DatabaseName" "SELECT Name
From dbo.SysUsers WHERE HasDBAccess=1 ORDER BY Name"
GOTO:EOF
```

Create a User

To create a SQL user for an existing login, create and then execute a shell script containing the following:

```
CALL :ExecSQLQuery "ServerName" "" "" "DatabaseName" "EXEC
sp_grantdbaccess 'LoginName'"
GOTO:EOF
```

Deleting a User

To delete a SQL user, create and then execute a shell script containing the following:

```
CALL :ExecSQLQuery "ServerName" "" "" "DatabaseName" "EXEC
sp_revokedbaccess 'UserName'"
GOTO:EOF
```

NOTE: *The highlighted code above must be placed on one line.*

Scripting Linked Servers

In all of the examples presented in this section, *LinkedServerName* is the name of the linked SQL server.

Listing Linked Servers

To list linked server names for a given SQL server, create and then execute a shell script containing the following:

```
CALL :ExecSQLQuery "ServerName" "" "" "Master" "SELECT srvName
FROM dbo.SysServers WHERE IsRemote=1 ORDER BY srvName"
GOTO:EOF
```

Deleting a Linked Server

To delete a linked server, create and then execute a shell script containing the following:

```
CALL :ExecSQLQuery "ServerName" "" "" "Master" "EXEC sp_dropserver
'LinkedServerName'"
GOTO:EOF
```

NOTE: *The highlighted code above must be placed on one line.*

Scripting SQL with Windows Script Host

In all of the examples presented in this section, **ServerName** is the name of the SQL server (or "" to connect to the local server) you wish to target. You will also need to append the **GetSQLServer** routine, listed next in this chapter, to all scripts in this section in order for the scripts to run. In all of the examples, no username and password are passed to the **GetSQLServer** routine, thus using the Windows credentials of the logged-on user. You may change these credentials if needed.

Connecting to a SQL Server

Before controlling a SQL sever through WSH, you must first connect to it. Here is a function to connect to a SQL server:

```
Function GetSQLServer(ByRef SQLServer, ServerName, Username,
Password, WindowsAccount)
  Set SQLServer = CreateObject("SQLDMO.SQLServer2")
  SQLServer.LoginTimeout = 15
  If ServerName="" Then ServerName="(local)"
  If Username="" Then
    SQLServer.LoginSecure = true
    SQLServer.Connect ServerName
  Else
    SQLServer.LoginSecure = WindowsAccount
```

```
      SQLServer.Connect ServerName, Username, Password
    End If
End Function
```

NOTE: *The highlighted code above must be placed on one line.*

Here, ***SQLServer*** is the SQL server object, ***ServerName*** is the name of the SQL server (or "" to connect to the local server), ***Username*** is a Windows or SQL username to use (or "" to use the currently logged on username), ***Password*** is the password for the username, and ***WindowsAccount*** indicates true or false if the ***Username*** is a Windows username (as opposed to a SQL username).

Listing SQL Object Properties

Once you have access to a SQL object, you can easily view the properties of that object by name. For example, if you wanted to know the size of a database, you would just connect to the database and view the **size** property:

```
Dim SQLServer, oDatabase
GetSQLServer SQLServer, "ServerName","","", True

Set oDatabase = SQLServer.Databases("DatabaseName")
Wscript.Echo oDatabase.Size
```

To display all of the properties of any SQL object, you can use the following routine:

```
Sub ListSQLObjectProperties(ByRef SQLObject)
  On Error Resume Next
  WScript.Echo SQLObject.Name
  For Each Prop in SQLObject.Properties
    WScript.Echo vbTab & Prop.Name & ":" & Prop.Value
  Next
End Sub
```

Scripting SQL Servers

The following section will introduce you to the basic techniques of WSH scripting the core SQL services and returning basic server information like the service pack and server edition.

Starting/Stopping the SQL Service

To stop the SQL service for a given SQL server, create and then execute a WSH script containing the following:

```
Dim SQLServer
GetSQLServer SQLServer, "ServerName", "", "", True
SQLServer.Shutdown(Wait)
```

Here, **Wait** is either **True** to wait for processes and transactions to complete (which is the nice thing to do) or **False** to perform an abrupt, immediate shutdown.

To start the SQL service for a given SQL server, create and then execute a WSH script containing the following:

```
Dim SQLServer
Set SQLServer = CreateObject("SQLDMO.SQLServer2")
SQLServer.Start False, "ServerName"
```

NOTE: *You do not need to append the GetSQLServer routine, listed earlier in this chapter, to this script in order for it to run.*

Displaying the SQL Edition

The **VersionString** property displays different information about a SQL server. Since we are only interested in the version, we will have to strip out the version from the rest of the information shown. To display the edition of a given SQL server, create and then execute a WSH containing the following:

```
Dim SQLServer
GetSQLServer SQLServer, "ServerName","","", True
VersionArray = Split(SQLServer.VersionString,Chr(10))
For Each Sentence In VersionArray
  If Instr(Sentence," on Windows ") > 0 Then
    Version = Mid(Sentence, 1, Instr(Sentence," on Windows "))
  End If
Next
Version = Replace(Version, vbTab, "")
WScript.Echo Version
```

Displaying the SQL Product Level

The **ProductLevel** property returns a string describing the installed product level of a SQL server. Once your SQL server has a service pack installed, this property will return a string like "SP4." If your SQL server has no service pack installed, it may display "RTM" (Release to Manufacturing—this is the original product version), "B1" (Beta 1), or something else. To display the service pack for a given SQL server, create and then execute a WSH script containing the following:

```
Dim SQLServer
GetSQLServer SQLServer, "ServerName","","", True
Wscript.Echo SQLServer.ProductLevel
```

Listing SQL Servers

The **ListAvailableSQLServers** method allows you to enumerate SQL
server instances that are online. To list SQL servers, create and then
execute a WSH script containing the following:

```
ListAvailableSQLServers

Sub ListAvailableSQLServers
Dim SQLDMO, i
 Set SQLDMO = CreateObject("SQLDMO.Application")

 For i = 1 To SQLDMO.ListAvailableSQLServers.Count
   WScript.Echo SQLDMO.ListAvailableSQLServers.Item(i)
 Next
End Sub
```

Displaying SQL Server Properties

The SQLServer object exposes various properties (version, if it's clus-
tered, timeout, connection, and so on). It is helpful when troubleshooting, inventorying, or auditing. To display the properties of a SQL server,
create and then execute a WSH script containing the following:

```
Dim SQLServer
GetSQLServer SQLServer, "ServerName","","", True
ListSQLObjectProperties SQLServer
```

Scripting Databases

In all of the examples presented in this section, *DatabaseName* is
the name of the job you wish to target and *FilePath* is the complete
path of a file that will contain the exported database structure.

Listing Databases

To list databases for a given SQL server, create and then execute a
WSH script containing the following:

```
Dim SQLServer, oDatabase
GetSQLServer SQLServer, "ServerName", "", "", True

Set oDatabase = CreateObject("SQLDMO.Database2")
For Each oDatabase In SQLServer.Databases
  WScript.Echo oDatabase.Name
```

```
Next
```

Displaying Database Properties

To display all of the properties of a SQL database, create and then execute a WSH script containing the following:

```
Dim SQLServer, Database
GetSQLServer SQLServer, "ServerName","","", True

Set Database = SQLServer.Databases("DatabaseName")
ListSQLObjectProperties Database
```

NOTE: You need to append the **ListSQLObjectProperties** routine, listed earlier in this chapter, to this script in order for it to run.

Shrinking a Database

If a SQL database is set to automatically grow, it will continue to grow as data is added and will not shrink even if you delete all the data. To shrink a SQL database, create and then execute a WSH script containing the following:

```
Dim SQLServer, Database
GetSQLServer SQLServer, "ServerName","","", True

Set Database = SQLServer.Databases("DatabaseName")
Database.Shrink -1,0
```

Here, *-1* instructs to shrink the database to the smallest size possible and *0* instructs to use the default truncate method.

Exporting a Database to a Script

To export a database to a script, create and then execute a WSH script containing the following:

```
Dim SQLServer, Database
GetSQLServer SQLServer, "ServerName","","", True

Set Database = SQLServer.Databases("DatabaseName")
Database.Script 4, "FilePath"
```

Here, *4* instructs SQLDMO to use the default scripting method.

Deleting a Database

To delete a SQL database, create and then execute a WSH script containing the following:

```
Dim SQLServer
GetSQLServer SQLServer, "ServerName","","", True
SQLServer.Databases("DatabaseName").Remove
```

Scripting Tables

In all of the examples presented in this section, **DatabaseName** is the name of the database you wish to target, **TableName** is the name of the table you wish to target, and **FilePath** is the complete path of a file that will contain the exported database structure.

Listing Tables

To list both user and system tables for a given SQL server database, create and then execute a WSH script containing the following:

```
Dim SQLServer, Table
GetSQLServer SQLServer, "ServerName", "", "", True

For Each Table In SQLServer.Databases("DatabaseName").Tables
  WScript.Echo Table.Name
Next
```

To list just user tables for a given SQL server database, create and then execute a WSH script containing the following:

```
Dim SQLServer, Table
GetSQLServer SQLServer, "ServerName", "", "", True

For Each Table In SQLServer.Databases("DatabaseName").Tables
  If Not Table.SystemObject Then
    WScript.Echo Table.Name
  End If
Next
```

Displaying Table Properties

To display the properties of a table from a given SQL server database, create and then execute a WSH script containing the following:

```
Dim SQLServer, Table
GetSQLServer SQLServer, "ServerName","","", True

Set Table =
SQLServer.Databases("DatabaseName").Tables("TableName")
```

```
ListSQLObjectProperties Table
```

Updating Table Statistics

To update the statistics of a table from a given SQL server database, create and then execute a WSH script containing the following:

```
Dim SQLServer, Table
GetSQLServer SQLServer, "ServerName","","", True

Set Table =
SQLServer.Databases("DatabaseName").Tables("TableName")
Table.UpdateStatistics
```

Exporting a Table to a Script

To export a table to a script, create and then execute a WSH script containing the following:

```
Dim SQLServer, Table
GetSQLServer SQLServer, "ServerName","","", True

Set Table =
SQLServer.Databases("DatabaseName").Tables("TableName")
Table.Script 4, "FilePath"
```

Here, *4* instructs SQLDMO to use the default scripting method.

Deleting Tables

To delete a table from a given SQL server database, create and then execute a WSH script containing the following:

```
Dim SQLServer
GetSQLServer SQLServer, "ServerName","","", True

SQLServer.Databases("DatabaseName").Tables("TableName").Remove
```

Scripting Stored Procedures

In all of the examples presented in this section, ***DatabaseName*** is the name of the database you wish to target, ***StoredProcedure*** is the name of the stored procedure you wish to target, and ***Parameters*** are the parameters (if any) you wish to pass to the stored procedure.

Listing Stored Procedures

To list both user and system stored procedures in a given SQL server database, create and then execute a WSH script containing the following:

```
Dim SQLServer, StoredProcedure
GetSQLServer SQLServer, "ServerName", "", "", True

For Each StoredProcedure In
SQLServer.Databases("DatabaseName").StoredProcedures
  WScript.Echo StoredProcedure.Name
Next
```

To list only user stored procedures in a given SQL server database, create and then execute a WSH script containing the following:

```
Dim SQLServer, StoredProcedure
GetSQLServer SQLServer, "ServerName", "", "", True

For Each StoredProcedure In
SQLServer.Databases("DatabaseName").StoredProcedures
  If Not StoredProcedure.SystemObject Then
    WScript.Echo StoredProcedure.Name
  End If
Next
```

Displaying Stored Procedure Code

To display the code of a stored procedure in a given SQL server database, create and then execute a WSH script containing the following:

```
Dim SQLServer, StoredProcedure
GetSQLServer SQLServer, "ServerName","","", True

Set StoredProcedure =
SQLServer.Databases("DatabaseName").StoredProcedures("StoredProcedure")
WScript.Echo StoredProcedure.Text
```

Running Stored Procedures

To run a stored procedure in a given SQL server database, create and then execute a WSH script containing the following:

```
Dim SQLServer, Database
GetSQLServer SQLServer, "ServerName", "", "", True
```

```
Set Database = SQLServer.Databases("DatabaseName")
Database.ExecuteImmediate("EXEC StoredProcedure Parameters")
```

For example, if you wanted to run the stored procedure **DeleteCustomer** to delete customer 24, your script would contain:

```
Dim SQLServer, oDatabase
GetSQLServer SQLServer, "ServerName", "", "", True

Set oDatabase = SQLServer.Databases("DatabaseName")
oDatabase.ExecuteImmediate("EXEC DeleteCustomer 24")
```

Exporting a Stored Procedure to a Script

To export a stored procedure to a script, create and then execute a WSH script containing the following:

```
Dim SQLServer, StoredProcedure
GetSQLServer SQLServer, "ServerName","","", True

Set StoredProcedure =
SQLServer.Databases("DatabaseName").StoredProcedures("StoredProcedureName")
StoredProcedure.Script 4, "FilePath"
```

Here, **4** instructs SQLDMO to use the default scripting method.

Deleting Stored Procedures

To delete a stored procedure in a given SQL server database, create and then execute a WSH script containing the following:

```
Dim SQLServer
GetSQLServer SQLServer, "ServerName", "", "", True
SQLServer.Databases("DatabaseName").StoredProcedures("ProcedureName").Remove
```

Scripting Jobs

In all examples in this section, **JobName** is the name of the job you wish to target, **JobStepName** is the name of the job step you wish to target, and **JobStepNumber** is the number of the job step you wish to target.

Starting/Stopping the SQL Agent Service

Unlike shell scripting the SQL Agent service, the **JobServer** object does not required us to know the instance or service names if we want to stop or start the service. To start/stop the SQL Agent Service, create and then execute a WSH script containing the following:

```
Dim SQLServer
GetSQLServer SQLServer, "ServerName","","", True
SQLServer.JobServer.Action
```

Here, **Action** is either **Start** or **Stop** to start or stop the SQL Agent service.

Listing Jobs

To list SQL jobs, create and then execute a WSH script containing the following:

```
Dim SQLServer, Job
GetSQLServer SQLServer, "ServerName", "", "", True

Set Job = CreateObject("SQLDMO.Job")
For Each Job In SQLServer.JobServer.Jobs
   Wscript.Echo Job.Name
Next
```

Displaying Job Properties

To display all the properties of a SQL job, create and then execute a WSH script containing the following:

```
Dim SQLServer, Job
GetSQLServer SQLServer, "ServerName", "", "", True

Set Job = SQLServer.JobServer.Jobs("JobName")
ListSQLObjectProperties Job
```

NOTE: You need to append the **ListSQLObjectProperties** routine, listed earlier in this chapter, to this script in order for it to run.

Listing Job Steps

To list the steps in a SQL job, create and then execute a WSH script containing the following:

```
Dim SQLServer
GetSQLServer SQLServer, "ServerName", "", "", True

For Each JobStep In SQLServer.JobServer.Jobs("JobName").JobSteps
   WScript.Echo JobStep.Name
Next
```

Displaying Job Step Properties

To display all of the properties of a SQL job step, create and then execute a WSH script containing the following:

```
Dim SQLServer, JobStep
GetSQLServer SQLServer, "ServerName", "", "", True

Set JobStep =
SQLServer.JobServer.Jobs("JobName").JobSteps("JobStepName")
ListSQLObjectProperties JobStep
```

NOTE: *You need to append the **ListSQLObjectProperties** routine, listed earlier in this chapter, to this script in order for it to run.*

Starting/Stopping a Job

While the SQL Agent service is responsible for starting and stopping your SQL jobs when needed, there may be times when you need to start and even stop a SQL job using scripting. To start/stop a SQL job, create and then execute a WSH script containing the following:

```
Dim SQLServer
GetSQLServer SQLServer, "ServerName", "", "", True
SQLServer.JobServer.Jobs("JobName").Action
```

Here, *Action* is either the word "Stop" or "Start" depending on if you want to stop or start the job.

Starting a Job at a Specific Step

To start a SQL job at a specific step, create and then execute a WSH script containing the following:

```
Dim SQLServer
GetSQLServer SQLServer, "ServerName", "", "", True
SQLServer.JobServer.Jobs("JobName").Start "JobStepName"
```

Enabling/Disabling a Job

To enable/disable a SQL job, create and then execute a WSH script containing the following:

```
Dim SQLServer
GetSQLServer SQLServer, "ServerName", "", "", True
SQLServer.JobServer.Jobs("JobName").Enabled = State
```

Here, **State** is either the word "True" or "False" depending on if you want to enable or disable the job.

Exporting a Job to a Script
To export a SQL job to a script, create and then execute a WSH script containing the following:

```
Dim SQLServer, Job
GetSQLServer SQLServer, "ServerName","","", True

Set Job = SQLServer.JobServer.Jobs("JobName")
Job.Script 4, "FilePath"
```

Here, **4** instructs SQLDMO to use the default scripting method.

Deleting a Job
To delete a SQL job, create and then execute a WSH script containing the following:

```
Dim SQLServer, Job
GetSQLServer SQLServer, "ServerName", "", "", True
Set Job = SQLServer.JobServer.Jobs("JobName")
Job.Remove
```

Deleting a Job Step
To delete a step within a SQL job, create and then execute a WSH script containing the following:

```
Dim SQLServer, JobStep
GetSQLServer SQLServer, "ServerName", "", "", True
Set JobStep =
SQLServer.JobServer.Jobs("JobName").JobSteps("JobStepName")
JobStep.Remove
```

Scripting Linked Servers
In all of the examples presented in this section, **LinkedServerName** is the name of the linked server you wish to target.

Listing Linked Servers
To list linked servers in a given SQL server database, create and then execute a WSH script containing the following:

```
Dim SQLServer, LinkedServer
GetSQLServer SQLServer, "ServerName", "", "", True
```

```
For Each LinkedServer In SQLServer.LinkedServers
  WScript.Echo LinkedServer.Name
Next
```

Displaying a Linked Server's Properties

To display the properties for a linked server, create and then execute a WSH script containing the following:

```
Dim SQLServer, LinkedServer
GetSQLServer SQLServer, "ServerName", "", "", True

Set LinkedServer = SQLServer.LinkedServers("LinkedServerName")
ListSQLObjectProperties LinkedServer
```

NOTE: *You need to append the **ListSQLObjectProperties** routine, listed earlier in this chapter, to this script in order for it to run.*

Deleting a Linked Server

To delete a linked server, create and then execute a WSH script containing the following:

```
Dim SQLServer, LinkedServer, LinkedServerLogin
GetSQLServer SQLServer, "ServerName", "", "", True
Set LinkedServer = SQLServer.LinkedServers("LinkedServerName")

For Each LinkedServerLogin in LinkedServer.LinkedServerLogins
  LinkedServerLogin.Remove
Next
LinkedServer.Remove
```

Scripting Queries

In all of the examples presented in this section, *DatabaseName* is the name of the database you wish to target and *Query* is a string containing the SQL query to run.

Executing a Query

To execute a SQL query without return results, create and then execute a WSH script containing the following:

```
Dim SQLServer, Database
GetSQLServer SQLServer, "ServerName", "", "", True

Set Database = SQLServer.Databases("DatabaseName")
Database.ExecuteImmediate("Query")
```

Executing a Query with Results

SQLDMO returns query results as a **QueryResults** object. Through this object, you can access the result's rows and columns to retrieve your desired data. To execute a SQL query and return results, create and then execute a WSH script containing the following:

```
Dim SQLServer, Database, Results, Row, Column
GetSQLServer SQLServer, "ServerName", "", "", True
Set Database = SQLServer.Databases("DatabaseName")

Set Results = Database.ExecuteWithResults("Query")
For Each Row in Results.Rows
  For Column in Results.Columns
    Wscript.Echo "Row " & Row & ", Col " & Column & ":" &
oResults.GetColumnString(Row, Column)
  Next
Next
```

NOTE: *The highlighted code above must be placed on one line.*

Scripting Logins

In all of the examples presented in this section, *LoginName* is the name of the SQL login you wish to target and *Password* is the password to assign to the SQL login.

Listing Logins

To list SQL logins for a given SQL server, create and then execute a WSH script containing the following:

```
Dim SQLServer, Login
GetSQLServer SQLServer, "ServerName", "", "", True

Set Login = CreateObject("SQLDMO.Login2")
For Each Login In SQLServer.Logins
  WScript.Echo Login.Name
Next
```

Displaying Login Properties

To display the properties of a SQL login, create and then execute a WSH containing the following:

```
Dim SQLServer, Login
GetSQLServer SQLServer, "ServerName", "", "", True

Set Login = SQLServer.Logins("LoginName")
ListSQLObjectProperties Login
```

NOTE: *You need to append the* **ListSQLObjectProperties** *routine, listed earlier in this chapter, to this script in order for it to run.*

Creating a Login

To create a SQL login, create and then execute a WSH containing the following:

```
Dim SQLServer, Login
GetSQLServer SQLServer, "ServerName", "", "", True

Set Login = CreateObject("SQLDMO.Login")
With Login
  .Name = "LoginName"
  .SetPassword "", "LoginPassword"
  .Database = "master"
  .Type = 2
End With
SQLServer.Logins.Add Login
```

Here, *2* instructs SQLDMO to create a SQL login. To add a Windows login or group, create and then execute a shell script containing the following:

```
Dim SQLServer, Login
GetSQLServer SQLServer, "ServerName", "", "", True

Set Login = CreateObject("SQLDMO.Login")
With Login
  .Name = "LoginName"
  .Database = "master"
  .Type = LoginType
End With
SQLServer.Logins.Add Login
```

Here, *LoginType* is 0 when creating a login for a Windows user and 1 when creating a login for a Windows group.

Exporting a Login to a Script

To export a login to a script, create and then execute a WSH script containing the following:

```
Dim SQLServer, Login
GetSQLServer SQLServer, "ServerName","","", True
```

```
Set Login = SQLServer.Logins("LoginName")
Login.Script 4, "FilePath"
```

Here, *4* instructs SQLDMO to use the default scripting method.

Deleting a Login

To delete a login, create and then execute a WSH script containing the following:

```
Dim SQLServer, Login
GetSQLServer SQLServer, "ServerName", "", "", True
Set Login = SQLServer.Logins("LoginName")
Login.Remove
```

Scripting Users

In all examples in this section, ***UserName*** is the name of the SQL login you wish to target.

Listing Users

To list all user names of a specific SQL database, create and then execute a WSH script containing the following:

```
Dim SQLServer, User
GetSQLServer SQLServer, "ServerName", "", "", True

For Each User In SQLServer.Databases("DatabaseName").Users
  WScript.Echo User.Name
Next
```

Displaying User Properties

To display the properties of a user, create and then execute a WSH script containing the following:

```
Dim SQLServer, User
GetSQLServer SQLServer, "ServerName","","", True

Set User = SQLServer.Databases("DatabaseName").Users("UserName")
ListSQLObjectProperties User
```

NOTE: *You need to append the* **ListSQLObjectProperties** *routine, listed earlier in this chapter, to this script in order for it to run.*

Creating a User

To create a user in a specific SQL database, create and then execute a
WSH script containing the following:

```
Dim SQLServer, User
GetSQLServer SQLServer, "ServerName", "", "", True

Set User = CreateObject("SQLDMO.User")
With User
  .Login = "LoginName"
End With
SQLServer.Databases("DatabaseName").Users.Add User
```

Exporting a User to a Script

To export a user to a script, create and then execute a WSH script
containing the following:

```
Dim SQLServer, User
GetSQLServer SQLServer, "ServerName","","", True

Set User = SQLServer.Databases("DatabaseName").Users("UserName")
User.Script 4, "FilePath"
```

Here, *4* instructs SQLDMO to use the default scripting method.

Deleting a User

To delete a user, create and then execute a WSH script containing the
following:

```
Dim SQLServer
GetSQLServer SQLServer, "ServerName", "", "", True
SQLServer.Databases("DatabaseName").Users("UserName").Remove
```

Chapter 16

Exchange Server Scripting

(continued)

In Brief

Microsoft Exchange is an enterprise messaging solution. It allows users to send and receive email and instant messages. It also provides features such as calendar, contact, task, journal, and others. While users typically connect via Outlook, they also can connect using the included browser-based, Outlook-mimicked client without having to have Outlook installed. Exchange is a huge product and can at times leave the administrator with repetitive or overwhelming tasks, such as creating the mailboxes for hundreds of users, renaming tons of public folders, and so on. While most Exchange administrators are aware of the GUI administrative tools used for Exchange management, they may not be aware that they can write scripts to automate some of the management tasks. This chapter will provide you an introduction of Exchange and the various ways to automate its management through scripting.

TIP: *If you don't have the highest level of permissions on the Active Directory and the Exchange server, you may have to modify permissions to allow the scripts to run properly. Testing scripts in a test environment where you have complete control can help you distinguish a permissions issue from a functional one.*

The Insides of Exchange

Microsoft Exchange is a very complicated product. While its main goal of providing enterprise email and communications is simple, its internal system and how it works is where the complication sets in. Before you start scripting, you need to have an understanding of the basics of Exchange and its objects. Due to the size of this book, I can't discuss and show you how to script every Exchange object. This is why I decided to focus on the most common objects and tasks.

16. Exchange Server Scripting

Active Directory

Let's admit it; before Exchange 2000, Microsoft Exchange was a mess. It had its own proprietary authentication, permission system, and directory service. If you wanted your Exchange 5.5 information to sync up with Active Directory, you had to use the Active Directory Connector which introduced a whole new set of problems (mismatched accounts, synchronization issues, and so on). With Exchange 2000, all that nonsense went away. We now have full, working (mostly) Active Directory integration and the removal of Exchange proprietary directory services. The directory information includes information about the users and groups, email addresses, lists, and more. The configuration information includes settings, routing information, and more. In addition to using the directory for storage, Exchange also extends the directory to include management methods on various objects (e.g., CreateMailbox, HideFromAddressBook, MailDisable, and so on). Exchange 2000 and later versions require an Active Directory and cannot operate without one.

Mailboxes

A mailbox is a secured area where email messages and other information are stored. Typically, a mailbox is secured to and used by a single user, but mailboxes can also have permissions that allow others to view, send, and receive for the mailbox as well. Since Exchange 2000 and up integrates with the Active Directory, you can perform minimal mailbox management (creating mailboxes, enabling/disabling email) through the "Active Directory Users and Computers" snap-in and perform advanced management (setting quotas,) through the "Exchange System Manager."

Stores

While Exchange does store some information in Active Directory, most data is stored in databases called "stores." There are two types of stores: mailbox stores and public folder stores. Mailbox stores (not to be confused with a mailbox) are containers for mailboxes while Public Folder stores are containers for Public Folders. By default, Exchange includes a single mailbox store cleverly called "Mailbox Store" and a public folder store ingeniously called "Public Folder Store."

Storage Groups

A storage group is simply a collection of Exchange stores (mailbox and public folder stores). All stores in a storage group share the same backup settings and transaction log. This provides for organization and backup/restore simplification.

Public Folders

Public folders provide a way for messages and files to be shared by all or a specific group of Exchange users. Depending on the type, public folders can contain mail messages, contacts, appointments, notes, tasks, and journals.

Scripting Exchange

Microsoft Exchange can be an extremely easy product to manage and maintain if you only have one of everything (one server, one storage group, one mailbox, and so on). Unfortunately, most companies have a handful of Exchange servers with hundreds of mailboxes and public folders, making it difficult to manage. Fortunately for us, Microsoft has provided several ways to script or automate Exchange administration through ADSI, WMI, CDOEXM, and others.

ADSI

Starting with Exchange 2000, Exchange stores its directory and configuration information in the Active Directory. Using ADSI to script Exchange is limited in that ADSI can only query and modify data and objects in the Active Directory and cannot interact directly with the Exchange server. While ADSI does not provide a complete scripting solution for Exchange, it does provide a quick and easy to use solution that focuses on the related Active Directory objects as opposed to the Exchange objects.

CDOEXM

Collaboration Data Objects for Exchange Management (let's just call this CDOEXM from now on) is a COM library of management classes for Exchange. You can access CDOEXM through any programming language that supports COM (VBScript, KiXtart, VB/VB.NET/C#, and so on) and automate just about every Exchange task you can think of. CDOEXM was designed to give programmers access to what users can access using GUI tools. (It's very extensive.) While ADSI focuses on Active Directory objects (users, groups, and so on), CDOEXM focuses on Exchange objects—mailboxes, storage groups, and so on. CDOEXM provides a very straight forward, comprehensive library to automate the management of Exchange servers.

16. Exchange Server Scripting

NOTE: *If you plan to run CDOEXM scripts from a machine that does not have Exchange installed, you will need to minimally install the Exchange Administrative Tools.*

WMI

Starting with Exchange 2000 and expanded with Exchange 2003, you can script Exchange through its included WMI providers. Once Exchange is installed, you can access its core two WMI namespaces: root\cimv2\applications\exchange and root\microsoftexchangev2. The root\cimv2\applications\exchange namespace was the original one included with Exchange 2000 while root\microsoftexchangev2 is the extension provided with Exchange 2000, Service Pack 2. While WMI is slightly harder to use than CDOEXM, it does provide access to a wealth of Exchange information and management methods.

The Scripting Advantage

Since all of the scripting methods covered in this chapter are implemented through COM, Windows Script Host and KiXtart have the clear advantage. Due to the size limitations of this book and the popularity of the scripting language, this chapter will provide COM examples in Windows Script Host only. (It should be easy to convert the scripts to KiXtart.) While Shell and AutoIt cannot directly interact with these scripting methods, you can still use them to run any of the shell and Windows Script Host scripts presented in this chapter.

A Word of Caution

This chapter contains many scripting examples on modifying and deleting Exchange objects (storage groups, mailboxes, and so on). As with all scripts, you should first test each script in an isolated testing environment to ensure that the script produces the desired results before using it in a production environment.

NOTE: *All scripts in this chapter are designed and have been tested with Exchange 2003. To obtain the highest compatibility, ensure that your Exchange server is running the latest service pack.*

Immediate Solutions

Enabling/Disabling Mail for an Object

In order for a user, contact, group, or folder to be able to receive mail, it must be mail enabled. A mail enabled object has its Exchange attributes set in the Active Directory (home server, email addresses, nickname, and so on). The **MailDisable** method allows you to easily prevent mail usage for an object, clearing the associated Exchanges attributes. To mail disable an object, create and then execute a WSH script containing the following:

```
SET Obj = GetObject("LDAP://ObjectDN")
Obj.MailDisable
Obj.SetInfo()
```

Here, *ObjectDN* is the name of the object for which you wish to mail disable. You can also enable mail for an object using the **MailEnable** method:

```
SET Obj = GetObject("LDAP://ObjectDN")
Obj.MailEnable
Obj.SetInfo()
```

TIP: You can use the above scripts to mail enable or disable users, groups, contacts, and folders.

Scripting Exchange Users and Contacts

In all the examples presented in this section, *ServerName* is the name of the Exchange server you wish to target.Creating Logon Scripts with Shell Scripting

Disabling/Enabling Mail for a User

To mail disable a user, create and then execute a WSH script containing the following:

```
SET Obj = GetObject("LDAP://UserDN")
Obj.MailDisable
Obj.SetInfo()
```

Here, *UserDN* is the name of the user for which you wish to mail disable. You can also enable mail for a user using the **MailEnable** method:

```
SET Obj = GetObject("LDAP://UserDN")
Obj.MailEnable
Obj.SetInfo()
```

Listing User Email Addresses

For each email recipient in an Exchange server, their email address information (protocol and name) is stored in the **proxyAddresses** attribute in the Active Directory user object. To display the protocol and email addresses for all users in the current domain, create and then execute a WSH script containing the following:

```
SET RootDSE = GetObject("LDAP://RootDSE")
DNC = RootDSE.Get("defaultNamingContext")

SET Conn = CreateObject("ADODB.Connection")
SET RS = CreateObject("ADODB.Recordset")

Conn.Provider = "ADSDSOObject"
Conn.Open "ADs Provider"

Query = "<LDAP://" & DNC & ">;" & _
  "(&(objectCategory=Person)" & _
  "(objectClass=User)(proxyaddresses=*)" & _
  "(homeMDB=*)(msExchHomeServerName=*))" & _
  ";adspath;subtree"

Set RS = Conn.Execute(Query)

Do While Not RS.EOF
  Set User = GetObject(RS.Fields(0))
  Wscript.Echo "User: " & User.displayName
  For Each EmailAddress in User.proxyAddresses
    Wscript.Echo EmailAddress
  Next
  Wscript.Echo ""
  RS.MoveNext
Loop
```

Hiding a User from the Address Book

The **HideFromAddressBook** property allows you to easily hide a user from the address book. To hide a user from the address book, create and then execute a WSH script containing the following:

```
SET Obj = GetObject("LDAP://UserDN")
Obj.HideFromAddressBook = True
Obj.SetInfo()
```

Here, *UserDN* is the name of the user (e.g., cn=joe.smith, cn=Users, dc=YourDomain, dc=com) of which you wish to hide.

Listing Contacts

To list all contacts, create and then execute a WSH script containing the following:

```
SET RS = CreateObject("ADODB.Recordset")
SET Conn = CreateObject("ADODB.Connection")

Conn.Provider = "ADsDSOObject"
Conn.Open "ADs Provider"

Set RS = Conn.Execute("Select name FROM 'LDAP://ServerName' WHERE
ObjectClass='Contact'")

Do While Not RS.EOF
  Wscript.Echo RS.Fields("name")
  RS.MoveNext
Loop
```

NOTE: *The highlighted code above must be placed on one line.*

Creating a Contact

To create a contact, create and then execute a WSH script containing the following:

```
Set Path = GetObject("LDAP://ContactPath ")
Set Contact = Path.Create("Contact","cn=My Contact")
Contact.Alias = "MyContact"
Contact.Company = "Test Company"
Contact.DisplayName = "My Contact"
Contact.GivenName = "My"
Contact.Mail = "MyContact@test.local"
Contact.SN = "Contact"
Contact.TargetAddress = "SMTP:MyContact@test.local"
Contact.PutEx 2, "proxyAddresses",
```

```
Array("SMTP:MyContact@test.local")
Contact.SetInfo
```

Here, *ContactPath* is the location where the new contact should be created (e.g., CN=Users,DC=Test,DC=local).

Disabling/Enabling Mail for a Contact

To mail disable a contact, create and then execute a WSH script containing the following:

```
SET Contact = GetObject("LDAP://ContactDN")
Contact.MailDisable
Contact.SetInfo()
```

Here, *ContactDN* is the name of the contact for which you wish to mail disable. You can also enable mail for a contact using the **MailEnable** method:

```
SET Contact = GetObject("LDAP://ContactDN")
Contact.MailEnable
Contact.SetInfo()
```

Deleting a Contact

To delete a contact, create and then execute a WSH script containing the following:

```
Set Path = GetObject("LDAP://ContactPath")
Path.Delete "Contact","cn=ContactCN"
```

Here, *ContactPath* is the location of the contact (ex. CN=Users, DC=Test,DC=local) and *ContactCN* is the common name of the contact.

Scripting Exchange Servers

In all of the examples presented in this section, *ServerName* is the name of the Exchange server you wish to target. Creating Logon Scripts with Shell Scripting

Listing Exchange Servers

The **msExchExchangeServer** object category provides a way to easily identify Exchange servers in the Active Directory. To list exchange servers, create and then execute a WSH script containing the following:

```
SET RootDSE = GetObject("LDAP://RootDSE")
SET Conn = CreateObject("ADODB.Connection")
SET CMD = CreateObject("ADODB.Command")
SET RS = CreateObject("ADODB.Recordset")

Config = RootDSE.Get("configurationNamingContext")
Conn.Provider = "ADsDSOObject"
Conn.Open "ADs Provider"

Query = "<LDAP://" & Config & ">;" & _
  (objectCategory=msExchExchangeServer)" & _
  ";name;subtree"
CMD.ActiveConnection = Conn
CMD.CommandText = Query

Set RS = CMD.Execute

Do While Not RS.EOF
  Wscript.Echo RS.Fields("Name")
  RS.MoveNext
Loop
```

In this script, we connect to the configuration container of the current domain to query for all Exchange server object names. By connecting to the RootDSE, we serverlessly bind to the Active Directory, saving us from having to specify the distinguished path of a domain controller.

TIP: *If you need to perform an action on all the Exchange servers in your environment, use this script to pass the server name to and execute others scripts mentioned in this chapter.*

Stopping Exchange Services

If you run Exchange 2003 on a Domain controller, you are probably aware of how painfully slow it takes to shutdown the computer. This is a documented issue (**http://support.microsoft.com/kb/829361**) and the solution is to stop all the services manually. To use a script to stop all the Exchange services, you can use any of the service control scripts from Chapters 7 and 8. For example, using information we learned in Chapter 8, we could stop the Exchange services on a remote machine called **BumbleBee** using the Windows 2000 resource kit utility NETSVC by starting a command prompt and entering the following:

```
NETSVC /STOP MSExchangeES \\BumbleBee
NETSVC /STOP MSExchangeIS \\BumbleBee
NETSVC /STOP MSExchangeMTA \\BumbleBee
NETSVC /STOP MSExchangeSA \\BumbleBee
NETSVC /STOP WinHttpAutoProxySvc \\BumbleBee
```

Displaying Exchange Server Information

The **Exchange_Server** WMI class allows you to obtain information about a local or remote Exchange server. To display basic information about an exchange server, create and then execute a WSH script containing the following:

```
SET WMI = GetObject("winmgmts:" _
    & "{impersonationLevel=impersonate}!\\ServerName" & _
    "\ROOT\MicrosoftExchangeV2").InstancesOf("Exchange_Server")

DisplayWMIProperties WMI
```

NOTE: You need to append the DisplayWMIProperties routine, listed in chapter 8, to this script in order for it to run.

Displaying Exchange Server Type

To display the type of an exchange server (Standard, Enterprise, and Conferencing), create and then execute a WSH script containing the following:

```
Set WMI = GetObject("winmgmts:" _
    & "{impersonationLevel=impersonate}!\\ServerName" & _
        "\ROOT\MicrosoftExchangeV2")

Set Servers = WMI.ExecQuery("Select * from Exchange_Server")

For Each Server in Servers
  SELECT CASE Server.Type
    CASE 0
      Wscript.Echo "Standard"
    CASE 1
      Wscript.Echo "Enterprise"
    CASE 2
      Wscript.Echo "Conferencing"
  End Select
Next
```

Displaying Exchange Server Version

To display the version of an Exchange server, create and then execute a WSH script containing the following:

```
SET ES = CreateObject("CDOEXM.ExchangeServer")
ES.DataSource.Open "ServerName"
Wscript.Echo ES.ExchangeVersion
```

Displaying Exchange's Directory Server

Starting with Microsoft Exchange 2000, Exchange is integrated and heavily relies on the Active Directory to store and retrieve information. Exchange regularly performs LDAP queries to communicate with the Global Catalog server. Exchange automatically picks a global catalog server to communicate with. To display the server Exchange has picked, create and then execute a WSH script containing the following:

```
SET ES = CreateObject("CDOEXM.ExchangeServer")
ES.DataSource.Open "ServerName"
Wscript.Echo ES.DirectoryServer
```

Displaying Exchange State Information

The **ExchangeServerState** WMI class allows you to obtain information about a local or remote Exchange server's state (e.g., service, CPU, memory, cluster, and so on). To display state information about an exchange server, create and then execute a WSH script containing the following:

```
Set WMI = GetObject("winmgmts:" _
    & "{impersonationLevel=impersonate}!\\ServerName" & _
    "\ROOT\CIMV2\APPLICATIONS\EXCHANGE").InstancesOf("ExchangeServerState")

DisplayWMIProperties WMI
```

NOTE: *You need to append the DisplayWMIProperties routine, listed in chapter 8, to this script in order for it to run.*

Scripting Exchange Mailboxes

In all examples in this section, *ServerName* is the name of the Exchange server you wish to target.

Listing Mailboxes

The **Exchange_Mailbox** WMI class allows you to access the mailboxes on a local or remote Exchange server. To list all the mailboxes, create and then execute a WSH script containing the following:

```
Set WMI = GetObject("winmgmts:" _
    & "{impersonationLevel=impersonate}!\\ServerName" & _
    "\ROOT\MicrosoftExchangeV2").InstancesOf("Exchange_Mailbox")

For Each Mailbox In WMI
  Wscript.Echo Mailbox.MailboxDisplayName
Next
```

Displaying Mailbox Properties

To display the properties of all mailboxes on an Exchange server, create and then execute a WSH script containing the following:

```
SET WMI = GetObject("winmgmts:" _
    & "{impersonationLevel=impersonate}!\\ServerName" & _
    "\ROOT\MicrosoftExchangeV2").InstancesOf("Exchange_Mailbox")

DisplayWMIProperties WMI
```

To display the properties of a specific mailbox, create and then execute a WSH script containing the following:

```
SET WMI = GetObject("winmgmts:" _
    & "{impersonationLevel=impersonate}!\\ServerName" & _
    "\ROOT\MicrosoftExchangeV2").ExecQuery _
    ("Select * From Exchange_Mailbox" & _
    " Where MailboxDisplayName='MailboxName'")

DisplayWMIProperties WMI
```

Here, *MailboxName* is the name of the mailbox as displayed in the Exchange Server Manager.

NOTE: You need to append the DisplayWMIProperties routine, listed in chapter 8, to these scripts in order for them to run.

Creating a User's Mailbox

The **CreateMailbox** method allows you to create a mailbox for a specific user. To create a mailbox for a user, create and then execute a WSH script containing the following:

```
SET User = GetObject("LDAP://UserDN")
User.CreateMailBox "homeMDB"
User.SetInfo()
```

Here, *UserDN* is the name of the user and *homeMDB* is the URL of the mailbox store to contain the new mailbox.

Deleting a User's Mailbox

The **DeleteMailbox** method allows you to delete a mailbox for a specific user. To delete the mailbox of a user, create and then execute a WSH script containing the following:

```
SET User = GetObject("LDAP://UserDN")
User.DeleteMailbox
User.SetInfo()
```

Here, *UserDN* is the distinguished name of the user that contains the mailbox to delete.

NOTE: *Exchange 2003 mailbox recovery causes a deleted mailbox to remain for 30 days in a disconnected state. To immediately remove a disconnected mailbox, you must purge the mailbox from the server.*

Purging a User's Mailbox

The **Purge** WMI method allows you to permanently remove a disconnected (deleted) mailbox for a specific user. To purge the mailbox of a user, create and then execute a WSH script containing the following:

```
SET WMI = GetObject("winmgmts:\\ServerName" & _
  "\root\MicrosoftExchangeV2")
SET MailBoxes = WMI.ExecQuery("Select * from Exchange_Mailbox
WHERE " _
  & "MailboxDisplayName='" & "MailBoxName" & "'")
FOR EACH MailBox IN MailBoxes
  MailBox.Purge
NEXT
```

Here, *UserDN* is the name of the user and *MailBoxName* is the display name of the mailbox to purge.

NOTE: *The highlighted code above must be placed on one line.*

WARNING! The Purge method will error if the mailbox is not already disconnected (deleted).

16. Exchange Server Scripting

Scripting Exchange Public Folders

In all of the examples presented in this section, **ServerName** is the name of the Exchange server you wish to target.

Listing Public Folders

The **Exchange_PublicFolder** WMI class allows you to access the public folders on a local or remote Exchange server. To list all public folder names and their paths, create and then execute a WSH script containing the following:

```
Set WMI = GetObject("winmgmts:" _
    & "{impersonationLevel=impersonate}!\\ServerName" & _
    "\ROOT\MicrosoftExchangeV2").InstancesOf("Exchange_PublicFolder")

For Each PublicFolder In WMI
   Wscript.Echo PublicFolder.Name & ":" & PublicFolder.Path
Next
```

Displaying Public Folder Properties

To display the properties of all public folders, create and then execute a WSH script containing the following:

```
Set WMI = GetObject("winmgmts:" _
    & "{impersonationLevel=impersonate}!\\ServerName" & _
    "\ROOT\MicrosoftExchangeV2").InstancesOf("Exchange_PublicFolder")

DisplayWMIProperties WMI
```

To display the properties of a specific public folder, create and then execute a WSH script containing the following:

```
Set WMI = GetObject("winmgmts:" _
    & "{impersonationLevel=impersonate}!\\ServerName" & _
    "\ROOT\MicrosoftExchangeV2").ExecQuery _
    ("Select * From Exchange_PublicFolder" & _
    " Where Path='FolderPath'")

DisplayWMIProperties WMI
```

Here, *FolderPath* is the path of the desired public.

NOTE: You need to append the DisplayWMIProperties routine, listed in chapter 8, to these scripts in order for them to run.

Creating a Public Folder

To create a public folder, create and then execute a WSH script containing the following:

```
Set WshShell = WScript.CreateObject("WScript.Shell")
UserDNSDomain =
WshShell.Environment("PROCESS").Item("UserDNSDomain")

Set PublicFolder = GetObject("winmgmts:" _
    & "{impersonationLevel=impersonate}!\\ServerName" & _
    "\ROOT\MicrosoftExchangeV2").Get("Exchange_PublicFolder").SpawnInstance_()

PublicFolder.Name = "FolderName"
PublicFolder.ParentFriendlyUrl = "http://ServerName" & _
    "/ExAdmin/Admin/" & UserDNSDomain & "/Public%20Folders/"
PublicFolder.Put_ (0 OR 2)
```

Here, *FolderName* is the name of the new public folder. In the script above, we dynamically generate the parent friendly URL to create the public folder in the root Public Folders tree. You can change this to the location of your choosing.

Renaming a Public Folder

To rename a public folder, create and then execute a WSH script containing the following:

```
Set WMI = GetObject("winmgmts:" _
    & "{impersonationLevel=impersonate}!\\ServerName" & _
    "\ROOT\MicrosoftExchangeV2").ExecQuery _
    ("Select * From Exchange_PublicFolder" & _
    " Where Path='FolderPath'")

For Each PublicFolder In WMI
  PublicFolder.Rename "NewName"
Next
```

Here, *FolderPath* is the path of the folder, and *NewName* is the name to rename the folder to.

Deleting a Public Folder

To delete a public folder, create and then execute a WSH script containing the following:

```
Set WMI = GetObject("winmgmts:" _
    & "{impersonationLevel=impersonate}!\\ServerName" & _
    "\ROOT\MicrosoftExchangeV2").ExecQuery _
```

16. Exchange Server Scripting

```
("Select * From Exchange_PublicFolder" & _
" Where Path='FolderPath'")

For Each PublicFolder In WMI
  PublicFolder.Delete_
Next
```

Here, *FolderPath* is the path of the folder to delete.

Scripting Exchange Stores

Remember that Exchange supports two types of stores: Mailbox and Public. This section will show you how to perform various tasks for both types. In all of the examples in this section, ***ServerName*** is the name of the Exchange server you wish to target, ***GroupName*** is the name of the storage group containing the target store, and ***StoreName*** is the name of the store you wish to target.

Get Mailbox Store

The following subroutine provides an easy way to connect to a mailbox store by name:

```
Sub GetMailboxStore(ByRef MailboxStore, ServerName, GroupName,
StoreName)
  SET ES = CreateObject("CDOEXM.ExchangeServer")
  SET SG = CreateObject("CDOEXM.StorageGroup")
  SET Stores = CreateObject ("CDOEXM.MailboxStoreDB")
  ES.DataSource.Open ServerName

  StorageGroups = ES.StorageGroups
  StorageGroup = MID(StorageGroups(0), INSTR(2, StorageGroups(0),
"CN"))

  URL = "LDAP://" & ES.DirectoryServer & "/CN=" & _
    GroupName & "," & StorageGroup

  SG.DataSource.Open URL
  For Each Store In SG.MailboxStoreDBs
    Stores.DataSource.Open Store
    If Stores.Name = StoreName Then
      SET MailboxStore = Stores
      Exit Sub
    End If
  Next
End Sub
```

Get Public Store

The following subroutine provides an easy way to connect to a public store by name:

```
Sub GetPublicStore(ByRef PublicStore, ServerName, GroupName,
StoreName)
  SET ES = CreateObject("CDOEXM.ExchangeServer")
  SET SG = CreateObject("CDOEXM.StorageGroup")
  SET Stores = CreateObject ("CDOEXM.PublicStoreDB")
  ES.DataSource.Open ServerName

  StorageGroups = ES.StorageGroups
  StorageGroup = MID(StorageGroups(0), INSTR(2, StorageGroups(0),
"CN"))

  URL = "LDAP://" & ES.DirectoryServer & "/CN=" & _
    GroupName & "," & StorageGroup

  SG.DataSource.Open URL
  For Each Store In SG.PublicStoreDBs
    Stores.DataSource.Open Store
    If Stores.Name = StoreName Then
      SET PublicStore = Stores
      Exit Sub
    End If
  Next
End Sub
```

Listing Mailbox Stores

To display mailbox stores and their parent storage group, create and then execute a WSH script containing the following:

```
SET ES = CreateObject("CDOEXM.ExchangeServer")
SET SG = CreateObject("CDOEXM.StorageGroup")
SET Stores = CreateObject("CDOEXM.MailboxStoreDB")
ES.DataSource.Open "ServerName"

For Each Group In ES.StorageGroups
  SG.DataSource.Open Group
  For Each Store In SG.MailboxStoreDBs
    Stores.DataSource.Open Store
```

```
      Wscript.Echo SG.Name & ":" & Stores.Name
   Next
Next
```

Listing Public Stores

To display public stores and their parent storage group, create and then execute a WSH script containing the following:

```
SET ES = CreateObject("CDOEXM.ExchangeServer")
SET SG = CreateObject("CDOEXM.StorageGroup")
SET Stores = CreateObject ("CDOEXM.PublicStoreDB")
ES.DataSource.Open "ServerName"

For Each Group In ES.StorageGroups
  SG.DataSource.Open Group
  For Each Store In SG.PublicStoreDBs
    Stores.DataSource.Open Store
    Wscript.Echo SG.Name & ":" & Stores.Name
  Next
Next
```

Displaying Mailbox Store Properties

To display the properties of a mailbox store, create and then execute a WSH script containing the following:

```
GetMailboxStore MailboxStore, "ServerName", "GroupName",
"StoreName"

Wscript.Echo "DaysBeforeGarbageCollection:" & _
   MailboxStore.DaysBeforeGarbageCollection
Wscript.Echo "DBPath:" & MailboxStore.DBPath
Wscript.Echo "Enabled:" & MailboxStore.Enabled
Wscript.Echo "GarbageCollectOnlyAfterBackup:" & _
   MailboxStore.GarbageCollectOnlyAfterBackup
Wscript.Echo "HardLimit:" & MailboxStore.HardLimit
Wscript.Echo "LastFullBackupTime:" & _
   MailboxStore.LastFullBackupTime
Wscript.Echo "Name:" & MailboxStore.Name
Wscript.Echo "OverQuotaLimit:" & _
   MailboxStore.OverQuotaLimit
Wscript.Echo "SLVPath:" & MailboxStore.SLVPath
Wscript.Echo "Status:" & MailboxStore.Status
Wscript.Echo "StoreQuota:" & _
   MailboxStore.StoreQuota
```

NOTE: You need to append the GetMailboxStore routine, listed earlier in this chapter, to this script in order for it to run.

Displaying Public Store Properties

To display the properties of a public store, create and then execute a WSH script containing the following:

```
GetPublicStore PublicStore, "ServerName", "GroupName", "StoreName"

Wscript.Echo "DaysBeforeGarbageCollection:" & _
   PublicStore.DaysBeforeGarbageCollection
Wscript.Echo "DaysBeforeItemExpiration:" & _
   PublicStore.DaysBeforeItemExpiration
Wscript.Echo "DBPath:" & PublicStore.DBPath
Wscript.Echo "Enabled:" & PublicStore.Enabled
Wscript.Echo "FolderTree:" & PublicStore.FolderTree
Wscript.Echo "GarbageCollectOnlyAfterBackup:" & _
   PublicStore.GarbageCollectOnlyAfterBackup
Wscript.Echo "HardLimit:" & PublicStore.HardLimit
Wscript.Echo "ItemSizeLimit:" & _
   PublicStore.ItemSizeLimit
Wscript.Echo "LastFullBackupTime:" & _
   PublicStore.LastFullBackupTime
Wscript.Echo "Name:" & PublicStore.Name
Wscript.Echo "SLVPath:" & PublicStore.SLVPath
Wscript.Echo "Status:" & PublicStore.Status
Wscript.Echo "StoreQuota:" & PublicStore.StoreQuota
```

NOTE: *You need to append the GetPublicStore routine, listed earlier in this chapter, to this script in order for it to run.*

Dismounting/Mounting a Mailbox Store

Dismounting a mailbox store provides a way to prevent users from connecting to the store but still allows administrators to access it. To dismount a mailbox store, create and then execute a WSH script containing the following:

```
GetMailboxStore MailboxStore, "ServerName", "GroupName",
"StoreName"
MailboxStore.Dismount
```

To mount a mailbox store, create and then execute a WSH script containing the following:

```
GetMailboxStore MailboxStore, "ServerName", "GroupName",
"StoreName"
MailboxStore.Mount
```

NOTE: *You need to append the GetMailboxStore routine, listed earlier in this chapter, to this script in order for it to run.*

Dismounting/Mounting a Public Store

Dismounting a public store provides a way to prevent users from connecting to the store but still allowing administrators to access it. To dismount a public store, create and then execute a WSH script containing the following:

```
GetPublicStore PublicStore, "ServerName", "GroupName", "StoreName"
PublicStore.Dismount
```

To mount a public store, create and then execute a WSH script containing the following:

```
GetPublicStore PublicStore, "ServerName", "GroupName", "StoreName"
PublicStore.Mount
```

NOTE: *You need to append the GetPublicStore routine, listed earlier in this chapter, to this script in order for it to run.*

Deleting a Mailbox Store

To delete a mailbox store, create and then execute a WSH script containing the following:

```
GetMailboxStore MailboxStore, "ServerName", "GroupName",
"StoreName"
MailboxStore.Delete
```

NOTE: *You need to append the GetMailboxStore routine, listed earlier in this chapter, to this script in order for it to run.*

Deleting a Public Store

To delete a public store, create and then execute a WSH script containing the following:

```
GetPublicStore PublicStore, "ServerName", "GroupName", "StoreName"
PublicStore.Delete
```

NOTE: *You need to append the GetPublicStore routine, listed earlier in this chapter, to this script in order for it to run.*

Scripting Exchange Storage Groups

In all examples in this section, *ServerName* is the name of the Exchange server you wish to target, and *GroupName* is the name of the group you wish to target.

Listing Storage Groups

To list the storage groups for a given exchange server, create and then execute a WSH script containing the following:

```
SET ES = CreateObject("CDOEXM.ExchangeServer")
SET SG = CreateObject("CDOEXM.StorageGroup")
ES.DataSource.Open "ServerName"

For Each StorageGroup In ES.StorageGroups
  SG.DataSource.Open StorageGroup
  Wscript.Echo SG.Name
Next
```

Displaying Storage Group Properties

To display the properties of all storage groups on an Exchange server, create and then execute a WSH script containing the following:

```
SET ES = CreateObject("CDOEXM.ExchangeServer")
SET SG = CreateObject("CDOEXM.StorageGroup")
ES.DataSource.Open "ServerName"

For Each Group In ES.StorageGroups
  SG.DataSource.Open Group
  Wscript.Echo "Name:" & SG.Name
  Wscript.Echo "LogFilePath:" & SG.LogFilePath
  Wscript.Echo "SystemFilePath:" & SG.SystemFilePath
  Wscript.Echo "CircularLogging:" & SG.CircularLogging
  Wscript.Echo "ZeroDatabase:" & SG.ZeroDatabase
  Wscript.Echo ""
Next
```

To display the properties of a specific storage group, create and then execute a WSH script containing the following:

```
SET ES = CreateObject("CDOEXM.ExchangeServer")
SET SG = CreateObject("CDOEXM.StorageGroup")
ES.DataSource.Open "ServerName"
```

```
StorageGroups = ES.StorageGroups
StorageGroup = MID(StorageGroups(0), INSTR(2, StorageGroups(0),
"CN"))

URL = "LDAP://" & ES.DirectoryServer & "/CN=" & _
    "GroupName" & "," & StorageGroup

SG.DataSource.Open URL
Wscript.Echo "Name:" & SG.Name
Wscript.Echo "LogFilePath:" & SG.LogFilePath
Wscript.Echo "SystemFilePath:" & SG.SystemFilePath
Wscript.Echo "CircularLogging:" & SG.CircularLogging
Wscript.Echo "ZeroDatabase:" & SG.ZeroDatabase
```

Creating a Storage Group

To create a storage group, create and then execute a WSH script containing the following:

```
SET ES = CreateObject("CDOEXM.ExchangeServer")
SET SG = CreateObject("CDOEXM.StorageGroup")
ES.DataSource.Open "ServerName"

StorageGroups =  ES.StorageGroups
StorageGroup =
MID(StorageGroups(0),INSTR(2,StorageGroups(0),"cn",1))

URL = "LDAP://" & ES.DirectoryServer & "/CN=" & _
    "GroupName" & "," & StorageGroup

SG.DataSource.SaveTo URL
```

Disabling/Enabling Storage Group Circular Logging

By default, circular logging is disabled. When an Exchange transaction log reaches its maximum size, a new log is created. Enabling circular logging instructs the Exchange server to overwrite the logs when they reach their maximum size, thus saving disk space. The main disadvantage to enabling circular logging (and why the default is and recommended to leave disabled) is that you make transaction logs ineffective. When circular logging is disabled, Exchange can recover from a system failure by committing the uncommitted transactions right up to the point of failure. If circular logging is enabled and a system failure occurs, you may have to restore Exchange from the last full backup.

To disable/enable circular logging for a storage group, create and then execute a WSH script containing the following:

16. Exchange Server Scripting

```
SET ES = CreateObject("CDOEXM.ExchangeServer")
SET SG = CreateObject("CDOEXM.StorageGroup")
ES.DataSource.Open "ServerName"

StorageGroups = ES.StorageGroups
StorageGroup = MID(StorageGroups(0), INSTR(2, StorageGroups(0),
"CN"))

URL = "LDAP://" & ES.DirectoryServer & "/CN=" & _
    "GroupName" & "," & StorageGroup

SG.DataSource.Open URL
SG.CircularLogging = State
SG.DataSource.Save
```

Here, *State* is either true or false, depending on whether you want circular logging enabled or disabled.

Deleting a Storage Group

To delete a storage group, create and then execute a WSH script containing the following:

```
SET ES = CreateObject("CDOEXM.ExchangeServer")
SET SG = CreateObject("CDOEXM.StorageGroup")
ES.DataSource.Open "ServerName"

StorageGroups = ES.StorageGroups
StorageGroup = MID(StorageGroups(0), INSTR(2, StorageGroups(0),
"CN"))

URL = "LDAP://" & ES.DirectoryServer & "/CN=" & _
    "GroupName" & "," & StorageGroup

SG.DataSource.Open URL
SG.DataSource.Delete
```

NOTE: *The highlighted code above must be placed on one line.*

16. Exchange Server Scripting

Chapter 17

Fun with Multimedia

In Brief

If you're not having complete and utter fun yet, this chapter is for you. In this chapter, you will learn how to use simple scripts to play and control multimedia files. You will also learn how to script the Office Assistant and Microsoft Agent characters to interact with your users.

The Dreaded Office Assistant

Office assistants are animated characters designed to help and entertain users of Microsoft Office. These characters provide tips, accept natural language queries (such as "How do I hide the Office Assistant?"), and perform animations based on the actions of the user. In theory, these assistants sound like a good idea. However, soon after the release of these assistants with Office 97, a flood of complaints followed denouncing them. The main problem was the over-interaction of these assistants.

To turn on the Office Assistant, choose Help|Show the Office Assistant. Once the assistant is visible, right-click on it and choose Options. Under the Options tab, you can disable the Office Assistant by unchecking Use the Office Assistant. Under the Gallery tab, you can choose which assistant you want to use. The default assistant is called Clippit, a hyperactive paper clip that doesn't know when to be quiet.

The Office Assistant Object Model

The Office Assistant object model is a limited one. At the top of the model is the assistant object. An instance of the Office Assistant object model is created whenever an instance of an office application is created. Once the instance is created, you can make the assistant visible by setting the **Visible** property to **True**:

```
officeapp.Assistant.Visible = True
```

Once the assistant is visible, you can move, resize, or animate the assistant:

```
officeapp.Assistant.Left = 500
officeapp.Assistant.Top = 500
```

Office assistants display messages to users through the **Balloon** object. You can use the **NewBalloon** property to create an instance of the **Balloon** object:

```
Set Balloon = officeapp.Assistant.NewBalloon
```

Once an instance of the **Balloon** object has been created, you can create text messages and check boxes, and then show these messages using the **Show** property:

```
Balloon.Heading = "Some Text Heading"
Balloon.Text = "Some Body Text"
Balloon.CheckBoxes(1).Text = "An example check box"
Balloon.Show
```

TIP: *If you have Microsoft Office 2000 with the VBA help files installed, the complete Office Assistant object model can be found in the file VBAOFF9.CHM.*

Under Office 97, office assistants are stored in actor files, with an ACT (Actor) extension (typically located in C:\Program Files\Microsoft Office\Office). Office 2000 uses the Microsoft Agent ActiveX technology and stores its assistants in ACS (Agent Character) files, allowing for more animations and interaction with the user.

Microsoft Agent

Microsoft Agent, originally called Microsoft Interactive Agent, is an ActiveX technology that allows you to display and animate characters to interact with the computer user. Agent characters are cartoon-like animations stored in agent character (ACS) files. Each character contains its own set of animations and voice patterns. You can use Microsoft Agent within Microsoft Office, script files, Web pages, and applications.

The Microsoft Agent Support Files

In order to run Microsoft Agent, you need to download and install the following items:

- *Microsoft Agent core components*—These are the core components that allow you to access and control a Microsoft Agent character.

- *Microsoft Agent character files*—These are the agent characters you can use to interact with the computer user.

17. Fun with Multimedia

- *Text-to-speech engines*—These engines allow the Microsoft Agent characters to translate text to speech, giving these characters the ability to "speak."

You can obtain these components from the Microsoft Agent Web site, **msdn.microsoft.com/workshop/imedia/agent/**.

The Microsoft Agent Process

All agent character commands and requests are exposed through the agent object model, MSAgent.ocx. After you create an instance of the object model, the character can be loaded and is ready to receive requests. When a request for a character animation is made, the data provider (AgentDPV.dll) decompresses the graphic and audio files, and passes them to the automation server (AgentSvr.exe). The automation server renders the files to use transparent backgrounds and borders, giving them the appearance of hovering on top of the screen.

Scripting the Microsoft Agent Using Windows Script Host

The first step to accessing the Microsoft Agent character methods is to create an instance of the Microsoft Agent Control:

```
Set ACTL = CreateObject("Agent.Control.2")
```

Once a connection has been established, you can load one of the preinstalled Microsoft Agent characters and set a reference to it:

```
ACTL.Characters.Load charactername, "charactername.acs"
Set CREF = ACTL.Characters(charactername)
```

Here, ***charactername*** is the name of the Microsoft Agent character, such as Merlin or Peedy. After the character has been loaded, you can make the character visible using the **Show** method:

```
CREF.Show
```

Once the character is visible, you can call on any of the character's methods to perform an animation or to speak. Each agent contains a set of unique animations. To make a character use a specific animation, you use the **Play** method:

```
CREF.Play "animation"
```

NOTE: *For a complete list of animations, consult the character's animation reference file.*

Here, ***animation*** is the type of animation to perform, such as greet or sad. You can use the **Speak** method to make the character say a specific phrase:

```
CREF.Speak "text"
```

Finally, you can cause the character to move to a specific location using the **MoveTo** method:

```
CREF.MoveTo x,y
```

Here, ***x*** is the horizontal pixel location, and ***y*** is the vertical pixel location.

TIP: *Specifying 0,0 will move the characters to the upper left corner of the screen.*

The Scripting Advantage

Through COM, you can script audio, video, and even animated characters to speak or sing. While both KiXtart and WSH can access these objects through COM, due to size limitations of this book and the popularity of the scripting language, this chapter will provide these examples in Windows Script Host only. (It should be simple to convert the scripts to KiXtart). AutoIt's unique ability to directly control the CD tray and play audio files provides an advantage of methods like KiXtart which only includes the ability to play WAV of SPK files. Finally, shell scripting has limited ability to play audio and video files, making it the least powerful scripting method in this chapter.

A Word of Caution

This chapter contains many scripting examples to play audio/video files and display animated characters. As with all scripts, you should first test each script in an isolated testing environment to ensure the script produces the desired results before using it in a production environment.

Immediate Solutions

Playing an Audio File Using AutoIt

AutoIt has the built-in ability to play a WAV or MP3 file using the **SoundPlay** command. To play an audio file, create and execute an AutoIt script that contains the following:

```
SoundPlay("filename", wait)
```

Here, *filename* is the full path and file name of the audio file to play and *wait* is either 1 to wait for the audio file to finish playing before the script continues or 0 to immediately continue the script.

Playing an Audio File Using KiXtart

KiXtart has the built-in ability to play a WAV or SPK file using the **Play** command. To play an audio file, create and execute a KiXtart script containing the following:

```
$Aud = "filename"
Play File $Aud
```

Here, *filename* is the full path and file name of the WAV or SPK file to play.

Scripting the Microsoft Media Player

Windows 2000/XP/2003 includes a free application called Media Player, designed to play audio and video files. Mplay32.exe is the 32-bit version of the standard Media Player, and this utility can play audio, video, and DirectShow files. This utility supports a limited amount of command-line switches.

Microsoft Media Player is a Windows utility that provides extremely enhanced functionality when compared to the older Windows multimedia players. Some of these features include media rights, MP3 (Motion Pictures Expert Group Layer 3 Audio) support, video streaming, radio tuners, and play list support. This player is intended to be the core Windows multimedia player and manager while replacing the older, built-in multimedia players, such as CDPlayer.exe and Mplay32.exe.

Playing a Media File from the Command Line

To play and then close a media file using Mplay32.exe, create and execute a shell script containing the following:

```
@Echo Off
MPLAY32 /PLAY /CLOSE "filename"
```

Here, *filename* is the full path and file name to play.

Playing an Audio File Using Windows Script Host

To play an audio file using the media player object model, create and execute a WSH script containing the following:

```
PlayAudio "filename"

Sub PlayAudio(AudioFile)
  Set Player = CreateObject("WMPlayer.OCX")
  Player.URL = AudioFile
  Do While Player.playState <> 1
    WScript.Sleep(500)
  Loop
End Sub
```

Here, *filename* is the full path and file name to play. Notice how no GUI player is shown.

Playing a Video File Using Windows Script Host

To play a video file using the media player object model, create and execute a WSH script containing the following:

```
PlayVideo "filename"

Sub PlayVideo(VideoFile)
  Set Player = CreateObject("WMPlayer.OCX")
  Player.openPlayer(VideoFile)
End Sub
```

17. Fun with Multimedia

415

Here, *filename* is the full path and file name to play. Notice how the GUI player is shown and not closed.

Scripting the CD Tray

While you may have legitimate reasons for needing to programmatically control the CD tray, my typical use is to surprise and annoy. Practical applications may be to prevent media access after a certain time, prepare for media exchange, or simply alert the user. This section will show you how to script the CD tray, regardless of the reason.

Ejecting a CD Using AutoIt

The AutoIt CDTray command allows you to control a CD tray by drive letter. To eject a CD, create and execute an AutoIt script containing the following:

```
CDTray("Drive", "Open")
```

Here, **Drive** is the drive letter (e.g., D:) to eject.

Closing a CD Tray Using AutoIt

To close a CD tray, create and execute an AutoIt script containing the following:

```
CDTray("Drive", "Closed")
```

Here, **Drive** is the drive letter (e.g., D:) to close.

Eject All CDs Using AutoIt

To eject all CDs, create and execute an AutoIt script containing the following:

```
$Drives = DriveGetDrive("all")
If NOT @error Then
  For $i = 1 to $Drives[0]
    CDTray($Drives[$i], "open")
  Next
EndIf
```

Ejecting a CD Using Windows Script Host

To eject a CD using the Media Player object model, create and execute a WSH containing the following:

```
On Error Resume Next
Set MPlayer = CreateObject("WMPlayer.OCX")

MPlayer.cdromCollection.item(x).eject()
```

Here, *x* is the number of the CD-ROM drive (starting at 0).

Ejecting All CDs Using Windows Script Host

To eject all CDs using the Media Player object model, create and execute a WSH containing the following:

```
On Error Resume Next
Set MPlayer = CreateObject("WMPlayer.OCX")
Set FSO = CreateObject("Scripting.FileSystemObject")
Count=-1

For Each Drive in FSO.Drives
  If Drive.DriveType = 4 Then
    Count=Count+1
  End If
Next

If Count > -1 Then
  For x = 0 to Count
    MPlayer.cdromCollection.item(x).eject()
  Next
End If
```

Here, a **DriveType** value of **4** indicates a CD-ROM player.

Scripting RealOne

RealOne is an advanced multimedia player from RealNetworks (**www.real.com**). Although this player is commonly used to play streaming media on the Internet, you can use these same ActiveX control calls to script RealPlayer using Windows Script Host.

17. Fun with Multimedia

Playing an Audio File

To play an audio file using the RealPlayer ActiveX control and Windows Script Host, proceed as follows:

1. Create a new directory to store all files included in this example.

2. Download and install the latest version of Windows Script Host, from **www.microsoft.com**, to the new directory.

3. Download and install the latest version of RealOne, from **www.real.com**, to the new directory.

4. Select Start|Run and enter "cscript *scriptfile*.vbs."

Here, **scriptfile** is the full path and file name of a script file that contains the following:

```
On Error Resume Next
Set RPlayer = CreateObject("rmocx.RealPlayer G2 Control.1")

RPlayer.SetSource "file:filename"
RPlayer.DoPlay

Wscript.Echo "Press OK to end."
```

Here, **filename** is the full path and file name to play.

Playing an Audio File

To play an audio file with basic controls using the RealPlayer ActiveX control and Windows Script Host, proceed as follows:

1. Create a new directory to store all files included in this example.

2. Download and install the latest version of Windows Script Host, from **www.microsoft.com**, to the new directory.

3. Download and install the latest version of RealOne, from **www.real.com**, to the new directory.

4. Select Start|Run and enter "cscript *scriptfile*.vbs."

Here, **scriptfile** is the full path and file name of a script file that contains the following:

```
On Error Resume Next
Set RPlayer = CreateObject("rmocx.RealPlayer G2 Control.1")

CMD = 2

Do While CMD <> 10
```

```
Select Case CMD
  Case 0
   RPlayer.DoPlay
  Case 1
   RPlayer.DoPause
  Case 2
 If AUD = "" Then AUD = "filename"
 AUD = InputBox("Please enter the name of the audio file
 to play", "Audio File", AUD)
 RPlayer.SetSource "file:" & AUD
  Case 3
   WScript.Quit
 End Select
  Message = "Choose a command:" & vblf & vblf & _
  "0: Play file" & vblf & _
  "1: Pause file" & vblf & _
  "2: Choose file" & vblf & _
  "3: Quit" & vblf
 CMD = InputBox(Message, "RealPlayer Commands", "0")
Loop
```

NOTE: *The highlighted code above must be entered as one paragraph.*

Here, *filename* is the full path and file name to play.

Playing Multiple Audio Files Using a Play List

Many new audio players (for example, winamp) utilize play lists to play one audio file after another. To play multiple media files using a play list, the RealPlayer ActiveX control, and Windows Script Host, proceed as follows:

1. Create a new directory to store all files included in this example.

2. Download and install the latest version of Windows Script Host, from **www.microsoft.com**, to the new directory.

3. Download and install the latest version of RealOne, from **www.real.com**, to the new directory.

4. Select Start|Run and enter "cscript *scriptfile*.vbs."

Here, *scriptfile* is the full path and file name of a script file that contains the following:

```
On Error Resume Next
Set RPlayer = CreateObject("rmocx.RealPlayer G2 Control.1")
Set FSO = CreateObject("Scripting.FileSystemObject")
Set readfile = FSO.OpenTextFile(TXTfile, 1, false)
```

17. Fun with Multimedia

```
PlayList ("playlist")
Wscript.Echo "Press OK to end."

SUB PlayList(TXTfile)
  Do while readfile.AtEndOfStream <> true
    filename = Trim(readfile.Readline)
      If filename <> "" Then
          RPlayer.SetSource "file:filename"
          RPlayer.DoPlay
        End If
    Loop
End Sub
```

Here, *filename* is the full path and file name to play.

Scripting the Office Assistant

The Office Assistant is an interactive animated character used to help
and entertain users of Microsoft Office. You can only access the assistant object model through an Office application object model. This
means that you must have an Office application installed in order to
automate an office assistant. To script the Office Assistant in Excel
using Windows Script Host, proceed as follows:

1. Create a new directory to store all files included in this example.

2. Install the latest version of Microsoft Excel.

3. Download and install the latest version of Windows Script Host,
    from **www.microsoft.com**, to the new directory.

4. Select Start|Run and enter "cscript *scriptfile*.vbs."

Here, *scriptfile* is the full path and file name of a script file that contains the following:

```
On Error Resume Next
Set FSO = CreateObject("Scripting.FileSystemObject")
Set objXL = CreateObject("Excel.Application")

objXL.Workbooks.Add
objXL.Visible = False
objXL.Assistant.Visible = True

With objXL.Assistant
   .Reduced = True
```

```
    .Left = 300
    .Top = 300
    .MoveWhenInTheWay = True
End With

Set Balloon =
objXL.Assistant.NewBalloon

Balloon.Heading = "Multiple Selections"
Balloon.Text = "Please make a selection"
Balloon.CheckBoxes(1).Text = "Selection 1"
Balloon.CheckBoxes(2).Text = "Selection 2"
Balloon.Show

If Balloon.CheckBoxes(1).Checked Then
   Wscript.Echo "You selected check box 1."
End If
If Balloon.CheckBoxes(2).Checked Then
   Wscript.Echo "You selected check box 2."
End If

objXL.quit
```

Related solution:	*Found on page:*
Automating Applications through an Application Object	98

Scripting Microsoft Agent Using Windows Script Host

Microsoft Agent is an ActiveX technology that allows you to use animated characters to present information to your users. This technology can be used in presentations, logon scripts, new user setups, and any other situation where an interaction is needed.

Scripting a Character to Speak

Many developers use Microsoft Agent to entertain, educate, or guide their users through a process. To script a Microsoft Agent character to speak using Windows Script Host, proceed as follows:

1. Create a new directory to store all files included in this example.

17. Fun with Multimedia

2. Download and install the latest version of Microsoft Agent, a text-to-speech engine, a Microsoft Agent character, and Windows Script Host, from **www.microsoft.com**, to the new directory.

3. Select Start|Run and enter "cscript *scriptfile*.vbs."

Here, *scriptfile* is the full path and file name of a script file that contains the following:

```
On Error Resume Next
Set SHELL = CreateObject("wscript.shell")
Set FSO = CreateObject("Scripting.FileSystemObject")
aCHAR = "charname"

Set ACTL = CreateObject("Agent.Control.2")
  ACTL.Connected = True
  If Not IsObject(ACTL) Then
    Wscript.Echo "Microsoft Agent was not found on your " & _
      "system." & vblf & "Please install and try again."
    Wscript.Quit
  End If
ACTL.Connected = True

ACTL.Characters.Load aCHAR, aCHAR & ".acs"
If Err.Number <> 0 Then
  Wscript.Echo "Could not locate the Agent called " & aCHAR
  Wscript.Quit
End If

Set CREF = ACTL.Characters(aCHAR)
CREF.Show
CREF.Speak "Hello there!"

WScript.Echo "Press OK to close"
```

Here, *charname* is the name of the agent character to use.

Scripting a Character to Speak a WAV File

Microsoft Agent has the ability to accept a WAV (WAVeform Audio) file and appear to speak it based on the gaps of silence detected. This allows you to use a real voice, as opposed to a synthesized voice, to speak to your users. To use Microsoft Agent to speak a WAV file, proceed as follows:

1. Create a new directory to store all files included in this example.

2. Download and install the latest version of Microsoft Agent, a text-to-speech engine, a Microsoft Agent character, and Windows Script Host, from **www.microsoft.com**, to the new directory.

3. Select Start|Run and enter "cscript *scriptfile*.vbs."

Here, ***scriptfile*** is the full path and file name of a script file that contains the following:

```
On Error Resume Next
Set SHELL = CreateObject("wscript.shell")
Set FSO = CreateObject("Scripting.FileSystemObject")
aCHAR = "charname"

Set ACTL = CreateObject("Agent.Control.2")
  ACTL.Connected = True
  If Not IsObject(ACTL) Then
    Wscript.Echo "Microsoft Agent was not found on your " & _
      "system." & vblf & "Please install and try again."
    Wscript.Quit
  End If
ACTL.Connected = True

ACTL.Characters.Load aCHAR, aCHAR & ".acs"
If Err.Number <> 0 Then
  Wscript.Echo "Could not locate the Agent called " & aCHAR
  Wscript.Quit
End If

Set CREF = ACTL.Characters(aCHAR)
CREF.Show
CREF.Speak "", "WAVFile"

WScript.Echo "Press OK to close"
```

Here, ***charname*** is the name of the agent character to use, and ***WAVFile*** is the full path and file name of the WAV file to use.

Scripting a Character to Sing

You can make the Microsoft Agent appear to sing by modifying the pitch and speed of the agent's voice. To make a Microsoft Agent character sing the Imperial March from Star Wars, proceed as follows:

1. Create a new directory to store all files included in this example.

2. Download and install the latest version of Microsoft Agent, a text-to-speech engine, a Microsoft Agent character, and Windows Script Host, from **www.microsoft.com**, to the new directory.

3. Select Start|Run and enter "cscript *scriptfile*.vbs."

Here, **scriptfile** is the full path and file name of a script file that contains the following:

```
On Error Resume Next
Set SHELL = CreateObject("wscript.shell")
Set FSO = CreateObject("Scripting.FileSystemObject")
aCHAR = "charname"

Set ACTL = CreateObject("Agent.Control.2")

ACTL.Connected = True
  If Not IsObject(ACTL) Then
    Wscript.Echo "Microsoft Agent was not found on your " & _
      "system." & vblf & "Please install and try again."
    Wscript.Quit
  End If
ACTL.Connected = True

ACTL.Characters.Load aCHAR, aCHAR & ".acs"
If Err.Number <> 0 Then
  Wscript.Echo "Could not locate the Agent called " & aCHAR
  Wscript.Quit
End If

Set CREF = ACTL.Characters(aCHAR)
CREF.Show
CREF.Speak "\Chr=""Monotone""\\Map=""\Pit=98\\Spd=50\DUN DUN
\Spd=134\DUN \Spd=50\DUN \Pit=78\DUN \Pit=117\\Spd=200\DUN
\Pit=98\\Spd=50\DUN \Pit=78\DUN \Pit=117\\Spd=150\DUN
\Pit=98\\Spd=50\DUN""=""""\"

CREF.Speak "\Chr=""Monotone""\\Map=""\Pit=147\\Spd=50\DUN
DUN DUN \Pit=156\\Spd=67\DUN \Pit=117\\Spd=134\DUN
\Pit=92\\Spd=67\DUN \Pit=78\\Spd=80\DUN \Pit=117
\\Spd=77\DUN \Pit=98\\Spd=67\DUN""=""""\"

Wscript.Echo "Press OK to end the show"
```

NOTE: *The highlighted code above must be placed on one line.*

Here, ***charname*** is the name of the agent character to use.

Scripting a Character to Read

You can make the Microsoft Agent speak any text that you can interpret in Windows Script Host. To make a Microsoft Agent character read a text file using Windows Script Host, proceed as follows:

1. Create a new directory to store all files included in this example.

2. Download and install the latest version of Microsoft Agent, a text-to-speech engine, a Microsoft Agent character, and Windows Script Host, from **www.microsoft.com**, to the new directory.

3. Select Start|Run and enter "cscript *scriptfile*.vbs."

Here, ***scriptfile*** is the full path and file name of a script file that contains the following:

```
On Error Resume Next
Set SHELL = CreateObject("wscript.shell")
Set FSO = CreateObject("Scripting.FileSystemObject")
aCHAR = "charname"

Set ACTL = CreateObject("Agent.Control.2")
  ACTL.Connected = True
  If Not IsObject(ACTL) Then
    Wscript.Echo "Microsoft Agent was not found on your " & _
      "system." & vblf & "Please install and try again."
    Wscript.Quit
  End If
ACTL.Connected = True

ACTL.Characters.Load aCHAR, aCHAR & ".acs"
If Err.Number <> 0 Then
  Wscript.Echo "Could not locate the Agent called " & aCHAR
  Wscript.Quit
End If

Set CREF = ACTL.Characters(aCHAR)
CREF.Show
ReadTXT ("textfile")

WScript.Echo "Press OK to close"

SUB ReadTXT(TXTfile)
  Set FSO = CreateObject("Scripting.FileSystemObject")
```

```
        Set readfile = FSO.OpenTextFile(TXTfile, 1, false)
        Do while readfile.AtEndOfStream <> true
          contents = readfile.Readline
          If contents <> "" THEN
            CREF.Speak contents
          End IF
        Loop

        contents = NULL
        readfile.close
End Sub
```

Here, ***charname*** is the name of the agent character to use, and
textfile is the full path and file name of the text file to read.

Scripting a Character to Check for Events

In Chapter 8, you learned how to check for events using Windows
Management Instrumentation. To make a Microsoft Agent character
notify you of events using WMI and Windows Script Host, proceed as
follows:

1. Create a new directory to store all files included in this example.

2. Download and install the latest version of Microsoft Agent, a
   text-to-speech engine, the Merlin Microsoft Agent character,
   and Windows Script Host, from **www.microsoft.com**, to the
   new directory.

3. Select Start|Run and enter "cscript *scriptfile*.vbs."

Here, ***scriptfile*** is the full path and file name of a script file that contains the following:

```
On Error Resume Next
Set SHELL = CreateObject("wscript.shell")
Set FSO = CreateObject("Scripting.FileSystemObject")
aCHAR = "Merlin"

Set ACTL = CreateObject("Agent.Control.2")
 ACTL.Connected = True
 If Not IsObject(ACTL) Then
   Wscript.Echo "Microsoft Agent was not found on your " & _
     "system." & vblf & "Please install and try again."
   Wscript.Quit
  End If
ACTL.Connected = True

ACTL.Characters.Load aCHAR, aCHAR & ".acs"
If Err.Number <> 0 Then
```

```
    Wscript.Echo "Could not locate the Agent called " & aCHAR
    Wscript.Quit
End If

Wscript.Echo "Press CTRL+C to end this script."

Set CREF = ACTL.Characters(aCHAR)
CREF.MoveTo 200,200
CREF.Show
CREF.Play "Wave"
CREF.Play "Restpose"
CREF.Speak "Hello, my name is Merlin!"
CREF.Play "Greet"
CREF.Play "Restpose"
CREF.Speak "I am your personal CPU monitoring assistant!"
CREF.Play "Announce"
CREF.Play "Restpose"
CREF.MoveTo 0,0
CREF.Speak "I will now monitor your CPU usage and notify " & _
    "you when an overload occurs."
CREF.Play "StartListening"

Computer = InputBox("Enter the computer name",
"CPU Monitor", "localhost")

CPULoad = InputBox("Enter the CPU overload threshhold",
"CPU threshhold", "75")

Poll = InputBox("Enter the polling interval",
"Poll Interval", "5")
If Computer = "" Then Computer = "Localhost"
If CPULoad = "" Then CPULoad = 75
If Poll = "" Then Poll = 5

Set ProLoad = GetObject("winmgmts:{impersonationLevel=
impersonate}!\\" &
Computer & "\root\cimv2")
.ExecNotificationQuery("SELECT * FROM
__InstanceModificationEvent WITHIN " & Poll & " WHERE
TargetInstance ISA 'Win32_Processor' and
TargetInstance .LoadPercentage > " &
CPULoad)
If Err.Number <> 0 then
    WScript.Echo Err.Description, Err.Number, Err.Source
End If
```

```
Do
  Set ILoad = ProLoad.nextevent
  If Err.Number <> 0 then
    WScript.Echo Err.Number, Err.Description, Err.Source
    Exit Do
  Else
    AMessage = ILoad.TargetInstance.DeviceID & _
    " is overloaded at " & _
    ILoad.TargetInstance.LoadPercentage & "%!"
    CREF.Stop
    CREF.Show
    CREF.Play "GetAttention"
    CREF.Play "GetAttentionContinued"
    CREF.Play "GetAttentionReturn"
    CREF.Speak AMessage
    RandomAction
  End If
Loop

Sub RandomAction()
  ulimit = 5.0
  llimit = 1.0

  Randomize
  X = Int((ulimit - llimit)*Rnd() + llimit)
  Select Case X
  Case 1
    CREF.Play "Acknowledge"
  Case 2
    CREF.Play "Alert"
  Case 3
    CREF.Play "Explain"
  Case 4
    CREF.Play "Sad"
  Case 5
    CREF.Play "Uncertain"
  End Select
End Sub
```

NOTE: *The highlighted code above must be placed on one line.*

Here, **computer** is the name of the system to monitor; **CPULoad** is the CPU utilization threshold to monitor for (1-100); and **poll** is the number of seconds to set as the polling interval to check for events. The subprocedure **RandomAction** creates a random number and then specifies an animation based on that number.

WARNING! If you run this script with WSCRIPT, you will only be able to terminate the script by ending the WSCRIPT.EXE process through the Task Manager.

Related solution:	Found on page:
Monitoring CPU Utilization	185

17. Fun with Multimedia

Chapter 18

Special Scripting for Windows XP and 2003

In Brief

It seems a new operating system comes out almost every year. While the constant upgrading, bugs, and change makes support more difficult, the new and improved features can help ease some of your pain. This final chapter will show you scripting techniques and examples designed specifically for the new features of Windows XP and 2003. And who said having the "latest and greatest" doesn't have its benefits?

Product Activation

Software piracy continues to be a huge problem for software vendors. Product activation is a technology designed to reduce the piracy of Microsoft applications and operating systems. Through product activation, Microsoft is ensured that their end users have legally obtained the software, and their end users are ensured that they have obtained an official, supported product from Microsoft. Microsoft has included this protection mechanism in their products since Windows XP.

How Product Activation Works

Before using a protected product, the product first needs to be "activated." Without activation, a product will stop working after a certain time frame or usage amount (grace period) and may prevent you from using the entire product or advanced features. The activation process generates a "hardware code" which is unique to the hardware installed in your computer. This code is transmitted to Microsoft over the Internet. (It can also be transmitted by phone.) Once transmitted, it is verified by Microsoft servers and a confirmation ID is returned when successful. Once the ID is returned, the product has been activated.

The Activation Blues

While activation may help Microsoft reduce piracy for its products, it also causes aggravation for its users. With every rebuild of your system, you will have to reactivate your protected product. Since the "hardware code" is based on the hardware configuration in your computer, you may also be forced to reactivate after adding or removing a few hardware components. Finally, users without Internet access will be forced to call Microsoft every time they need to activate.

System Restore

Windows XP and 2003 include a feature called System Restore designed to quickly resolve problems to the operating system. Originally introduced in Windows ME, System Restore provides a method to revert a system back to a previously known working state in the event a serious issue occurs.

Restore Points

A restore point is a compressed snapshot of your system's key files and registry entries. System restore creates restore points daily, on demand, and when certain events occur. These events include application installs that use the windows installer, updates applied by Windows Update (**http://windowsupdate.microsoft.com**), and when System Restore rolls back to a restore point.

MMC 2.0

Windows XP and 2003 contain the latest version of the Microsoft Management Console (MMC), version 2.0. MMC 2.0 includes many new features such as automatic saving of settings, smaller console file sizes, view extensions, enhanced drag and drop support, and the much needed Automation Object Model.

Automation Object Model

The MMC 2.0 Automation object allows you interface with the MMC through scripting. This is the first time Microsoft has exposed the MMC to scripting. The object model allows you to modify console files, snapins, documents, views, and more.

As you learned in Chapter 1, in order to gain access to an object, you must first use the **CreateObject** method and set it to a variable:

```
Set variable = CreateObject("MMC20.Application")
```

While the application object is not the only object in the MMC 2.0 Automation object model, for administrators it is the most important as it allows us to initiate, control, and terminate MMC sessions. For more information about the MMC 2.0 Automation object model, please visit the following site:

http://msdn.microsoft.com/library/default.asp?url=/library/en-us/mmc/mmc/document_object.asp

18. Special Scripting for Windows XP and 2003

433

The Scripting Advantage

This entire chapter revolves around scripting through COM objects or WMI. While both KiXtart and WSH can access these items through COM, due to the size limitations of this book and the popularity of the scripting language, this chapter will provide these examples in Windows Script Host only. (It should be simple to convert the scripts to KiXtart.) AutoIt and shell scripting are not appropriate and not discussed in this chapter.

A Word of Caution

This chapter contains scripting examples on managing Windows Activation, restore points, MMCs, and more. As with all scripts, you should first test each script in an isolated testing environment to ensure the script produces the desired results before using it in a production environment.

Immediate Solutions

Working with Windows Product Activation

While working with Windows XP/2003 Windows Product Activation (WPA), you will definitely run into your share of "activation" support calls. Luckily, Microsoft has had the foresight to include the ability to script common activation tasks.

Determining Windows Product Activation Status

To determine the activation status, create and then execute a WSH containing the following:

```
Set objWMI = GetObject("winmgmts:{" & _
  "impersonationLevel=impersonate}!\\" & _
  computer & "\root\cimv2")

Set objWPA = objWMI.ExecQuery(_
  "Select * from " & _
  "Win32_WindowsProductActivation")

For Each PA in objWPA
 If PA.ActivationRequired = 0 Then
   Wscript.Echo _
     "Product Already Activated"
 Else
   Wscript.Echo _
     "Product Not Activated" & vbcrlf & _
     "Remaining Evaluation Period: " & _
     PA.RemainingEvaluationPeriod & _
     vbcrlf & _
     "Remaining Grace Period: " & _
     PA.RemainingGracePeriod
   End If
Next
```

Here, ***computer*** is the computer name to query.

Disabling Windows Product Activation Notices

To prevent Windows Product Activation notices reminding you to activate, create and then execute a WSH containing the following:

```
Set objWMI = GetObject("winmgmts:{" & _
  "impersonationLevel=impersonate}!\\" & _
  computer & "\root\cimv2")

Set objWPA = objWMI.ExecQuery(_
  "Select * from " & _
  "Win32_WindowsProductActivation")

For Each PA in objWPA
 PA.SetNotification(0)
Next
```

Here, *computer* is the computer name to disable notices.

NOTE: *Disabling activation notices does not prevent the need to activate; it only prevents the reminder notices.*

Activating Windows

To activate Windows XP/2003, create and then execute a WSH containing the following:

```
Set objWMI = GetObject("winmgmts:{" & _
  "impersonationLevel=impersonate}!\\" & _
  computer & "\root\cimv2")

Set objWPA = objWMI.ExecQuery(_
  "Select * from " & _
  "Win32_WindowsProductActivation")

For Each PA in objWPA
  PA.ActivateOnline()
Next
```

Here, *computer* is the computer name to activate.

Scripting the System Restore

While system restores are normally performed through the System Restore Utility, you can also script restores through WMI. The WMI

system restore class (SystemRestore) provides methods to enable/
disable the system restore feature, create restore points, list restore
points, and roll back to a restore point.

Enabling/Disabling System Restore

To enable system restore on all drives through WMI, create and then
execute a WSH containing the following:

```
Set objWMI = GetObject("winmgmts:\\" & computer & "\root\default")
Set objSR = objWMI.Get("SystemRestore")
objSR.Enable("")
```

Here, **computer** is the name of the remote computer.

To disable system restore on all drives, change the method name "Enable" to "Disable."

```
Set objWMI = GetObject("winmgmts:\\" & computer & "\root\default")
Set objSR = objWMI.Get("SystemRestore")
objSR.Disable("")
```

Creating a System Restore Point

To create a restore point through WMI, create and then execute a
WSH containing the following:

```
Set objWMI = GetObject("winmgmts:\\" & computer & _
  "\root\default:SystemRestore")
objWMI.CreateRestorePoint "Scripted Restore Point", 0, 100
```

Here, **computer** is the name of the remote computer.

Listing All System Restore Points

To list all system restore points through WMI, create and then execute
a WSH containing the following:

```
Set objSR = GetObject("winmgmts:\\" & computer & _
  "\root\default").InstancesOf("SystemRestore")
If objSR.Count = 0 Then
  WScript.Echo "No restore points found."
Else
  Set objWMIDate = CreateObject("WbemScripting.SWbemDateTime")
  For Each RP in objSR
    Select Case RP.RestorePointType
      Case 0
        RPT = "Application install"
      Case 1
```

```
                    RPT = "Application Uninstall"
              Case 2
                 RPT = "Desktop Settings"
              Case 3
                 RPT = "Accessibility Settings"
              Case 4
                 RPT = "Outlook Express Settings"
              Case 5
                 RPT = "Application Run"
              Case 6
                 RPT = "Restore"
              Case 7
                 RPT = "Checkpoint"
              Case 8
                 RPT = "Windows Shutdown"
              Case 9
                 RPT = "Windows Boot"
              Case 10
                 RPT = "Device Drive install"
              Case 11
                 RPT = "First Run"
              Case 12
                 RPT = "Modify Settings"
              Case 13
                 RPT = "Cancelled Operation"
              Case 14
                 RPT = "Backup Recovery"
              Case Else
                 RPT = "Unknown"
          End Select

          objWMIDate.Value = RP.CreationTime

          Wscript.Echo "Date: " & objWMIDate.GetVarDate & vbcrlf & _
             "Number: " & RP.SequenceNumber & vbcrlf & _
             "Description: " & RP.Description & vbcrlf & _
             "Type: " & RPT
       Next
    End If
```

Here, **computer** is the name of the remote computer.

Rollback to a Restore Point

To roll back to an existing restore point through WMI, create and then execute a WSH containing the following:

```
Set objWMI - GetObject("winmgmts:\\" & computer & _
   "\root\default:SystemRestore")
objWMI.Restore RestoreNumber

Set OS - GetObject("winmgmts:{impersonationLevel-impersonate}!\\"
   & computer & "\root\cimv2").ExecQuery
("select * from Win32_ OperatingSystem where Primary-true")

For each System in OS
 System.Reboot()
Next
```

Here, **computer** is the name of the remote computer and **RestoreNumber** is the restore point sequence number. The actual restore occurs during the reboot process.

NOTE: *The highlighted code on the previous page must be placed on one line.*

Related solution:	Found on page:
Rebooting a System	186

Scripting the MMC Using Windows Script Host

In Chapter 8 you learned how to script the MMC from the command line. This section will show you how to script the MMC using the MMC 2.0 Automation object and Window Script Host.

Loading a Console File

To load a console file using Windows Script Host, create and then execute a WSH containing the following:

```
Set objMMC - CreateObject("MMC20.Application")
objMMC.Load("ConsoleFile")
objMMC.Show
objMMC.UserControl - 1
```

Here, **ConsoleFile** is the location of the console file to load.

Saving a Console File

To save a console file using Windows Script Host, create and then execute a WSH containing the following:

```
Set objMMC = CreateObject("MMC20.Application")
Set objDOC  = objMMC.Document

objDOC.SaveAs("ConsoleFile")
objDOC .Close(true)
```

Here, **ConsoleFile** is the location of the console file to save.

Adding a Snapin

To add a snapin to an MMC using Windows Script Host, create and then execute a WSH containing the following:

```
Set objMMC = CreateObject("MMC20.Application")
Set objDOC = objMMC.Document

objDOC.SnapIns.Add "snapinname"
objMMC.show
objMMC.UserControl = 1
```

Here, **snapinname** is the name of the snapin to add (i.e. "Event Viewer", "Local Users and Groups").

WMI Improvements

Starting with Windows XP/2003, Microsoft has included a few new classes and objects to WMI. While the sections below explore a few additions, you can visit the following site for a complete list:

http://msdn.microsoft.com/library/default.asp?url=/library/ enus/wmisdk/wmi/what_s_new_in_wmi.asp

Converting WMI Dates

WMI uses the Common Information Model (CIM) DateTime format for date and time values which displays dates and times as $yyyymmddHHMMSS.mmmmmmsUUU$ or $yyyy-mm-dd$ $HH:MM:SS:mmm$. You can use the **sWbemDateTime** object to translate CIM formatted dates and time. To translate a WMI CIM formatted date and time using the **sWbemDateTime** object, create and then execute a WSH containing the following:

```
Set objDT = CreateObject("WbemScripting.SWbemDateTime")
Set objWMI = GetObject("winmgmts:\\" & Computer & "\root\cimv2")
Set objOS = objWMI.ExecQuery("Select LocalDateTime " & _
  "from Win32_OperatingSystem")

For Each OS in objOS
    objDT.Value = OS.LocalDateTime
    WScript.Echo "Original: " & OS.LocalDateTime & vbcrlf & _
      "Formatted: " & objDT.GetVarDate
Next
```

Here, *computer* is the name of the remote system. The example above retrieves the current time of a *computer* and displays both the original CIM formatted date/time and the translated date/time.

Pinging a Network Device

You can use the WMI **Win32_PingStatus** class to ping a network device and retrieve the returned results through scripting. To ping a network device and display the results using WMI, create and then execute a WSH containing the following:

```
set objPING = GetObject("winmgmts:{impersonationLevel=impersonate}")._
  ExecQuery ("select * from Win32_PingStatus where address ='"
_ & NetworkDevice & "'")

For Each PING In objPing
  Select Case PING.StatusCode
    Case 0
      Wscript.Echo "Reply from " & PING.ProtocolAddress & _
        ": bytes=" & PING.BufferSize & " " & _
        "time=" & PING.ResponseTime & " " & _
        "TTL=" & PING.ResponseTimeToLive
    Case 11001
      wscript.echo "Buffer Too Small"
    Case 11002
      wscript.echo "Destination Net Unreachable"
    Case 11003
      wscript.echo "Destination Host Unreachable"
    Case 11004
      wscript.echo "Destination Protocol Unreachable"
    Case 11005
      wscript.echo "Destination Port Unreachable"
    Case 11006
      wscript.echo "No Resources"
    Case 11007
      wscript.echo "Bad Option"
    Case 11008
      wscript.echo "Hardware Error"
```

```
         Case 11009
           wscript.echo "Packet Too Big"
         Case 11010
           wscript.echo "Request Timed Out"
         Case 11011
           wscript.echo "Bad Request"
         Case 11012
           wscript.echo "Bad Route"
         Case 11013
           wscript.echo "TimeToLive Expired Transit"
         Case 11014
           wscript.echo "TimeToLive Expired Reassembly"
         Case 11015
           wscript.echo "Parameter Problem"
         Case 11016
           wscript.echo "Source Quench"
         Case 11017
           wscript.echo "Option Too Big"
         Case 11018
           wscript.echo "Bad Destination"
         Case 11032
           wscript.echo "Negotiating IPSEC"
         Case 11050
           wscript.echo "General Failure"
      End Select
Next
```

Here, ***networkdevice*** is the name or IP address of the device to ping.

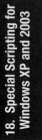

Resources

This appendix lists various web sites and newsgroups where you can gather more information or download some of the tools used in this book.

ADSI

The following sites provide information on Active Directory Services Interface (ADSI):

**msdn.microsoft.com/library/default.asp?url=/library/en-us/adsi/
adsi/adsi_objects_of_winnt.asp**

**www.microsoft.com/windows2000/techinfo/howitworks/activedirectory/
adsilinks.asp**

Newsgroups

microsoft.public.adsi.general

microsoft.public.platformsdk.adsi

Antivirus

The following sites provide information on antivirus:

www.networkassociates.com/us/security/vil.htm

www.symantec.com/avcenter/

Newsgroups

alt.comp.virus

alt.comp.virus.source.code

microsoft.public.scripting.virus.discussion

symantec.support.winnt.nortonantivirus.general

AutoItAutoIt

AutoIt is a free automation tool to send key presses, manipulate the mouse, modify files and the registry, control dialog boxes, and more.

Site: **www.autoitscript.com**

KiXtart KiXtart.org

KiXtart.org, formerly **kixtart.to**, is the premiere Web site for KiXtart scripting. The heart of this site is its bulletin board where you can find hundreds of KiXtart tips, tricks, facts, and scripts.

Site: **www.KiXtart.org**

Microsoft Agent

The following sites provide information on Microsoft Agent.

MASH (Microsoft Agent Scripting Helper)

MASH, by BellCraft Technologies, is the easiest and quickest way to script Microsoft Agent. This advanced tool allows you to browse through character animations and create complex script files with absolutely no prior scripting or programming experience.

Site: **www.bellcraft.com/mash/**

Microsoft Agent Web Ring

The Microsoft Agent Web Ring is the one place on the Web that tries to bring all Microsoft Agent Web sites together. This site is full of examples, applications, characters, and links to other Microsoft Agent Web sites.

Site: **www.msagentring.org**

Microsoft Agent in the MSDN Library

This is the official site for Microsoft Agent. Here you will find the latest news and downloads regarding Microsoft Agent.

Site: **www.microsoft.com/msagent/default.asp**

Newsgroups

microsoft.public.msagent

Other

The following sites provide information on other helpful sites.

ActiveWin.com

This site is truly an Internet resource center for the Windows platform. Here you will find all sorts of information, drivers, articles, tools, tips, and tricks for the Windows operating system of your choice.

Site: **www.activewin.com**

JesseWeb

This is my own personal Web site. Here you will find updates and support material for the book, scripts, tricks, tips, security documents, music, and more. If you visit any site on this page, this should be the place to start.

Site: **www.jesseweb.com**

JSIInc

Glad to see that this site is still alive and well. JSIInc contains an extensive amount of registry tips, tricks, and hacks. The site also contains administrative utilities, tips, and tricks for almost anything you can think of. A definite bookmark.

Site: **www.jsiinc.com/reghack.htm**

Sysinternals

The site for the true Windows administrator. From the guys that brought you NTFSDOS, ERD Commander, and FAT32 for Windows NT (**www.wininternals.com**), this site contains many free and invaluable utilities that you may find yourself using on a daily basis.

Site: **www.sysinternals.com**

FAQ for Windows

Formerly Windows 2000 FAQ, this site contains the answers to hundreds of Windows 2000/XP/2003 questions on just about every topic. A good site for quick questions and answers.

Site: **www.winnetmag.com/windowsnt20002003faq/**

Shell Scripting

The following sites provide information on shell scripting.

BatFiles

It's amazing that with the growth of all the other scripting languages, a site like this could still exist. BatFiles is a Web site purely devoted to the DOS shell scripter. Here you will find tons of examples, tricks, FAQs, links, and downloads.

Site: **bigfoot.com/~batfiles/**

The DOS Command Index

This site contains a comprehensive list of shell scripting commands and their usage.

Site: **www.easydos.com/dosindex.html**

Newsgroups

alt.msdos.batch
alt.msdos.batch.nt

Scripting: General

The following sites provide information on scripting in general.

DevGuru

DevGuru is an Internet learning center providing downloads, tutorials, and references for scripters and ASP developers.

Site: **www.devguru.com**

Microsoft Windows Script Technologies

This Web site is Microsoft's central location to obtain scripting downloads, documentation, news, and support. Here you can download the latest versions of Windows Script Host, Microsoft Script Encoder, and the complete VBScript documentation.

Site: **msdn.microsoft.com/scripting/**

PrimalSCRIPT

PrimalSCRIPT, by Sapien Technologies, is by far the leader of script editors. Packed with advanced features and providing support for more than 30 scripting and programming languages including Microsoft .NET, PrimalSCRIPT is my tool of choice and should be for any scripting professional.

Site: **www.sapien.com**

Technet Script Center

Run by Microsoft, this site contains tons and tons of useful Windows scripts. This site should be a scripter's first stop before attempting to write any new Windows scripts.

Site: **www.microsoft.com/technet/scriptcenter/default.mspx**

UltraEdit-32

UltraEdit-32, by IDM Computer Solutions, Inc., is an award-winning script editor that provides for quick and painless editing. This compact editing tool contains many of the advanced features of other editors, at a fraction of the cost. With features like project management, macros, keyboard mapping, automatic backup, and unlimited file sizes, this little tool packs a big punch.

Site: **www.ultraedit.com**

Win32 Scripting

Win32 Scripting is the Web center for the serious scripter. Packed with code and custom tools for all types of scripting languages, this site proves that nothing is unscriptable.

Site: **cwashington.netreach.net**

Windows Scripting Solutions

Windows and .NET Magazine's Windows Scripting Solutions is a 15-page monthly publication focused on task automation for the Windows administrator. The site is generally restricted to its publication subscribers, but is full of scripting articles and examples.

Site: **www.winnetmag.com/WindowsScripting/**

Appendix: Resources

Newsgroups

microsoft.public.scripting.vbscript

microsoft.public.scripting.jscript

microsoft.public.scripting.remote

microsoft.public.scripting.scriptlets

Windows Management Instrumentation

The following sites provide information on Windows Management Instrumentation (WMI):

http://msdn.microsoft.com/library/default.asp?url=/library/en-us/wmisdk/wmi/wmi_reference.asp

msdn.microsoft.com/library/default.asp?url=/library/en-us/wmisdk/wmi/wmi_start_page.asp

www.microsoft.com/whdc/hwdev/driver/wmi/default.mspx

Newsgroups

microsoft.public.wbem

microsoft.public.dotnet.framework.wmi

Windows Script Host

The following sites provide information on Windows Script Host.

Windows Script Host Bazaar

Gunter Born's Windows Script Host Bazaar is packed with samples, ActiveX controls, book reviews, newsletters, tools, links, and more.

Site: : people.freenet.de/gborn/WSHBazaar/WSHBazaar.htm

Windows Script Host FAQ

This site is an excellent resource for anyone interested in Windows Script Host. This site is loaded with information, tutorials, FAQs, links, reviews, and more. A definite starting point for the new WSH scripter.

Site: groups.msn.com/windowsscript

WinScripter

Although most of the scripts at this site are written in Jscript (and the scripts in this book were written in VBScript), this site is an excellent resource for articles, tutorials, and examples.

Site: **www.winscripter.com**

Newsgroups

Microsoft.Public.Scripting.wsh

Security

The following sites provide information on security issues.

Microsoft Security

Microsoft's official security site providing the latest security news, fixes, and links.

Site: **www.microsoft.com/security/**

SANS (System Administration, Networking, and Security)

SANS is a research community, composed of over 156,000 security personnel and system administrators. Here you'll find the latest security news, events, resources, and more.

Site: **www.sans.org**

Windows IT Security

Windows 2000 Magazine's central site for IT security news, FAQS, files, articles, and more.

Site: **www.winnetmag.com/WindowsSecurity/**

Newsgroups

microsoft.public.security

microsoft.public.win2000.security

microsoft.public.windowsxp.security_admin

VBA

The following sites provide information on Visual Basic for Applications (VBA).

directory.google.com/Top/Computers/Programming/Languages/VBA/outlookvba.com

Newsgroups

microsoft.public.word.vba.beginners

microsoft.public.word.vba.customization

microsoft.public.word.vba.general

Index

B

C

G

H

I

N